- **SCHIZOPHRENIA AND OTHER PSYCHOTIC DISORDERS**

Schizophrenia
    Paranoid Type
    Disorganized Type
    Catatonic Type
    Undifferentiated Type
    Residual Type
Schizophreniform Disorder
Schizoaffective Disorder
Delusional Disorder
Brief Psychotic Disorder
Shared Psychotic Disorder
Psychotic Disorder Due to General Medical Condition
Substance-Induced Psychotic Disorder

- **MOOD DISORDERS**

Depressive Disorders
Major Depressive Disorder
Dysthymic Disorder

Bipolar Disorders
Bipolar I Disorder
Bipolar II Disorder
Cyclothymic Disorder
Mood Disorder Due to General Medical Condition
Substance-Induced Mood Disorder

- **ANXIETY DISORDERS**

Panic Disorder without Agoraphobia
Panic Disorder with Agoraphobia
Agoraphobia without History of Panic Disorder
Specific Phobia
Social Phobia
Obsessive-Compulsive Disorder
Posttraumatic Stress Disorder
Acute Stress Disorder
Generalized Anxiety Disorder
Anxiety Disorder Due to General Medical Condition
Substance-Induced Anxiety Disorder

- **SOMATOFORM DISORDERS**

Somatization Disorder
Undifferentiated Somatoform Disorder
Conversion Disorder
Pain Disorder
Hypochondriasis
Body Dysmorphic Disorder

- **FACTITIOUS DISORDERS**

- **DISSOCIATIVE DISORDERS**

Dissociative Amnesia
Dissociative Fugue
Dissociative Identity Disorder
Depersonalization Disorder

- **SEXUAL AND GENDER IDENTITY DISORDERS**

Sexual Dysfunctions

Sexual Desire Disorders
Hypoactive Sexual Desire Disorder
Sexual Aversion Disorder

Sexual Arousal Disorders
Female Sexual Arousal Disorder
Male Erectile Disorder

Orgasmic Disorders
Female Orgasmic Disorder
Male Orgasmic Disorder
Premature Ejaculation

Sexual Pain Disorders
Dyspareunia
Vaginismus

Sexual Dysfunction Due to General Medical Condition
Substance-Induced Sexual Dysfunction

Paraphilias
Exhibitionism
Fetishism
Frotteurism
Pedophilia
Sexual Masochism
Sexual Sadism
Transvestic Fetishism
Voyeurism

Gender Identity Disorders

- **EATING DISORDERS**

Anorexia Nervosa
Bulimia Nervosa

- **SLEEP DISORDERS**

Primary Sleep Disorders

Dyssomnias
Primary Insomnia
Primary Hypersomnia
Narcolepsy
Breathing-Related Sleep Disorder
Circadian Rhythm Sleep Disorder

Parasomnias
Nightmare Disorder
Sleep Terror Disorder
Sleepwalking Disorder

Sleep Disorders Related to Another Mental Disorder

Other Sleep Disorders

- **IMPULSE-CONTROL DISORDERS NOT ELSEWHERE CLASSIFIED**

Intermittent Explosive Disorder
Kleptomania
Pyromania
Pathological Gambling
Trichotillomania

- **ADJUSTMENT DISORDERS**

- **PERSONALITY DISORDERS (AXIS II)**

Paranoid Personality Disorder
Schizoid Personality Disorder
Schizotypal Personality Disorder
Antisocial Personality Disorder
Borderline Personality Disorder
Histrionic Personality Disorder
Narcissistic Personality Disorder
Avoidant Personality Disorder
Dependent Personality Disorder
Obsessive-Compulsive Personality Disorder

- **OTHER CONDITIONS THAT MAY BE A FOCUS OF CLINICAL ATTENTION**

Psychological Factors Affecting Medical Condition

Medication-Induced Movement Disorders

Other Medication-Induced Disorders

Relational Problems
Relational Problem Related to a Mental Disorder or General Medical Condition
Parent-Child Relational Problem
Partner Relational Problem
Sibling Relational Problem

Problems Related to Abuse or Neglect
Physical Abuse of Child
Sexual Abuse of Child
Neglect of Child
Physical Abuse of Adult
Sexual Abuse of Adult

Additional Conditions that May Be a Focus of Clinical Attention
Noncompliance with Treatment
Malingering
Adult Antisocial Behavior
Child or Adolescent Antisocial Behavior
Borderline Intellectual Functioning
Age-Related Cognitive Decline
Bereavement
Academic Problem
Occupational Problem
Identity Problem
Religious or Spiritual Problem
Acculturation Problem
Phase of Life Problem

- **ADDITIONAL CODES**

Unspecified Mental Disorder (nonpsychotic)
No Diagnosis or Condition on Axis I
Diagnosis or Condition Deferred on Axis I
No Diagnosis on Axis II
Diagnosis Deferred on Axis II

ABNORMAL PSYCHOLOGY

ABNORMAL PSYCHOLOGY

Clinical Perspectives on Psychological Disorders

SEVENTH EDITION

SUSAN KRAUSS WHITBOURNE

University of Massachusetts Amherst

RICHARD P. HALGIN

University of Massachusetts Amherst

McGraw Hill

Connect
Learn
Succeed™

ABNORMAL PSYCHOLOGY: CLINICAL PERSPECTIVES ON PSYCHOLOGICAL DISORDERS, SEVENTH EDITION

This book is printed on acid-free paper.

1 2 3 4 5 6 7 8 9 0 DOW/DOW 1 0 9 8 7 6 5 4 3 2

ISBN   978-0-07-803527-2
MHID   0-07-803527-9

Senior Vice President, Products & Markets: *Kurt L. Strand*
Vice President, General Manager: *Michael Ryan*
Vice President, Content Production & Technology Services: *Kimberly Meriwether David*
Managing Director: *William Glass*
Director: *Krista Bettino*
Senior Director of Development: *Dawn Groundwater*
Development Manager: *Barbara A. Heinssen*
Content Development Editor: *Thomas Sigel*
Editorial Coordinator: *Chantelle C. Walker*
Digital Development Editor: *Sarah Coldwell*
Marketing Managers: *AJ Laferrera/ Ann Helgerson*
Director, Content Production: *Terri Schiesl*
Project Manager/Content Project Manager: *Anne Fuzellier*
Buyer: *Debra Sylvester*
Designer: *Srdjan Savanovic*
Cover/Interior Designer: *Cara Hawthorme, cara david DESIGN*
Cover Image: © *JGI/Jamie Grill/Blend Images/Corbis*
Content Licensing Specialist: *Karyn Morrison*
Photo Researcher: *Keri Johnson*
Media Project Manager: *Katie Klochan*
Typeface: *10/12 Times LT*
Compositor: *Aptara®, Inc.*
Printer: *R. R. Donnelley Willard*

Library of Congress Cataloging-in-Publication Data
Whitbourne, Susan Krauss.
  Abnormal psychology : clinical perspectives on psychological disorders / Susan Whitbourne, Halgin, Richard.—7th ed.
        p. cm.
  Rev. ed. of: Abnormal psychology / Richard P. Halgin, Susan Krauss Whitbourne. c2010. 6th ed.
  Includes bibliographical references and index.
  ISBN 978-0-07-803527-2
  1. Psychology, Pathological.   2. Mental illness.   I. Halgin, Richard P.   II. Halgin, Richard P. Abnormal psychology.   III. Title.
  RC454.H334 2013
  616.89—dc23
                                        2012032968

www.mhhe.com

To our families, with love and appreciation

Susan Krauss Whitbourne and **Richard Halgin** are Professors of Psychology at the University of Massachusetts Amherst. Both teach large undergraduate classes in addition to teaching and supervising doctoral students in developmental and clinical psychology. Their clinical experience has covered both inpatient and outpatient settings. Professors Whitbourne and Halgin are Fellows of the American Psychological Association. They co-edited *A Case Book in Abnormal Psychology: From the Files of Experts* (Oxford University Press), containing case studies written by leading international authorities in the field of psychopathology.

Professor Whitbourne received her PhD from Columbia University and has dual specializations in life-span developmental psychology and clinical psychology. She taught at the State University of New York at Geneseo and the University of Rochester. At the University of Massachusetts, she received the University's Distinguished Teaching Award, the Outstanding Advising Award, and the College of Arts and Sciences Outstanding Teacher Award. In 2001, she received the Psi Chi Eastern Region Faculty Advisor Award and in 2002, the Florence Denmark Psi Chi National Advisor Award. In 2003, she received both the APA Division 20 and Gerontological Society of America Mentoring Awards. She served as the Departmental Honors Coordinator from 1990–2010 and currently is the Psi Chi Faculty Advisor and the Director of the Office of National Scholarship Advisement in the Commonwealth Honors College. The author of sixteen books and over 160 journal articles and book chapters, Professor Whitbourne is regarded as an expert on personality development in mid- and late life. She is on the APA Membership Board, was Chair of APA's Policy and Planning Board, and was a member of the APA Committee for the Structure and Function of Council. She is APA Council Representative to Division 20 (Adult Development and Aging), having also served as Division 20 President. She is a Fellow of APA's Divisions 20, 1 (General Psychology), 2 (Teaching of Psychology), 12 (Clinical Psychology), and 35 (Society for the Psychology of Women). A Fellow of the Gerontological Society of America, she serves on the Executive Board of the Behavioral and Social Sciences Section. In 2007, she was the Psi Chi Eastern Region Vice President and in 2009 was the Program Chair of the 2009 National Leadership Conference. Professor Whitbourne served as an item writer for the Educational Testing Service, was a member of APA's High School Curriculum National Standards Advisory Panel, wrote the APA High School Curriculum Guidelines for Life-Span Developmental Psychology, and serves as an item writer for the Examination for Professional Practice of Psychology and as Chair of the Council of Professional Geropsychology Training Programs. Her 2010 book, "The Search for Fulfillment" was nominated for an APA William James Award. In 2011, she was recognized with a Presidential Citation from APA. In addition to her academic writing, she edits a blog on *Psychology Today* entitled "Fulfillment at Any Age."

Professor Halgin received his PhD from Fordham University and completed a fellowship in the Department of Psychiatry at New York Hospital-Cornell Medical Center prior to joining the faculty of the University of Massachusetts in 1977. He is a Board-Certified Clinical Psychologist with over four decades of clinical, supervisory, and consulting experience. At the University of Massachusetts, he received the Distinguished Teaching Award, the Alumni Association's Distinguished Faculty Award, and was nominated for the Carnegie Foundation's U.S. Professor of the Year Award. His teaching was recognized by the Danforth Foundation and the Society for the Teaching of Psychology. Professor Halgin is the author of sixty journal articles and book chapters in the fields of psychotherapy, clinical supervision, and professional issues in psychology. He is also the editor of *Taking Sides: Controversial Issues in Abnormal Psychology*, Sixth Edition (McGraw-Hill). Professor Halgin served as Chair of the Committee of Examiners for the Psychology Graduate Record Examination, as an Associate Member of the Ethics Committee of the American Psychological Association, and currently serves on the Massachusetts Board of Registration of Psychologists.

BRIEF CONTENTS

CONTENTS

CHAPTER 7
Sexual Disorders   146

CHAPTER 8
Mood Disorders   174

McGraw-Hill Connect Abnormal Psychology

Abnormal Psychology is available to instructors and students in traditional print format as well as online within McGraw-Hill's Connect **Abnormal Psychology,** an integrated assignment and assessment platform. Connect **Abnormal Psychology's** online tools make managing assignments easier for instructors—and make learning and studying more motivating and efficient for students.

Experience a new classroom dynamic with *LearnSmart*

How many students *think* they know what they know but struggle on the first exam? *LearnSmart,* McGraw-Hill's adaptive learning system, identifies students' metacognitive abilities and limitations, identifying what they know—and more importantly, what they don't know. Using Bloom's Taxonomy and a highly sophisticated "smart" algorithm, LearnSmart creates a customized study plan, unique to every student's demonstrated needs. With virtually no administrative overhead, instructors using LearnSmart are reporting an increase in student performance by one letter grade or more.

New *Faces: Interactive*

Faces: Interactive is a unique digital learning environment, now available exclusively through Connect, which has been significantly updated as an assignable and assessable database to provide students with an opportunity to observe real patients through a series of case studies on 12 different psychological disorders. The disorders include Attention-Deficit/Hyperactivity Disorder, Bipolar Disorder, Borderline Personality Disorder, Bulimia Nervosa, Dysthymic Disorder, Major Depression, Obsessive-Compulsive Disorder, Panic Disorder with Agoraphobia, Paranoid Schizophrenia, Post-Traumatic Stress Disorder,

Tourette's Syndrome, and Substance Abuse. Each case study takes students through four stages of a patient's experience: diagnosis, case history, interview, and treatment. Students are able to explore the diagnostic processes, improve their understanding of clinical practice, and gain experience documenting their findings in a case study report project. After using *Faces: Interactive,* students will have a wealth of information about, and a humanistic outlook on, these disorders. These modules are available http://via/ in

Integrated eBook

A fully loaded eBook allows students to review **Abnormal Psychology** anytime and anywhere. They can highlight, take notes, and quickly search for key terms and phrases.

Assignable and Assessable Activities

Instructors can easily deliver assignments and tests online, and students can practice skills that fulfill learning objectives at their own pace and on their own schedule.

Real-time Reports

These printable, exportable reports show how well each student (or section) is performing on each course segment. Instructors can use this feature to spot problem areas before they crop up on an exam.

Accessible Storytelling Approach and Empirically Supported Research

The seventh edition of *Abnormal Psychology* focuses on providing an accurate, understandable, concise, and up-to-date view of this rapidly evolving field. In particular, we have taken a thorough look at the literature and synthesized the information to provide the most relevant theories and research for you to study. We have added new features to give you an appreciation for the ethical issues that confront mental health professionals and the current controversies in the field around changes in the diagnostic system. **"You Be the Judge"** presents you with controversial ethical questions specific to the content of the chapter. **"Towards the DSM-5"** boxes summarize the most recent DSM-5 proposed revisions. We have also revised each chapter based on principles of what is called "evidence-based treatment." These features will give you a contemporary view of the field as it is now and will also provide you with a solid basis for understanding how this ever-changing field continues to progress.

In writing the seventh edition, we have significantly sharpened the focus of each chapter to provide you with as vibrant a picture as possible of this remarkable field in psychology. If you've seen a previous edition, you will notice a distinct change that, while still focused on "talking to the student," does so in a way that reflects the learning style of today's students. We realize that students take many credit hours and that each course (particularly in psychology) seems to be getting increasingly demanding. Therefore, we want you to be able to grasp the material in the least amount of time, but with similar depth as students found in our previous editions.

You Be the Judge

Prescribing Psychiatric Medications to Children

Research on human participants of any age requires that investigators adhere strictly to the APA Ethical Guidelines. In the case of children, however, the issues shift considerably given that they are "vulnerable populations." This means that they may be at increased risk for abuse and exploitation. Consequently, for decades, researchers avoided conducting studies to test the efficacy of psychotherapeutic medications on children to avoid exposing them to unnecessary harm during research trials. With no conclusive data about effectiveness, safety, and pharmacological action on which to base treatment recommendations, psychiatrists treated their pediatric patients using so-called "off-label" prescriptions which had not received U.S. Food and Drug Administration (FDA) approval.

The practice of prescribing these off-label medications for disorders is widespread in the U.S., but because of the problems of conducting research on children, these prescriptions are often targeted toward this population. The FDA has no authority to regulate the way in which physicians practice medicine, so they must make their own decisions about whether or not to prescribe an off-label medication to a child. In the process, physicians must balance the potential benefits with the risks of the medication. With few studies of the safety and efficacy of the medications, physicians must rely on their own experience (Spetie & Arnold, 2007).

Children may therefore be at greater risk of side effects than other populations about whom extensive data exists. The situation was brought to light in a dramatic manner in 2003 when the FDA received reports showing an association between SSRI use in adolescents and a heightened risk of self-harm and suicidal thoughts. By 2007, these medications received "black box" warnings from the FDA that applied not only to children and adolescents, but also to young adults. Because the FDA did not have extensive data on the use of these medications for young people, they used the information they had at their disposal to make this ruling. There is now considerably more information about these medications present, suggesting that antidepressants may, in fact, reduce suicide risks in this population, a risk that decreases steadily with length of treatment (Dudley, Goldney, & Hadzi-Pavlovic, 2010).

Q: *You be the judge:* Should researchers conduct more research on psychopharmacological treatments on children? Do the risks of side effects that may occur during this research justify these investigations? Furthermore, if researchers discover that a medication has harmful side effects, how should prescribing health professionals weigh these against possible benefits?

Toward the DSM-5: Schizophrenia Dimensions

The *DSM-5* authors are suggesting a major change in their approach to diagnosing schizophrenia. As we mentioned at the beginning of the chapter, it is likely that they will eliminate the types of schizophrenia. Instead, clinicians will assign a diagnosis of schizophrenia to which they will add a rating of the individual's symptoms along a set of dimensions, as Table 9.3 shows.

Using this system, then, clinicians will rate each individual whom they diagnose with schizophrenia on each dimension. A rating of two or higher will be sufficient to determine that the individual fits a Criterion A diagnostic indicator. Clinicians will base their ratings on the individual's behavior within the past month. As of now, the diagnostic criteria for schizophrenia will not change other than to remove the stipulation that a client needs only one symptom from Category A if the delusions are bizarre or hallucinations consist of a voice keeping up a running commentary or two or more voices talking with each other.

By eliminating the subtypes of schizophrenia, the *DSM-5* authors are hoping to improve both the diagnostic reliability and validity of the system, but also allow researchers and clinicians to have a more quantifiable basis for research on the disorder's causes as well as for treatment planning. For example, a clinician evaluating the results of cognitive behavioral therapy could use the ratings of hallucination and delusion severity to determine whether the intervention is reducing the specific symptoms toward which they are targeting treatment.

The *DSM-5* authors also decided to include cognitive impairment as a dimension, given the importance of cognitive deficits in current understandings of the individual's ability to carry out social and occupational activities and to carry out the tasks involved in everyday living. Recognizing the importance of cognitive symptoms as central to the disorder, the *DSM-5* authors are considering whether or not to require that clinicians conduct a neuropsychological assessment as part of the diagnostic process (Reichenberg, 2010).

The *DSM-5* authors also plan to include ratings of depression and mania for all psychotic disorders. Schizoaffective disorder as a separate entity will most likely eventually disappear as a diagnosis, because evidence continues to accumulate showing that it should not be a separate category.

Although not there yet, the *DSM-5* authors believe that clinicians will eventually diagnose schizophrenia as a "spectrum" disorder. This would mean, potentially, that even diagnoses long in use in psychiatry would disappear, including schizophreniform disorder, schizoaffective disorder, and the two personality disorders associated with schizophrenic-like symptoms. As we mentioned in the chapter, the *DSM-5* authors will almost certainly decide to diagnose catatonia not as a type of schizophrenia, but as an associated condition with other psychiatric disorders and/or general medical conditions. They also will be eliminating shared psychotic disorder in the interests of reducing the number of different disorders within the overall category.

If carried out, these changes in the *DSM-5* will represent a hybrid between the old categorization system and the newer, dimensional approach. By including severity ratings rather than subtypes, they are making it possible for clinicians and researchers to track individuals over time in a quantifiable fashion.

How Will You Study "Abnormal" Human Behavior?

The field of abnormal psychology covers the full spectrum of human behavior throughout the life span. From infancy through later adulthood, the process of development propels us through a vast range of experiences. Some of these experiences, invariably, include encounters with distressing emotions, behaviors, inner experiences, and interactions with other people. There is no sharp dividing line between "normal" and "abnormal," as you will learn in this book, nor do people spend their entire lives in one or the other of these realms.

Abnormal psychology is particularly fascinating because it reflects so many possible variations in human behavior, particularly as these evolve over time in an individual's life. Learning about abnormal psychology can be a goal for you in and of itself, but you more than likely will find yourself drawn to its practical applications as a basis for learning how to help others. Whether or not you decide to enter a helping profession, however, you will find knowledge of this field useful in whatever profession you decide to pursue as well as your everyday life.

Clinical Perspectives on Psychological Disorders

The subtitle of this seventh edition, *Clinical Perspectives on Psychological Disorders*, reflects the emphasis in each of the prior editions on the experience of clients and clinicians in their efforts to facilitate each individual's maximum functioning. We present an actual case study at the beginning of each chapter that typifies the disorders in that chapter. At the end of the chapter, we return to the case study with the outcome of a prescribed treatment on the basis of the best available evidence. Throughout the chapter, we translate the symptoms of each disorder into terms that capture the core essence of the disorder. Our philosophy is that students should be able to appreciate the fundamental nature of each disorder without necessarily having to memorize diagnostic criteria. In that way, students can gain a basic understanding that will serve them well regardless of their ultimate professional goals.

The Biopsychosocial Approach

An understanding of psychological disorders requires an integrative approach, particularly as researchers begin to understand increasingly the connections among the multiple dimensions that influence people throughout life.

We are adopting the *biopsychosocial* approach—incorporating biological, psychological, and sociocultural contributions to psychological disorders. Neuroscience research is increasingly becoming relevant to the understanding of psychopathology, but at the same time, so are issues related to social context including diversity of social class, race, and ethnicity. These factors combine in complex ways, and throughout the book, we explain how they apply to particular psychological disorders.

The Life-Span Approach

Individuals grow and change throughout life, and we feel that it is essential to capture the developmental dimension in helping students understand the evolution of psychological disorders over time. Therefore, we have incorporated research and theories that provide relevant understandings of how the disorders that we cover emerge and modulate from childhood through adulthood. We also emphasize the interactive and reciprocal effects of "nature" (genetics) and "nurture" (the environment) as contributors to psychological disorders.

The Human Experience of Psychological Disorders

Above all, the study of abnormal psychology is the study of profoundly human experiences. To this end, we have developed a biographical feature entitled **"Real Stories."** You will read narratives from the actual experiences of celebrities, sports figures, politicians, authors, musicians and artists ranging from Beethoven to Herschel Walker. Each Real Story is written to provide insight into the particular disorder covered within the chapter. By reading these fascinating biographical pieces, you will come away with a more in-depth personal perspective to use in understanding the nature of the disorder.

The Scientist-Practitioner Framework

We have developed this text using a scientist-practitioner framework. In other words, you will read about research informed by clinical practice. We present research on theories and treatments for each of the disorders based on the principles of "evidence-based practice." This means that the approaches that we describe are tested through extensive research informed by clinical practice. Many researchers in the field of abnormal psychology also treat clients in their own private offices, hospitals, or group practices. As a result, they approach their work in the lab with the knowledge that their findings can ultimately provide real help to real people.

Chapter-by-Chapter Changes

One major change you will notice is in the order of authors. After many years of teaching, research, and writing, the new first author (Professor Whitbourne) is bringing her classroom style into the writing of this text. Professor Whitbourne also writes a popular *Psychology Today* blog called "Fulfillment at Any Age," and she has adapted the material in the previous editions to reflect the empirically informed but accessible reading style that has contributed to the success of this blog.

In addition, we added a research assistant to the team who brings a more youthful and contemporary perspective to particular features within the text. An advanced clinical psychology graduate student at American University at the time of this writing, Jennifer O'Brien wrote the "Real Story" features and the case studies that begin and end each chapter. Changing any identifiable details, she brought her work into these cases from her practicums at a college counseling center, a Veterans Administration Hospital, a judicial court system, and a women's therapy clinic. In addition to her outstanding academic credentials, Jennifer happens to be Professor Whitbourne's younger daughter. She is a member of Psi Chi, APAGS (the APA Graduate Student association), and the recipient of an outstanding undergraduate teaching assistant award. Her dissertation research, on the therapeutic alliance, will provide new insights into understanding this fundamental component of effective psychotherapy. She currently works as a researcher at the Veterans Administration Medical Center in Jamaica Plain, Boston, MA.

We have added two particularly exciting features to the Seventh Edition found in most chapters:

- **"Toward the DSM-5"** This boxed feature summarizes the current state of the DSM-5 proposals as of mid-2012, when the DSM-5 is close to its final form. In addition to this boxed feature, we discuss the DSM-5 within the chapters where we think the changes are of importance for understanding contemporary views of the disorder.

- **"You Be the Judge"** The ethical issues that psychologists grapple with are an integral part of research and practice. In these boxed features, we highlight a specific aspect of one of the disorders that we discuss in the chapter and present a question for you to answer. You will be the judge in deciding which position you want to take, after we inform you of both sides of the issue at stake.

To make it easier for previous users of the text to see what's changed, a summary of the most important revisions to each chapter follows.

CHAPTER 1: Overview to Understanding Abnormal Behavior

- Reduced length of sections on history of abnormal psychology
- Clarified the biopsychosocial perspective section
- Added a section on Behavioral Genetics
- Expanded the discussion of the developmental perspective

CHAPTER 2: Classification and Treatment Plans

- Tightened the description of the DSM-IV-TR
- Added a section on the International Classification of Diseases (ICD) system
- Provided greater focus on evidence-based practice

CHAPTER 3: Assessment

- Provided up-to-date information on the WAIS-IV and its use in assessment
- Greatly expanded the section on neuropsychological assessment including computerized testing
- Updated and expanded treatment of brain imaging methods
- Retained projective testing but with less focus on detailed interpretation of projective test data

CHAPTER 4: Theoretical Perspectives

- Retained the classic psychodynamic theories, but with updates from current research
- Expanded greatly the discussion of biological theories, and moved these to the beginning of the chapter
- Provided more detail on the cognitive-behavioral perspective to use as a basis for subsequent chapters that rely heavily on treatment based on this perspective

CHAPTERS 5-14: Anxiety Disorders to Eating and Impulse-Control Disorders

- Where appropriate, incorporated information about how DSM-5 will change conceptualization of these disorders, including what will be accepted changes in terminology

- Expanded the coverage of biological theories, including studies on genetics, epigenetics, and neuroimaging

- Completely updated treatment sections, giving emphasis to those approaches to treatment recommended through Evidence-Based Practice.

- Included newer therapies including mindfulness/meditation, relaxation, and Acceptance and Commitment Therapy

- Revised tables and figures to provide more readily accessible pedagogy

CHAPTER 15: Ethical and Legal Issues

- Expanded the discussion of APA's Ethics Code, including a table that summarizes its most important features

- Updated the cases with newer information, including a section on Kendra's Law

- Revised the section on forensic psychology, including examples from relevant case law

Do More

MCGRAW-HILL/BB/DO MORE

Through McGraw-Hill's partnership with Blackboard, *Abnormal Psychology: Clinical Perspectives on Psychological Disorders* offers a seamless integration of content and tools:

- Seamless gradebook between Blackboard and Connect

- Single sign-on providing seamless integration between McGraw-Hill content and Blackboard

- Simplicity in assigning and engaging your students with course materials

create Craft your teaching resources to match the way you teach! With McGraw-Hill Create, **www.mcgrawhillcreate.com,** you can easily rearrange chapters, combine material from other content sources, and quickly upload content you have written, such as your course syllabus or teaching notes. Find the content you need in Create by searching through thousands of leading McGraw-Hill textbooks. Arrange your book to fit your teaching style. Create even allows you to personalize your book's appearance by selecting the cover and adding your name, school, and course information. Order a Create book and you'll receive a complimentary print review copy in 3–5 business days or a complimentary electronic review copy (eComp) via e-mail in about an hour. Go to **www.mcgrawhillcreate.com** today and register. Experience how McGraw-Hill Create empowers you to teach *your* students *your* way.

Tegrity campus Tegrity Campus is a service that makes class time available all the time by automatically capturing every lecture in a searchable format for students to review when they study and complete assignments. With a simple one-click start and stop process, users capture all computer screens and corresponding audio. Students replay any part of any class with easy-to-use browser-based viewing on a PC or Mac. Educators know that the more students can see, hear, and experience class resources, the better they learn. With Tegrity Campus, students quickly recall key moments by using Tegrity Campus's unique search feature. This search helps students efficiently find what they need, when they need it, across an entire semester of class recordings. Help turn all your students' study time into learning moments immediately supported by your lecture.

CourseSmart CourseSmart e-Textbook This text is available as an eTextbook at **www.CourseSmart.com.** At CourseSmart your students can take advantage of significant savings off the cost of a print textbook, reduce their impact on the environment, and gain access to powerful Web tools for learning. CourseSmart eTextbooks can be viewed online or downloaded to a computer. The eTextbooks allow students to do full text searches, add highlighting and notes, and share notes with classmates. CourseSmart has the largest selection of eTextbooks available anywhere. Visit **www.CourseSmart.com** to learn more and to try a sample chapter.

Support Materials

The following ancillaries are available to accompany *Abnormal Psychology,* Seventh Edition. Please contact your McGraw-Hill sales representative for details concerning policies, prices, and availability, as some restrictions may apply.

For the Instructor

The password-protected instructor side of the Online Learning Center at www.mhhe.com/whitbourne7e contains the Instructor's Manual, Test Bank files, PowerPoint slides, Image Gallery, and other valuable material to help you design and enhance your course. Ask your local McGraw-Hill representative for your password.

The **Instructor's Manual** provides many tools useful for teaching the seventh edition. For each chapter, the Instructor's Manual includes an overview of the chapter, teaching objectives, suggestions and resources for lecture topics, classroom activities, and essay questions designed to help students develop ideas for independent projects and papers.

The **Test Bank** contains over 2,000 testing items. All testing items are classified as conceptual or applied, and referenced to the appropriate learning objective. All test questions are compatible with EZTest, McGraw-Hill's Computerized Test Bank program, which runs on both Macintosh and Windows computers and includes an editing feature that enables instructors to import their own questions, scramble items, and modify questions to create their own tests.

The **PowerPoint Presentations** are the key points of each chapter and contain key illustrations, graphs, and tables for instructors to use during their lectures.

Acknowledgments

The following instructors were instrumental in the development of the text, offering their feedback and advice as reviewers:

David Alfano, *Community College of Rhode Island*
Bryan Cochran, *University of Montana*
Julie A. Deisinger, *Saint Xavier University*
Angela Fournier, *Bemidji State University*
Richard Helms, *Central Piedmont Community College*
Heather Jennings, *Mercer County Community College*
Joan Brandt Jensen, *Central Piedmont Community College*
Cynthia Kalodner, *Towson University*
Patricia Kemerer, *Ivy Tech Community College*
Barbara Kennedy, *Brevard Community College-Palm Bay*
Joseph Lowman, *University of North Carolina-Chapel Hill*
Don Lucas, *Northwest Vista College*
James A. Markusic, *Missouri State University*
Mark McKellop, *Juniata College*
Maura Mitrushina, *California State UniversityNorthridge*
John Norland, *Blackhawk Technical College*
Karen Clay Rhines, *Northampton Community College*
Ty Schepis, *Texas State University*

William R. Scott, *Liberty University*
Dr. Wayne S. Stein, *Brevard Community College*
Marla Sturm, *Montgomery County Community College*
Terry S. Trepper, *Purdue University Calumet*
Naomi Wagner, *San Jose State University*
Nevada Winrow, *Baltimore City Community College*

A great book can't come together without a great publishing team. We'd like to thank our editorial team, all of whom worked with us through various stages of the publishing process. Special gratitude goes to our editor, Krista Bettino, whose vision helped us present the material in a fresh and student-oriented manner. Barbara Heinssen, Development Manager, aided in development and redesign of this new edition. Anne Fuzellier, Managing Editor, and Chantelle Walker, Editorial Coordinator, assisted us through the complex publication process. Sarah Colwell, Digital Development Editor, and Neil Kahn, Digital Product Analyst, ensured that the material is translated into digital media, allowing greater access for students and instructors. Laura Byrnes, Marketing Coordinator, also deserves our special thanks.

A Letter from the Author

I am very glad that you are choosing to read my textbook. The topic of abnormal psychology has never been more fascinating or relevant. We constantly hear media reports of celebrities having meltdowns for which they receive quickie diagnoses that may or may not be accurate. Given all of this misinformation in the mind of the public, I feel that it's important for you to be educated in the science and practice of abnormal psychology. At the same time, psychological science grabs almost as many headlines in all forms of news media. It seems that everyone is eager to learn about the latest findings ranging from the neuroscience of behavior to the effectiveness of the newest treatment methods. These advances in brain scanning methods and studies of psychotherapy effectiveness are greatly increasing our understanding of how to help people with psychological disorders.

Particularly fascinating are the changes that will lead to the DSM-5. Each revision of the DSM brings with it controversies and challenges, and the DSM-5 is no exception. At the time of this writing, the American Psychological Association and other mental health organizations had submitted challenges to the new ways that the DSM-5 will define and categorize psychological disorders. Yet, the DSM-5 is perhaps based more so than any earlier edition on a strong research base. Scientists and practitioners will continue to debate the best ways to interpret this research. We all will benefit from these dialogues.

The profession of clinical psychology is also undergoing rapid changes. With changes in health care policy, it is very likely that more and more professionals ranging from psychologists to mental health counselors will be employed in providing behavioral interventions. By taking this first step toward your education now, you will be preparing yourself for a career that is increasingly being recognized as vital to helping individuals of all ages and all walks of life to achieve their greatest fulfillment.

I hope you find this text as engaging to read as I found to write. Please feel free to e-mail me with your questions and reactions to the material. As a user of McGraw-Hill's Connect in my own introductory psychology class, I can also vouch for its effectiveness in helping you achieve mastery of the content of abnormal psychology. I am also available to answer any questions you have, from an instructor's point of view, about how best to incorporate this book's digital media into your own teaching.

Thank you again for choosing to read my book!

Best,
Susan Krauss Whitbourne, PhD
swhitbo@psych.umass.edu

Overview to Understanding Abnormal Behavior

OUTLINE

Learning Objectives

1.1 Distinguish between normal but unusual behavior and between unusual but abnormal behavior.

1.2 Understand how explanations of abnormal behavior have changed through time.

1.3 Articulate the strengths and weaknesses of research methods.

1.4 Describe types of research studies.

CHAPTER 1

Case Report: Rebecca Hasbrouck

Demographic information: 18-year-old Caucasian female.

Presenting problem: Rebecca self-referred to the university psychotherapy clinic. She is a college freshman, living away from home for the first time. After the first week of school, Rebecca reports that she is having trouble sleeping, is having difficulty concentrating in her classes, and often feels irritable. She is frustrated by the difficulties of her coursework and states she is worried that her grades are beginning to suffer. She also reports that she is having trouble making friends at school and that she has been feeling lonely because she has no close friends here with whom she can talk openly. Rebecca is very close to her boyfriend of three years, though they have both started attending college in different cities. She was tearful throughout our first session, stating that, for the first time in her life, she feels overwhelmed by feelings of sadness. She reports that although the first week at school felt like "torture," she is slowly growing accustomed to her new lifestyle, but she still struggles with missing her family and boyfriend, as well as her friends from high school.

Relevant past history: Rebecca has no family history of psychological disorders. She reported that sometimes her mother tends to get "really stressed out" though she has never received treatment for this.

Symptoms: Depressed mood, difficulty falling asleep (insomnia), difficulty concentrating on schoolwork. She reported no suicidal ideation.

Case formulation: Although it appeared at first as though Rebecca was suffering from a major depressive episode, she did not meet the diagnostic criteria. In order to qualify as a major depressive episode, individuals must display at least five out of the nine criteria, and she only displayed three (insomnia, depressed mood, and difficulty concentrating). While the age of onset for depression tends to be around Rebecca's age, given her lack of a family history of depression and that her symptoms were occurring in response to a major stressor, the clinician determined that Rebecca was suffering from an Adjustment Disorder with depressed mood.

Treatment plan: The counselor will refer Rebecca for psychotherapy. Therapy should focus on improving her mood, and also should allow her a space to discuss her feelings surrounding the major changes that have been occurring in her life.

Sarah Tobin, PhD
Clinician

Rebecca Hasbrouck's case report summarizes the pertinent features that a clinician would include when first seeing a client after an initial evaluation. Each chapter of this book begins with a case report for a client whose characteristics are related to the chapter's topic. A fictitious clinician, Dr. Sarah Tobin, who supervises a clinical setting that offers a variety of services, writes the case reports. In some instances, she provides the services, and in others, she supervises the work of another psychologist. For each case, she provides a diagnosis using the official manual adopted by the profession known as *The Diagnostic and Statistical Manual of Mental Disorders, Fourth Text Revision (DSM-IV-TR)* (American Psychiatric Association, 2000).

At the end of the chapter, after you have developed a better understanding of the client's disorder, we will return to Dr. Tobin's description of the treatment results and expected future outcomes for the client. We also include Dr. Tobin's personal reflections on the case so that you will gain insight into the clinician's experience in working with psychologically disordered individuals.

The field of abnormal psychology is filled with countless fascinating stories of people who suffer from psychological disorders. In this chapter, we will try to give you some sense of the reality that psychological disturbance is certain to touch everyone, to some extent, at some point in life. As you progress through this course, you will almost certainly develop a sense of the challenges people associate with psychological problems. You will find yourself drawn into the many ways that mental health problems affect the lives of individuals, their families, and society. In addition to becoming more personally exposed to the emotional aspects of abnormal psychology, you will learn about the scientific and theoretical basis for understanding and treating the people who suffer from psychological disorders.

This young woman's apparent despair may be the symptoms of a psychological disorder.

1.1 What Is Abnormal Behavior?

It's possible that you know someone very much like Rebecca, who is suffering from more than the average degree of adjustment difficulties in college. Would you consider that person psychologically disturbed? Would you consider giving this person a diagnosis? What if a person you knew was not only depressed, but also showed up on your floor seemingly ready to harm herself? At what point do you draw the line between someone who has a psychological disorder and someone who, like Rebecca, has an adjustment disorder? Is it even necessary to give Rebecca any diagnosis at all? Questions about normality and abnormality such as these are basic to our understanding of psychological disorders.

Conditions like Rebecca's are likely to affect you in a very personal way. Perhaps you have been unusually depressed, fearful, or anxious, or maybe the emotional distress has been a step removed from you: Your father struggles with alcoholism, your mother has been hospitalized for severe depression, a sister has an eating disorder, or your brother has an irrational fear. If you have not encountered a psychological disorder within your immediate family, you have very likely encountered one in your extended family and circle of friends. You may not have known the formal psychiatric diagnosis for the problem, and you may not have understood its nature or cause, but you knew that something was wrong and recognized the need for professional help.

Until they are forced to face such problems, most people believe that "bad things" happen only to other people. Other people have car accidents, succumb to cancer, or become severely depressed.

We hope that reading this textbook will help you go beyond this "other people" syndrome. Psychological disorders are part of the human experience, touching the life—either directly or indirectly—of every person. As you read about these disorders and the people who suffer with them, you will find that most of these problems are treatable, and many are preventable.

1.2 The Social Impact of Psychological Disorders

Put yourself in the following situation. An urgent message awaits you from Jeremy's mother. Your best friend in high school, Jeremy has just been admitted to a psychiatric hospital and begs to see you, because only you can understand what he is going through. You are puzzled and distressed by this news. You had no idea that he had any psychological problems. What will you say to him? Can you ask him what's wrong? Can you ask him how he feels? Do you dare inquire about what his doctors have told him about his chances of getting better? What will it be like to see him in a psychiatric hospital? Do you think you could be friends with someone who has spent time in such a place?

Now imagine the same scenario, but instead you receive news that Jeremy was just admitted to the emergency room of a general hospital with an acute appendicitis. You know exactly how to respond when you go to see him. You will ask him how he feels, what exactly is wrong with him, and when he will be well again. Even though you might not like hospitals very much, at least you have a pretty good idea about what hospital patients are like. It does not seem peculiar to imagine Jeremy as a patient in this kind of hospital. It would probably be much easier for you to understand and accept your friend's physical illness than his psychological disorder, and you would probably not even consider whether you could be friends with him again after he is discharged.

People with psychological disorders often face situations like Jeremy's in which the people close to them aren't sure how to respond to their symptoms. Even worse, they experience profound and long-lasting emotional and social effects even after their

The family of individuals with psychological disorders face significant stress when their relatives must be hospitalized.

symptoms are brought under control and they can resume their former lives. They also must cope with the personal pain associated with the disorder itself. Think about Rebecca and her unhappiness. Rather than enjoying her newly found independence while at college like her classmates, she is experiencing extreme amounts of sadness and loneliness. She is unable to focus on her studies, make new friends, or even sleep.

Social attitudes toward people with psychological disorders range from discomfort to outright prejudice. Language, humor, and stereotypes all portray psychological disorders in a negative light and people often fear that people suffering from these disorders are violent and dangerous. There seems to be something about a psychological disorder that makes people want to distance themselves from it as much as possible. The result of these stereotypes is social discrimination, which only serves to complicate the lives of the afflicted even more.

In the chapters that follow, you will read about a wide range of disorders involving mood, anxiety, substance abuse, sexuality, and thought disturbance. The case descriptions will give you a glimpse into the feelings and experiences of people who have these disorders, and you may find that some of these individuals seem similar to you or to people you know. As you read about the disorders, put yourself in the place of the people who have these conditions. Consider how they feel and how they would like people to treat them. We hope that you will realize that our discussion is not about disorders, but about the people with these disorders.

1.3 Defining Abnormality

How would you define abnormal behavior? Read the following examples. Which of these behaviors do you regard as abnormal?

- Finding a "lucky" seat in an exam
- Inability to sleep, eat, study, or talk to anyone else for days after a lover says, "It's over between us"
- Breaking into a cold sweat at the thought of being trapped in an elevator
- Swearing, throwing pillows, and pounding fists on the wall in the middle of an argument with a roommate
- Refusing to eat solid food for days at a time in order to stay thin
- Engaging in a thorough hand-washing after coming home from a bus ride
- Believing that the government has agents who are eavesdropping on telephone conversations
- Drinking a six-pack of beer a day in order to be "sociable" with friends after work

If you're like most people, you probably found it difficult to decide between normal and abnormal. It is surprisingly difficult to make this distinction, but it is important to establish some criteria for abnormality.

The mental health community currently uses diagnostic procedures to decide on whether a given individual fits the criteria for abnormality. There are currently five criteria for a psychological disorder. The first is that of "clinical significance," meaning that the behavior involves a measurable degree of impairment. Second, the individual must be experiencing distress or must be engaging in behaviors that present the risk of death, hospitalization, or incarceration. Third, the individual's behavior cannot be a socially expectable response to a particular event such as the death of a close friend or relative. Fourth, the behavior must be linked to some underlying disturbance within the individual, whether psychological or biological. Fifth, the individual's behavior cannot be defined solely in terms of social rebellion or deviance. Thus, in some oppressive political symptoms, people were "diagnosed" as having a psychological disorder when in reality, the government sought to find a way to silence protestors.

This young woman is distressed over her inability to fall asleep, but does this mean she has a psychological disorder?

1.4 What Causes Abnormal Behavior?

However defined, we can best conceptualize abnormal behavior from multiple perspectives that incorporate biological, psychological, and sociocultural factors.

Biological Causes

The biological domain includes genetic and environmental influences on physical functioning. People with psychological disorders may inherit a predisposition to developing behavioral disturbances. Of particular interest are inherited factors that alter the functioning of the nervous system. There are also physiological changes that affect behavior, which other conditions in the body cause, such as brain damage or exposure to harmful environmental stimuli. For example, a thyroid abnormality can cause a person's moods to fluctuate widely. Brain damage resulting from a head trauma can result in aberrant thought patterns. Toxic substances or allergens in the environment can also cause a person to experience disturbing emotional changes and behavior.

Psychological Causes

Psychological causes of abnormal behavior involve disturbances in thoughts and feelings. As you will learn in this book, there are a variety of alternative explanations of abnormal behavior that focus on factors such as past learning experiences, maladaptive thought patterns, and difficulties coping with stress. The varying theoretical perspectives within abnormal psychology reflect differences in assumptions about the underlying causes of human behavior. Treatment models based on these theoretical perspectives reflect these varying assumptions.

Sociocultural Causes

The term *sociocultural* refers to the various circles of influence on the individual ranging from close friends and family to the institutions and policies of a country or the world as a whole. Discrimination, whether based on social class, income, race and ethnicity, or

TABLE 1.1 **Causes of Abnormal Behavior**

Biological	Genetic inheritance
	Physiological changes
	Exposure to toxic substances
Psychological	Past learning experiences
	Maladaptive thought patterns
	Difficulties coping with stress
Sociocultural	Social policies
	Discrimination
	Stigma

stigma
A label that causes certain people to be regarded as different, defective, and set apart from mainstream members of society.

gender, can influence the development of abnormal behavior. For people who are diagnosed with a psychological disorder, social stigmas associated with being "mental patients" can further affect their symptoms. A **stigma** is a label that causes us to regard certain people as different, defective, and set apart from mainstream members of society. In addition to increasing the burden for them and for their loved ones, a stigma deters people from obtaining badly needed help, and thereby perpetuates a cycle in which many people in need become much worse. The stigma of psychological disorders affects people from ethnic and racial minorities more severely than those from mainstream society. For example, European-American adolescents and their caregivers are twice as likely as members of minority groups to define problems in mental health terms or to seek help for such problems (Roberts, Alegría, Roberts, & Chen, 2005).

The Biopsychosocial Perspective

Table 1.1 summarizes the three categories of the causes of abnormality. Disturbances in any of these areas of human functioning can contribute to the development of a psychological disorder. However, we cannot so neatly divide the causes of abnormality. There is often considerable interaction among the three sets of influences.

biopsychosocial
A model in which the interaction of biological, psychological, and sociocultural factors is seen as influencing the development of the individual.

Social scientists use the term **biopsychosocial** to refer to the interaction in which biological, psychological, and sociocultural factors play a role in the development of an individual's symptoms. The biopsychosocial perspective incorporates a developmental viewpoint. This means that individuals must be seen as changing over time. Biopsychosocial factors interact to alter the individual's expression of behavioral patterns over time. Thus, it is important to examine early risk factors that make an individual vulnerable to developing a disorder. Similarly, risk factors may vary according to the individual's position in the life span (Whitbourne & Meeks, 2011).

As you will see when reading about the conditions in this textbook, the degree of influence of each of these variables differs from disorder to disorder. For some disorders, such as schizophrenia, biology plays a dominant role. For other disorders, such as stress reactions, psychological factors predominate. For other conditions, such as post-traumatic stress disorder, that result, for example, from experiences under a terrorist regime, the cause is primarily sociocultural.

However, certain life experiences can protect people from developing conditions to which they are vulnerable. Protective factors, such as loving caregivers, adequate health care, and early life successes, reduce vulnerability considerably. In contrast, low vulnerability can heighten when people receive inadequate health care, engage in risky behaviors (such as using drugs), and get involved in dysfunctional relationships. The bottom line is that we can best conceptualize abnormal behavior as a complex interaction among multiple factors.

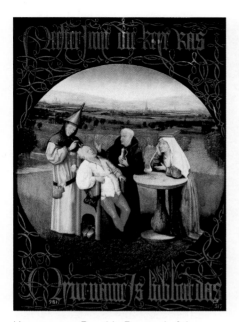

Hieronymous Bosch's *Removal of the Stone of Folly* depicted a medieval "doctor" cutting out the presumed source of madness from a patient's skull. The prevailing belief was that spiritual possession was the cause of psychological disorder.

The Greeks sought advice from oracles, wise advisors who made pronouncements from the gods.

1.5 Prominent Themes in Abnormal Psychology throughout History

The greatest thinkers of the world, from Plato to the present day, have attempted to explain the varieties of human behavior that constitute abnormality. Three prominent themes in explaining psychological disorders recur throughout history: the spiritual, the scientific, and the humanitarian. **Spiritual explanations** regard abnormal behavior as the product of possession by evil or demonic spirits. **Humanitarian explanations** view psychological disorders as the result of cruelty, stress, or poor living conditions. **Scientific explanations** look for causes that we can objectively measure, such as biological alterations, faulty learning processes, or emotional stressors.

Spiritual Approach

The earliest approach to understanding abnormal behavior is spiritual; the belief that people showing signs of behavioral disturbance were possessed by evil spirits. Archeological evidence dating back to 8000 B.C. suggests that the spiritual explanation was prevalent in prehistoric times. Skulls of the living had holes cut out of them, a process called "trephining," apparently in an effort to release the evil spirits from the person's head (Maher & Maher, 1985). Archeologists have found evidence of trephining from many countries and cultures, including the Far and Middle East, the Celtic tribes in Britain, ancient and recent China, India, and various peoples of North and South America, including the Mayans, Aztecs, Incas, and Brazilian Indians (Gross, 1999).

Another ancient practice was to drive away evil spirits through the ritual of exorcism, a physically and mentally painful form of torture carried out by a shaman, priest, or medicine man. Variants of shamanism have appeared throughout history. The Greeks sought advice from oracles who they believed were in contact with the gods. The Chinese practiced magic as a protection against demons. In India, shamanism flourished for centuries, and it still persists in Central Asia.

spiritual explanations
Regard psychological disorders as the product of possession by evil or demonic spirits.

humanitarian explanations
Regard psychological disorders as the result of cruelty, stress, or poor living conditions.

scientific explanations
Regard psychological disorders as the result of causes that we can objectively measure, such as biological alterations, faulty learning processes, or emotional stressors.

In this modern-day re-enactment of the Salem Witchcraft trials, a woman is tortured for her supposed crimes.

During the Middle Ages, people widely practiced magical rituals and exorcism, and administered folk medicines. Society considered people with psychological difficulties sinners, witches, or embodiments of the devil, and they were punished severely. Malleus Malificarum, an indictment of witches written by two Dominican monks in Germany in 1486, became the Church's justification for denouncing witches as heretics and devils whom it had to destroy in the interest of preserving Christianity. The Church recommended "treatments" such as deportation, torture, and burning at the stake. Women were the main targets of persecution. Even in the late 1600s in colonial America, the Puritans sentenced people to burning at the stake, as evidenced by the famous Salem Witchcraft trials.

Humanitarian Approach

Dorothea Dix was a Massachusetts reformer who sought to improve the treatment of people with psychological disorders in the mid-1800s.

The humanitarian approach developed throughout history, in part as a reaction against the spiritual approach and its associated punishment of people with psychological disorders. Poorhouses and monasteries became shelters, and although they could not offer treatment, they provided some protective measures. Unfortunately, these often became overcrowded, and rather than provide protection themselves, they became places where abuses occurred. For example, society widely believed that psychologically disturbed people were insensitive to extremes of heat and cold, or to the cleanliness of their surroundings. Their "treatment" involved bleeding, forced vomiting, and purging. It took a few courageous people, who recognized the inhumanity of the existing practices, to bring about sweeping reforms. By the end of the eighteenth century, hospitals in France, Scotland, and England attempted to reverse these harsh practices. The idea of "moral treatment" took hold—the notion that people could develop self-control over their behaviors if they had a quiet and restful environment. Institutions used restraints only if absolutely necessary, and even in those cases the patient's comfort came first.

Conditions in asylums again began to worsen in the early 1800s as facilities suffered from overcrowding and staff resorted to physical punishment to control the patients. In 1841, a Boston schoolteacher named Dorothea Dix (1802–1887) took up the cause of reform. Horrified by the inhumane conditions in the asylums, Dix appealed to the Massachusetts Legislature for more state-funded public hospitals to provide humane treatment for mental patients. From Massachusetts, Dix spread her message throughout North America and Europe.

Although deinstitutionalization was designed to enhance the quality of life for people who had been held years in public psychiatric hospitals, many individuals left institutions only to find a life of poverty and neglect on the outside.

Over the next 100 years, governments built scores of state hospitals throughout the United States. Once again, however, it was only a matter of time before the hospitals became overcrowded and understaffed. It simply was not possible to cure people by providing them with the well-intentioned, but ineffective, interventions proposed by moral treatment. However, the humanitarian goals that Dix advocated had a lasting influence on the mental health system. Her work was carried forward into the twentieth century by advocates of what became known as the mental hygiene movement.

Until the 1970s, despite the growing body of knowledge about the causes of abnormal behavior, the actual practices in the day-to-day care of psychologically disturbed people were sometimes as barbaric as those in the Middle Ages. Even people suffering from the least severe psychological disorders were often housed in the "back wards" of large and impersonal state institutions, without adequate or appropriate care. Institutions restrained patients with powerful tranquilizing drugs and straitjackets, coats with sleeves long enough to wrap around the patient's torso. Even more radical was the indiscriminate use of behavior-altering brain surgery or the application of electrical shocks—so-called treatments that were punishments intended to control unruly patients (see more on these procedures in Chapter 2).

Public outrage over these abuses in mental hospitals finally led to a more widespread realization that mental health services required dramatic changes. The federal government took emphatic action in 1963 with the passage of groundbreaking legislation. The Mental Retardation Facilities and Community Mental Health Center Construction Act of that year initiated a series of changes that would affect mental health services for decades to come. Legislators began to promote policies designed to move people out of institutions and into less restrictive programs in the community, such as vocational rehabilitation facilities, day hospitals, and psychiatric clinics. After their discharge from the hospital, people entered halfway houses, which provided a supportive environment in which they could learn the necessary social skills to re-enter the community. By the mid-1970s, the state mental hospitals, once overflowing with patients, were practically deserted. These hospitals freed hundreds of thousands of institutionally confined people to begin living with greater dignity and autonomy. This process, known as the deinstitutionalization movement, promoted the release of psychiatric patients into community treatment sites.

Unfortunately, the deinstitutionalization movement did not completely fulfill the dreams of its originators. Rather than abolishing inhumane treatment, deinstitutionalization created another set of woes. Many of the promises and programs hailed as alternatives to institutionalization ultimately failed to come through because of inadequate

Table 1.2 **Healthy People 2020 Goals**

In late 2010, the U.S. government's Healthy People project released goals for the coming decade. These goals are intended both to improve the psychological functioning of individuals in the U.S. and to expand treatment services.

- Reduce the suicide rate.
- Reduce suicide attempts by adolescents.
- Reduce the proportion of adolescents who engage in disordered eating behaviors in an attempt to control their weight.
- Reduce the proportion of persons who experience major depressive episodes.
- Increase the proportion of primary care facilities that provide mental health treatment onsite or by paid referral.
- Increase the proportion of children with mental health problems who receive treatment.
- Increase the proportion of juvenile residential facilities that screen admissions for mental health problems.
- Increase the proportion of persons with serious mental illness (SMI) who are employed.
- Increase the proportion of adults with mental disorders who receive treatment.
- Increase the proportion of persons with co-occurring substance abuse and mental disorders who receive treatment for both disorders.
- Increase depression screening by primary care providers.
- Increase the proportion of homeless adults with mental health problems who receive mental health services.

SOURCE: http://www.healthypeople.gov/2020/topicsobjectives2020/pdfs/MentalHealth.pdf

planning and insufficient funds. Patients shuttled back and forth between hospitals, halfway houses, and shabby boarding homes, never having a sense of stability or respect. Although the intention of releasing patients from psychiatric hospitals was to free people who had been deprived of basic human rights, the result may not have been as liberating as many had hoped. In contemporary American society, people who would have been in psychiatric hospitals four decades ago are moving through a circuit of shelters, rehabilitation programs, jails, and prisons, with a disturbing number of these individuals spending long periods of time as homeless and marginalized members of society.

Contemporary advocates of the humanitarian approach suggest new forms of compassionate treatment for people who suffer from psychological disorders. These advocates encourage mental health consumers to take an active role in choosing their treatment. Various advocacy groups have worked tirelessly to change the way the public views mentally ill people and how society deals with them in all settings. These groups include the National Alliance on Mental Illness (NAMI), as well as the Mental Health Association, the Center to Address Discrimination and Stigma, and the Eliminate the Barriers Initiative. The U.S. federal government has also become involved in antistigma programs as part of efforts to improve the delivery of mental health services through the President's New Freedom Commission (Hogan, 2003). Looking forward into the next decade, the U.S. government has set the 2020 Healthy People initiative goals as focused on improving significantly the quality of treatment services (see Table 1.2).

Scientific Approach

Early Greek philosophers were the first to attempt a scientific approach to understanding psychological disorders. Hippocrates (ca. 460–377 B.C.), considered the founder of modern medicine, believed that there were four important bodily fluids that influenced physical and mental health, leading to four personality dispositions. To treat a psychological disorder would require ridding the body of the excess fluid. Several hundred years later, the Roman physician Claudius Galen (A.D. 130–200) developed a system of medical knowledge based on anatomical studies.

Dr. Benjamin Rush, founder of American psychiatry, was an ardent reformer who promoted the scientific study of psychological disorders.

Scientists made very few significant advances in the understanding of abnormality until the eighteenth century. Benjamin Rush (1745–1813), the founder of American psychiatry, rekindled interest in the scientific approach to psychological disorders. In 1783, Rush joined the medical staff of Pennsylvania Hospital. Appalled by the poor hospital conditions, he advocated for improvements such as placing psychologically disturbed patients in their own wards, giving them occupational therapy, and prohibiting visits from curiosity seekers who would visit the hospital for entertainment.

Reflecting the prevailing methods of the times, Rush also supported the use of bloodletting and purging in the treatment of psychological disorders as well as the "tranquilizer" chair, intended to reduce blood flow to the brain by binding the patient's head and limbs. Rush also recommended submerging patients in cold shower baths and frightening them with death threats. He thought that fright inducement would counteract the overexcitement that he believed was responsible for the patients' violent behavior (Deutsch, 1949).

In 1844, a group of 13 mental hospital administrators formed the Association of Medical Superintendents of American Institutions for the Insane. The organization eventually changed its name to the American Psychiatric Association. German psychiatrist Wilhelm Greisinger published *The Pathology and Therapy of Mental Disorders* in 1845, which proposed that "neuropathologies" were the cause of psychological disorders. Another German psychiatrist, Emil Kraepelin, promoted a classification system much like that applied to medical diagnoses. He proposed that disorders could be identified by their patterns of symptoms. Ultimately, this work provided the scientific basis for current diagnostic systems.

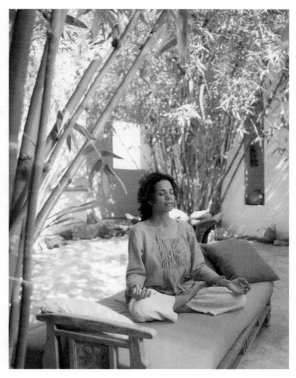

Positive psychology emphasizes personal growth through meditation and other alternate routes to self-discovery.

The scientific approach to psychological disorders also gained momentum as psychiatrists and psychologists proposed behavior models that included explanations of abnormality. In the early 1800s, European physicians experimented with hypnosis for therapeutic purposes. Eventually, these efforts led to the groundbreaking work of Viennese neurologist Sigmund Freud (1856–1939), who in the early 1900s developed psychoanalysis, a theory and system of practice that relied heavily on the concepts of the unconscious mind, inhibited sexual impulses, and early development.

Throughout the twentieth century, psychologists developed models of normal behavior, which eventually became incorporated into systems of therapy. The work of Russian physiologist Ivan Pavlov (1849–1936), known for his discovery of classical conditioning, became the basis for the behaviorist movement begun in the United States by John B. Watson (1878–1958). B. F. Skinner (1904–1990) formulated a systematic approach to operant conditioning, specifying the types and nature of reinforcement as a way to modify behavior. In the twentieth century, these models continued to evolve into the social learning theory of Albert Bandura (1925–), the cognitive model of Aaron Beck (1921–), and the rational-emotive therapy approach of Albert Ellis (1913–2007).

In the 1950s, scientists experimenting with pharmacological treatments invented medications that for the first time in history could successfully control the symptoms of psychological disorders. Now, patients could receive treatments that would allow them to live for extended periods of time on their own outside psychiatric hospitals. In 1963, the Mental Retardation Facilities and Community Mental Health Center Construction Act proposed patient treatment in clinics and treatment centers outside of mental hospitals. This legislation paved the way for the deinstitutionalization movement and subsequent efforts to continue to improve community treatment.

Most recently, the field of abnormal psychology is benefiting from the **positive psychology** movement, which emphasizes the potential for growth and change throughout life. The movement views psychological disorders as difficulties that inhibit the individual's ability to achieve highly subjective well-being and feelings of fulfillment. In addition, the positive psychology movement emphasizes prevention rather than intervention. Instead of fixing

positive psychology
Perspective that emphasizes the potential for growth and change throughout life.

problems after they occur, it would benefit people more if they could avoid developing symptoms in the first place. Although its goals are similar to those of the humanitarian approach, the positive psychology movement has a strong base in empirical research and as a result is gaining wide support in the field.

1.6 Research Methods in Abnormal Psychology

As you've just learned, the scientific approach led to significant advances in the understanding and treatment of abnormal behavior. The essence of the scientific method is objectivity, the process of testing ideas about the nature of psychological phenomena without bias before accepting these ideas as adequate explanations.

The scientific method involves a progression of steps from posing questions of interest to sharing the results with the scientific community. Throughout the scientific method, researchers maintain the objectivity that is the hallmark of the scientific approach. This means that they do not let their personal biases interfere with the data collection or interpretation of findings. In addition, researchers must always be open to alternative explanations that could account for their findings.

Although the scientific method is based on objectivity, this does not mean that scientists have no personal interest in what they are studying. In fact, it is often quite the opposite. Many researchers become involved in the pursuit of knowledge in areas that relate to experiences in their own lives, particularly in the field of abnormal psychology. They may have relatives afflicted with certain disorders or they may have become puzzled by a client's symptoms. In conducting their research, however, they cannot let these personal biases get in the way.

Thus, in posing questions of interest, psychological researchers may wonder whether a particular kind of experience led to an individual's symptoms, or they may speculate about the role of particular biological factors. Clinical psychologists are also interested in finding out whether a certain treatment will effectively treat the symptoms of a disorder. In either case, the ideal approach to answering these questions involves a progression through a set of steps in which the psychologist proposes a hypothesis, conducts a study, and collects and analyzes the data. Eventually, they communicate results through publication in scientific journals.

1.7 Experimental Design

independent variable
The variable whose level is adjusted or controlled by the experimenter.

dependent variable
The variable whose value is the outcome of the experimenter's manipulation of the independent variable.

When using experimental design in research, an investigator sets up a test of a hypothesis by constructing a manipulation of a key variable of interest. The variable that the investigator manipulates is called the **independent variable,** meaning that the investigator controls it. The investigator sets up at least two conditions that reflect different levels of the independent variable. In most cases, these conditions are the "experimental" or treatment group (the group that receives the treatment) and the "control" group (the group that receives no treatment or a different treatment). The researchers then compare the groups on the **dependent variable,** which is the variable that they observe. Key to the objectivity of experimental research is the requirement that the researchers always randomly assign participants to the different groups. A study would be flawed if all the men were in the experimental group, for example, and all the women were in the control group.

In research on the causes of abnormal behavior, it may be difficult to set up a true experimental study. Many of the variables that are of most interest to psychologists are ones that the investigator cannot control; hence, they are not truly "independent." For example, depression can never be an independent variable because the investigator cannot manipulate it. Similarly, investigators cannot randomly assign people to groups based on their biological sex. Studies that investigate differences among groups not determined by random assignment are known as "quasi-experimental."

The majority of true experimental studies in abnormal psychology, at least those on humans, test not the causes of abnormal behavior, but the effectiveness of particular treatments where it is possible to design randomly assigned control and experimental groups. Investigators evaluate a treatment's effectiveness by comparing the groups on dependent variables such as symptom alleviation. There may be more than one experimental group, depending on the nature of the particular study.

It is common practice in studies evaluating therapy effectiveness to have a **placebo condition** in which participants receive a treatment similar to the experimental treatment, but lacking the key feature of the treatment of interest. If the study is evaluating effectiveness of medication, the placebo has inert ingredients. In studies evaluating effectiveness of therapy, scientists must design the placebo in

---

Toward the DSM-5

Definition of a Mental Disorder

There are five criteria for a mental disorder in the *DSM-5*, the same number as was included in *DSM-IV*. There will be slight wording changes, but the criteria still refer to "clinically significant" to establish the fact that the behaviors under consideration are not passing symptoms or minor difficulties. *DSM-5* refers to the behaviors as having a "psychobiological function," a term that *DSM-IV* does not use. Both the *DSM-IV* and *DSM-5* state that disorders must occur outside the norm of what is socially accepted and expected for people experiencing particular life stresses. *DSM-5* also specifies that the disorder must have "diagnostic validity," meaning that, for example, the diagnoses predict future behavior or responses to treatment. The diagnosis of abnormality also must be clinically useful, meaning that it provides either a better understanding of the disorder or leads to better assessment and treatment than would otherwise be the case. Finally, the authors of *DSM-5* provide a caution against changing the lists of disorders (either adding to or subtracting) without taking into account potential benefits and risks. For example, adding a new diagnosis might lead to labeling as "abnormal" a behavior previously considered "normal." The advantage of having the new diagnosis must outweigh the harm of categorizing a "normal" person as having a "disorder." Similarly, deleting a diagnosis for a disorder that requires treatment (and hence insurance coverage) might leave individuals who still require that treatment vulnerable to withholding of care or excess payments for treatment.

---

a way that mimics, but is not the same as the actual therapy. Ideally, the researchers would want the placebo participants to receive treatments of the same frequency and duration as the experimental group participants who are receiving psychotherapy.

Expectations about the experiment's outcome can affect both the investigator and the participant. These so-called "demand characteristics" can compromise the conclusions about the intervention's true effectiveness. Obviously, the investigator should be as unbiased as possible, but there still may be subtle ways that he or she communicates cues that affect the participant's response. The participant may also have a personal agenda in trying to prove or disprove the study's supposed true intent. The best way to eliminate demand characteristics is to use a **double-blind** method, which shields both investigator and participant from knowing either the study's purpose or the nature of the patient's treatment.

In studies involving medication, a completely inert placebo may not be sufficient to establish true experimental control. In an "active placebo" condition, researchers build the experimental medication's side effects into the placebo. If they know that a medication produces dry mouth, difficulty swallowing, or upset stomach, then the placebo must also mimic these side effects or participants will know they are receiving placebos.

placebo condition
Condition in an experiment in which participants receive a treatment similar to the experimental treatment, but lacking the key feature of the treatment of interest.

double-blind
An experimental procedure in which neither the person giving the treatment nor the person receiving the treatment knows whether the participant is in the experimental or control group.

1.8 Correlational Design

Studies based on a correlational design involve tests of relationships between variables that researchers cannot experimentally manipulate. We express the correlation statistic in terms of a number between +1 and −1. Positive numbers represent positive correlations, meaning that, as scores on one variable increase, scores on the second variable increase. For example, because one aspect of depression is that it causes a disturbance in normal sleep patterns, you would expect then that scores on a measure of depression would be positively correlated with scores on a measure of sleep disturbances. Conversely, negative correlations indicate that, as scores on one variable increase, scores on the second variable decrease. An example of a negative correlation is the relationship between depression and self-esteem. The more depressed people are, the lower their scores are on a measure of self-esteem. In many cases, there is no correlation between

Being Sane in Insane Places

In the early 1970s, psychologist David Rosenhan embarked upon a groundbreaking study that was to shatter people's assumptions about the difference between "sane" and "insane." Motivated by what he regarded as a psychiatric diagnostic system that led to the hospitalization of people inappropriately diagnosed as having schizophrenia, Rosenhan and his co-workers decided to conduct their own experiment to put the system to the test. See whether you think their experiment proved the point.

Eight people with no psychiatric history of symptoms of any kind, employed in a variety of professional occupations, checked themselves into psychiatric hospitals complaining about hearing voices that said, "Empty," "Hollow," and "Thud." These were symptoms that psychiatric literature never reported. In every other way, the "pseudopatients" provided factual information about themselves (except their names and places of employment). Each pseudopatient was admitted to his or her respective hospital; once admitted, they showed no further signs of experiencing these symptoms. However, the hospital staff never questioned their need to be hospitalized; quite the contrary, their behavior on the hospital wards, now completely "normal," was taken as further evidence of their need for continued hospitalization. Despite the efforts of the pseudopatients to convince the staff that there was nothing wrong with them, it took from 7 to 52 days for their discharge. Upon their release, they received the diagnosis of "schizophrenia in remission" (meaning that they, for the moment, no longer would have a diagnosis of schizophrenia).

There was profound reaction in the psychiatric community to the Rosenhan study. If it was so easy to institutionalize nonpatients, wasn't there something wrong with the diagnostic system? How about the tendency to label people as "schizophrenic" when there was nothing wrong with them, and to hang on to the label even when they no longer showed any symptoms? Additionally, the pseudopatients reported that they felt dehumanized by the staff and failed to receive any active treatment. Once on the outside, they could report to the world at large about the failings of psychiatric hospitals to provide appropriate treatment. True patients would not have received so much sympathetic press, and therefore, would not have paved the way for the deinstitutionalization movement that was to follow the study's widespread dissemination.

Now, you be the judge. Do you think that it was unethical for Rosenhan to devise such a study? The mental health professionals at the hospitals had no idea that they were the "subjects" of the study. They had responded to what seemed to them to be serious psychological symptoms by individuals voluntarily seeking admission. At the point of discharge, the fact that the doctors labeled the pseudopatients as being in remission implied that they were symptom-free, but there was no reason for the staff to doubt the truth of the symptoms. On the other hand, had the staff known they were in a study, they might have reacted very differently, and as a result, the study would not have had an impact.

How about the quality of this study from a scientific point of view? There was no control condition so it was not truly an experiment. Moreover, the study did not take objective measures of the staffs' behavior, nor were there direct outcome measures that the researchers could statistically analyze.

Q: *You be the judge:* Was Rosenhan's study, with its flaws, worthwhile? Did the ends justify the means?

two variables. In other words, two variables show no systematic relationship with each other. For example, depression is unrelated to height.

Just knowing that there is a correlation between two variables does not tell you whether one variable causes the other. The correlation simply tells you that the two variables are associated with each other in a particular way. Sleep disturbance might cause a higher score on a measure of depression, just as a high degree of depression might cause more disturbed sleep patterns. Or, a third variable that you have not measured could account for the correlation between the two variables that you have studied. Both depression and sleep disturbance could be due to an underlying physiological dysfunction.

Investigators who use correlational methods in their research must always be on guard for the potential existence of unmeasured variables influencing the observed results. However, beyond simply linking two variables to see if they are correlated, researchers can use advanced methods that take more complex relationships into account. For example, we can assess the relative contributions of sleep disturbances, self-esteem, gender, and social class with correlational methods that evaluate several related variables at the same time.

1.9 Types of Research Studies

How do investigators gather their data? There are several types of studies that psychologists use. The type of study depends in large part upon the question and the resources available to the investigator. Table 1.3 summarizes these methods.

Survey

Investigators use a **survey** to gather information from a sample of people representative of a particular population. They use surveys primarily in studies involving a correlational design when investigators seek to find out whether potentially related variables actually do relate to each other as hypothesized. In a survey, investigators design sets of questions to tap into these variables. They may conduct a survey to determine whether age is correlated with subjective well-being, controlling for the influence of health. In this case, the researcher may hypothesize that subjective well-being is higher in older adults, but only after taking into account the role of health.

Researchers also use surveys to gather statistics about the frequency of psychological symptoms. For example, the Substance Abuse and Mental Health Services Administration of the United States government (SAMHSA) conducts yearly surveys to establish the frequency of use of illegal substances within the population. The World Health Organization (WHO) conducts surveys comparing the frequency by country of psychological disorders. These surveys provide valuable epidemiological data that can assess the health of the population.

survey
A research tool used to gather information from a sample of people considered representative of a particular population, in which participants are asked to answer questions about the topic of concern.

Table 1.3 Research Methods in Abnormal Psychology

Type of Method	Purpose	Example
Survey	Obtain population data	Researchers working for a government agency attempt to determine disease prevalence through questionnaires administered over the telephone.
Laboratory study	Collect data under controlled conditions	An experiment is conducted to compare reaction times to neutral and fear-provoking stimuli.
Case study	An individual or a small group of individuals is studied intensively	A therapist describes the cases of members of a family who share the same unusual disorder.
Single case experimental design	The same person serves as subject in experimental and control conditions	Researchers report on the frequency of a client's behavior while the client is given attention (experimental treatment) and ignored (control condition) for aggressive outbursts in a psychiatric ward.
Behavioral genetics	Attempt to identify genetic patterns in inheritance of particular behaviors	Genetic researchers compare the DNA of people with and without symptoms of particular psychological disorders

REAL STORIES

Vincent van Gogh: Psychosis

"There is safety in the midst of danger. What would life be if we had no courage to attempt anything? It will be a hard pull for me; the tide rises high, almost to the lips and perhaps higher still, how can I know? But I shall fight my battle . . . and try to win and get the best of it."
Vincent van Gogh, December, 1881.

Vincent van Gogh, a Dutch-born post-impressionist painter, lived most of his life in poverty and poor physical and mental health. After his death, his work grew immensely in recognition and popularity. His now instantly recognizable paintings sell for tens of millions of dollars, while during his lifetime his brother, Theo, mainly supported the painter, sending him art supplies and money for living expenses. Van Gogh struggled with mental illness for much of his life, spending one year in an asylum before the last year of his life, when he committed suicide in 1890 at the age of 37.

Though the specific nature of van Gogh's mental illness is unknown, his 600 or so letters to Theo offer some insight into his experiences. Published in 1937, *Dear Theo: The Autobiography of Vincent van Gogh* provides an unfiltered glimpse into all aspects of his life including art, love, and his psychological difficulties. Van Gogh never received a formal diagnosis in his lifetime, and to this day many psychologists argue over the disorder from which he may have been suffering. Psychologists have suggested as many as 30 possible diagnoses ranging from schizophrenia and bipolar disorder to syphilis and alcoholism. Van Gogh's constant poor nutrition, excessive consumption of absinthe, and a tendency to work to the point of exhaustion undoubtedly contributed to and worsened any psychological issues he experienced.

Van Gogh's romantic life was highlighted by a series of failed relationships, and he never had children. When he proposed marriage to Kee Vos-Stricker in 1881, she and her parents turned him down because he was having difficulty supporting himself financially at the time. Kee was a widow with a child and van Gogh would not have been able to support the family fully. In response to this rejection, van Gogh held his hand over a lamp flame, demanding her father that he be allowed see the woman he loved, an event he was later unable to recall entirely. Unfortunately for van Gogh, the affection was never reciprocated. His longest known romantic relationship lasted for one year, during which he lived with a prostitute and her two children.

Van Gogh first learned to draw in middle school, a hobby that he carried on throughout his failed attempt at becoming a religious missionary. He failed his entrance exam for theology school in Amsterdam, and later failed missionary school. In 1880 he decided to devote his life to painting. After attending art school in Brussels, van Gogh moved around the Netherlands and fine-tuned his craft, often living in poverty and squalid conditions. He spent some time living with his parents, but never stayed with them long due to his tumultuous relationship with his father. By 1885, he began to gain recognition as an artist and had completed his first major work, *The Potato Eaters.* The following year, he moved to Paris where he lived with his brother and began to immerse himself in the thriving art world of the city. Due to his poor living conditions, van Gogh's health began to deteriorate, and so he moved to the countryside in the south of France. There he spent two months living with and working alongside his good friend and fellow painter Paul Gauguin. Their artistic differences led to frequent disagreements that slowly eroded their amiable companionship. In *Dear Theo*, Johanna van Gogh, Vincent's sister-in-law, writes about

Vincent Van Gogh's *Starry Night over the Rhone*, painted in 1888, one year before his death.

the notorious incident that took place on December 23, 1888. Van Gogh, "in a state of terrible excitement and high fever, had cut off a piece of his own ear, and had brought it as a gift to a woman in a brothel. There had been a violent scene; Roulin, the postman, managed to get him home, but the police intervened, found Vincent bleeding and unconscious in bed, and sent him to the hospital."

After the incident, van Gogh was committed to an asylum in Saint-Remy de Provence, France, for about one year. While in the hospital, he often reflected on the state of his mental health in letters to his brother:

"These last three months do seem so strange to me. There have been moods of indescribable mental anguish, sometimes moments when the veil of time and of inevitable circumstance seemed for the twinkling of an eye to be parted. After all, you are certainly right,

damn well right; even making allowance for hope, the thing is to accept the probably disastrous reality. I am hoping to throw myself once again wholly into my work, which has got behindhand."

While hospitalized and working on recovering from his "attacks," van Gogh spent most of his time working feverishly on painting, often finding inspiration in the scenery surrounding the asylum. For van Gogh, painting was a welcome relief that he hoped would cure his illness. Of his experiences with mental illness, he wrote "... I am beginning to consider madness as a disease like any other, and accept the thing as such; whereas during the crises themselves I thought that everything I imagined was real." It is clear from many of his letters that he had been experiencing hallucinations and perhaps delusions—two hallmark symptoms of psychological disorders involving psychosis, such as schizophrenia.

After his release from the asylum, van Gogh participated in art shows in Brussels and Paris. Though he remained artistically productive, his depression deepened until on July 29, 1890, he walked into a field and shot himself in the chest with a revolver, dying two days later. Van Gogh's last words, according to his brother who had rushed to be at his side at his deathbed, were "the sadness will last forever."

In his lifetime, Vincent van Gogh sold only one painting; in 1990 his *Portrait of Dr. Gachet* sold for $82.5 million, making it one of the most expensive paintings ever sold. His priceless work graces galleries around the globe and has an invaluable influence in the art world. Had his story taken place now, with many different options for psychological treatment of psychotic symptoms and depression, his life might not have been cut short so tragically.

Researchers report epidemiological data about the occurrence of psychological symptoms and disorders in terms of the time frame over which it occurs. The **incidence** of a disorder is the frequency of *new* cases of a disorder within a given time period. Respondents providing incidence data state whether they now have a disorder that they have never had before but now are experiencing. Incidence information can cover any time interval; people tend to report it in terms of one month, six months, and one year. Investigators use incidence data when they are interested in determining how quickly a disorder is spreading. For example, during an epidemic, health researchers need to know how to plan for controlling the disease, and so incidence data is most pertinent to this question.

The **prevalence** of a disorder refers to the number of people who have *ever* had the disorder over a specified period of time. To collect prevalence data, investigators ask respondents to state whether, during this period of time, they experienced the symptoms of the disorder. The time period of reference can be the day of the survey, in which case we call it point prevalence. There is also one-month prevalence, which refers to the 30 days preceding the study, and lifetime prevalence, which refers to the entire life of the respondent. For example, researchers may ask respondents whether they smoked cigarettes at any time during the past month (one-month prevalence) or whether they ever, in their lifetimes, used cigarettes (lifetime prevalence). Typically, lifetime prevalence is higher than one-month or point prevalence because the question captures all past experience of a disorder or a symptom.

incidence
The frequency of new cases within a given time period.

prevalence
The number of people who have ever had a disorder at a given time or over a specified period.

Laboratory Studies

Researchers carry out most experiments in psychological laboratories in which participants provide data under controlled conditions. Participants are exposed to conditions based upon the nature of the experimental manipulation. For example, investigators may show participants stimuli on computer screens and ask them to respond. The collected data might include speed of reaction time or memory for different types of stimuli.

Laboratory studies may also involve comparison of brain scan responses taken under differing conditions. Another type of laboratory study may involve observing people in small group settings in which the investigators study their interactions.

Although laboratories are ideal for conducting such experiments, they may also be appropriate settings for self-report data such as responses to questionnaires. Researchers can ask participants to complete their responses in a fixed period of time and under conditions involving a minimum of distractions. They may also provide them with self-report instruments to complete on a computer, allowing for the investigator to collect data in a systematic and uniform fashion across respondents.

The Case Study Method

case study
An intensive study of a single person described in detail.

Many of the researchers, from what the profession regards as classic studies in early abnormal psychology, based their findings on the **case study,** which is an intensive investigation of an individual or small group of individuals. For example, Freud based much of his theory on reports of his own patients—the development of their symptoms and their progress in therapy. In current research, investigators carry out case studies for a number of reasons. They afford the opportunity to report on rare cases, or the development of a disorder over time may be the focus of the study. For example, a clinical psychologist may write a report in a published journal about how she provided treatment to a client with a rare type of fear.

qualitative research
A method of analyzing data that provides research with methods of analyzing complex relationships that do not easily lend themselves to conventional statistical methods.

The advantage of an in-depth case study is also a potential disadvantage in that it does not involve enough experimental control to make a useful addition to the literature. Investigators using case studies, therefore, must be extremely precise in their methods and, as much as possible, take an objective and unbiased approach. There are standards for use in **qualitative research** that can ensure that researchers present case study data in a way that will be valuable to other investigators.

Single Case Experimental Design

single case experimental design
Design in which the same person serves as the subject in both the experimental and control conditions.

In a **single case experimental design (SCED)**, the same person serves as the subject in both the experimental and control conditions. Particularly useful for studies of treatment effectiveness, a single-subject design typically involves alternating off-on phases of the baseline condition ("A") and the intervention ("B"). The profession also refers to SCEDs as "ABAB" designs, reflecting the alternation between conditions A and B. Figure 1.1 shows an example of an SCED involving self-injurious behavior.

In cases where withholding the treatment in the "B" phase would present an ethical problem (because of an elimination of an effective treatment), researchers use a variation called the multiple baseline method. In a multiple baseline design, the researcher applies the treatment in an AB fashion so that it is never removed. The observation occurs across different subjects, for different behaviors, or in different settings. The researcher takes repeated measures of behavior in relation to introduction of the treatment. For example, in treating a suicidal client, an investigator may first target suicidal thoughts, and second, target suicidal behaviors. The power of the design is in showing that the behaviors change only when the researcher introduces specific treatments (Rizvi & Nock, 2008).

Investigations in Behavioral Genetics

concordance rate
Agreement ratios between people diagnosed as having a particular disorder and their relatives.

Researchers in the field of behavioral genetics and psychopathology attempt to determine the extent to which people inherit psychological disorders. Behavioral geneticists typically begin an investigation into a disorder's genetic inheritance after observing that the disorder shows a distinct pattern of family inheritance. This process requires obtaining complete family histories from people whom they can identify as having symptoms of the disorder. The investigators then calculate the **concordance rate,** or agreement ratios, between people diagnosed as having the disorder and their relatives. For example, a

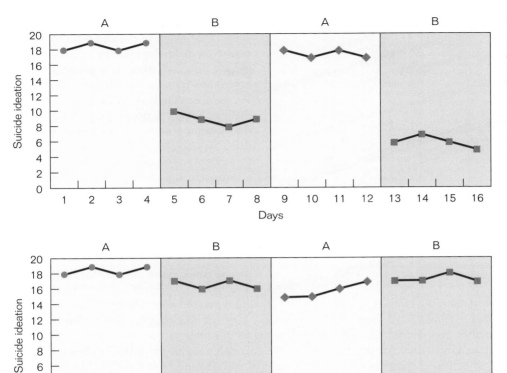

FIGURE 1.1 **SCED**

In an ABAB design, researchers observe behaviors in the "A" phase, institute treatment in the "B" phase, and then repeat the process. In this hypothetical study, suicide ideation seems to improve with treatment in the top set of graphs but shows no effect of treatment in the bottom set of graphs (Rizvi & Nock, 2008).

researcher may observe that 6 out of a sample of 10 twin pairs have the same diagnosed psychological disorder. This would mean that, among this sample, there is a concordance rate of .60 (6 out of 10). We would expect an inherited disorder to have the highest concordance between monozygotic or identical twins (whose genes are the same), with somewhat lower rates between siblings and dizygotic or fraternal twins (who are no more alike genetically than siblings of different ages), and even lower rates among more distant relatives.

A second approach in behavioral genetics is to study families who have adopted. The most extensive evidence available from these studies comes from the Scandinavian countries, where the governments maintain complete birth and adoption records. The research studies two types of adoptions. The first is an adoption study in which researchers establish the rates of the disorder in children whose biological parents have diagnosed psychological disorders, but whose adoptive parents do not. If the children have the disorder, this suggests that genetic factors play a stronger role than the environment. In the second adoption study, referred to as "cross-fostering," researchers examine the frequency of the disorder in children whose biological parents had no disorder, but whose adoptive parents do.

Twin studies are a third method of behavioral genetics. In these studies, researchers compare monozygotic twins reared together to those reared apart. Theoretically, if twins reared apart share a particular disorder, this suggests that the environment played a relatively minor role in causing that behavior.

These kinds of studies enable researchers to draw inferences about the relative contributions of biology and family environment to the development of psychological disorders. However, they are imprecise and have several potential serious flaws. Adoption studies can be suggestive, but are hardly definitive. There may be unmeasured characteristics of the adoptive parents that influence the development of the disorder in the children. The most significant threat to the usefulness of twin studies is the fact that the majority of monozygotic twins do not share the same amniotic sac during prenatal development (Mukherjee et al., 2009). They may not even share 100 percent of the same DNA (Ollikainen et al., 2010).

Gene mapping is revolutionizing the way that scientists understand and treat psychological disorders.

gene mapping
The attempt by biological researchers to identify the structure of a gene and the characteristics it controls.

molecular genetics
The study of how genes translate hereditary information.

In **gene mapping** researchers examine and connect variations in chromosomes to performance on psychological tests or diagnosis of specific disorders. **Molecular genetics** studies how genes translate hereditary information. We use these methods in the study of abnormal psychology to determine how hereditary information translates into behavior disorders. They have led to widespread advances in the understanding of such disorders as autism, schizophrenia, and various anxiety disorders (Hoffman & State, 2010).

Bringing It All Together: Clinical Perspectives

As you come to the close of this chapter, you now have an appreciation of the issues that are central to your understanding of abnormal psychology. We have tried to give you a sense of how complex it is to define abnormality, and you will find yourself returning to this issue as you read about many of the disorders in the chapters that follow. We will elaborate on the historical perspective in subsequent chapters as we look at theories of and treatments for specific disorders. Currently, developments are emerging in the field of abnormal psychology at an unbelievable pace due to the efforts of researchers applying the techniques described here. You will learn more about some of these research methods in the context of discussions regarding specific disorders. You will also develop an understanding of how clinicians, such as Dr. Sarah Tobin, look at the range of psychological disorders that affect people throughout the life span. We will give particular attention to explaining how disorders develop and how we can best treat them. Our discussion of the impact of psychological disorders forms a central theme for this book, as we return time and again to consideration of the human experience of psychological disorders.

Return to the Case: Rebecca Hasbrouck

An intern saw Rebecca at the counseling center once a week for 12 consecutive weeks. During the first few sessions she was often tearful, especially when talking about her boyfriend and how lonely she was feeling. In therapy, we worked on identifying her emotions and finding coping skills for dealing with stress. Eventually, Rebecca's feelings of sadness lifted as she became accustomed to her life on campus and was able to make a few close friends. Since she was feeling better, her sleeping also improved, which helped her to concentrate in class more easily, allowing her to perform better, and thus, feel more confident in herself as a student.

Dr. Tobin's reflections: It was clear to me in our initial session that Rebecca was a young woman who was having a particularly difficult time dealing with ordinary adjustment issues in adapting to college. She was overwhelmed by the many new experiences confronting her as well, and she seemed particularly unable to cope with being on her own and being separated from her support network including her family and boyfriend. Her high academic standards added to her stress and because she didn't have social support, she was unable to talk about the difficulties she was having, which surely perpetuated her problems. I am glad that she sought help early on before her difficulties became exacerbated and that she responded so well to treatment.

SUMMARY

- Questions about normality and abnormality are basic to our understanding of psychological disorders. They can affect us in very personal ways.

- Social impact can affect psychological disorders. Social attitudes toward people with psychological disorders range from discomfort to prejudice. Language, humor, and stereotypes all portray psychological disorders in a negative light. Stereotypes then result in social discrimination, which only serves to complicate the lives of the affected even more.

- The mental health community currently uses diagnostic procedures to define four criteria for abnormality: 1) **distress,** 2) **impairment,** 3) **risk,** and 4) **behavior outside the norms of the social and cultural context within which it takes place.** While these four criteria can serve as the basis for defining abnormality, often there is an interaction.

- Causes of abnormality incorporate **biological, psychological,** and **sociocultural** factors.

- Three prominent themes in explaining psychological disorders that recur throughout history include 1) spiritual, 2) scientific, and 3) humanitarian. **Spiritual** explanations regard abnormal behavior as the product of possession by evil or demonic spirits. **Humanitarian** explanations view psychological disorders as the result of cruelty, stress, or poor living conditions. **Scientific** explanations look for causes that we can objectively measure, such as biological alterations, faulty learning processes, or emotional stressors.

- Researchers use various methods to study the causes and treatment of psychological disorders. These include 1) the **scientific method,** which involves a progression of steps from posing questions of interest to sharing the results with the scientific community, 2) **experimental design,** which testes a hypothesis by constructing a manipulation of a key variable interest, and 3) **correlational design,** which involves tests of relationships between variables that researchers cannot experimentally manipulate.

- Types of research studies include **surveys, laboratories,** and **case studies.** Surveys enable researchers to estimate the incidence and prevalence of psychological disorders. In a laboratory, participants are exposed to conditions based on the nature of the experimental manipulation. Case study enables the researcher to intensively study one individual. This can also involve single-subject design, where the researcher studies one person at a time in both the experimental and control conditions, as he or she applies and removes treatment in alternating phases.

- Investigations in the field of behavioral genetics and psychotherapy attempt to determine the extent to which people inherit psychological disorders. Different studies enable researchers to draw inferences about the relative contributions of biology and family environment to the development of psychological disorders, but they are imprecise and have potential serious flaws.

KEY TERMS

Classification and Treatment Plans

Learning Objectives

2.1 Describe the experiences of the client and the clinician

2.2 Assess the strengths and weaknesses of the *DSM* approach to psychological disorders

2.3 Identify the International Classification of Diseases (ICD)

2.4 Explain steps of the diagnostic process

2.5 Describe treatment planning and goals

2.6 Explain the course and outcome of treatment

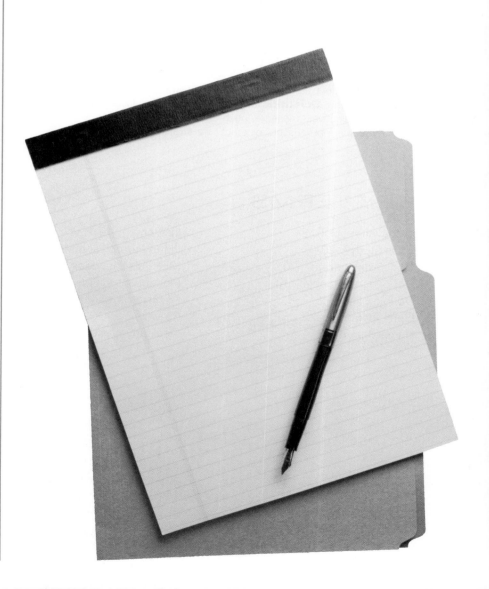

CHAPTER 2

Case Report: Peter Dickinson

Demographic information: 28-year-old Caucasian male.

Presenting problem: Peter's girlfriend of one year, Ashley, referred him to an outpatient mental health clinic. He is in his second year of working as a defense attorney at a small law firm. Ashley reported that about six months ago, Peter's parents began divorce proceedings, at which point she noticed some changes in his behavior. Although his job had always been challenging, Peter was a hard worker who devoted himself to his studies throughout his academic career and had been just as motivated at his current job. Since the divorce, however, Ashley reported that Peter had only been sleeping a few hours a night and was having trouble keeping up with his caseload at work. It had gotten so bad that the firm considered firing him.

When he was seen at the psychotherapy clinic, Peter reported that the past six months had been very difficult for him. Although he stated he had always been a "worrier," he couldn't get his parents' divorce off his mind, and it was interfering with his ability to focus and perform well at his job. He described most of the worried thoughts as fears that his parents' divorce would destroy their lives as well as his. He stated that he would worry that somehow their divorce was his fault, and that once the thought entered his mind, it would play on repeatedly like a broken record. He also explained that Ashley had threatened to break up with him if he didn't "get it together," about which he was also spending a great deal of time worrying. He stated that he constantly worried that he had ruined her life and that this thought was also very repetitive.

Peter was noticeably anxious and irritable throughout the session, especially when talking about his parents or about Ashley. Early in the

session, he expressed that he had been feeling very tense all day and that his stomach was "in knots." Throughout the session, his legs and hands were fidgety, and he stood up and sat down in his chair several times. He stated that since starting his new job, he had become very short-tempered with people, and often felt "wired" and tense, and as a result had a difficult time concentrating on his work and sleeping soundly. He explained that he couldn't remember the last time he felt calm or didn't worry about anything for an entire day. He also stated that he could barely think about anything other than his parents' divorce and his relationship problems with Ashley, even if he tried to get his mind off it. He reported that prior to learning of his parents' divorce, he was mainly "obsessive" about his work, which he noted was similar to how he was as an undergraduate and in law school. He stated that he was usually afraid that he would make an error, and would spend more time worrying about failing than actually doing his work. As a result, he said, he often had little time for friends or romantic relationships because he would feel guilty if he were engaging in pleasurable activities rather than focusing on his work. A serious relationship of four years ended after his ex-girlfriend grew tired of what she had called his "obsession" with working and his neglect of their relationship. Currently, faced with losing his job and another important relationship, Peter stated that he realizes for the first time that his anxiety might be interfering with his life.

Relevant history: Peter reported that his mother had a history of panic attacks and his father had taken anxiety medication, though he was unable to recall any further details of his family history. He stated that since he could remember he had "always" felt anxious and often worried about

Case Report *continued*

things more than other people. He remembered a particular instance in high school when he barely slept for two weeks because he was preparing for an argument for his school's debate team. Peter stated he has never had any psychotherapy or taken any psychiatric medication. He reported that although his worrying often makes him feel "down," he has never felt severely depressed and has no history of suicidal ideation.

Symptoms: Difficulty sleeping through the night, restlessness, difficulty concentrating, irritability. Peter stated that he found it difficult to control the worry and he spent most of his time worrying about either his parents' divorce, work, or his relationship with Ashley.

Case formulation: Peter meets all of the required *DSM-IV-TR* criteria for Generalized Anxiety Disorder (GAD). He had been displaying excessive worry for more days than not for at least the past six months, was unable to control his worry, and presented four of the six main symptoms associated with GAD. Additionally, Peter's worry was not related to fears of having a panic attack (as in Panic Disorder), or about being in social or public situations (as in Social Anxiety Disorder). His

anxiety was causing him significant problems at work and in his relationship with Ashley. Finally, Peter's anxiety was not the result of substance use.

Multiaxial assessment:

> Axis I: Generalized Anxiety Disorder
> Axis II: Deferred
> Axis III: None
> Axis IV: Parents' divorce, relationship problems, work-related stress

Treatment plan: Peter's treatment plan will involve a combination of two approaches. First, he will be referred to a psychiatrist for antianxiety medication to ease the physical symptoms of his anxiety. Cognitive behavioral psychotherapy will also be recommended, as this has been shown to be the most effective current therapeutic modality for treating GAD.

Sarah Tobin, Ph.D.
Clinician

Peter's life was thrown into havoc by the worsening of his anxiety symptoms, putting him at risk of losing his job and his relationship. Dr. Tobin's treatment plan suggests a set of steps to address Peter's immediate symptoms and ultimately to bring him longer-term relief. In this chapter, you will learn about how clinicians proceed through the steps of diagnosis and treatment planning. In order to help you understand these steps, we will introduce you to the fundamental concepts that guide these key processes.

2.1 Psychological Disorder: Experiences of Client and Clinician

psychologist
Health care professional offering psychological services.

client
A person seeking psychological treatment.

Psychologists working in the field of abnormal psychology examine not only the causes of abnormal behavior, but also the complex human issues involved in the therapeutic process. Throughout this text, you will read many cases of individual **clients** who seek treatment to alleviate their symptoms so they can lead more fulfilling lives. We begin this exploration by introducing you to the relevant players of "client" and "clinician."

The Client

patient
In the medical model, a person who receives treatment.

People working in the area of abnormal psychology refer to individuals seeking psychological intervention as "client" and **"patient."** In this book, our preference is to use the term *client,* reflecting the view that the people in treatment collaborate with those who treat them. We feel that the term *patient* carries with it the connotation of a passive rather than active participant. However, there are times when it is appropriate to use the term *patient* such as in the context of "outpatient treatment" and "patients' rights."

In this context, we wish to point out that you should definitely avoid some terminology and call people with psychological disorders by the name of their disorder. If you call someone a "schizophrenic" you are equating the person with the disorder. Instead, you will show greater sensitivity if you refer to the individual as "a person with schizophrenia." People are more than the sum of their disorders. By using your language carefully, you communicate greater respect for the total person.

The Clinician

In this book, we refer to the person providing treatment as the **clinician.** There are many types of clinicians who approach clinical work in a variety of ways, based on their training and orientation. **Psychiatrists** are people with degrees in medicine (MDs) who receive specialized advanced training in diagnosing and treating people with psychological disorders. **Clinical psychologists** have an advanced degree in the field of psychology and are trained in diagnosis and therapy. Clinical psychologists cannot administer medical treatments, but some U.S. states, such as Louisiana and New Mexico, as of 2011, grant them prescription privileges. Other states are also pushing to pass similar legislation.

There are two types of doctorates in psychology. The doctor of philosophy (PhD) is typically awarded for completing graduate training in research. In order to be able to practice, people who get their PhD's in clinical psychology also complete an internship. The doctor of psychology (PsyD) is the degree that professional schools of psychology award and typically involves less training in research. These individuals also must complete an internship in order to practice. Counseling psychologists, with either a doctorate in education (EdD) or (PhD) also serve as clinicians.

Professionals with master's degrees also provide psychological services. These include social workers, master's-level counselors, marriage and family therapists, nurse clinicians, and school psychologists. The mental health field also includes a large group of individuals who do not have graduate-level training but serve a critical role in the functioning and administration of the mental health system. Included in this group are occupational therapists, recreational therapists, and counselors who work in institutions, agencies, schools, and homes.

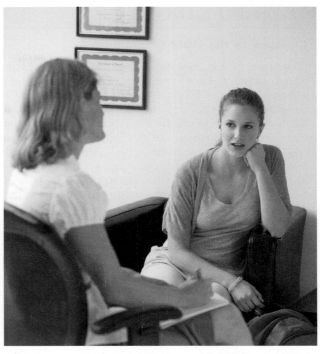

A trusting, positive relationship between therapist and client is crucial to a good therapeutic outcome.

clinician
The person providing treatment.

psychiatrists
People with degrees in medicine (MDs) who receive specialized advanced training in diagnosing and treating people with psychological disorders.

clinical psychologist
A mental health professional with training in the behavioral sciences who provides direct service to clients.

2.2 Diagnostic and Statistical Manual of Mental Disorders (DSM)

A diagnostic manual serves to provide consistent diagnoses across people based on the presence or absence of a set of specific symptoms. Without an accurate diagnostic manual, it is impossible for the clinician to decide on the best treatment path for a given client. Researchers also use diagnostic manuals to provide investigators with consistent terminologies to use when reporting their findings.

The profession uses two factors in evaluating a diagnostic manual's ability to do its job. The first is **reliability,** meaning that practitioners will apply the diagnoses consistently across individuals who have a particular set of symptoms. A manual would not be very useful if the symptom of sad mood led one clinician to assign a diagnosis of some sort of depressive disorder and another to assign a diagnosis of some type of anxiety disorder. The second factor is **validity,** meaning that the diagnoses represent real and distinct clinical phenomena.

Current diagnostic manuals are based on the medical model in that they focus on accurately labeling groups of symptoms with the intention of providing targeted treatments. Not everyone in the mental health system is comfortable with this model.

reliability
When used with regard to diagnosis, the degree to which clinicians provide diagnoses consistently across individuals who have a particular set of symptoms.

validity
The extent to which a test, diagnosis, or rating accurately and distinctly characterizes a person's psychological status.

Toward the DSM-5

Changes in the DSM-5 Structure

All editions of the *DSM* have generated considerable controversy, and the fifth edition seems to be no exception, at least so far. The most significant questions will concern the multiaxial system—the categorization of disorders along five separate axes. Task forces are attempting to determine whether they should follow the system in use by the World Health Organization's International Classification of Diseases (ICD). The first three axes would be collapsed into one axis that contains *all* diagnoses, including psychiatric and medical. Both Axes IV and V might be restructured so that they, too, are more similar to the ICD. In addition to overhauling the axes, the *DSM-5* Task Force is moving from a categorical to a dimensional rating system. The dimensional model would rate people according to the degree to which they experience a set of fundamental attributes, not whether or not they have an overall diagnosis. A dimensional system with numerical ratings would provide a clearer and perhaps more accurate representation of psychological disorders. The first and most significant change would eliminate most of the separate personality disorders, now found on Axis II. The second, almost equally important change would allow clinicians to assign severity ratings *within* a diagnosis. With the new system, clinicians could allow for gradations from minimal to severe. Along with changes in the classification of psychological disorders, the new approach would necessitate changes in assessment methods. We'll explore those in Chapter 3.

Those who object note that the current diagnostic systems assume that there is a recognizable distinction between normality and abnormality. In addition, by labeling a collection of behaviors as constituting a "disease," manual use can heighten the tendency to stigmatize those whose behavior falls outside the norm.

Despite these criticisms, mental health professionals must rely on diagnostic systems if for no other reason than to allow their clients to receive treatment in hospitals and reimbursement from health care providers. Insurance companies utilize the diagnostic codes they provide to determine payment schedules for both in-hospital and outpatient care.

It is worthwhile to be alert to the criticisms of these diagnostic systems, particularly since they serve as a reminder that it is the person, and not the disease, that clinicians aim to help.

Diagnostic and Statistical Manual of Mental Disorders (DSM)
A book published by the American Psychiatric Association that contains standard terms and definitions of psychological disorders.

axis
A class of information in *DSM-IV* regarding an aspect of the individual's functioning.

multiaxial system
A multidimensional classification and diagnostic system that summarizes a variety of relevant information about an individual's physical and psychological functioning.

As you learned in Chapter 1, clinicians use the standard terms and definitions contained in the ***Diagnostic and Statistical Manual of Mental Disorders (DSM)*** published by the American Psychiatric Association. We have organized this text according to the most recent version as the *DSM-IV* (fourth edition) - *TR* ("text revision") (American Psychiatric Association, 2000). The *DSM* organizes diagnoses using five separate axes. An **axis** is a category of information regarding one dimension of an individual's functioning. The **multiaxial system** in the *DSM-IV-TR* allows professionals to characterize clients in a multidimensional way, accommodating relevant information about their functioning in an organized and systematic fashion.

Axis I: Clinical Disorders

You can find the major clinical disorders, called "syndromes," on Axis I. Each syndrome is a collection of symptoms that constitute a particular psychological disorder. Many of the syndromes on Axis I represent a logical grouping of disorders that involve similar symptoms such as mood disturbances, anxiety, and substance abuse. However, the system doesn't always work that neatly, and as a result, the authors of *DSM-5* are rethinking both the groupings and the location of specific disorders within groupings. You can read the categories of disorders on Axis I along with examples of some of the disorders in each category in Table 2.1.

Axis II: Personality Disorders and Mental Retardation

The second axis includes disorders best thought of as enduring characteristics of an individual's personality or abilities. Personality disorders reflect disturbances in a person's underlying dispositions or traits. Personality traits that are inflexible and maladaptive, causing chronic distress or impairment, are characteristic of personality disorders. Mental retardation is also on Axis II. Although this is not a "disorder" in the same sense as personality disorders, the rationale is that they reflect fundamental qualities of an individual's ability to think and adapt to the world.

TABLE 2.1 Axis I Disorders of the DSM-IV-TR

Category	Description	Examples of diagnoses
Disorders usually first diagnosed in infancy, childhood, or adolescence	Disorders that usually develop during the earlier years of life, primarily involving abnormal development and maturation	Autistic disorders Learning disorders Attention-deficit disorders Learning disorders
Delirium, dementia, amnestic, and other cognitive disorders	Disorders involving impairments in thought processes caused by substances or medical conditions	Amnestic disorder Dementia (Alzheimer's type) Delirium
Substance-related disorders	Disorders related to the use or abuse of substances	Substance dependence Substance abuse
Schizophrenia and other psychotic disorders	Disorders involving symptoms that include distortion in perception of reality and impairment in thinking, behavior, affect, and motivation	Schizophrenia Brief psychotic disorder
Mood disorders	Disorders involving a disturbance in mood	Major depressive disorder Bipolar disorder
Anxiety disorders	Disorders involving the experience of intense anxiety, worry, or apprehension	Panic disorder Agoraphobia Social phobia Obsessive-compulsive disorder Post-traumatic stress disorder
Somatoform disorders	Disorders involving recurring complaints of physical symptoms with no medical causes	Hypochondriasis Body dysmorphic disorder
Dissociative disorders	Disorders in which the normal integration of consciousness, memory, sense of self, or perception is disrupted	Dissociative identity disorder Dissociative amnesia
Sexual and gender identity disorders	Disorders involving disturbance in the expression or experience of sexuality	Sexual dysfunctions Pedophilia Gender identity disorder
Eating disorders	Disorders characterized by severe disturbances in eating behavior	Anorexia nervosa Bulimia nervosa
Sleep disorders	Disorders involving disturbed sleep patterns	Insomnia Nightmare disorder
Impulse-control disorders	Disorders characterized by repeated expression of impulsive behaviors	Kleptomania Pathological gambling Trichotillomania
Adjustment disorders	Conditions characterized by the development of emotional and behavioral symptoms within 3 months after a clear stressor	Adjustment disorder with depressed mood Adjustment disorder with anxiety
Other conditions that may be a focus of clinical attention	Conditions or problems for which a person may seek professional help	Problems related to abuse or neglect Bereavement Occupational problem

SOURCE: Reprinted with permission from the *Diagnostic and Statistical Manual of Mental Disorders*, Fourth Edition, Text Revision. Copyright © 2000 American Psychiatric Association.

People can and often do have diagnoses on Axes I and II. For example, a young man may have a substance abuse disorder that we can find on Axis I. In addition, he may also behave manipulatively when dealing with others. He may chronically lie, and show lack of remorse for his harmful actions to others. We associate all these characteristics with the Axis II disorder that we call Antisocial Personality Disorder.

Axis III: General Medical Conditions

The clinician records the client's medical conditions using the medical profession's diagnostic numbering system, the ICD, which we discuss below. By specifying the client's physical illnesses, the clinician transmits information that has important therapeutic implications. For example, a person with chronic heart disease should not receive certain psychiatric medications. In addition, knowing about a client's medical condition can provide important information about the mental disorder's etiology, which is its presumed cause. It would be useful to know that a middle-aged man appearing in treatment for a depressive disorder for the first time had a heart attack six months ago. The heart attack may have constituted a risk factor for the development of depression, particularly in a person with no previous psychiatric history.

Axis IV: Psychosocial and Environmental Problems

In providing a total diagnostic picture of the client's psychological disorder, clinicians must evaluate the extent to which a person is under stress. Axis IV provides a place for the clinician to document events or pressures that may affect the diagnosis, treatment, or outcome of a client's psychological disorder. A person first showing signs of an anxiety disorder shortly after becoming unemployed presents a very different diagnostic picture than someone whose current life circumstances have not changed at all in several years. For the most part, the life events on Axis IV are negative. However, we might consider positive life events, such as a job promotion, as stressors. A person who receives a major job promotion may encounter psychological difficulties due to his or her increased responsibilities and demands with the new position. We have provided examples from Axis IV in Table 2.2.

TABLE 2.2 Examples from Axis IV of the *DSM-IV-TR*

Problem	Examples
Problems with primary support group	Death of significant family member, physical or sexual abuse, remarriage of parent (for a child), divorce (for an adult)
Problems related to the social environment	Social isolation, adjusting to life cycle transition (such as retirement), difficulty with acculturation
Occupational problems	Unemployment, job dissatisfaction, difficult work situation
Housing problems	Homelessness, unsafe neighbors, inadequate housing
Economic problems	Poverty, serious credit problems
Problems with access to health services	Inadequate health insurance
Problems related to the legal system	Incarceration, victim of crime
Other psychosocial problems	Exposure to disasters

Axis V: Global Assessment of Functioning

Clinicians rate the overall functioning of the client along Axis V, which documents the clinician's overall judgment of a client's psychological, social, and occupational functioning. The **Global Assessment of Functioning (GAF) scale,** which is the basis for Axis V, allows for a rating of the individual's overall level of psychological health. Table 2.3 illustrates the points in the full scale along with examples of each range of scores.

Clinicians make the GAF ratings for the client's current functioning at the point of admission or discharge, or the highest level of functioning during the previous year. The rating of the client's functioning during the preceding year provides the clinician with important information about the client's **prognosis,** or likelihood of recovering from the disorder. If a client has functioned effectively in the recent past, the clinician has more reason to hope for improvement. The prognosis may not be so bright if a client has a lengthy history of poor adjustment.

Global Assessment of Functioning (GAF) scale
Axis V of the *DSM-IV,* a scale that rates the individual's overall level of psychological health.

prognosis
A client's likelihood of recovering from a disorder.

Culture-Bound Syndromes

Within particular cultures, there are idiosyncratic patterns of symptoms, many of which have no direct counterpart to a specific *DSM-IV-TR* diagnosis. **Culture-bound syndromes** are behavior patterns that exist only within particular cultures. To qualify as a culture-bound syndrome, the symptoms must not have any clear biochemical or physiological sources. Only that particular culture, and not others, recognizes the symptoms of a culture-bound syndrome. Table 2.4 describes examples of some of the best-studied culture-bound syndromes.

culture-bound syndromes
Recurrent patterns of abnormal behavior or experience that are limited to specific societies or cultural areas.

TABLE 2.3 Axis V: Global Assessment of Functioning Scale

Rating	Level of Symptoms	Examples
91–100	Superior functioning; no symptoms	
81–90	No symptoms or minimal symptoms; generally good functioning in all areas; no more than everyday problems	Occasional worries such as feeling understandably anxious before taking examinations or feelings of disappointment following an athletic loss
71–80	Transient, slight symptoms that are reasonable responses to stressful situations; no more than slight impairment in social, occupational, or school functioning	Concentration difficulty following an exciting day; trouble sleeping after an argument with partner
61–70	Mild symptoms, or some difficulty in social, occupational, or school functioning	Mild insomnia; mild depression
51–60	Moderate symptoms or moderate difficulties in social, occupational, or school functioning	Occasional panic attacks; conflicts with roommates
41–50	Serious symptoms or any serious impairment in social, occupational, or school functioning	Suicidal thoughts; inability to keep job
31–40	Serious difficulties in thought or communication or major impairment in several areas of functioning	Illogical speech; inability to work; neglect of responsibilities
21–30	Behavior influenced by psychotic symptoms or serious impairment in communication or judgment or inability to function in almost all areas	Delusional and hallucinating; incoherent; preoccupied with suicide; stays in bed all day every day
11–20	Dangerous symptoms or gross impairment in communication	Suicide attempts without clear expectation of death; muteness
1–10	Persistent danger to self or others or persistent inability to maintain hygiene	Recurrent violence; serious suicidal act with clear expectation of death
0	Inadequate information	

SOURCE: Reprinted with permission from the *Diagnostic and Statistical Manual of Mental Disorders,* Fourth Edition, Text Revision. Copyright © 2000 American Psychiatric Association.

TABLE 2.4 Culture-Bound Syndromes in the *DSM-IV-TR*

Certain psychological disorders, such as depression and anxiety, are universally encountered. Within particular cultures, however, idiosyncratic patterns of symptoms are found, many of which have no direct counterpart to a specific *DSM-IV-TR* diagnosis. These conditions, called culture-bound syndromes, are recurrent patterns of abnormal behavior or experience that are limited to specific societies or cultural areas.

Culture-bound syndromes may fit into one or more of the *DSM-IV-TR* categories, just as one *DSM-IV-TR* category may be thought to be several different conditions by another culture. Some disorders recognized by the DSM-IV-TR are seen as culture-bound syndromes, because they are specific to industrialized societies (e.g., anorexia nervosa).

This table describes some of the best-studied culture-bound syndromes and forms of distress that may be encountered in clinical practice in North America, as well as the *DSM-IV-TR* categories they most closely resemble.

Term	Location	Description	*DSM-IV-TR* Disorders
Amok	Malaysia	Dissociative episode consisting of brooding followed by violent, aggressive, and possibly homicidal outburst. Precipitated by insult; usually seen more in males. Return to premorbid state following the outburst.	
Ataque de nervios	Latin America	Distress associated with uncontrollable shouting, crying, trembling, and verbal or physical aggression. Dissociation, seizure, and suicidal gestures possible. Often occurs as a result of a stressful family event. Rapid return to premorbid state.	Anxiety Mood Dissociative Somatoform
Bilis and colera	Latin America	Condition caused by strong anger or rage. Marked by disturbed core body imbalances, including tension, trembling, screaming, and headache, stomach disturbance. Chronic fatigue and loss of consciousness possible.	
Bouffée délirante	West Africa and Haiti	Sudden outburst of agitated and aggressive behavior, confusion, and psychomotor excitement. Paranoia and visual and auditory hallucinations possible.	Brief psychotic
Brain fag	West Africa	Difficulties in concentration, memory, and thought, usually experienced by students in response to stress. Other symptoms include neck and head pain, pressure, and blurred vision.	Anxiety Depressive Somatoform
Dhat	India	Severe anxiety and hypochondriacal concern regarding semen discharge, whitish discoloration of urine, weakness, and extreme fatigue.	
Falling out or *blacking out*	Southern United States and the Caribbean	A sudden collapse, usually preceded by dizziness. Temporary loss of vision and the ability to move.	Conversion Dissociative
Ghost sickness	American Indian tribes	A preoccupation with death and the deceased. Thought to be symbolized by bad dreams, weakness, fear, appetite loss, anxiety, hallucinations, loss of consciousness, and a feeling of suffocation.	
Hwa-byung (wool-hwa-byung)	Korea	Acute feelings of anger resulting in symptoms including insomnia, fatigue, panic, fear of death, dysphoria, indigestion, loss of appetite, dyspnea, palpitations, aching, and the feeling of a mass in the abdomen.	
Koro	Malaysia	An episode of sudden and intense anxiety that one's penis or vulva and nipples will recede into the body and cause death.	
Latah	Malaysia	Hypersensitivity to sudden fright, usually accompanied by symptoms including echopraxia (imitating the movements and gestures of another person), echolalia (irreverent parroting of what another person has said), command obedience, and dissociation, all of which are characteristic of schizophrenia.	

Term	Location	Description	*DSM-IV-TR* Disorders
Mal de ojo	Mediterranean cultures	Means "the evil eye" when translated from Spanish. Children are at much greater risk; adult females are at a higher risk than adult males. Manifested by fitful sleep, crying with no apparent cause, diarrhea, vomiting, and fever.	
Pibloktog	Arctic and sub-Arctic Eskimo communities	Abrupt dissociative episode associated with extreme excitement, often followed by seizures and coma. During the attack, the person may break things, shout obscenities, eat feces, and behave dangerously. The victim may be temporarily withdrawn from the community and report amnesia regarding the attack.	
Qi-gong psychotic reaction	China	Acute episode marked by dissociation and paranoia that may occur following participation in qi-gong, a Chinese folk health-enhancing practice.	
Rootwork	Southern United States, African American and European populations, and Caribbean societies	Cultural interpretation that ascribes illness to hexing, witchcraft, or sorcery. Associated with anxiety, gastrointestinal problems, weakness, dizziness, and the fear of being poisoned or killed.	
Shen-k'uei or *Shenkui*	Taiwan and China	Symptoms attributed to excessive semen loss due to frequent intercourse, masturbation, and nocturnal emission. Dizziness, backache, fatigue, weakness, insomnia, frequent dreams, and sexual dysfunction. Excessive loss of semen is feared, because it represents the loss of vital essence and therefore threatens one's life.	
Shin-byung	Korea	Anxiety and somatic problems followed by dissociation and possession by ancestral spirits.	
Spell	African American and European American communities in the southern United States	Trance state in which communication with deceased relatives or spirits takes place. Sometimes connected with a temporary personality change.	
Susto	Latinos in the United States and Mexico, Central America, and South America	Illness caused by a frightening event that causes the soul to leave the body. Causes unhappiness, sickness (muscle aches, stress headache, and diarrhea), strain in social roles, appetite and sleep disturbances, lack of motivation, low self-esteem, and death. Healing methods include calling the soul back into the body and cleansing to restore bodily and spiritual balance.	Major depressive Post-traumatic stress Somatoform
Taijin kyofusho	Japan	Intense fear that one's body parts or functions displease, embarrass, or are offensive to others regarding appearance, odor, facial expressions, or movements.	
Zar	Ethiopia, Somalia, Egypt, Sudan, Iran, and other North African and Middle Eastern societies	Possession by a spirit. May cause dissociative experiences characterized by shouting, laughing, hitting of one's head against a hard surface, singing, crying, apathy, withdrawal, and change in daily habits.	

SOURCE: Reprinted with permission from the *Diagnostic and Statistical Manual of Mental Disorders*, Fourth Edition, Text Revision. Copyright © 2000 American Psychiatric Association.

2.3 The International Classification of Diseases (ICD)

Most mental health professionals outside the U.S. and Canada use the World Health Organization's (WHO) diagnostic system, which is the International Classification of Diseases (ICD). WHO developed the ICD as an epidemiological tool. With a common diagnostic system, the 110 member nations can compare illness rates and have assurance that countries employ the same terminology for the sake of consistency. The tenth edition (ICD-10) is currently in use; it is undergoing a major revision, and WHO projects that ICD-11 will be available no earlier than 2014. The ICD is available in WHO's six official languages (Arabic, Chinese, English, French, Russian, and Spanish), as well as in 36 other languages.

2.4 The Diagnostic Process

The diagnostic process involves using all relevant information to arrive at a label that characterizes the client's disorder. This information includes the results of any tests given to the client, material gathered from interviews, and knowledge about the client's personal history. Clinicians use the first phase of working with clients to gather this information prior to proceeding with the treatment itself.

Diagnostic Procedures

Key to diagnosis is gaining as clear a description as possible of a client's symptoms, both those that the client reports and those that the clinician observes. Dr. Tobin, when hearing Peter describe himself as "anxious," immediately assumes that he *may* have an anxiety disorder. However, clients do not always label their internal states accurately. Therefore, the clinician also must attend carefully to the client's behavior, emotional expression, and apparent state of mind. The client may express anxiety, but his behavior may suggest that instead he is experiencing a mood disorder.

Clinicians first listen to clients as they describe the experience of their symptoms, but they must next follow this up with a more systematic approach to diagnosis. As you will learn in Chapter 3, a variety of assessment tools give the clinician a framework for determining the extent to which these symptoms coincide with the diagnostic criteria of a given disorder. The clinician must determine the exact nature of a client's symptoms, the length of time the client has experienced these symptoms, and any associated symptoms. In the process, the clinician also obtains information about the client's personal and family history. By asking questions in this manner, the clinician begins to formulate the **principal diagnosis**—namely, the disorder most closely aligned with the primary reason the individual is seeking professional help.

For many clients, the symptoms they experience reflect the presence of more than one principal diagnosis. In these cases, we use the term **comorbid,** meaning literally two (or more) disorders. Comorbidity is remarkably common. A major investigation, known as the National Comorbidity Survey (NCS), showed that over half of respondents with one psychiatric disorder also had a second diagnosis at some point in their lives. The most common comorbidities involve drug and/or alcohol abuse with other psychiatric disorders.

Differential diagnosis, the ruling out of alternative diagnoses, is a crucial step in the diagnostic process. It is important for the clinician to eliminate the possibility that the client is experiencing a different disorder or perhaps an additional disorder. Peter states that he is anxious, and his symptoms suggest the disorder known as "general anxiety disorder," but Dr. Tobin needs to consider whether this diagnosis best suits his symptoms or not. It is possible that Peter suffers from panic disorder, another anxiety disorder involving the experience of panic attacks. His symptoms may also suggest social

principal diagnosis
The disorder that is considered to be the primary reason the individual seeks professional help.

comorbid
The situation that occurs when multiple diagnostic conditions occur simultaneously within the same individual.

differential diagnosis
The process of systematically ruling out alternative diagnoses.

anxiety disorder. Alternatively, he might be suffering from adjustment difficulties following the divorce of his parents or the stress of his job. He may even have a substance abuse disorder, an undiagnosed medical condition, or even a third disorder. Dr. Tobin's initial diagnostic must be tested against these possibilities during the assessment period of treatment.

The diagnostic process can take anywhere from a few hours to weeks depending on the complexity of the client's presenting symptoms. The client and clinician may accomplish therapeutic work during this time, particularly if the client is in crisis. For example, Dr. Tobin will start Peter on antianxiety medications right away to help him feel better. However, her ultimate goal is to arrive at as thorough an understanding as possible of Peter's disorder. This paves the way for her to work with Peter throughout the treatment process.

Case Formulation

Once the clinician makes a formal diagnosis, he or she is still left with a formidable challenge—to piece together a picture of how the disorder evolved. With the diagnosis, the clinician can assign a label to the client's symptoms. Although informative, this label tells the client's full story. To gain a full appreciation of the client's disorder, the clinician develops a **case formulation:** an analysis of the client's development and the factors that might have influenced his or her current psychological status. The case formulation provides an analysis that transforms the diagnosis from a set of code numbers to a rich piece of descriptive information about the client's personal history. With this descriptive information, the clinician can design a treatment plan that is attentive to the client's symptoms, unique past experiences, and future potential for growth.

case formulation
A clinician's analysis of the factors that might have influenced the client's current psychological status.

Understanding the client from a developmental perspective is crucial to provide a thorough case formulation. In Dr. Tobin's work with Peter, she will flesh out the details of her case formulation as she gets to know him better in the initial therapy phases. Her case formulation will expand to include Peter's family history, focusing on the divorce of his parents, as well as the possible causes of his perfectionism and concern over his academic performance. She will try to understand why he feels so overwhelmed at work and gain a perspective on why his relationship with Ashley has been so problematic. Finally, she will need to investigate the possible role of his mother's panic attacks and how they relate to Peter's experience of anxiety symptoms. To aid in differential diagnosis, Dr. Tobin will also evaluate Peter's pattern of substance use as well as any possible medical conditions that she did not detect during the initial assessment phase.

Cultural Formulation

Clinicians need to account for the client's cultural background in making diagnoses. A **cultural formulation** includes the clinician's assessment of the client's degree of identification with the culture of origin, the culture's beliefs about psychological disorders, the ways in which the culture interprets particular events, and the cultural supports available to the client.

cultural formulation
Includes the clinician's assessment of the client's degree of identification with the culture of origin, the culture's beliefs about psychological disorders, the ways in which the culture interprets particular events, and the cultural supports available to the client.

We might expect cultural norms and beliefs to have a stronger impact on clients who strongly identify with their culture of origin. The client's familiarity with and preference for using a certain language is one obvious indicator of cultural identification. A culture's approach to understanding the causes of behavior may influence clients who strongly identify with their culture. Exposure to these belief systems may influence the expression of a client's symptoms.

Even if a client's symptoms do not represent a culture-bound syndrome, clinicians must consider the individual's cultural framework as a backdrop. Members of a given culture attach significant meanings to particular events. For example, within certain

Symptoms of psychological disorders often vary based on the culture the individual belongs to.

Asian cultures, an insult may provoke the condition known as *amok*, where a person (usually male) enters an altered state of consciousness in which he becomes violent, aggressive, and even homicidal. In Peter's case, although he is a product of middle-class white background, it is possible that cultural factors are influencing his extreme preoccupation with his academic performance. Perhaps his family placed pressure on him to succeed due to their own incorporation of belief in the importance of upward mobility. They may have pressured him heavily to do well in school, and as a result, he felt that his self-worth as an individual depended on his grades. As an adult, he is unable to shake himself from this overly harsh set of values.

Clinicians should look within the client's cultural background as a way of determining available cultural supports. Clients from certain cultures, particularly Black, Hispanic, Latino, and Asian, have extended family networks and religion, which provide emotional resources to help individuals cope with stressful life events.

Cultural formulations are important to understanding psychological disorders from a biopsychosocial perspective. The fact that psychological disorders vary from one society to another supports the claim of the sociocultural perspective that cultural factors play a role in influencing the expression of abnormal behavior.

Psychologists are increasingly gaining education in training in working within the multicultural framework to take into account not only a client's race and ethnicity, but also age, gender, sexual orientation, and disability status, among others (American Psychological Association, 2002). Through such education, clinicians can learn how to adapt not only their diagnostic methods more generally but to adopt a multicultural approach throughout treatment.

2.5 Planning the Treatment

treatment plan
The outline for how therapy should take place.

Clinicians typically follow up the diagnosis phase by setting up a **treatment plan,** the outline for how therapy should take place. In the treatment plan, the clinician describes the treatment goals, treatment site, modality of treatment, and theoretical approach. The decisions the clinician makes while putting the treatment plan together reflect what he or she knows at the time about the client's needs and the available resources. However, clinicians often revise the treatment plan once they see how the proposed intervention methods are actually working.

Psychologists as Prescribers

In 2002, New Mexico became the first state to approve prescription privileges for psychologists. Louisiana followed shortly thereafter, passing similar legislation in 2004. These landmark pieces of legislation are paving the way for other states to take similar action. However, the question remains controversial. In 2010, the Oregon legislature passed a bill (SB 1046) granting prescriptive authority to psychologists, but Governor Ted Kulongoski vetoed the bill, in response to pressure from various lobbying groups, including psychiatrists.

There are several arguments against the granting of prescription privileges to psychologists. Unlike psychiatrists, psychologists do not receive medical training and therefore do not have the undergraduate pre-medical training or the years of medical school, internship, and residency that physicians receive. Philosophically, research-oriented psychologists argue that the granting of prescription privileges takes away from the notion that psychologists are scientists as well as practitioners. Psychologists should not be in the business, they argue, of handing out medication. A second argument against prescription privileges concerns the role of medication in psychological treatment. From this perspective, psychologists should be focused on psychotherapy. The long-term benefits of psychotherapy, these critics argue, are equal to if not greater than the long-term benefits of medication for the majority of disorders including major depression, anxiety disorders, and other nonpsychotic disorders. In the exceptional cases of serious mental illness, such as schizophrenia and bipolar disorder, psychologists can work as a team with psychiatrists to maintain their clients on long-term medication regimens.

The arguments in favor of prescription privileges are also compelling. If psychologists have the power to prescribe medications, they can do a better job than psychiatrists do integrating medication into psychotherapy. From the client's point of view, there is greater continuity of care, in that the individual does not need to see more than one mental health practitioner. Psychologists in favor of prescription privileges also point to the fact that specialized training is required for a clinical psychologist to be able to prescribe medications aimed at psychological disorders. Therefore, the psychologists who do prescribe have an equal knowledge base as do physicians. A second argument in favor of prescription privileges is that there are other nondoctoral level health professionals with this legal power including psychiatric nurse practitioners and psychiatric nurse specialists, among others, although the exact nature of their privileges varies across states.

The American Psychological Association's Practice Directorate continues to lobby in favor of more widespread acceptance of prescription privileges across the United States. However, as the Oregon case demonstrates, this legislation is likely to face a rocky road in other states.

Q: *You be the judge:* Does having prescription privileges reduce the scientific status of psychology as a profession? Would you prefer that the psychologist you might see for treatment can also incorporate medications into your treatment?

Goals of Treatment

The first step in treatment planning is for the clinician to establish treatment goals, ranging from immediate to long term. Ideally, treatment goals reflect what we know about both the disorder and the recommended therapy, and the particular needs and concerns of the individual client.

The immediate goal of treating clients in crisis is to ensure that their symptoms are managed, particularly if they are at risk to themselves or others. Peter, for example, needs psychiatric treatment in order to bring his anxiety symptoms under control. The

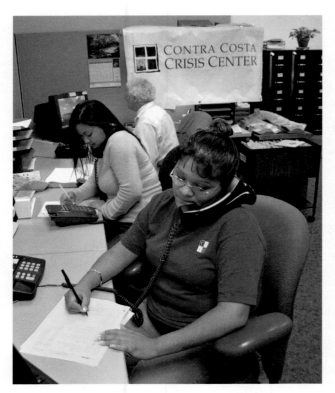

At this crisis center, telephone counselors are available 24 hours a day.

clinician may need to hospitalize a client who is severely depressed and suicidal. The treatment plan may only include this immediate goal until the clinician gains a broader understanding of the client's situation.

Short-term goals are aimed at alleviating the client's symptoms by addressing problematic behavior, thinking, or emotions. The plan at this point might include establishing a working relationship between the clinician and client, as well as setting up specific objectives for therapeutic change. Another short-term goal might be to stabilize a client taking medications, a process that might take as long as several weeks or longer if the first round of treatment is unsuccessful. In Peter's case, Dr. Tobin will need to ensure that the medications he is receiving are in fact helping to alleviate his anxiety. She will also need to work with the psychiatrist to monitor any adverse side effects. Her short-term goals with Peter will also include beginning to examine the nature of his anxiety and how he can start to manage his symptoms using psychological interventions.

Long-term goals include more fundamental and deeply rooted alterations in the client's personality and relationships. These are the ultimate aims of therapeutic change. Ideally, the long-term goals for any client are to cope with the symptoms of the disorder and to develop a strategy to manage them, if not achieve complete recovery. Depending on the nature of the client's disorder, available supports, and life stress, these long-term goals may take years to accomplish. Dr. Tobin's long-term goals with Peter are to take him off the medication. At the same time, she would plan to help him gain an understanding of the causes of his symptoms, and in the process, reduce their severity if not eliminate them altogether.

In many cases, clinicians carry out treatment goals in a sequential manner. First the clinician deals with the crisis, then handles problems in the near future, and finally addresses issues that require extensive work well into the future. However, many clients experience a cyclical unfolding of stages. New sets of immediate crises or short-term goals may arise in the course of treatment. Or there may be a redefinition of long-term goals as the course of treatment progresses. It is perhaps more helpful to think of the three stages not as consecutive stages per se, but as implying different levels of treatment focus.

Treatment Site

Clinicians juggle a number of issues when recommending which treatment site will best serve the client. Treatment sites vary in the degree to which they provide a controlled environment and in the nature of the services that clients will receive. Clients who are in crisis or are at risk of harming themselves or others need to be in controlled environments. However, there are many other considerations including cost and insurance coverage, the need for additional medical care, availability of community support, and the projected length of treatment. In some cases, clinicians recommend client treatment in outpatient settings, schools, or the workplace.

Psychiatric Hospitals In a psychiatric hospital, a client receives medical interventions and intensive forms of psychotherapy. These settings are most appropriate for clients at risk of harming themselves or others and who seem incapable of self-care. In some cases, clinicians may involuntarily hospitalize clients through a court order until they can bring the symptoms under control (we will discuss this in more detail in Chapter 15).

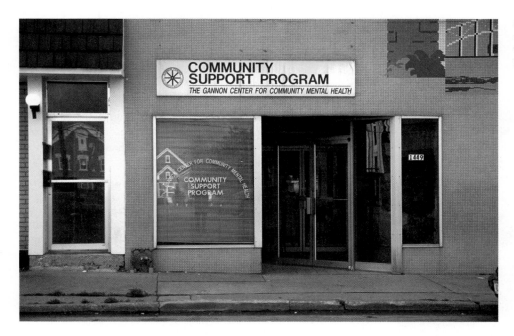

Community treatment centers, like this one, provide much needed care to individuals with a wide range of psychological disorders.

Specialized Inpatient Treatment Centers Clients may need intensive supervision, but not actual hospital care. For these individuals, specialized inpatient treatment centers provide both supportive services and round-the-clock monitoring. These sites include recovery treatment centers for adults seeking to overcome substance addiction. Clinicians may also recommend this treatment site to children who need constant monitoring due to severe behavioral disturbances.

Outpatient Treatment By far, the most common treatment site is a private therapist's outpatient clinic or office. **Community mental health centers (CMHCs)** are outpatient clinics that provide psychological services on a sliding fee scale for individuals who live within a certain geographic area. Professionals in private practice offer individual or group sessions. Some prepaid health insurance plans cover the cost of such visits, either to a private practitioner or to a clinician working in a health maintenance organization (HMO). Agencies supported partially or completely by public funds may also offer outpatient treatment. Dr. Tobin will see Peter in outpatient treatment because his symptoms are not sufficiently severe to justify hospitalization.

community mental health center (CMHC)
Outpatient clinic that provides psychological services on a sliding fee scale to serve individuals who live within a certain geographic area.

Clients receiving outpatient services will, by necessity, receive more limited care than what they would encounter in a hospital, in terms of both the time involved and the nature of the contact between client and clinician. Consequently, clinicians may advise that their clients receive additional services, including vocational counseling, in-home services, or the support of a self-help organization, such as Alcoholics Anonymous.

Halfway Houses and Day Treatment Programs Clients with serious psychological disorders who are able to live in the community may need the additional support that they will receive in sites that are intended to serve the needs of this specific population. These facilities may be connected with a hospital, a public agency, or a private corporation. **Halfway houses** are designed for clients who have been discharged from psychiatric facilities, but who are not yet ready for independent living. A halfway house provides a living context with other deinstitutionalized people, and it is staffed by professionals who work with clients in developing the skills they need to become employed and to set up independent living situations. **Day treatment programs** are designed for formerly hospitalized clients as well as for clients who do not need hospitalization, but do need a structured program during the day, similar to what a hospital provides.

halfway house
A community treatment facility designed for deinstitutionalized clients leaving a hospital who are not yet ready for independent living.

day treatment program
A structured program in a community treatment facility that provides activities similar to those provided in a psychiatric hospital.

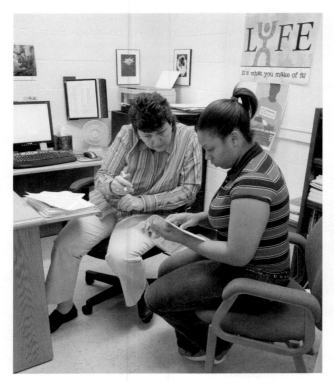

Guidance counselors are often the first professionals to whom troubled students turn for professional assistance.

modality
Form in which the clinician offers psychotherapy.

individual psychotherapy
Psychological treatment in which the therapist works on a one-to-one basis with the client.

family therapy
Psychological treatment in which the therapist works with several or all members of the family.

group therapy
Psychological treatment in which the therapist facilitates discussion among several clients who talk together about their problems.

milieu therapy
A treatment approach, used in an inpatient psychiatric facility, in which all facets of the milieu, or environment, are components of the treatment.

Other Treatment Sites Clinicians may recommend that their clients receive treatment in the places where they work or go to school. School psychologists are trained to work with children and teenagers who require further assessment or behavioral interventions. In the workplace, Employee Assistance Programs (EAP) provide employees with a confidential setting in which they can seek individual treatment in the form of counseling, assistance with substance abuse, and family treatment. These resources may prove important for clinicians who wish to provide their clients with as many resources over the long term as possible.

Modality of Treatment

The **modality,** or form in which the clinician offers psychotherapy, is another crucial component of the treatment plan. Clinicians recommend one or more modalities depending on the nature of the client's symptoms and whether or not other people in the client's life should be involved.

Clients receive treatment on a one-to-one basis in **individual psychotherapy.** In couples therapy, both partners in a relationship, and in **family therapy,** several or all family members are involved in treatment. In family therapy, family members may identify one person as the "patient." The therapist, however, views the whole family system as the target of the treatment. **Group therapy** provides a modality in which clients who face similar issues can openly share their difficulties with others, receive feedback, develop trust, and improve their interpersonal skills.

A clinician may recommend any or all of these modalities in any setting. Specific to psychiatric hospitals is **milieu therapy,** which is based on the premise that the milieu, or environment, is a major component of the treatment. Ideally, the milieu is organized in a way that allows clients to receive consistently therapeutic and constructive reactions from all who live and work there. In addition to traditional psychotherapy, clients participate in other therapeutic endeavors through group or peer counseling, occupational therapy, and recreational therapy.

Milieu therapy involves many patients participating within a community setting.

Determining the Best Approach to Treatment

Whatever treatment modality a clinician recommends, it must be based on the choice of the most appropriate theoretical perspective or combination of perspectives. Many clinicians are trained according to a particular set of assumptions about the origins of psychological disorders and the best methods of treating these disorders. Often, this theoretical orientation forms the basis for the clinician's treatment decisions. However, just as frequently, clinicians adapt their theoretical orientation to fit the client's needs.

After decades of debate regarding which treatments are most effective, and for whom, psychologists adopted the principles of **evidence-based practice in psychology**—clinical decision making that integrates the best available research evidence and clinical expertise in the context of the cultural background, preferences, and characteristics of clients (American Psychological Association Presidential Task Force on Evidence-Based Practice, 2006). In other words, clinicians should base their treatments on state-of-the-art research findings that they adapt to the particular features of the client, taking into account the client's background, needs, and prior experiences. Clinicians currently use these criteria as the basis for curricula in graduate programs and postdoctoral continuing education (Collins, Leffingwell, & Belar, 2007).

As you read in this book about various disorders and the most effective treatments, it will be important to keep in mind the empirical basis for the treatment conclusions. Findings from efficacy studies shed light on appropriate interventions, but they are insufficient for conclusively determining what is most effective with real people with complex problems.

evidence-based practice in psychology
Clinical decision making that integrates the best available research evidence and clinical expertise in the context of the cultural background, preferences, and characteristics of clients.

2.6 The Course of Treatment

The way treatment proceeds is a function of the clinician's and client's contributions. Each has a part to play in determining the outcome of the case, as does the unique interaction of their personalities, abilities, and expectations.

The Clinician's Role in Treatment

Above and beyond whatever techniques a clinician uses to treat a client's problems, the quality of the relationship between the client and clinician is a crucial determinant of whether therapy will succeed or not. A good clinician does more than objectively administer treatment to a client. The best clinicians infuse a deep personal interest, concern, and respect for the client into the therapeutic relationship. Dr. Tobin will work with Peter in the initial weeks of therapy to establish this solid basis for their further work together.

The Client's Role in Treatment

In optimal situations, psychotherapy is a joint enterprise in which the client plays an active role. It is largely up to the client to describe and identify the nature of his or her disorder, to describe personal reactions as treatment progresses, and to initiate and follow through on changes.

The client's attitudes toward therapy and the therapist are an important part of the contribution the client makes to the therapeutic relationship. There is a special quality to the help that the client is requesting; it involves potentially painful, embarrassing, and personally revealing material that the client is not accustomed to disclosing to someone else. Most people are much more comfortable discussing their medical, legal, financial, and other problems outside the realm of emotions. Social attitudes toward psychological disorders also play a role. People may feel that they should be able to handle their emotional problems without seeking help. They may believe that, if they can't solve their

REAL STORIES

Daniel Johnston: Mood Disturbance

"Wherever I am, I have music in my heart."

Daniel Johnston, born on January 22, 1961, is an American singer-songwriter well known for his unique musical talent as well as his life-long struggle with bipolar disorder. The 2005 documentary, *The Devil and Daniel Johnston*, depicts his incredible story from childhood in West Virginia to the present day. Though Daniel has had an extraordinary musical career, his tumultuous journey with mental illness is not unlike that of many other individuals who suffer from severely debilitating psychological disorders. Through his music, Daniel expresses both the soaring, sometimes delusional manias and the dark, unbearable depths of depression he has faced throughout his life.

The youngest of five children, Daniel's mother, Mabel, recalls that ". . . he was different . . . I noticed that from the start." As a teenager, inspired mostly by comic books, he took on countless artistic endeavors including drawing and making playful movies about his life at home. His creativity helped him gain attention from friends and classmates, but also endlessly frustrated his highly religious and traditional parents, who would rather he spend his time attending church, working, and helping out around the house. Daniel's passion for creating has remained with him his entire life. In the words of Daniel's best friend, David Thornberry, "He exudes art . . . he can't stop making art."

As with many individuals with severe mood disorders, Daniel's behavior began to change for the worse after leaving home for college. His family was used to him acting differently than his peers, but in college Daniel started to become confused and disoriented. A visit to the family physician resulted in a diagnosis of manic-depression (bipolar disorder). Unable to continue

with the challenges he faced at school, he returned home and enrolled in a small arts college in nearby Ohio. In art school, Daniel met and subsequently fell in love with his classmate Laurie. Though they never had a romantic relationship and she went on to marry another man, Daniel's unrequited love for her has been one of his most powerful creative muses and also caused his first major depressive episode. It was at this point, his mother recalls, that he began to play the piano and write songs.

Daniel was having trouble in his courses at art school, and so his family once again took him out of school. This time they sent him to live with his older brother in Houston, in hopes that he could start building a productive life. Daniel worked part-time at a local amusement park and began recording music in his brother's garage. After his brother grew frustrated that Daniel was not finding stable work, he sent him to live with his sister, Margie. One morning, Margie noticed that Daniel had never returned home the night before. His family did not hear from Daniel for months; when they did, they learned that he had spontaneously purchased a moped and joined a traveling carnival. When the carnival stopped in Austin, Texas, Daniel was assaulted on the fair grounds and fled to a local church for help. He was able to find housing in Austin and began taking his homemade tape-recorded albums to local musicians and newspapers. One of the local musicians he met was Kathy McCarthy. The two briefly dated, and after meeting him,

Kathy remembers, "It was undeniable after one or two weeks that something was dreadfully wrong with him."

In one scene of *The Devil and Daniel Johnston*, he reads a detailed account of the characteristics of an individual with his condition, stating, "There you have it. I'm a manic depressive with grand delusions." The majority of his delusions were paranoid and religious in nature, perhaps the result of his highly religious upbringing. Although Daniel was well aware of his illness, at the time he was doing little to assuage it. In Austin, Daniel began to smoke marijuana and regularly experimented with LSD, causing several bizarre and sometimes violent episodes. Simultaneously, Daniel's music career began to blossom as he gained recognition as well as notoriety for his music and his often bizarre live performances.

In 1986, a Christmas gathering with his siblings soon turned into a horrifying event. Daniel began preaching about Satan to his family, and began attacking his brother,

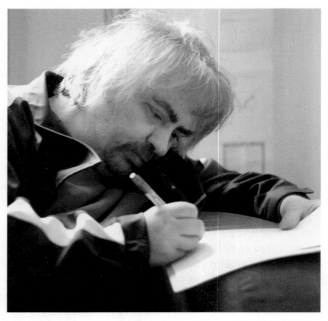

Daniel Johnston's songs provide a glimpse into his struggles with mental illness.

breaking his rib. Frightened by his behavior, and unsure of what to do, his siblings drove him to a nearby bus station. Soon after, the police discovered Daniel at the University of Austin, splashing in the middle of a pond and again preaching about Satan. It was at this point that his friends and family began to realize that, as one friend put it, "he was a really sick person." While his music had been a way for him to filter the demons in his mind, Daniel's illness was beginning to wreak havoc on his life, and drastic measures were necessary to ensure he did no further harm to others or to himself. Doctors prescribed Daniel the antipsychotic medication, Haldol, and he spent the entire year of 1987 in bed (what he called his "lost year"). Although he was stabilized, Daniel found himself unable to write any music during this period. Indeed, throughout his life and like many individuals with bipolar disorder, Daniel often struggled with

medication compliance. He felt that he was better at creating and performing when his mind was allowed to run free rather than be confined to the numbness he felt while on medication.

Because he often went off his medication, Daniel experienced a five-year whirlwind of breakdowns that cycled between delusional mania and clinical depression, resulting in numerous hospitalizations that lasted months at a time. When first going off his medication, Daniel's behavior and mood were normal for up to a few days until he would quickly and unexpectedly take a turn for the bizarre. In one particular instance, Daniel had stopped taking his medication before playing to a large auditorium for a music festival in Austin, Texas. The appearance was one of the most acclaimed performances of his career. Shortly afterwards however, when he and his father boarded the two-person plane to take them home

to West Virginia, Daniel seized the controls from his father, sending their plane crashing toward the ground. Luckily, Daniel's father was able to regain control of the plane in time, and they survived after landing on a treetop. Daniel's father now recalls that at the time Daniel believed he was Casper (from the children's cartoon about Casper the friendly ghost), and that taking over the plane was a heroic act.

Since that dark period of his life, Daniel has been stable in large part because of his supportive network of family and friends. He lives with his parents in Waller, Texas, and continues to write music and tour around the world. Many regard Daniel Johnston as one of the most brilliant singer-songwriters in American history. His heartbreaking battle with mental illness has been a destructive yet inspiring force in his work that blurs the line between artistic creativity and mental illness.

---

own emotional problems, it means they are immature or incompetent. Moreover, having to see a clinician may make a person believe that he or she is "crazy." Although attitudes toward therapy are becoming more accepting in current Western culture, there is still a degree of potential shame or embarrassment that clients must confront.

Most people would, though, feel less inclined to mention to acquaintances that they are in psychotherapy for personal problems. The pressure to keep therapy secret usually adds to a client's anxiety about seeking professional help. To someone who is already troubled by severe problems in living, this added anxiety can be further inhibiting. With so many potential forces driving the individual away from seeking therapy, the initial step is sometimes the hardest to take. Thus, the therapeutic relationship requires the client to be willing to work with the clinician in a partnership and to be prepared to endure the pain and embarrassment involved in making personal revelations. Moreover, it also requires a willingness to break old patterns and to try new ways of viewing the self and relating to others.

2.7 The Outcome of Treatment

In the best of all possible worlds, the treatment works. The client remains in treatment until the treatment runs its course, shows improvement, and maintains this improved level of functioning. Many times, though, the road is not so smooth, and either the client does not attain the treatment plan goals or unanticipated problems arise.

Clinicians find it particularly frustrating when their clients do not seem willing to follow through on their desire to change. Change is very difficult, and many clients have become so accustomed to living with their symptoms that the necessary effort to solve the problem seems overwhelming. At times, clinicians also face frustration over financial constraints. They may recommend a treatment that they are confident can succeed, but that is financially infeasible. In other cases, people in the client's life refuse to participate in the treatment, even though they play central roles. Other pragmatic issues can disrupt therapy: Clients may move, lose jobs, or lack consistent transportation to the clinic. Over time, those in the mental health field learn that they are limited in how effective they can be in changing the lives of people who go to them for help. However, as you will learn in this book, therapy is usually effective and the majority of treatments do result in significant improvement.

Return to the Case: Peter Dickinson

Peter was prescribed antianxiety medication through the psychiatrist at the mental health clinic. Within four weeks, he reported that he was able to sleep through the night and was feeling less restless. His psychotherapy focused on relaxation techniques such as deep breathing as well as cognitive techniques such as labeling and challenging his worrying, and coming up with various ways to cope with stress rather than worrying excessively. Therapy was also helpful for Peter to discuss and sort through his feelings about his parents' divorce, and to understand how his anxiety affected his romantic relationships.

Dr. Tobin's reflections: Typical of many individuals with GAD, Peter has always felt like a constant "worrier," but this anxiety was recently aggravated by a stressful event: his parents' divorce. Additionally, his lack of sleep was likely contributing to his difficulty with the concentration that is necessary for keeping up with the standards of work required by his career. Since he had been doing well at work up until this point, he may not have felt that his anxiety was a problem. His anxiety may

have also gone unnoticed due to the intense pressure and sacrifice that face all individuals who work in Peter's career area. It was clear however, that Peter worried about many issues to a greater degree than do others in his situation. At the time he presented for treatment, however, it was clear that his inability to control his worry over his parents and his girlfriend were causing major problems in his work and social life. Not only that, but his past anxiety had caused problems that he did not recognize at that time. For many people who suffer from GAD, the longer it goes untreated the worse it may get. Fortunately for Peter, his girlfriend recognized that he was struggling and was able to obtain help for his overwhelming anxiety. I am pleased with the progress of therapy so far, and am hopeful that given his many strengths, Peter will be able to manage his symptoms through the psychological methods over which he is gaining mastery. Peter has the potential to be a successful lawyer, and given the strength of his relationship with Ashley, I am hopeful that he will be able to turn his life around with only a slight chance of re-experiencing these symptoms.

SUMMARY

The field of abnormal psychology goes beyond the academic concern of studying behavior. It encompasses the large range of human issues involved when a client and a clinician work together to help the client resolve psychological difficulties.

- People working in the area of abnormal psychology use both "**client**" and "**patient**" to refer to those who use psychological services. Our preference is to use the term "client," reflecting the view that clinical interventions are a collaborative endeavor.

- The person providing the treatment is the **clinician.** There are many types of clinicians who approach clinical work in a variety of ways based on training and orientation. These include psychiatrists, clinical psychologists, social workers,

counselors, therapists, and nurses. The field also includes those who do not have graduate-level training. These include occupational therapists, recreational therapists, and counselors who work in institutions, agencies, schools, and homes.

- Clinicians and researchers use the *Diagnostic and Statistical Manual of Mental Disorders,* fourth edition (*DSM-IV-TR*), which contains descriptions of all psychological disorders. In recent editions, the authors of the *DSM* have strived to meet the criterion of reliability so that a clinician can consistently apply a diagnosis to anyone showing a particular set of symptoms. At the same time, researchers have worked to ensure the validity of the classification system so that the various diagnoses represent real and distinct clinical phenomena.

- The *DSM-IV-TR* presents diagnoses using five separate **axes,** categories of information. The classification system is descriptive rather than explanatory, and it is categorical rather than dimensional. The axes include: Axis I (Clinical Disorders), Axis II (Personality Disorders and Mental Retardation), Axis III (General Medical Conditions), Axis IV (Psychosocial and Environmental Problems), and Axis V (Global Assessment of Functioning).

- The diagnostic process involves using all relevant information to arrive at a label that characterizes a client's disorder. Key to diagnosis is gaining as clear a description as possible of a client's symptoms, both those that the client reports and those that the clinician observes. **Differential diagnosis,** the ruling out of alternative diagnoses, is a crucial step in the diagnostic process.

- To gain full appreciation of the client's disorder, the clinician develops a **case formulation:** analysis of the client's development and the factors that might have influenced his or her current psychological status.

- A **cultural formulation** accounts for the client's cultural background in making diagnoses.

- **Culture-bond syndromes** are behavior patterns that we find only within particular cultures.

- Clinicians typically follow up the diagnosis phase by setting up a **treatment plan,** the outline for how therapy should take place. The first step in a treatment plan is for the clinician to establish treatment goals, ranging from immediate to long-term.

- Treatment sites vary in the degree to which they provide a controlled environment and in the nature of the services that clients receive. These include psychiatric hospitals, specialized inpatient treatment centers, outpatient treatment ranging from a private therapist's outpatient clinic or office, or a community based mental health center. Other treatment sites include halfway houses, day treatment programs, or places of work or school.

- **Modality,** or the form in which one offers psychotherapy, is also a crucial component of the treatment plan. It can be **individual, family, group,** or **milieu** therapy. Whatever treatment of modality a clinician recommends, it must be based on the choice of the most appropriate theoretical or combination of perspectives.

- In optimal situations, psychotherapy is a joint enterprise in which clients play an active role. In the best of all possible worlds, the client remains in treatment until the treatment runs its course, and the client shows improvement and maintains the improved level of functioning. While not always successful, therapy is usually effective, and the majority of treatments do result in significant improvement.

KEY TERMS

Axis   28
Case formulation   35
Client   26
Clinician   27
Clinical psychologist   27
Community mental health
   center (CMHC)   39
Comorbid   34
Culture-bound syndromes   31
Cultural formulation   34
Day treatment program   39

*Diagnostic and Statistical Manual of
   Mental Disorders (DSM)*   28
Differential diagnosis   34
Evidence-based practice in
   psychology   41
Family therapy   40
Global Assessment of Functioning
   (GAF) scale   31
Group therapy   40
Halfway house   39
Individual psychotherapy   40

Milieu therapy   40
Modality   40
Multiaxial system   28
Patient   26
Principal diagnosis   34
Prognosis   31
Psychiatrist   27
Psychologist   26
Reliability   27
Treatment plan   36
Validity   27

Assessment

Learning Objectives

3.1 Define key concepts of assessment

3.2 Describe clinical interviews

3.3 Identify mental status examination

3.4 Explain intelligence testing

3.5 Describe personality testing

3.6 Recognize behavioral assessment

3.7 Identify multicultural assessment

3.8 Explain neuropsychological assessment

3.9 Describe neuroimaging

Case Report: Ben Robsham

Reason for referral: Ben is a 22-year-old Caucasian male with 12 years of formal education who was referred to the clinic by his supervisor following an incident in which he hit his head while operating a subway train. While driving above ground, Ben reported that the brakes had jammed while he was coming to an intersection where pedestrians were crossing. Using the emergency brake, Ben was able to stop the train, but the abrupt halt caused him to hit his head on the glass window and temporarily lose consciousness. He is unable to recall what happened directly after hitting his head. Ben took a two-week leave of absence after the incident, and continued to avoid going to work for the two following weeks. When the supervisor called him, Ben stated, "I can't leave my house. They'll come and get me."

Relevant history: Ben has no history of psychiatric treatment. He stated that he has never experienced depression or anxiety, and that he typically feels "just fine," which has made the recent changes in his psychological state all the more disturbing to him. Ben reported that he has never used drugs and only occasionally drinks when he is in a social environment. Additionally, Ben reported that his maternal grandfather and uncle had both been diagnosed with schizophrenia. Finally, Ben reported having no remarkable past or current medical history.

Case formulation: Because Ben's symptoms emerged following the incident, Ben will be referred for neuropsychological testing to rule out possible traumatic brain injury.

Multiaxial assessment:

Axis I: Rule out personality change due to traumatic brain injury, paranoid type

Axis II: Deferred

Axis III: Traumatic brain injury

Axis IV: Recent accident

Axis V: 55

Treatment plan: After an initial intake interview at the university, Ben was referred for further psychological evaluation and psychiatric consultation to Dr. Martin Washington, a neuropsychologist.

Sarah Tobin, PhD
Referring Clinician

TABLE 3.1 Tests Administered to Ben

Clinical Interview
Wechsler Adult Intelligence Scale, Fourth Edition (WAIS-IV)
Trail-Making Test, Parts A and B
Clock Drawing Test
Paced Auditory Serial Addition Test (PASAT)
Boston Naming Test, Second Edition (BNT)
Wechsler Memory Scale (WMS)
Minnesota Multiphasic Personality Inventory-2 (MMPI-2)

3.1 Characteristics of Psychological Assessments

psychological assessment
A broad range of measurement techniques, all of which involve having people provide scorable information about their psychological functioning.

A **psychological assessment** is a procedure in which a clinician provides a formal evaluation of an individual's cognitive, personality, and psychosocial functioning. As you will see in Ben's case, a comprehensive assessment proved valuable in helping to understand the nature of his symptoms and potential directions for treatment.

Clinicians conduct assessments under a variety of conditions. In many cases, clinicians use the assessment process to provide a diagnosis, or at least a tentative diagnosis, of an individual's psychological disorder. However, clinicians may also use assessments for a variety of other reasons. For example, in forensic assessments, clinicians determine whether a suspect meets the criteria of being competent to stand trial. Clinicians might also provide information that employers can use to evaluate an individual's appropriateness for a particular job. Assessments are also useful when clinicians consult about an individual's level of functioning in a specific area. An older woman experiencing memory problems may seek neuropsychological assessment to determine whether she has a cognitive impairment that will require further intervention.

For Ben, the assessment process is critical to understanding the nature of his current symptoms. The clinician must evaluate the potential roles of both brain injury and what may have been the appearance of symptoms unrelated to the train incident. His immediate treatment plan and his long-term psychological development will depend on the outcome of the evaluation. Dr. Tobin provided an initial evaluation, and as a result of this assessment, she decided to refer Ben to a neuropsychologist.

To be useful, clinicians must hold assessments to standards that ensure that they provide the most reproducible and accurate results. The reliability of a test indicates the consistency of the scores it produces. In other words, it should produce the same results regardless of when it is given, and the individual should answer test items in similar fashion. The test's validity reflects the extent to which a test measures what it is designed to measure. An intelligence test should measure intelligence, not personality. Before using a given test, clinicians should be aware of its reliability and validity, information that is readily available in the published literature about the instrument.

standardization
a psychometric criterion that clearly specifies a test's instructions for administration and scoring.

The profession strives to design tests so that the results they produce don't vary from clinician to clinician. The criterion of **standardization** clearly specifies a test's instructions for administration and scoring. Each individual receiving the test should have the same amount of time, and each person scoring the test should do so in the same manner according to the same, predefined criteria. Furthermore, a given score on the test that one person obtains should have a clear meaning. Ideally, the test's designers have a substantial enough database against which to compare each test-taker's scores.

In addition to determining a test's reliability and validity, it is important to take into account its applicability to test-takers from a diversity of backgrounds. Increasingly, test publishers are designing their measures for usage with a variety of individuals in terms of ability level, first language, cultural background, and age. For example, clinicians may need to adapt assessment instruments for use with older adults, who may require larger print, slower timing, or special writing instruments for use with those who have arthritis (Edelstein, Martin, & McKee, 2000). Even so, clinicians need to ensure that they are using the most appropriate instrument for a given client.

When interpreting test results, clinicians need to ensure that they don't fall into the trap of the so-called "Barnum Effect." Named after legendary circus owner P. T. Barnum, this is the tendency for clinicians unintentionally to make generic and vague statements about their clients that do not specifically

A patient completes a visual-spatial task as part of a neuropsychological assessment.

characterize the client. Here's an example of a Barnum Effect statement: "Julia is often shy around other people, but at times she can be very outgoing. When presented with a challenge, she can often perform very well, but she occasionally becomes nervous and intimidated." These two sentences *could* apply to Julia, but they could also apply to most other people. Therefore, they don't say anything special about Julia. Furthermore, most people would find it difficult to disagree with this feedback. You are most likely to encounter the Barnum Effect in situations such as reading your horoscope or a fortune cookie, which are written so generally that they could apply to anyone. These are relatively harmless situations, unless you decide to invest a great deal of money on the basis of such an unreliable prognosticator. In a clinical situation, the problem is that such statements are not particularly insightful or revealing and do not help inform the assessment process.

Clinicians should keep up with the literature to ensure that they are using the best assessment methods possible. Evidence-based assessment includes (1) relying on research findings and scientifically viable theories; (2) using psychometrically strong measures; and (3) empirically evaluating the assessment process (Hunsley & Mash, 2007). By following these guidelines, clinicians ensure that they will evaluate their clients using the most current and appropriate materials available. For example, a seasoned clinician may have a preference for using the assessment methods she learned about in graduate school, but she should be constantly alert for newer procedures that rely on newer technology or research. According to criterion (3), she should also develop evaluation methods to assess whether her assessments are providing useful information about her clients.

For example, consider the case of an assessment suggesting that a client is experiencing significant depressive symptoms even though she seeks help for what she describes as attacks of anxiety. Following the criteria for evidence-based assessment, the clinician would determine whether the tool or tools she used to make the diagnosis provided an accurate characterization of the woman's symptoms as they evolved over the course of treatment. Similarly, in Ben's case, the clinician must validate the findings from neuropsychological assessment carefully by obtaining multiple measures to assess possible brain injury.

3.2 Clinical Interview

Clinicians typically begin their assessment with the **clinical interview,** a series of questions that they administer in face-to-face interaction with the client. The answers the client gives to these questions provide important background information on clients, allow them to describe their symptoms, and enable clinicians to make observations of their clients that can guide decisions about the next steps, which may include further testing.

The least formal version of the clinical interview is the **unstructured interview,** which consists of a series of open-ended questions regarding the client's symptoms, health status, family background, life history, and reasons for seeking help. In addition to noting the answers to these questions, the clinician also observes the client's body language. By noting the client's nonverbal cues, the clinician can gain an understanding of whether the client is experiencing, for example, anxiety, attentional difficulties, unwillingness to cooperate, or unusual concern about testing. The clinician may also use cues from the client's appearance that give further indication of the client's symptoms, emotional state, or interpersonal difficulties. The typical clinical interview covers the areas outlined in Table 3.2. The clinician can vary the order of questions and the exact wording he or she used to obtain this information.

In Ben's case, the clinical interview provided Dr. Tobin with key information about his history including not only his educational and vocational background, but also his relationship history. She determined that, prior to the incident, he enjoyed engaging with others, so his current isolation is a change from his previous pattern of social functioning.

clinical interview
a series of questions that clinicians administer in face-to-face interaction with the client.

unstructured interview
A series of open-ended questions aimed at determining the client's reasons for being in treatment, symptoms, health status, family background, and life history.

TABLE 3.2 Areas Covered in a Clinical Interview

Topic	Purpose
Age and sex	Obtain basic demographic information
Reason for referral	Hear client's reason for seeking treatment, in his or her own words.
Education and work history	Obtain socioeconomic status and determine whether client is still working.
Current social situation	Find out whether client is currently in a relationship and how much social support is potentially available.
Physical and mental health history	Determine whether client has any medical illnesses and whether there has been a recent change in health.
	Find out about history of present problem including past diagnoses and treatments and whether treatment was helpful or not.
Drug/alcohol use and current medication	Ascertain whether client is using psychoactive drugs (including alcohol and caffeine). Obtain list of medications to avoid potential interactions with any psychopharmacological interventions.
Family history	Find out whether client's family has medical and psychological disorders, particularly any relevant to client's current symptoms.
Behavioral observations	Note behaviors, including nonverbal behaviors, which indicate whether client is experiencing anxiety or altered mood. Also note whether client seems to be experiencing difficulties in attention or compliance. Attempt to determine client's mental status. Compare client's appearance with stated age. Determine whether client is oriented to time, place, and person. Observe any unusual motor behaviors.

Dr. Washington obtained more detailed information from his clinical interview with Ben. Upon further questioning about his symptoms, Ben stated that he has difficulty concentrating, but that his main symptom is the occurrence of "very strange thoughts" that have been quite troubling to him. Specifically, he feels too afraid to leave his apartment because he believes that the police will apprehend and arrest him as punishment for "what [he] did." He worries that others blame him for killing people in the incident and that if he returned to work the passengers would turn on him, thus resulting in his apprehension. He states that he spends several hours a day worrying about the consequences of the incident and sometimes hears accusatory voices blaming him for hurting people and telling him that he is a "monster." He reported that he has only heard these voices a few times in the past four weeks. As Dr. Tobin noted, though, no one was injured in the incident.

Though Ben reports that he feels distressed about his recent psychological problems, he stated that he had no thoughts of hurting or killing himself. Ben also reported that he has been unable to get a full night's sleep since the incident. At times he is unable to fall asleep, and when he does, frequent nightmares awaken him about the incident, and he feels that those he believes he killed in the incident are "haunting" him.

Ben stated that although he was worried about what he had been experiencing recently, he had been too embarrassed to tell anyone, worrying that he was "going crazy." As he had not spent time with friends or family, and had not been to work, the people in his life had been unaware of the extent of his psychological problems following the incident. Ben took a leave of absence for the first two weeks following the incident and has since been calling in sick daily. When the suggestion of psychological testing came up, Ben reports that he was hoping that it might help reveal the nature of his troubling symptoms.

As you can see, the clinical interview is a key step in the diagnostic process because of the information it provides regarding the client's current symptoms, history, and availability of social support. In addition, Dr. Washington used the interview as an opportunity to establish rapport with Ben. Over the course of a 30- to 45-minute interview, the clinician must help the client feel as relaxed as possible. Because the client is providing highly personal information, the clinician attempts to draw the client out with questioning that is respectful, but also matter-of-fact. The clinical interview is not like an ordinary conversation in that respect.

Unlike the clinical interview, the **structured interview** provides standardized questions that are worded the same way for all clients. A structured interview can either provide a diagnosis on which to further base treatment or classify the client's symptoms into a *DSM* disorder.

One of the most widely used clinical interviews is the **Structured Clinical Interview for *DSM-IV* Disorders (SCID)**. Though the title uses the word "Structured," clinicians who administer the SCID modify the wording and order of questions to accommodate the particular individual whom they are examining. Clinicians use the SCID-I to make Axis I diagnoses and the SCID-II to make Axis II diagnoses. Both SCIDs are designed so that the clinician can adapt to the interviewee's particular answers. The questions are worded in standard form, but the interviewer chooses which questions to ask based on the client's answers to previous questions. For example, if a client states that she experiences symptoms of anxiety, the interviewer would follow up with specific questions

structured interview
A standardized series of assessment questions, with a predetermined wording and order.

Structured Clinical Interview for *DSM-IV* Disorders (SCID)
A widely used clinical interview.

TABLE 3.3 Example of SCID Questions for Current Major Depressive Episode

Current Major Depressive Episode	MDE Criteria	
Now I am going to ask you some more questions about your mood	A. Five (or more) of the following symptoms have been present during the same two-week period and represent a change from previous functioning; at least one of the symptoms is either (1) depressed mood, or (2) loss of interest or pleasure.	
In the last month . . . . . . has there been a period of time when you were feeling depressed or down most of the day nearly every day? (What was that like?) If yes: How long did it last? (As long as two weeks?)	(1) depressed mood most of the day, nearly every day, as indicated either by subjective report (e.g., feels sad or empty) or observation made by others (e.g., appears tearful).	? 1 2 3
. . . what about losing interest or pleasure in things you usually enjoyed? If Yes: Was it nearly every day? How long did it last? (As long as two weeks?)	(2) markedly diminished interest or pleasure in all, or almost all, activities most of the day, nearly every day (as indicated either by subjective account or observation made by others).	? 1 2 3 If neither item (1) nor (2) is coded "3," go to
	Note: When rating the following items, code "1" if clearly due to a general medical condition, or to mood-incongruent delusions or hallucinations	

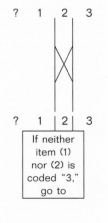

SOURCE: First, M. B., & Gibbon, M. (2004). "The structured clinical interview for *DSM-IV* Axis I Disorders (SCID-I) and the structured clinical interview for *DSM-IV* Axis II Disorders (SCID-II). In M. J. Hilsenroth & D. L. Segal (Eds.), *Comprehensive handbook of psychological assessment*, Vol. 2: *Personality assessment.* (pp. 134–143). Hoboken, NJ: John Wiley & Sons Inc.

about these symptoms. The interviewer would only ask follow-up questions if the client stated that she was experiencing anxiety symptoms. If she stated that she had different symptoms, such as depressed mood, then the follow-up questions would inquire further about her mood (First & Gibbon, 2004). The SCID-I takes 45 to 90 minutes to administer, depending on the complexity of the client's symptoms.

An advantage of a structured interview is that it is a systematic approach that is less subject to variations from clinician to clinician than an unstructured interview. Furthermore, anyone with the proper training can administer the SCID, not necessarily just licensed mental health professionals. This has practical value in that clients can receive initial screening prior to their beginning a course of therapy. Furthermore, there is a research version of the SCID that professionals can use to provide systematic diagnostic information across different investigations. Researchers can feel confident that an SCID-based diagnosis of a mood disorder means the same thing regardless of who conducted the study.

3.3 Mental Status Examination

mental status examination
A method of objectively assessing a client's behavior and functioning in a number of spheres, with particular attention to the symptoms associated with psychological disturbance.

A clinician uses a **mental status examination** to assess a client's current state of mind. In conducting a mental status examination, the clinician assesses a number of features of the client including appearance, attitudes, behavior, mood and affect, speech, thought processes, content of thought, perception, cognition, insight, and judgment. The outcome of the mental status examination is a comprehensive description of how the client looks, thinks, feels, and behaves.

The Mini-Mental State Examination (MMSE) is a structured tool that clinicians use as a brief screening device to assess dementia. The clinician administers a set of short memory tasks and compares the client's scores to established norms. If the client scores below a certain cutoff, the clinician then can (and should) continue to more in-depth testing of potential cognitive impairments.

In Ben's case, Dr. Washington noted that Ben was not experiencing an altered mental state at the time of the interview. He arrived on time and was alert and fully oriented. His conversational speech was normal in tone, rhythm, volume, rate, and prosody. The clinician noted that his receptive language appeared intact, and he was able to understand novel test instructions. However, his general appearance was slightly disheveled (i.e., his clothes were wrinkled and he was unshaven). His affect was appropriate, meaning that his apparent emotional state matched that expected in the situation, though he made a few jokes when he became frustrated during the administration of a test he found difficult. In general, though, throughout testing he cooperated with the examiner and appeared motivated and interested in the tests themselves. Dr. Washington decided not to administer a formal mental status examination. Instead he proceeded directly to further neuropsychological and personality testing.

3.4 Intelligence Testing

Many professions (i.e., mental health, academia, business, government agencies) use intelligence (IQ) tests for a variety of assessments, including overall cognitive evaluation, diagnosis of learning disabilities, determination of giftedness or mental retardation, and prediction of future academic achievement. Clinicians also sometimes use IQ tests in the diagnosis of neurological and psychiatric disorders, in which cases they are a component of a more comprehensive assessment procedure. Finally, human resource departments often use IQ tests in personnel selection to evaluate the potential for employees to perform in specific conditions.

Through intelligence testing, clinicians can obtain standardized scores that allow them to evaluate the cognitive strengths and weaknesses of their clients. The most commonly used intelligence tests in clinical settings are on a one-to-one basis, providing a comprehensive view of the client's abilities to perform a range of perceptual, memory, reasoning, and speeded tasks.

TABLE 3.4 Types of Abilities Assessed by the Stanford-Binet 5 (SB5)

Scale	Definition	Example
Fluid Reasoning	Ability to solve novel problems	Sort picture chips into groups of three
Knowledge	Accumulated fund of general information	Show how to perform a given action
Quantitative Reasoning	Ability to solve problems with numbers or numerical concepts	Count a set of items
Visual-Spatial Reasoning	Ability to analyze spatial relationships and geometric concepts	Assemble puzzle-like forms
Working Memory	Ability to store, transform, and retrieve information in short-term memory	Recall a sequence of taps

SOURCE: Roid & Barram, 2004.

Stanford-Binet Intelligence Test

First developed in the early 1900s by Alfred Binet, the Stanford-Binet is now in its fifth edition, known as the Stanford-Binet 5 (SB5). Children taking this test receive a **deviation intelligence (IQ)** score, calculated by converting their raw scores to standardized scores that reflect where a child stands in relation to others of similar age and gender. The average deviation IQ score is set at 100 with a standard deviation of 15. If a child receives an SB5 IQ score of 115, this means that the child stands at above the IQ of 68 percent of the population.

In addition to yielding an overall IQ score, the SB5 yields scores on measures of scales labeled Fluid Reasoning, Knowledge, Quantitative Reasoning, Visual-Spatial Reasoning, and Working Memory (Table 3.4). These scales are intended to provide greater understanding of the child's cognitive strengths and weaknesses not necessarily conveyed in an overall IQ score.

deviation intelligence (IQ)
An index of intelligence derived from comparing the individual's score on an intelligence test with the mean score for that individual's reference group.

Wechsler Intelligence Scales

The first comprehensive individual test that researchers specifically designed to measure adult intelligence was the Wechsler Adult Intelligence Scale (WAIS). Originally developed in 1939 by David Wechsler as the Wechsler-Bellevue test, the WAIS, first published in 1955, is now in its fourth edition (WAIS-IV) (D. Wechsler, 2008). Researchers subsequently developed parallel tests for children based on the same format as the adult scales. Those currently in use are the Wechsler Intelligence Scale for Children–Fourth Edition (WISC-IV) (D. Wechsler, 2003) and the Wechsler Preschool and Primary Scale of Intelligence–Third Edition (WPPSI-III) (D. Wechsler, 2002).

Wechsler originally sought to develop a tool for use in clinical settings, not just schools. He also believed that it was important to include both verbal and nonverbal tests. Originally he labeled these two categories "Verbal" and "Performance." For many years, clinicians reported the WAIS scores in terms of these two categories of subtests. However, over time it became increasingly evident that these two categorical scores didn't adequately capture the full complexity of intellectual functioning. Thus, the WAIS-III was substantially revised in 2008 to become the WAIS-IV, which now includes new tests and a different scoring system.

The WAIS-IV, like its predecessors and the SB5, produces an overall IQ score based on an age-normed mean of 100 and standard deviation of 15. However, the full scale IQ is not as useful for clinical purposes as are scores on Verbal Comprehension, Perceptual

TABLE 3.5 Scales on the Wechsler Adult Intelligence Scale-IV (WAIS-IV)

Scale	Tests	Type of Item
Verbal Comprehension	Vocabulary	Define the word "barrel"
	Information	How many minutes are there in an hour?
	Comprehension	Why do plants need water?
	Similarities	How are an elephant and a cat alike?
Perceptual Reasoning	Matrix reasoning	Choose which pattern logically follows after a set of patterns
	Visual puzzles	Arrange a set of blocks so that they reproduce a design
	Block design	State what is missing in a picture of a common object
	Picture completion	
Working Memory	Digit span forward	Recall a series of digits in forward order
	Digit span backward	Recall a series of digits in backward order
	Letter/number sequencing	Recall a set of digits from smallest to largest
		Recall a set of mixed letters and numbers from largest to smallest.
Processing Speed	Symbol search	
	Coding	Copy numbers that match symbols into appropriate boxes

Organization, Working Memory, and Processing Speed (Table 3.5). The intent of the WAIS-IV is to allow clinicians to examine in more depth the client's cognitive functioning along these key dimensions.

You can think of scores from the WAIS-IV as forming a triangle (see Figure 3.1). At the top is the Full Scale IQ (FSIQ), which reflects general cognitive functioning and is the best

FIGURE 3.1 Structure of the WAIS-IV

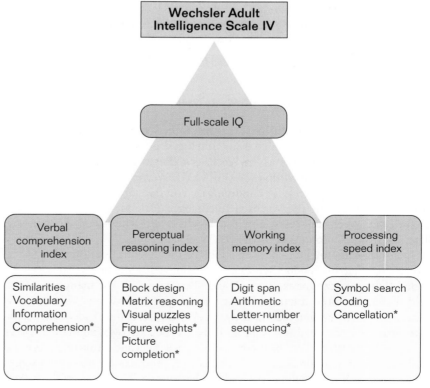

*Supplemental subtest

TABLE 3.6 Ben's WAIS-IV Scores

Full Scale: 115

Verbal Comprehension Index	132
Perceptual Reasoning Index	107
Working Memory Index	111
Processing Speed Index	97

Individual Subtests:

Vocabulary:	15	Picture Completion:	12
Similarities:	17	Coding:	7
Arithmetic:	13	Block Design:	10
Digit Span:	11	Matrix Reasoning:	14
Information:	14	Symbol Search:	12
Comprehension:	18	Figure Weights:	13
Letter-Number Seq.:	10	Visual Puzzles:	10
		Cancellation:	12

single predictor of school achievement on the WAIS-IV. Beneath the FSIQ score at the top of the pyramid are four index scores. Verbal Comprehension Index (VCI) assesses acquired knowledge and verbal reasoning skills. Perceptual Reasoning Index (PRI) measures visual-spatial and fluid reasoning. Working Memory Index (WMI) measures the capacity to hold and process information in memory. Processing Speed Index (PSI) measures the ability to process nonverbal information quickly. Beyond interpreting the index scores, clinicians propose hypotheses about individuals' performance based on an interpretation of clinical clusters, which are comprised of various combinations of individual subscale scores.

Because the WAIS-IV is given on an individual basis, clinicians have ample opportunities to observe the test-taker's behavior during the test, possibly gaining valuable diagnostic information to complement the test scores. In fact, the instructions for the WAIS-IV scoring include suggestions for the examiner to include behavioral observations such as the individual's fluency in English; physical appearance; problems with vision, hearing, or motor behavior; difficulties with attention and concentration; motivation for testing; and any unusual behaviors that the test-taker shows.

Table 3.6 shows Ben's performance on the WAIS-IV. Ben's FSIQ was 115, indicating that he has an above average level of performance (higher than 68 percent of the population). However, if you look across the entire pattern of his scores, you'll notice that Ben demonstrated high variability among the index scores that make up the FSIQ. This type of variability suggests that there is a wide range to Ben's cognitive abilities. The clinician found it noteworthy that Ben's Processing Speed cluster score was low (higher than only 40 percent of the population). This would suggest that Ben struggles with the perception of visual patterns and stimuli, particularly when speed is a factor. The appearance of this low test score where he should have performed well given his job suggests that there may be injury to the areas of his brain involved in processing of spatial information.

While administering the WAIS-IV, Dr. Washington carefully recorded Ben's behaviors, further fleshing out the picture provided by the test scores themselves. Ben stated several times throughout the testing session that "they give you fake confidence early on," referring to his frustration as the test became more difficult. Despite his frustration, Ben remained determined to complete the test. For example, he took nearly six minutes to complete the final Block Design item, and finally stated, "It doesn't make sense—there aren't enough blocks." On the Matrix Reasoning subtest, Ben took nearly one minute for each response toward the end of the task. While completing the Figure Weights subtest, Ben commented on what the shapes in the stimulus book looked like and made several jokes throughout the subtest administration. On the Letter-Number Sequencing task, before giving his response to each item, Ben described how each correlated with the name of a different type of army ship or plane. As the tests became more difficult toward the end of the testing session, Ben appeared visibly restless and began to tap his fingers and tap on his legs. On tasks requiring verbal responses, Ben provided long elaborations, and when the test required a short answer, he would sometimes respond in a sing-song voice.

3.5 Personality Testing

Clinicians use tests of personality to understand a person's thoughts, behaviors, and emotions. There are two main forms of personality tests: self-report and projective. These tests differ in the nature of their items and in the way they are scored.

Self-Report Tests

self-report clinical inventory
A psychological test with standardized questions having fixed response categories that the test-taker completes independently, self-reporting the extent to which the responses are accurate characterizations.

A **self-report clinical inventory** contains standardized questions with fixed response categories that the test-taker completes independently either on paper or on the computer. Test-takers rate the appropriateness of the item to themselves on a fixed scale. These tests are objective in the sense that the scoring does not involve any form of subjective judgment on the part of the examiner. In fact, computers can both score these tests and produce brief explanatory reports. However, clinicians need to balance the advantages of their objectivity against the possibility that these reports are subject to the Barnum Effect. Because computer programs rely on a set of algorithms to produce their reports, they run the risk of being overly generic and not tapered to the particular test-taker's idiosyncrasies.

Nevertheless, a major advantage of self-report inventories is that they are relatively easy to administer and score. Consequently, large numbers of people can take these in an efficient manner. Clinicians can take advantage of the wealth of information on the validity and reliability of the better-known self-report inventories when interpreting the scores of their own clients.

There are literally hundreds of self-report clinical inventories, many of which researchers developed specifically to investigate particular clinical problems or research areas. These inventories can range from a few dozen to several hundred items. As with tests such as the MMPI, clinicians must take care to ensure that the measures meet standards of reliability and validity before interpreting their scores.

The most popular self-report inventory by far is the Minnesota Multiphasic Personality Inventory (MMPI), originally published in 1943. The current version of the test is the 1989 revision known as the MMPI-2 (Table 3.7). There are 567 true-false items on the MMPI-2, which are all in the form of statements that describe the individual's thoughts, behaviors, feelings, and attitudes. The original intent of the MMPI was to provide scores on 10 so-called "clinical scales" corresponding to major diagnostic categories such as schizophrenia, depression, and anxiety. The text developers built an additional 3 "validity" scales into the test in order to guard against people trying to feign either exceptional psychological health or illness.

In the decades after its publication, researchers and clinicians became aware of limitations in MMPI-2 clinical scale scores. They did not correspond to the original clinical categories, meaning that they could not interpret them as the scale's developers originally planned (i.e., a high "Schizophrenia" scale score did not imply that the individual had a diagnosis of schizophrenia). Consequently, MMPI-2 users are incorporating the MMPI's newer, restructured clinical scales (RC's). In fact, the newest version of the MMPI is the MMPI-2-RF, published in 2008 (Table 3.8). The MMPI-RF is based entirely on the restructured scales. Containing only 338 items, this latest version of the MMPI-2 also provides scores for so-called "higher order" factors that indicate a client's overall emotional, cognitive, and behavioral functioning.

TABLE 3.7 Clinical and Validity Scales of the MMPI-2, with Adapted Items

Scale	Scale Name	Type of Content	Adapted Item
Clinical scales			
1	**Hypochondriasis**	Bodily preoccupations and concerns, fear of illness and disease.	I have a hard time with nausea and vomiting.
2	**Depression**	Unhappiness and feelings of low personal worth.	I wish I were as happy as others appear to be.
3	**Hysteria**	Denial of psychological problems and over-reactions to stressful situations, various bodily complaints.	Frequently my head seems to hurt everywhere.
4	**Psychopathic deviate**	Antisocial tendencies and delinquency.	I was occasionally sent to the principal's office for bad behavior.
5	**Masculinity-femininity**	Adoption of stereotypic sex-role behaviors and attitudes.	I like reading romantic tales (female item).
6	**Paranoia**	Feelings of persecution and suspiciousness of others.	I would have been a lot more successful had others not been vindictive toward me.
7	**Psychasthenia**	Uncontrollable urges to think and act; unreasonable fears.	Sometimes I think thoughts too awful to discuss.
8	**Schizophrenia**	Disturbances of thinking, mood, and behavior.	I have had some rather bizarre experiences.
9	**Hypomania**	Elevated mood, accelerated speech and motor activity.	I become excited at least once a week.
10	**Social introversion**	Tendency to withdraw from social situations.	I usually do not speak first. I wait for others to speak to me.
Validity scales (composed of items from clinical scales)			
L	**Lie scale**	Unrealistically positive self-representation	
K	**Correction**	Similar to L scale—more sophisticated indication of tendency toward positive self-presentation	
F	**Infrequency**	Presenting oneself in an unrealistically negative light	

SOURCE: *MMPI®-2 (Minnesota Multiphasic Personality Inventory®-2) Manual for Administration, Scoring, and Interpretation.* Copyright © 2001 by the Regents of the University of Minnesota. All rights reserved. Used by permission of the University of Minnesota Press.

TABLE 3.8 Clinical Scales of the MMPI-2-RF

Scale	Scale Name	Type of Content
RCd	Demoralization	General unhappiness and dissatisfaction
RC1	Somatic complaints	Diffuse physical health complaints
RC2	Low positive emotions	Lack of positive emotional responsiveness
RC3	Cynicism	Non self-referential beliefs expressing
RC4	Antisocial behavior	Rule breaking and irresponsible behavior
RC6	Ideas of persecution	Belief that others pose a threat to the self
RC7	Dysfunctional negative emotions	Maladaptive anxiety, anger, and irritability
RC8	Aberrant experiences	Unusual thoughts or perceptions
RC9	Hypomanic activation	Over-activation, aggression, impulsivity, and grandiosity.

SOURCE: Ben-Porath, 2010.

The Personality Assessment Inventory (PAI) (Morey, 1992) consists of 344 items organized into 11 clinical scales, 5 treatment scales, 2 interpersonal scales, and 4 validity scales. One advantage of the PAI is that clinicians can use it with clients who may not have the language or reading skills to complete the MMPI-2. A second advantage is that, unlike the MMPI, one calculates the validity scale independently of any of the content scales.

The SCL-90-R (Derogatis, 1994) measures the test-taker's current experiencing of 90 physical and psychological symptoms. One advantage of the SCL-90-R is that it focuses on the client's current status rather than asking about symptoms over a previous period of time. Consequently, clinicians can track the progress of their clients over multiple occasions.

Less oriented toward clinical use is the NEO Personality Inventory (Revised) (NEO-PI-R)(Costa & McCrae, 1992), a 240-item questionnaire that measures five personality

FIGURE 3.2

Ben's MMPI-2 profile

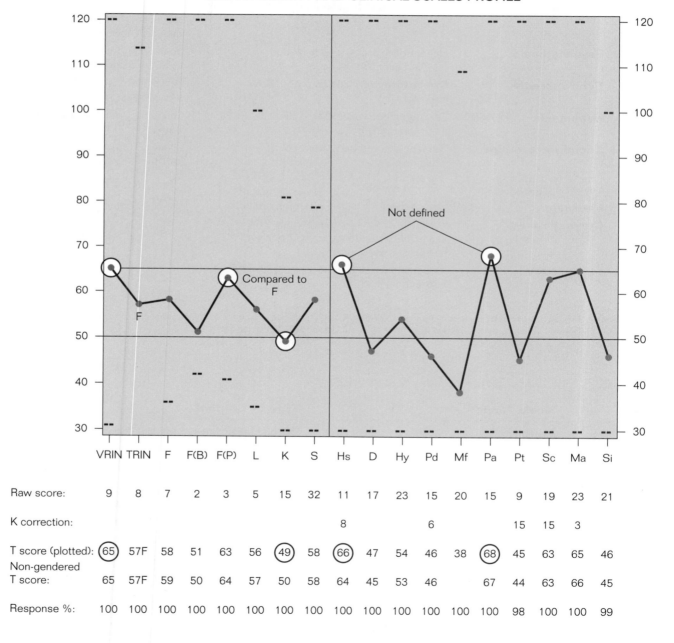

MMPI-2 VALIDITY AND CLINICAL SCALES PROFILE

	VRIN	TRIN	F	F(B)	F(P)	L	K	S	Hs	D	Hy	Pd	Mf	Pa	Pt	Sc	Ma	Si
Raw score:	9	8	7	2	3	5	15	32	11	17	23	15	20	15	9	19	23	21
K correction:									8			6			15	15	3	
T score (plotted):	65	57F	58	51	63	56	49	58	66	47	54	46	38	68	45	63	65	46
Non-gendered T score:	65	57F	59	50	64	57	50	58	64	45	53	46		67	44	63	66	45
Response %:	100	100	100	100	100	100	100	100	100	100	100	100	100	100	98	100	100	99

dimensions, or sets of traits. The scales are designed so the test-taker can complete them as well as individuals who know the test-taker, such as spouses, partners, or relatives (Form R). People use the NEO-PI-R less in clinical settings than in personality research or in personnel selection, although it can be of value in describing a client's "personality" as distinct from the client's symptoms.

Clinicians and researchers may also use specific self-report inventories designed to investigate specific disorders or research questions for which a general test may not be as relevant. There are literally hundreds of these developed for such specific purposes. These inventories may also supplement more general assessment methods.

You can see Ben's MMPI-2 scores in Figure 3.2. His scores on the Paranoia scale were slightly elevated and he endorsed several critical items relating directly to psychosis such

MMPI-2 RESTRUCTURED CLINICAL SCALES PROFILE

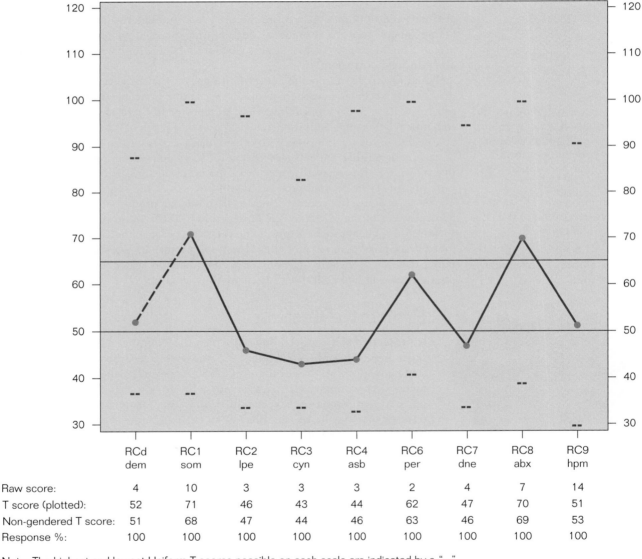

	RCd dem	RC1 som	RC2 lpe	RC3 cyn	RC4 asb	RC6 per	RC7 dne	RC8 abx	RC9 hpm
Raw score:	4	10	3	3	3	2	4	7	14
T score (plotted):	52	71	46	43	44	62	47	70	51
Non-gendered T score:	51	68	47	44	46	63	46	69	53
Response %:	100	100	100	100	100	100	100	100	100

Note: The highest and lowest Uniform T scores possible on each scale are indicated by a "--".

Legend
dem = Demoralization   cyn = Cynicism   dne = Dysfunctional negative emotions
som = Somatic complaints   asb = Antisocial behavior abx = Aberrant experiences
lpe = Low positive emotions per = Ideas of persecution hpm = Hypomanic Activation

as "I have no enemies who really wish to harm me" (False), "I have strange and peculiar thoughts" (True), and "At times my thoughts have raced ahead faster than I could speak them" (True). According to his responses, he may have unusual thought content and may often feel suspicious that others are saying bad things about him. As a result, he may feel disconnected from reality. He may believe that his feelings and thoughts are controlled by others. His abnormal thought content was evidenced at times throughout the WAIS-IV administration in his unusual reactions to certain test items. His scores on the MMPI-2, however, indicate that he does not tend to be impulsive or take physical risks and generally follows rules and laws. These may be protective factors for Ben in that he may be able to maintain some control of his abnormal thoughts, which may differentiate him from those with diagnosable psychotic disorders.

From looking at Ben's scores, Dr. Washington concluded that his limited coping resources may be a more situational than long-standing problem. Further, his clinical profile suggests that he may be excessively sensitive and overly responsive to the opinions of others. He may overemphasize rationality and be moralistic and rigid in his attitudes and opinions. As a result, he may be argumentative and have a tendency to blame others and act suspicious, hostile, and guarded in relationships. This may account for his report of having few close friends at school and his preference to be alone in his dorm room.

Based on his scores on the MMPI-2, it appears that Ben has a traditional sense of masculinity and may have stereotypically masculine preferences in work, hobbies, and other activities. In the clinical interview, he reported having had no previous significant romantic relationships with women, which may be a result of his tendency to be guarded and hostile in his relationships with others. Ben's scores on the MMPI-2-R suggest that he does endorse aberrant experiences, but his score on persecution is within the normative range. He also received scores above the norm on somatic complaints.

Clinicians typically interpret the MMPI-2 scores in the context of other test scores. They also may use the content scales to flesh out the profiles provided by the basic 10 clinical scales of the MMPI-2. The Restructured MMPI-2 also provides a different perspective on a client's current psychological state, because the content scales provide a more descriptive summary of the client's symptoms. In Ben's case, Dr. Washington noted that his score was high on the Demoralization scale, suggesting that Ben felt discouraged and hopeless about his current life situation.

projective test
A technique in which the test-taker is presented with an ambiguous item or task and is asked to respond by providing his or her own meaning or perception.

behavioral assessment
A form of measurement based on objective recording of the individual's behavior.

target behavior
A behavior of interest or concern in an assessment.

Projective Testing

A **projective test** is a technique in which the examiner asks the test-taker questions about an ambiguous item. The underlying idea behind projective tests is that people cannot or will not provide accurate statements on self-report inventories. For example, clients may not wish to say that they are experiencing unusual symptoms or have qualities that they deem negative. On projective tests, clients may be less guarded about their responses because they don't know how the assessor will interpret their answers. Projective tests are most useful when combined with self-report inventories rather than used as the sole basis for diagnosing or evaluating a client.

The most famous projective technique is the Rorschach Inkblot Test, named after Swiss psychiatrist Hermann Rorschach, who developed the method in 1911. To administer the test, the examiner shows the test-taker a set of 10 cards (5 black and white, 5 with color), one by one. The test-taker's job is to describe what the inkblot looks like. Although the method sounds simple enough, over the last century researchers and clinicians continue to refine the scoring methods.

The Thematic Apperception Test (TAT) presents test-takers with a very different task than does the Rorschach. Test-takers look at black-and-white drawings that portray people in a variety of ambiguous situations. Their task is to tell a story about what is happening in each scene, focusing on such details as what the characters in the picture are thinking and feeling. The TAT's original

Ben's perception of this Rorschach-like inkblot was "An evil mask that's jumping out to get you. Also a seed, some kind of seed which is dividing itself into two equal halves. It could be a sign of conception and yet it's dying. It's losing part of itself, falling apart, raging."

purpose was to evaluate motivation such as the need for achievement or need for power. Like the Rorschach, its use has evolved over time and clinicians can administer it as part of a larger test battery.

In Ben's case, Dr. Washington decided not to conduct projective testing until he completed the neuropsychological assessment. Clinicians typically do not administer these instruments as part of a standard battery, particularly if there is the potential that the client's symptoms are related to a trauma or injury.

3.6 Behavioral Assessment

Unlike psychological tests, **behavioral assessments** record actions rather than responses to rating scales or questions. The **target behavior** is what the client and clinician wish to change. Behavioral assessments include descriptions of the events that precede or follow the behaviors. We call events that precede the behavior antecedents and events following the behavior consequences.

For example, a child in a classroom may be unusually disruptive immediately following recess, but not immediately following lunch. When clinicians record behavior in its natural context, such as the classroom or the home, this is called *in vivo* **observation.** However, it's not always possible or practical to conduct an *in vivo* observation. The teacher or a teacher's aide is most likely too busy to record the behavior of one child, and having a clinician in the room would create a distraction or influence the behavior he or she is observing.

Patients often complete individual self-reports of behavioral patterns as part of a comprehensive psychological assessment.

Analog observations take place in a setting or context such as a clinician's office or a laboratory specifically designed for observing the target behavior. A clinician assessing the disruptive child would need to arrange a situation as comparable as possible to the natural setting of the classroom for the analog observation to be useful.

Clients may also report on their own behavior rather than having someone observe them. In a **behavioral self-report** the client records the target behavior, including the antecedents and consequences of the behavior. **Self-monitoring** is a form of behavioral self-report in which the client keeps a record of the frequency of specified behaviors, such as the number of cigarettes he or she smoked or calories he or she consumed, or the number of times in a day that a particular unwanted thought comes to the client's mind. Clinicians may also obtain information from their clients using **behavioral interviewing** in which they ask questions about the target behavior's frequency, antecedents, and consequences.

3.7 Multicultural Assessment

When psychologists conduct an assessment, they must take into account the person's cultural, ethnic, and racial background, performing a **multicultural assessment.** Clinicians evaluating clients who speak English as a second language, or do not speak English at all, must ask a number of questions: Does the client understand the assessment process sufficiently to provide informed consent? Does the client understand the instructions for the instrument? Are there normative data for the client's ethnic group? Even if clients appear as fairly fluent, they may not understand idiomatic phrases for which there are multiple meanings (Weiner & Greene, 2008).

Publishers of psychological tests are continually re-evaluating their instruments to ensure that a range of clients can understand the items. At the same time, graduate trainees in clinical programs are trained to understand the cultural backgrounds of the clients who

in vivo observation
Process involving the recording of behavior in its natural context, such as the classroom or the home.

analog observations
Assessments that take place in a setting or context such as a clinician's office or a laboratory specifically designed for observing the target behavior.

behavioral self-report
A method of behavioral assessment in which the individual provides information about the frequency of particular behaviors.

self-monitoring
A self-report technique in which the client keeps a record of the frequency of specified behaviors.

behavioral interviewing
Assessment process in which clinicians ask questions about the target behavior's frequency, antecedents, and consequences.

multicultural assessment
Assessment process in which clinicians take into account the person's cultural, ethnic, and racial background.

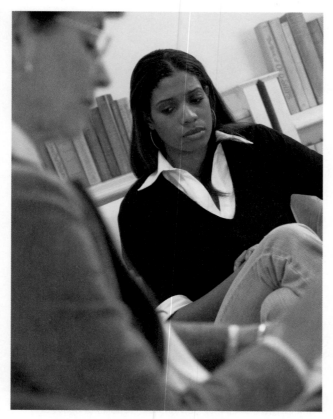

It is important for psychologists to take multicultural considerations into account throughout each part of the assessment process.

neuropsychological assessment

A process of gathering information about a client's brain functioning on the basis of performance on psychological tests.

they assess. They are also learning to evaluate assessment instruments critically and to recognize when they need further consultation (Dana, 2002).

3.8 Neuropsychological Assessment

Neuropsychological assessment is the process of gathering information about a client's brain functioning on the basis of performance on psychological tests. Clinicians use neuropsychological assessment measures to attempt to determine the functional correlates of brain damage by comparing a client's performance on a particular test with normative data from individuals who are known to have certain types of injuries or disorders. There is no one set procedure for conducting a neuropsychological assessment. Particular clinicians may have preferences for certain tests, but these preferences are not set in stone. Moreover, neuropsychologists typically choose tests that will help them understand the client's presenting symptoms and possible diagnoses. The client's age is another factor that the clinician takes into account. Tests appropriate for older adults are not necessarily either appropriate or useful for diagnosing a child or adolescent.

Certain neuropsychological tests are derived from or the same as tests on the WAIS-IV, such as Digit Span (used to assess verbal recall and auditory attention) and Similarities (used to assess verbal abstraction abilities). Developers think that each of these tests is related to brain damage in particular areas. Developers have also created other tests, such as the Trail Making Tests, also called "Trails." Figure 3.3 shows a sample item from the Trail Making Test A. This test evaluates frontal lobe functioning, and focuses on attention, scanning of visual stimuli, and number sequencing.

In a neuropsychological assessment, the clinician can choose from tests that measure attention and working (short-term) memory, processing speed, verbal reasoning and comprehension, visual reasoning, verbal memory, and visual memory. A number of tests evaluate what clinicians call "executive function," the ability to formulate goals, make plans, carry out those plans, and then complete the plans in an effective way. There are a variety of available tests within each category. If a clinician wishes to investigate one area in depth for a particular client, then he or she will administer more tests from that category.

FIGURE 3.3 Trail Making Test

There are a large number of tests that measure visuospatial ability. Many neuropsychologists rely on the Clock Drawing Test (Sunderland et al., 1989) a simple procedure that involves giving the client a sheet of paper with a large predrawn circle on it. Then the examiner asks the client to draw the numbers around the circle to look like the face of an analog clock. Finally, the examiner asks the client to draw the hands of the clock to read "10 after 11." The clinician then rates the client's drawing according to number of errors. The most impaired clients are unable to reproduce a clock face at all, or make mistakes in writing the numbers or placing them around the clock.

The Wisconsin Card Sorting Test (WCST) (see Figure 3.3) requires that the client match a card to one of a set of cards that share various features. Originally developed using the physical cards, the clinician typically administers the test in its computerized format. The test requires that the client shift mental set because the basis for a correct match shifts from trial to trial. In the example we've shown in Figure 3.3, the client could match the card on the basis of color, number of items, or shape. The profession regards the WCST as a test of executive functioning (Rabin, Barr, & Burton, 2005) that is sensitive to injury of the frontal lobes, but also assesses damage in other cortical areas (Nagahama, Okina, Suzuki, Nabatame, & Matsuda, 2005).

Toward the DSM-5

Changes in Diagnostic Assessments

The *DSM-5* Task Force is recommending a major shift in diagnostic assessments. First, they propose including dimensional assessments along with the existing categorical diagnoses. Such assessments would allow clinicians to employ "measurement-based care," meaning that they could more readily quantify the impact of treatment. The technology in this new approach would include traditional paper-and-pencil measures, but would also expand to computerized adaptive testing. Dimensional assessment also makes it possible to evaluate a client's functioning in areas that span several diagnostic categories. For example, clinicians could measure depression, suicidality, and anxiety, symptoms that occur in people who would have a variety of possible diagnoses. By having access to this information, clinicians could establish a baseline of the client's functioning. As the client continues through treatment, the clinician could then measure whether changes are occurring in these dimensions of functioning.

The changes that the committee is considering in *DSM-5* assessments would mean that clinicians would ask clients to complete a brief "Level 1" screening in which they rate themselves in several key areas, simply described, and on a 0 to 4 or 5 scale. If they answer positively to these screening questions, they would then receive a "Level 2" set of ratings that would more precisely tap into that symptom category. For example, clients who rate themselves as "5" on anxiety, would then move on to questions that ask them to rate themselves on more specific symptoms such as whether or not they experience panic attacks.

One advantage of the new system is that clients (or informants) can answer these questions on their own without the need for a clinician to administer these questions. This would mean that clinicians could evaluate clients in a wider range of treatment settings. The National Institute of Health is supporting this effort as part of its larger "PROMIS®"initiative, a "Patient-Reported Outcomes Measurement System" (http://www.nihpromis.org). PROMIS will provide an opportunity to improve health care outcomes by "giving decision makers hard data on how health care affects what patients are able to do and how they feel." Clearly, with the development of more objective indexes of client functioning across a range of physical and psychological domains, clinicians will better be able to evaluate the effectiveness of their approaches both to assessment and treatment.

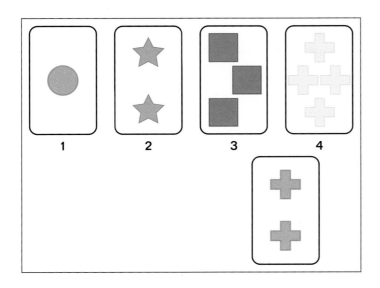

FIGURE 3.4 Sample item from the Wisconsin Card Sorting Test

Psychologists in the Legal System

Psychologists working within the legal system are frequently called on to serve as expert witnesses, and their testimony often relies on psychological assessments. Unlike the therapeutic setting, the forensic setting does not necessarily involve a positive relationship. In fact, the psychologist may face a malpractice suit from the clients if they wish to seek revenge for an assessment that led to a conviction or unfavorable decision, as in custody cases.

Knapp and VandeCreek (2001), though writing before the adoption of the 2002 APA Ethical Principles, present an interesting case history of a psychologist involved in a custody case who wrote in his report that the father had "authoritarian tendencies and could benefit from participating in parenting classes" (pp. 244–245). However, the psychologist had not actually interviewed the father; he based this statement on what the children told him. As a result, the psychologist was reprimanded by his state licensing board.

Psychologists are also mandated by the Ethics Code to practice within their field of competence. If they have not received training in forensic psychology, they are required to seek consultation from an expert colleague. A second case example presented by Knapp and VandeCreek involved the testimony by a psychologist proficient in assessment, but not forensic assessment, who testified that on the basis of elevated scores on the MMPI-2 scales 6 and 9, the defendant was indeed "insane." However, legal insanity is not the same as psychologically disordered, and therefore the psychologist's testimony was discredited in court.

Informed consent is another key ethical principle that applies not only to research but to assessment and treatment. When a defendant with a psychological disorder is interviewed for a forensic assessment, the psychologist must take all possible precautions to let the defendant know about the limits of confidentiality in this context. In another example presented by Knapp and VandeCreek, a defendant was genuinely startled to hear the psychologist report on the interview, because the defendant had not understood the nature of the informed consent.

As a final example, consider the prohibition in the Ethics Code against dual relationships. Psychologists providing therapy should not be providing information that could be used by a lawyer in a legal case. The example cited by Knapp and VandeCreek involved a psychologist treating the children of a separated couple. The children stated that they preferred to live with their mother. The mother later requested that the psychologist write a letter to her attorney. In turn, the attorney asked the psychologist to "share your opinions as to where the children should live" (p. 250).

The question here for you to judge is not which course of action is proper, as this is clearly stated in the APA Ethics Code. Instead, consider the complexities that psychologists face when interacting in the legal system. These examples are only a handful from the many possible scenarios that can ensue, placing psychologists in situations that require them to be entirely familiar with the principles that guide the profession.

Neuropsychologists use the Boston Naming Test (BNT) to assess language capacity. Containing 60 line drawings of objects ranging in familiarity, clinicians can use the test to examine children with learning disabilities and adults who suffer from brain injury or dementia. Simple items are those that have high frequency, such as a house. The client must choose from among four choices to identify correctly the object (e.g., chimney, church, school, and house).

The Paced Auditory Serial Addition Test (PASAT) assesses a client's auditory information processing speed, flexibility, and calculation ability. The tasks on the PASAT require that the client keep a running total of a series of numbers. For example, the examiner reads the numbers "6" and "8"; the correct total is 14. If the next number were "3," then the correct total would be 17. The client must respond before hearing the next digit to score the response correctly. In addition to its usage to assess traumatic brain injury, clinicians also use the PASAT extensively in assessing the functioning of individuals with multiple sclerosis (Tombaugh, Stormer, Rees, Irving, & Francis, 2006).

Other neuropsychological tests investigate a variety of memory functions, for example, the Wechsler Memory Scale, now in its fourth edition (WMS-IV). The WMS-IV includes tests of working (short-term) and long-term memory for visual and verbal stimuli. Examiners can choose from among the WMS-IV subscales according to which areas they believe are most critical to evaluate in particular clients. For example, when testing an older adult, the examiner may use only the scales assessing Logical Memory (recall of a story), Verbal Paired Associates (remembering the second in pairs of words), and Visual Reproduction (drawing a visual stimulus). However, neuropsychologists are cautious in accepting the newer versions of both the WMS-IV and the WAIS-IV, as they are too new to have accumulated sufficient validational data.

Increasingly, neuropsychologists are relying on computerized test batteries, which are easier to administer than paper-and-pencil tests. One advantage to computerized testing is that it provides the opportunity for **adaptive testing,** in which the client's responses to earlier questions determine the subsequent questions presented to them.

adaptive testing
Testing in which the client's responses to earlier questions determine the subsequent questions presented to them.

The Cambridge Neuropsychological Testing Automated Battery (CANTAB) consists of 22 subtests that assess visual memory, working memory, executive function and planning, attention, verbal memory, and decision making and response control. Before deciding whether to move to a computerized test, the clinician must weigh the advantages of ease of administration and scoring against the potential disadvantages that may exist for clients who are disadvantaged in their ability to use computers, such as young children (Luciana, 2003). However, given the relatively rapid growth of this field, more extensive normative data will be available that will allow clinicians to feel more confident about their utility.

Dr. Washington chose to administer tasks that would be sensitive to the type of injury that Ben might have sustained given his low WAIS-IV Coding score, which suggested that Ben may have suffered brain damage that led to changes in his ability to focus his visual attention and perform quickly on a psychomotor speed task. Unfortunately, because Dr. Washington saw Ben two weeks after the possible brain injury, Dr. Washington could not administer the Glascow Coma Scale (GCS), a common test that clinicians use in cases of possible traumatic brain injury. Included in the GCS are ratings, for example, of the individual's ability to hear and obey commands, open the eyes, and speak coherently.

neuroimaging
Assessment method that provides a picture of the brain's structures or level of activity and therefore is a useful tool for "looking" at the brain.

electroencephalogram (EEG)
A measure of changes in the electrical activity of the brain.

Ben's completion time on Trail Making Test Part A was in the marginally impaired range. On the Clock Drawing Test, Ben received a score of 5 out of a possible 10, erroneously crowding the numbers at one end of the clock. He received a score within the normal range on the PASAT, suggesting that the injury did not affect his auditory attentional functioning. On the WCST, Ben showed evidence of perseverative errors, meaning that he was unable to switch mental set in categorizing the cards according to different criteria. Ben's performance on the WMS-IV was within normal range, a finding consistent with his relatively high scores on the Verbal scales of the WAIS-IV, indicating that he has not suffered either short- or long-term memory loss.

3.9 Neuroimaging

Neuroimaging provides a picture of the brain's structures or level of activity and therefore is a useful tool for "looking" at the brain. There are several types of neuroimaging methods that vary in the types of results they provide.

The **electroencephalogram (EEG)** measures electrical activity in the brain. EEG activity reflects the extent to which an individual is alert, resting, sleeping, or dreaming. The EEG pattern also shows particular patterns of brain waves when an individual engages in particular mental tasks. Clinicians use EEGs to evaluate clients for conditions such as epilepsy, sleep disorders, and brain tumors.

A CAT scan of a patient's brain helps neuropsychologists to find brain structure abnormalities that may be causing cognitive dysfunction.

of brain chemicals. Vibrant colors at the red end of the spectrum represent higher levels of activity, and colors at the blue-green-violet end of the spectrum represent lower levels of brain activity. **Proton magnetic resonance spectroscopy (MRS)** is yields a multicolored image.

REAL STORIES

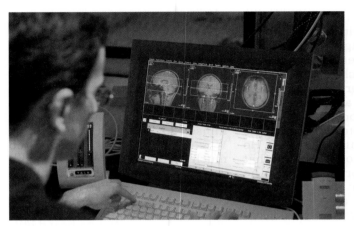

An fMRI is used to monitor changes in brain activity.

proton magnetic resonance spectroscopy (MRS)
A scanning method that measures metabolic activity of neurons, and therefore may indicate areas of brain damage.

functional magnetic resonance imaging (fMRI)
A variant of the traditional MRI, which makes it possible to construct a picture of activity in the brain.

single photon emission computed tomography (SPECT)
A variant of the PET scan that permits a longer and more detailed imaging analysis.

another scanning method that measures metabolic activity of neurons, and therefore may indicate areas of brain damage (Govind et al., 2010).

Functional magnetic resonance imaging (fMRI) provides a picture of how people react to stimuli virtually in real time, making it possible to present stimuli to an individual while the examiner monitors the individual's response. Researchers are increasingly using fMRIs to understand the brain areas involved in the processing of information. One major advantage of the fMRI is that it does not require injection of radioactive materials, like the PET or SPECT scans. However, because the fMRI uses magnetism to detect brain activity, people with artificial limbs made from metals such as titanium cannot use this testing method.

Brain scans can produce evidence of specific areas of damage, but they do not necessarily correspond to a specific loss of behavioral functioning (Meyers & Rohling, 2009). Upon evaluating Ben through neuropsychological testing, Dr. Washington decided to administer a CT scan (de Guise et al., 2010), because Ben showed some signs of frontal lobe damage (personality changes, some perseveration on the WCST, and marginal errors on the TMT). However, it was necessary to rule out parietal lobe damage, which can also contribute to this performance pattern as well as to visual attentional deficits. The CT scan revealed that Ben had suffered a traumatic brain injury as a result of the incident, perhaps in the form of a brain hemorrhage.

3.10 Putting It All Together

As we have just shown in Ben's case, clinicians face a formidable task when attempting to develop a diagnosis from the evidence that they obtain through the assessment process. They must evaluate each client on an individual basis and determine which combination of tests is most appropriate to identify as closely as possible the nature and cause of his or her behavioral symptoms. In addition, clinicians performing assessments attempt to understand a client's adaptive skills, so that they can make recommendations to build on his or her existing abilities and help address treatment to maximize his or her functioning in everyday life.

Return to the Case: Ben Robsham

Given the potential cause of his symptoms, Dr. Washington recommended that Ben will require rehabilitation to strengthen his existing skills so that he can return to his previous employment. Ben will also receive supportive therapy and possibly vocational counseling if he continues to demonstrate deficits in visual and spatial processing speed, skills that he clearly needs for his present job.

Dr. Tobin's reflections: It is somewhat reassuring to know that Ben's injury, though currently interfering with his ability to go to work, will most likely resolve on its own. A neuropsychological

assessment was clearly called for in this case; unfortunately, with increases in traumatic brain injuries in recent years, this type of assessment will be increasingly necessary. Ben's injury occurred at work, but many other young people are experiencing such injuries in areas of activity as diverse as playing hockey or football to involvement in war. With increases in the sophistication of computerized testing, we will be better prepared to assess individuals like Ben in the future, as well as those clients we see whose disorders are primarily psychological in nature.

SUMMARY

- A **psychological assessment** is a procedure in which a clinician provides a formal evaluation of an individual's cognitive, personality, and psychosocial functioning. Clinicians conduct assessments under a variety of conditions. In many cases, clinicians use the assessment process to provide a diagnosis, or at least a tentative diagnosis, of an individual's psychological disorder.

- To be useful, clinicians must hold assessments to standards that ensure that they provide the most reproducible and accurate results. The **reliability** of a test indicates the consistency of the scores it produces. The test's **validity** reflects the extent to which a test measures what it is designed to measure.

- Clinicians should use the best assessment methods possible. Evidence-based assessment includes (1) relying on research findings and scientifically viable theories; (2) using psychometrically strong measures; and (3) empirically evaluating the assessment process.

- The **clinical interview** is a series of questions that clinicians administer in face-to-face interaction with the client. The answers the client provides to these questions provide important background information on clients, allow them to describe their symptoms, and enable clinicians to make observations of their clients that can guide decisions about the next steps, which may include further testing. The format can be structured or unstructured.

- A clinician uses a **mental status examination** to assess a client's current state of mind. The clinician assesses a number of features of the client including appearance, attitudes, behavior, mood and affect, speech, thought processes, content of thought, perception, cognition, insight, and judgment. The outcome of the mental status examination is a comprehensive description of how the client looks, thinks, feels, and behaves.

- Intelligence tests such as the Stanford-Binet Intelligence Test, but particularly the Wechsler scales, provide valuable information about an individual's cognitive functioning.

- Clinicians use tests of personality to understand a person's thoughts, behaviors, and emotions. There are two main forms of personality tests: self-report and projective. Tests include the Minnesota Personality Inventory (MMPI), the Personality Assessment Inventory (PAI), the SCL-90-R, the NEO Personality Inventory, and other specific self-report inventories designed to investigate specific disorders or research questions for which a general test may not be relevant.

- Unlike psychological tests, **behavioral assessments** record actions rather than responses to rating scales or questions. The **target behavior** is what the client and clinician wish to change. Behavioral assessments include descriptions of the events that precede or follow the behaviors. *In vivo* **observation** takes place when clinicians record behavior in its natural context, such as the classroom or the home. **Analog observations** take place in a setting or context such as a clinician's office or a laboratory specifically designed for observing the target behavior. In a **behavioral self-report** the client records the target behavior, including the antecedents and consequences of the behavior. **Self-monitoring** is a form of behavioral self-report in which the client keeps a record of the frequency of specified behaviors.

- When psychologists conduct a **multicultural assessment,** they must take into account the person's cultural, ethnic, and racial background.

- **Neuropsychological assessment** is the process of gathering information about a client's brain functioning on the basis of performance on psychological tests. Clinicians use neuropsychological assessment measures to attempt to determine the functional correlates of brain damage by comparing a client's performance on a particular test with normative data from individuals who are known to have certain types of injuries or disorders. There are a variety of tests to assess verbal recall and auditory attention. Physiological measures include brain imaging techniques such as EEG, CT scan, MRI, fMRI, PET, and other techniques for assessing abnormalities in the body, particularly the brain.

KEY TERMS

Theoretical Perspectives

Learning Objectives

4.1 Assess the theories of the biological perspective and identify treatments

4.2 Describe trait theory

4.3 Compare and contrast Freud's theory to post-Freudian psychodynamic views and identify treatments

4.4 Assess the theories of the behavioral perspective and identify treatments

4.5 Assess the theories of the cognitive perspective and identify treatments

4.6 Assess the theories of the humanistic perspective and identify treatments

4.7 Assess the theories of the sociocultural perspective and identify treatments

4.8 Explain the biopsychosocial perspective

CHAPTER 4

Case Report: Meera Krishnan

Demographic information: 26-year-old Indian-American female.

Presenting problem: Meera self-referred to my office upon the urging of a friend. For the past three weeks she reports feeling "profoundly sad for no reason at all," lethargic, and preoccupied with thoughts of suicide, although she stated that she has no specific plan or intent to commit suicide. Her work performance has suffered. She oversleeps most days, has lost her appetite, and tries to avoid any social contact. She describes feeling that she has greatly let down her family and friends.

Relevant history: A college graduate, Meera works as a biologist in a hospital research laboratory. The younger of two daughters, Meera reported feeling that her parents favored her older sister. She feels that her parents disapprove of her current lifestyle in comparison to her sister, who married the son of family friends. Although she and her sister had once been very close, they no longer maintain regular contact, and she rarely visits her parents, although they live in a neighboring town.

Meera reported that she rarely drank alcohol and had never used any illicit drugs. She has no medical conditions and reported that, in general, her health is very good. Prior to the onset of her current depressive episode, Meera reported that she exercised regularly by participating in a long-distance running club and enjoyed cooking with her friends and listening to music.

This is Meera's third depressive episode since her junior year of high school. Each episode has lasted approximately two months or slightly longer. She has not previously sought treatment.

Symptoms: For three weeks, Meera has been experiencing overwhelming feelings of sadness, not accounted for by bereavement, substance use, or a medical condition. Her symptoms include feelings of worthlessness, tearfulness, loss of interest, sleep disturbance (oversleeping), and loss of appetite. She has experienced recurrent thoughts about death and passive suicidal ideation.

Case formulation: Meera meets *DSM-IV-TR* criteria for Major Depressive Disorder (MDD). The symptoms of her current depressive episode are interfering with her ability to carry out her normal daily functioning. Since Meera has experienced two previous depressive episodes that have been at least two months apart each, her Axis I diagnosis is Major Depressive Disorder, recurrent.

Multiaxial assessment:

> Axis I: Major Depressive Disorder, recurrent
> Axis II: Deferred
> Axis III: Deferred
> Axis IV: Work-related stress, family issues, social isolation
> Axis V: 45

Treatment plan: The principles of evidence-based practice suggest that the best treatment for Meera is cognitive behavioral therapy. Following intake, she will receive a complete psychological assessment and be referred to a psychiatrist for a medical evaluation.

Sarah Tobin, PhD

4.1 Theoretical Perspectives in Abnormal Psychology

theoretical perspective
An orientation to understanding the causes of human behavior and the treatment of abnormality.

Underlying **theoretical perspectives,** orientations to understanding the causes of human behavior and the treatment of abnormality all guide research and clinical work in abnormal psychology. In this chapter, we will explore the major theoretical perspectives that form the foundation for the book. You will read in more detail about each perspective and how it applies to specific disorders within the chapters covering the major psychological disorders. To facilitate your understanding of these perspectives, we will use Meera's case as an example to show how clinicians working within each perspective would address her treatment. Although Meera's plan calls for treatment within the cognitive behavioral perspective, her case has many facets that each of the major theories do address. These warrant discussion.

4.2 Biological Perspective

biological perspective
A theoretical perspective in which it is assumed that disturbances in emotions, behavior, and cognitive processes are caused by abnormalities in the functioning of the body.

Psychologists working within the **biological perspective** believe that abnormalities in the body's functioning are responsible for the symptoms of psychological disorders. In particular, they deem that we can trace the causes of psychological symptoms primarily to disturbances in the nervous system or other systems that have an impact on the nervous system.

Theories

neurotransmitter
A chemical substance released from a neuron into the synaptic cleft, where it drifts across the synapse and is absorbed by the receiving neuron.

The transmission of information throughout the nervous system takes place at synapses, or points of communication between neurons. Electrical signals containing information transmit chemically across the synapse from one neuron to the next. Through this transmission, neurons form complex pathways along which information travels from one part of the nervous system to another. **Neurotransmitters** are the chemical messengers that travel across the synapse, allowing neurons to communicate with their neighbors. Table 4.1 shows the proposed role of several major neurotransmitters in psychological disorders.

Apart from disturbances in neurotransmitters, abnormalities in the brain structures themselves can also cause psychological symptoms. Although it's not always possible to link brain structures that are too large or too small to behavioral impairments, researchers believe that some disturbances in behavior have a connection to abnormally developed or functioning brain structures. Because we cannot directly observe brain structures, researchers have developed sophisticated brain scanning methods to allow them to measure how an individual's brain is structured and, more importantly, how it performs while it is processing information.

The causes of nervous system dysfunction range from genetic abnormalities to brain damage. Genetic abnormalities can come about through the inheritance of particular combinations of genes, to faulty copying when cells reproduce, or to mutations that a person acquires over the course of life. Cells do possess the ability to repair many of these mutations. If these repair mechanisms fail, however, the mutation can pass along to the altered cell's future copies.

Genes contain the instructions for forming proteins, which, in turn, determine how the cell performs. In the case of neurons, genes control the manufacturing of neurotransmitters, as well as the way the neurotransmitters behave in the synapse. Genes also determine, in part, how the brain's structures develop throughout life. Any factor that can alter the genetic code can also alter how these structures perform.

genotype
The genetic makeup of an organism.

allele
One of two different variations of a gene.

Inherited disorders come about when the genes from each parent combine in such a way that the ordinary functioning of a cell is compromised. Your **genotype** is your genetic makeup, which contains the form of each gene that you inherit, called an **allele.** Let's say that Allele A causes a protein to form that leads a neuron to form abnormally.

TABLE 4.1 Selected Neurotransmitters Involved in Psychological Disorders

Neurotransmitter	Related disorders
Norepinephrine	Mood disorders
	Anxiety disorders (panic disorder)
Serotonin	Mood disorders
	Anxiety disorders
	Schizophrenia
	Eating disorders
	Substance abuse disorders
Gamma-aminobutyric acid (GABA)	Anxiety disorders
	Substance abuse disorders
Dopamine	Parkinson's disease
	Schizophrenia
	Eating disorders
	Substance abuse disorders
Acetylcholine	Alzheimer's disease
Opioids	Substance abuse disorders

Allele B causes the neuron to be entirely healthy. If you have inherited two genes containing Allele B, then you have no chance of developing that disease. If, on the other hand, you have inherited two genes containing Allele A, you will almost certainly get the disease. If you inherit one Allele A and one Allele B, the situation becomes more complicated. Whether or not you get the disease depends on whether Allele A is "dominant," meaning that its instructions to code the harmful protein will almost certainly prevail over those of Allele B. If Allele A is "recessive," then it alone cannot cause the harmful protein to form. However, because you are an AB combination, you are a carrier because should you produce a child with another AB carrier, that child could receive the two AAs, and therefore develop the disorder (Figure 4.1).

The dominant-recessive gene inheritance model rarely, if at all, can account for the genetic inheritance of psychological disorders. In some cases, inherited disorders come about through maternal linkages only, meaning that they transmit only through the mother. These disorders occur with defects in the mitochondrial DNA, which is the DNA that controls protein formation in the cell's mitochondria (energy-producing structures). Many psychological disorders reflect a **polygenic** model involving the joint impact of multiple gene combinations.

To complicate matters further, not only are multiple genes involved in the development of psychological disorders, but the environment plays an important role in contributing to the way our behavior reflects our genetic inheritance. Your **phenotype** is the observed and measurable characteristic that results from the combination of environmental and genetic influences. Some phenotypes are relatively close to their genotype. For example, your eye color does not reflect environmental influences. Complex organs such as the brain, however, often show a wide disparity between the genotype and phenotype because the environment to which people are exposed heavily influences brain development throughout life. Moreover, there are numerous genes that participate in building the structures in the brain and influencing their changes over time. The study of **epigenetics** attempts to identify the ways that the environment influences genes to produce phenotypes.

polygenic
A model of inheritance in which more than one gene participates in the process of determining a given characteristic.

phenotype
The expression of the genetic program in the individual's physical and psychological attributes.

epigenetics
The science that attempts to identify the ways that the environment influences genes to produce phenotypes.

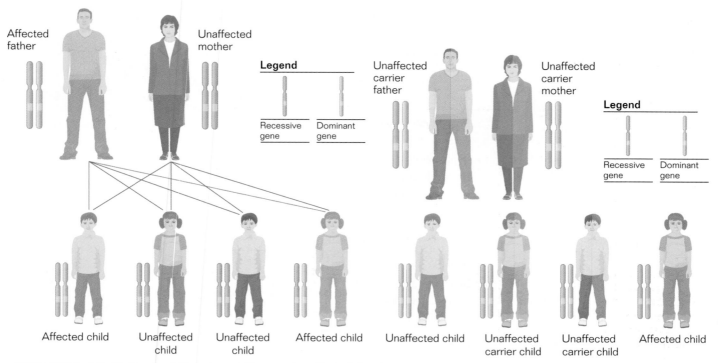

FIGURE 4.1 Pattern of Dominant-Recessive Trait Inheritance

endophenotypes
Biobehavioral abnormalities that are linked to genetic and neurobiological causes of mental illness.

Reflecting the complexity of the brain's structures and functions, leading researchers in schizophrenia (Gottesman & Shields, 1972; Gottesman & Shields, 1973) proposed the use of the term **"endophenotypes"** to characterize the combination of genetic and environmental contributors to complex behaviors. An endophenotype is an internal phenotype, that is, a characteristic that is not outwardly observable. In the case of schizophrenia, for example, there are several possible endophenotypes that may underlie the disease's outwardly observed symptoms. These include abnormalities in memory, sensory processes, and particular types of nervous system cells. The assumption is that these unobservable characteristics, which heredity and the environment influence, are responsible for the disease's behavioral expressions. The concept of endophenotypes was probably decades ahead of its time, because in the 1970s, researchers were limited in what they could study both in terms of genetics and the brain. With the development of sophisticated DNA testing and brain imaging methods, the concept is seeing a resurgence (Gottesman & Gould, 2003).

The relationships between genetic and environmental influences fall into two categories: gene-environment correlations and interactions between genes and the environment (Lau & Eley, 2010). Gene-environment correlations exist when people with a certain genetic predisposition are distributed unequally in particular environments (Scarr & McCartney, 1983). These correlations can come about in three ways. The first way is through passive exposure. Children with certain genetic predispositions can be exposed to environments that their parents create based on their genetic predispositions. For example, a child of two athletically gifted parents who participate in sports inherits genes that give this child athletic prowess. Because the parents themselves are involved in athletic activities, they have created an environment that fosters the child's own athletic development. This elicits the second gene-environment interaction and can occur when the parents treat the children with certain genetic predispositions in particular ways because their abilities bring out particular responses. Returning to our example, the school coach may recruit the athletically gifted child for sports teams starting in early life, leading the child to become even more athletically talented. We call the third gene-environment correlation "niche picking." The athletically gifted child may not wait for

MINI CASE

Biological Approaches to Treating Meera

A clinician working within a biological perspective would treat Meera's depression with antidepressant medications beginning, most likely, with SSRIs. Because these medications do not take effect for several weeks, the clinician would monitor her closely during this period to ensure that Meera remains stable. During this time, the clinician would meet with her on a weekly basis at least, to monitor Meera's progress, learn of any side effects that she is experiencing, and make adjustments as necessary particularly after four to six weeks. Meera is not a suitable candidate for more radical interventions because, although she has suicidal thoughts, she does not have plans and does not appear to be at significant risk. The clinician may also recommend that Meera attempt to resume her prior exercise routines to help augment the therapeutic effects of her medications.

recruitment, but instead seeks out opportunities to play sports, and in this process becomes even more talented. In terms of the development of psychological disorders, any three of these situations can occur, heightening the risk that children of parents with genetic predispositions are more likely to develop the disorder because of the environment's enhancing effect.

Gene-environment interactions occur when one factor influences the expression of the other. In the case of people with major depressive disorder, for example, researchers have found that people with high genetic risk are more likely to show depressive symptoms when placed under high stress than are people with low genetic risk. Thus, the same stress has different effects on people with different genetic predispositions. Conversely, the genetic risk of people exposed to higher stress levels becomes higher than that of people who live in low-stress environments. In other words, a person may have a latent genetic predisposition or vulnerability that only manifests itself when that individual comes under environmental stress. In these studies, the researchers defined genetic risk in terms of whether or not an individual had a close relative with disorder symptoms. The genetic risk presence did not predict whether or not the person developed major depressive disorder unless that individual was exposed to a high-stress environment (Lau & Eley, 2010).

Researchers studying psychopathology have long been aware of the joint contributions of genes and the environment to the development of psychological disorders. The **diathesis-stress model** proposed that people are born with a diathesis (genetic predisposition) or acquire vulnerability early in life due to formative events such as traumas, diseases, birth complications, or harsh family environments (Zubin & Spring, 1977). This vulnerability then places these individuals at risk for the development of a psychological disorder as they grow older (Johnson, Cohen, Kasen, Smailes, & Brook, 2001).

With advances in genetic science, researchers are now much better able to understand the precise ways in which genes and environmental factors interact. Usually, people inherit two copies of a gene, one from each parent, and both copies actively shape the individual's development. However, certain genes regulate through a process known as **epigenesis,** meaning that the environment causes them to turn "off" or "on." If the remaining working gene is deleted or severely mutated, then a person can develop an illness. The process of **DNA methylation** can turn off a gene as a chemical group, methyl, attaches itself to the gene (Figure 4.2) (http://www.nature.com/scitable/topicpage/the-role-of-methylation-in-gene-expression-1070).

Through the epigenetic processes of DNA methylation, maternal care, for example, can change gene expression. One study showed that during pregnancy, a mother's exposure to environmental toxins caused DNA methylation in her unborn child (Furness, Dekker, & Roberts, 2011). Studies on laboratory animals also show that stress can affect

diathesis-stress model
The proposal that people are born with a predisposition (or "diathesis") that places them at risk for developing a psychological disorder if exposed to certain extremely stressful life experiences.

epigenesis
Process through which the environment causes them to turn "off" or "on."

DNA methylation
The process that can turn off a gene as a chemical group, methyl, attaches itself to the gene.

FIGURE 4.2 Epigenesis

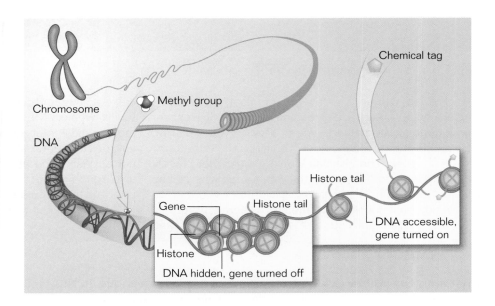

DNA in specific ways that alter brain development (Mychasiuk, Ilnytskyy, Kovalchuk, Kolb, & Gibb, 2011). Researchers believe that certain drugs that the mother uses during pregnancy cause DNA methylation, including nicotine, alcohol, and cocaine.

To understand the contributions of genetics to psychological disorders, researchers use three methods: family inheritance studies, DNA linkage studies, and genomics combined with brain scan technology. In family inheritance studies, researchers compare the disorder rates across relatives who have varying degrees of genetic relatedness. These studies examine disorder rates in different pairs of genetically related individuals. The highest degree of genetic relatedness is between identical or monozygotic (MZ) twins, who share 100 percent of their genotype. Dizygotic (DZ) or fraternal twins share, on the average, 50 percent of their genomes, but both types of twins share the same familial environment. Therefore, although MZ-DZ twin comparisons are useful, they do not allow researchers to rule out the impact of the environment. Similarly, studies of parents and children are confounded by the fact that the parents create the environment in which their children are raised. In order to separate the potential impact of the environment in studies comparing MZ and DZ twins, researchers turned long ago to adoption studies in which different families raised MZ twins, and therefore the twins experienced different environments.

For decades, family and twin studies were the only methods researchers had at their disposal to quantify the extent of genetic influences on psychological disorders. With the advent of genetic testing, however, researchers became able to examine specific genetic contributions to a variety of traits, including both physical and psychological disorders.

In a **genome-wide linkage study,** researchers study the families of people with specific psychological traits disorders. The principle behind a linkage study is that characteristics near to each other on a particular gene are more likely inherited together. With refined genetic testing methods available, researchers can now carry this task out with far greater precision than was true in the past.

Although useful, linkage studies have limitations primarily because they require the study of large numbers of family members and may produce only limited findings. In **genome-wide association studies (GWAS)**, researchers scan the entire genome of individuals who are not related to find the associated genetic variations with a particular disease. They are looking for a **single nucleotide polymorphism (SNP)** (pronounced "snip"), which is a small genetic variation that can occur in a person's DNA sequence. Four nucleotide letters—adenine, guanine, thymine, and cytosine (A, G, T, C)—specify the genetic code. A SNP variation occurs when a

genome-wide linkage study
Genetic method in which researchers study the families of people with specific psychological traits disorders.

genome-wide association studies (GWAS)
Genetic method in which researchers scan the entire genome of individuals who are not related to find the associated genetic variations with a particular disease.

single nucleotide polymorphism (SNP)
(pronounced "snip"): A small genetic variation that can occur in a person's DNA sequence.

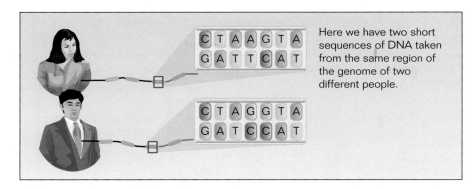

FIGURE 4.3 **SNP Detection**

Here we have two short sequences of DNA taken from the same region of the genome of two different people.

We can see that the sequences are almost exactly the same, except at one nucleotide position.

SNP

To keep things simple, we will just show one strand of the double-stranded DNA molecule

If we look at the same stretch of DNA from a larger group – say 1,000 people – we see that 72 percent of the time we find a G at this position, while 28 percent of the time we find an A.

single nucleotide, such as an A, replaces one of the other three. For example, a SNP is the alteration of the DNA segment AAGGTTA to ATGGTTA, in which a "T" replaces the second "A" in the first snippet (Figure 4.3). With high-tech genetic testing methods now more readily available, researchers are much better able to find SNPs that occur with particular traits (or diseases) across large numbers of people. Although many SNPs do not produce physical changes in people, researchers believe that other SNPs may predispose people to disease and even influence their response to drug regimens.

Imaging genomics increasingly augment genetic studies. Researchers can combine linkage or association methods with imaging tools to examine connections between gene variants and activation patterns in the brain.

Treatment

At the present time, biologically based treatment cannot address the disorder's cause in terms of fixing genetic problems. Instead, biological therapies either involve medications, surgery, or other direct treatment forms on the brain.

Psychotherapeutic medications are intended to reduce the individual's symptoms by altering the levels of neurotransmitters that researchers believe are involved in the disorder.

psychotherapeutic medications
Somatic treatments that are intended to reduce the individual's symptoms by altering the levels of neurotransmitters that researchers believe are involved in the disorder.

TABLE 4.2 Major Psychotherapeutic Medications

Used to Treat	Category
Schizophrenia and schizophrenia-related disorders	Antipsychotics Conventional or "typical" antipsychotic medications "Atypical" antipsychotic medications (also called "second generation")
Major depressive disorder	Selective serotonin reuptake inhibitors (SSRIs) Serotonin and norepinephrine reuptake inhibitors (SNRIs) Atypical antidepressants Tricyclic antidepressants Monoamine oxidase inhibitors (MAOIs) Mood stabilizers
Bipolar disorder	Anticonvulsants Atypical antipsychotics Antianxiety medications
Anxiety disorders	Benzodiazepines Atypical antidepressants MAOIs SSRIs SNRIs Tricyclics Stimulants
Attention deficit hyperactivity disorder	Stimulants Antidepressants

SOURCE: http://www.nimh.nih.gov/health/publications/mental-health-medications/complete-index.shtml

In 1950, a French chemist, Paul Charpentier, synthesized chlorpromazine (Thorazine). This medication gained widespread acceptance in the 1960s, and led the way toward the development of a wider range of psychotherapeutic agents.

Currently, the major categories of psychotherapeutic agents include antipsychotics, antidepressants, mood stabilizers, anticonvulsants, anti-anxiety medications, and stimulants (Table 4.2). As you can see from this table, some medication categories that pharmaceutical companies have designed to treat one disorder, such as antidepressants, also serve to treat other disorders, such as anxiety disorders. That clinicians use the same medications to treat different disorders suggests that abnormalities involving similar neurotransmitter actions may mediate these disorders.

Each of these medications can have serious side effects, leading patients experiencing these so-called adverse drug reactions to discontinue their use and try a different medication, perhaps from a different category. The Federal Drug Administration maintains a watch list of side effects with monthly updates (http://www.fda.gov/Safety/MedWatch/default.htm) and patients can sign up for a monthly newsletter by following a link on this website.

Biological treatments also include a second major category of interventions. **Psychosurgery**, or **psychiatric neurosurgery,** is a treatment in which a neurosurgeon operates

psychosurgery
A form of brain surgery, the purpose of which is to reduce psychological disturbance.

psychosurgery, or psychiatric neurosurgery
A treatment in which a neurosurgeon operates on brain regions,

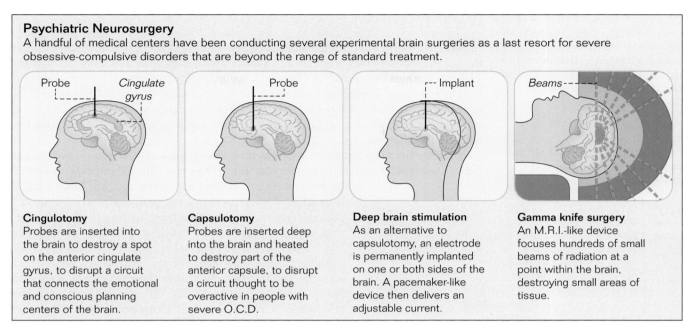

Psychiatric Neurosurgery
A handful of medical centers have been conducting several experimental brain surgeries as a last resort for severe obsessive-compulsive disorders that are beyond the range of standard treatment.

Cingulotomy
Probes are inserted into the brain to destroy a spot on the anterior cingulate gyrus, to disrupt a circuit that connects the emotional and conscious planning centers of the brain.

Capsulotomy
Probes are inserted deep into the brain and heated to destroy part of the anterior capsule, to disrupt a circuit thought to be overactive in people with severe O.C.D.

Deep brain stimulation
As an alternative to capsulotomy, an electrode is permanently implanted on one or both sides of the brain. A pacemaker-like device then delivers an adjustable current.

Gamma knife surgery
An M.R.I.-like device focuses hundreds of small beams of radiation at a point within the brain, destroying small areas of tissue.

FIGURE 4.4 **Forms of Psychosurgery for Treating Severe Obsessive-Compulsive Disorder That Are Beyond the Range of Standard Treatment**

on brain regions, most likely responsible for the individual's symptoms. The first modern use of psychosurgery was a prefrontal lobotomy, which the Portuguese neurosurgeon Egas Moniz developed in 1935. By severing the prefrontal lobes from the rest of the brain, Moniz found that he was able to reduce the patient's symptoms. Unfortunately, the procedure also caused severe changes in the patient's personality, including loss of motivation. The medical field considered the technique a major breakthrough at the time, leading Moniz to be honored with a Nobel Prize in 1949. In the 1960s, when psychotherapeutic medications became available, psychiatrists had an alternative to prefrontal lobotomies, allowing them to reduce a patient's symptoms without resorting to this extreme measure.

Modern psychosurgery relies on targeted interventions designed to reduce symptoms in patients who have proven otherwise unresponsive to less radical treatment (Figure 4.4). Each of these psychiatric neurosurgery forms targets a specific region of the brain that researchers believe are involved as a cause of symptoms. With higher levels of precision that reflect advances in surgical techniques, neurosurgeons can produce a lesion in a specific brain region to provide symptom relief. For individuals with severe obsessive-compulsive or major depressive disorder, the lesions target the cortex, striatum, and thalamus. **Deep brain stimulation (DBS),** also called **neuromodulation,** is another form of psychiatric neurosurgery in which permanently implanted electrodes trigger responses in specific brain circuits, as needed (Shah, Pesiridou, Baltuch, Malone, & O'Reardon, 2008).

In **electroconvulsive therapy (ECT),** attached electrodes across the head produce an electric shock that produces brief seizures. Ugo Cerletti, an Italian neurologist seeking a treatment for epilepsy, developed this method in 1937. ECT became increasingly popular in the 1940s and 1950s, but, as the movie *One Flew over the Cuckoo's Nest* depicts, staff in psychiatric hospitals also misused it as a way to restrain violent patients. Even though ECT had largely fallen into disuse by the mid-1970s, psychiatrists continued to use it to treat a narrow range of disorders. A comprehensive review of controlled studies using ECT for treatment of major depressive disorder showed that, in the short-term, ECT was more effective than medications in producing rapid improvement of symptoms. However, there are long-term ECT consequences including memory impairment (UK ECT Review Group, 2003).

deep brain stimulation (DBS)
A somatic treatment in which a neurosurgeon implants a microelectrode that delivers a constant low electrical stimulation to a small region of the brain, powered by an implanted battery.

neuromodulation
A form of psychiatric neurosurgery in which permanently implanted electrodes trigger responses in specific brain circuits, as needed.

electroconvulsive therapy (ECT)
The application of electrical shock to the head for the purpose of inducing therapeutically beneficial seizures.

4.3 Trait Theory

personality trait
An enduring pattern of perceiving, relating to, and thinking about the environment and others.

Five Factor Model (also called "Big Five")
Trait theory proposing that there are five basic dispositions in personality.

As much a theory about normal personality functioning as about psychological disorders, the trait theory approach proposes that abnormality occurs when the individual has maladaptive **personality traits.** In Chapter 3, we mentioned briefly that some assessment methods focus on measuring these qualities of personality, which we think of as stable, enduring dispositions that persist over time. For many personality trait theorists, these components of psychological functioning are long-standing qualities that are potentially biologically inherited.

It is easy for most people to relate to trait theory because it fits so closely with the use of the term "personality" in everyday life. When you think about how to describe the personality of someone you know, you will likely come up with a list of qualities that seem to fit the person's observable behavior. These characteristics typically take the form of adjectives such as "friendly," or "calm," or perhaps, "anxious" and "shy." Trait theories of personality propose that adjectives such as these capture the essence of the individual's psychological makeup. The fact that people use these adjectives in everyday life to describe themselves and others agrees with the basic principle of trait theory—namely, that personality is equivalent to a set of stable characteristic attributes.

The predominant trait theory in the field of abnormal psychology is the **Five Factor Model,** also called the "Big Five" (Figure 4.5) (McCrae & Costa, 1987). According to this theory, each of the basic five dispositions has six facets, which leads to a total of 30 personality components. The Five Factor Model includes the personality traits of neuroticism, extraversion, openness to experience, agreeableness, and conscientiousness (conveniently, they spell out "OCEAN" or "CANOE"). A complete characterization of an individual on the five factors involves providing scores or ratings on each facet.

According to trait theory, where they fall on the 30 facets strongly influences the shape of people's lives. People high on the traits that define the less psychologically healthy end of each continuum may be more likely to experience negative life events

Big Five		
	Low scorers	**High scorers**
1 Extroversion	Loner Quiet Passive Reserved	Joiner Talkative Active Affectionate
2 Agreeableness	Suspicious Critical Ruthless Irritable	Trusting Lenient Soft-hearted Good-natured
3 Conscientiousness	Negligent Lazy Disorganized Late	Conscientious Hard-working Well-organized Punctual
4 Neuroticism	Calm Even-tempered Comfortable Unemotional	Worried Temperamental Self-conscious Emotional
5 Openness to experience	Down-to-earth Uncreative Conventional Uncurious	Imaginative Creative Original Curious

FIGURE 4.5 Five Factor Model of Personality

MINI CASE

Trait Theory Approaches to Treating Meera

Because trait theory does not incorporate treatment, there are no obvious ways in which a clinician would apply this perspective to Meera's depression. However, as Dr. Tobin noted in the Case Report, Meera's Axis II diagnosis is deferred. Assessment of Meera's personality traits could assist in determining whether she in fact would receive such a diagnosis. Even if she does not have a personality disorder, it is possible that Meera's personality trait profile would be relevant to treatment. For example, she seems not to be overly introverted, as she interacts frequently with friends. Her depressive symptoms appear not to be overlaid onto personality traits that include high neuroticism. She seems to enjoy activities that involve creativity and exploration of the outdoors, indicating a normative personality for her age in openness to experience. Prior to her depressive episode, she was, at least, average in conscientiousness, as her successful work history indicated, and there is no evidence to suggest that she is unusually low in agreeableness. Meera's clinician would most likely order an assessment that includes a personality trait-based measure to confirm these hypotheses and to determine whether or not she has an Axis II disorder.

because their personalities make them more vulnerable to life stresses. People high on personality traits representing riskiness (thrill-seeking) are more likely to get hurt because their personalities lead them into situations that can land them in trouble. According to the Five Factor Model, although circumstances can change personality, it's more likely that personality molds circumstances.

However, according to research using highly sophisticated data analytic designs to follow up on people over time, people can change even their fundamental personality traits. Most of the research is based on samples whose scores fall within the normal range of functioning. For example, as people get older, they are less likely to act impulsively (Terracciano, McCrae, Brant, & Costa, 2005).

The main value of understanding personality trait theory is that it provides a perspective for examining personality disorders. Research based on the Five Factor Model became the basis for the current attempts to reformulate the personality disorders in the *DSM-5*. Although the Five Factor Model does not necessarily provide a framework for psychotherapy, it has proven valuable as a basis for personality assessment within the context of understanding an individual's characteristic behavior patterns (Bastiaansen, Rossi, Schotte, & De Fruyt, 2011).

Toward the DSM-5

Theoretical Approaches

Versions of the *DSM* prior to *DSM-III* were based almost entirely on clinical judgments framed within the psychodynamic model of abnormality. The DSM used terms such as "neurosis" and "psychosis," which had meaning in the psychodynamic world, to differentiate disorder categories. For example, anxiety disorders fell into the category of neurosis because their primary symptoms included irrational fears and worries. It labeled schizophrenia a psychotic disorder because its primary symptoms involve lack of contact with reality and other cognitive distortions. The *DSM-III* authors reconceptualized it along two major lines. First, they intended it to be atheoretical—meaning that there was no underlying theory, psychodynamic or otherwise. Second, they intended the diagnostic criteria to be ones that a variety of mental health professionals could reliably evaluate. The *DSM-III* Taskforce therefore commissioned studies in which researchers could evaluate the reliability of the diagnostic criteria. Rather than use the rather vague terminology (such as neurosis) that could be open to various interpretations, the *DSM-III* diagnostic spelled out criteria in exacting levels of detail. The *DSM-IV* and its later revision, the *DSM-IV-TR*, carried on this tradition of specifying diagnostic criteria in research-based, objective terms.

The *DSM-5* will continue this empirical tradition and will remain atheoretical. Critics now maintain that the authors should, instead, develop a system that recognizes the known (to date) underpinnings of many of the disorders (Hyman, 2011). Rather than maintain the distinct categorical system of previous *DSM*s, disorders that share common features, whether in terms of symptoms, risk factors, or shared neural abnormalities, the *DSM-5* should represent them on spectrums or larger grouping systems. Although the *DSM-5* task forces considered making this radical change, they eventually decided to maintain the previous categories, albeit with some alterations. The move away from categories and toward dimensions would have required not only a massive restructuring, but also a need to retrain clinicians who were trained on the previous *DSM*s. These changes would also reinforce the medical model because they would lead to a system more similar to the diagnosis of physical diseases than psychological.

Whether future *DSM*s move away from the present system will depend largely on developments in the field of psychopathology. The *DSM-5* will implement some dimensional changes, such as the reframing of personality disorders. It will move several diagnoses in *DSM-IV-TR* from their present location to groupings that share important symptoms. Ultimately, the authors will make decisions on empirical grounds, which will maintain the intent of *DSM* to maintain its atheoretical basis.

4.4 Psychodynamic Perspective

The **psychodynamic perspective** emphasizes unconscious determinants of behavior. Of all the psychological approaches, the psychodynamic gives greatest emphasis to the role of processes beneath the surface of awareness as influences on abnormality.

Freud's Theory

Emerging out of his interest in the cause of unusual symptoms in his patients, in the late 1800s, Sigmund Freud began to explore the idea that man could scientifically study and explain the causes of and symptoms of psychological disorders. By the time of his death in 1939, Freud had articulated a vision for psychological disorder cause and treatment with the basic tenet that most symptoms had roots buried deep within an individual's past.

According to Freud (1923), the mind has three structures: the id, the ego, and the superego. The **id** is the structure of personality hidden in the unconscious that contains instincts oriented toward fulfilling basic biological drives, including gratification of

psychodynamic perspective
The theoretical orientation in psychology that emphasizes unconscious determinants of behavior.

id
In psychoanalytic theory, the structure of personality that contains the sexual and aggressive instincts.

Sigmund Freud believed that an individual's dreams held vital information about their innermost wishes and desires that could be understood through dream analysis.

pleasure principle
In psychoanalytic theory, a motivating force oriented toward the immediate and total gratification of sensual needs and desires.

libido
An instinctual pressure for gratification of sexual and aggressive desires.

ego
In psychoanalytic theory, the structure of personality that gives the individual the mental powers of judgment, memory, perception, and decision making, enabling the individual to adapt to the realities of the external world.

reality principle
In psychoanalyic theory, the motivational force that leads the individual to confront the constraints of the external world.

secondary process thinking
In psychoanalytic theory, the kind of thinking involved in logical and rational problem solving.

superego
In psychoanalytic theory, the structure of personality that includes the conscience and the ego ideal; it incorporates societal prohibitions and exerts control over the seeking of instinctual gratification.

defense mechanisms
Tactics that keep unacceptable thoughts, instincts, and feelings out of conscious awareness and thus protect the ego against anxiety.

psychosexual stages
According to psychoanalytic theory, the normal sequence of development through which each individual passes between infancy and adulthood.

sexual and aggressive needs. The id follows the **pleasure principle,** a motivating force that seeks immediate and total gratification of sensual needs and desires. According to Freud, we can only obtain pleasure when the tension of an unmet drive reduces. The way the id attempts to achieve pleasure is not necessarily through the actual gratification of a need with tangible rewards. Instead, the id uses wish fulfillment to achieve its goals. Through wish fulfillment, the id conjures an image of whatever will satisfy the needs of the moment. We call the id's primal instincts the **libido.**

The center of conscious awareness in personality is the **ego,** which gives the individual the cognitive powers of judgment, memory, perception, and decision making. Freud (1911) described the ego as being governed by the **reality principle,** meaning that the ego uses rationality to achieve its goals. In contrast to the id's illogical primary process thinking, **secondary process thinking,** logical analytic approaches to problem solving, characterize the ego functions. The third part of the equation in psychodynamic theory is the **superego,** which is personality's seat of morality. The superego includes the conscience (sense of right and wrong), and the ego ideal, or aspirations.

According to Freud (1923), in a healthy individual's personality, the id achieves instinctual desires through the ego's ability to navigate in the external world within the confines that the superego places on it. Psychodynamics, or the interplay among the structures of the mind, is thus the basis for both normal and abnormal psychological functioning.

Freud believed that people need protection from knowing about their own unconscious desires. They do so by using **defense mechanisms** (Table 4.3). According to Freud, everyone uses defense mechanisms on an ongoing basis to prevent recognizing the existence of these desires. Although everyone uses defense mechanisms to some extent, they become problematic when an individual fails to come to terms completely with his or her true unconscious nature.

The topic of development forms an important piece of Freud's theory. In 1905, he proposed that there is a normal sequence of development through a series of what he called **psychosexual stages.** Freud claimed that children go through these stages in accordance

TABLE 4.3 Categories and Examples of Defense Mechanisms

Defense Mechanism	Definition
Displacement	Shifting unacceptable feelings or impulses from the target of those feelings to someone less threatening or to an object
Intellectualization	Resorting to excessive abstract thinking rather than focus on the upsetting aspects of response to issues that cause conflict or stress
Reaction formation	Transforming an unacceptable feeling or desire into its opposite in order to make it more acceptable
Repression	Unconsciously excluding disturbing wishes thoughts, or experiences from awareness
Denial	Dealing with emotional conflict or stress by refusing to acknowledge a painful aspect of reality or experience that would be apparent to others
Projection	Attributing undesirable personal traits or feelings to someone else to protect one's ego from acknowledging distasteful personal attributes
Sublimation	Transferring an unacceptable impulse or desire into a socially appropriate activity or interest
Regression	Dealing with emotional conflict or stress by reverting to childish behaviors

with the development of their libido. At each stage, the libido becomes fixated on a particular "erogenous" or sexually excitable zone of the body. According to Freud, an individual may regress to behavior appropriate to an earlier stage or may become stuck, or fixated, at that stage. For example, the so-called "*anal retentive*" personality is overly rigid, controlled, and perfectionistic. Freud believed that the adult personality reflects the way in which the individual resolves the psychosexual stages in early life, though some reworking may occur at least up through middle adulthood. Freud also believed that the child's feelings toward the opposite-sex parent set the stage for later psychological adjustment. The outcome of what he called the "Oedipus Complex" (named after a tragic character in ancient Greece), determined whether the individual has a healthy ego or would spend a life marred by anxiety and repressed conflictual feelings.

Post-Freudian Psychodynamic Views

Freud developed his theory in the context of his clinical practice, but he also encouraged like-minded neurologists and psychiatrists to work together to develop a new theory of abnormality. Over a period of years, they spent many hours comparing notes about their

MINI CASE

Psychodynamic Approaches to Treating Meera

A clinician working with Meera from a psychodynamic perspective would assume that her difficulties stem from conflicts in early life. For example, the clinician would explore the resentment that she feels toward her parents for favoring her sister and her possible guilt over breaking away from the family when she established her own independent life. In treatment, the clinician would observe whether Meera re-enacts the conflicted feelings she has toward her parents onto the relationships that Meera establishes with the clinician. CCRT would seem particularly appropriate for Meera, given the possible role of these difficult relationships in triggering her depressive disorder. Meera's depressive symptoms would warrant a time-limited approach focusing on her current episode with the option that she would seek treatment in the future if her depression recurs.

Carl Jung's archetype theory would explain that popular superheroes are outward representations of universal aspects of human personality.

clinical cases and trying to come to a joint understanding of the cause of abnormality. Although they shared many of the same views when they began their discussions, several went on to develop their own unique brand of psychodynamic theory and now have their own schools of thought.

The most notable departure from Freud's school of thought came when Swiss psychiatrist Carl Jung (1875–1961) revamped the definition of the unconscious. According to Jung (1961), the unconscious is formed at its very root around a set of images common to all human experience, which he called *archetypes*. Jung believed that people respond to events in their daily lives on the basis of these archetypes, because they are part of our genetic makeup. For example, Jung asserted that archetypal characters (such as today's Batman and Superman) are popular because they activate the "hero" archetype. In addition, Jung (1916) believed that abnormality resulted from an imbalance within the mind, especially when people fail to pay proper attention to their unconscious needs.

For Alfred Adler (1870–1937) and Karen Horney (1885–1952), the ego was the most important aspect of personality. Although their theories represented distinct contributions, and each associated with it a particular type of therapy, they both gave great emphasis to the role of a healthy self-concept in normal psychological functioning. Adler talked about the negative consequences of an "inferiority complex," and Horney proposed that unhappiness comes from trying to live up to a false self. Both Adler and Horney also emphasized social concerns and interpersonal relations in the development of personality. They saw close relationships with family and friends and an interest in the life of the community as gratifying in their own right, not because a sexual or an aggressive desire is indirectly satisfied in the process (as Freud might say).

Perhaps the only psychodynamic theorist to give attention to the whole of life, not just childhood, was Erik Erikson (1902–1994). Like Adler and Horney, Erikson gave greatest attention to the ego, or what he called "ego identity." For this reason, we refer to the theories of Adler, Horney, and Erikson as the **ego psychology** group. In fact, we associate Erikson with the term "identity crisis," a task that he believed was central to development in adolescence. Erikson believed that the ego goes through a series of transformations throughout life in which a new strength or ability can mature. He also believed that each stage builds on the one that precedes it, and in turn, influences all following stages. However, Erikson proposed that any stage could become a major focus at any age—identity issues can resurface at any point in adulthood, even after a person's identity is relatively set. For example, a middle-aged

ego psychology
Theoretical perspective based on psychodynamic theory emphasizing the ego as the main force in personality.

According to Alfred Adler's theory, this person may be portraying himself negatively to others due to a sense of low self-worth and inferiority.

Karen Horney believed the ego to be a central aspect of human functioning.

woman who is laid off from her job may once again question her occupational identity as she seeks to find a new position for herself in the workforce.

Yet another group of psychodynamically oriented theorists focused on what became **object relations,** namely, the relationships that people have with the others ("objects") in their lives. In particular, the object relations theorists believed that the individual's relationship with the caregiver (usually the mother) becomes a model for all close adult relationships. These theorists included John Bowlby (1907–1990), Melanie Klein (1882–1960), D. W. Winnicott (1896–1971), Heinz Kohut (1913–1981), and Margaret Mahler (1897–1995). As with the ego psychologists, the object relations theorists each have a particular model of therapy that we associate with their theories. However, they all agree that early childhood relationships are at the root of abnormality.

The work of object relations theorists led to the development of what is now a widely recognized framework for understanding adult personality, particularly as applied to romantic relationships. Canadian psychologist Mary Salter Ainsworth (1913–1999) and her associates (1978) studied differences among infants in **attachment style,** or the way of relating to a caregiver figure. She developed the "strange situation," an experimental setting in which researchers separated infants from and then reunited them with their mothers.

Although designed as a theory of child development, later researchers have adapted the concept of attachment style to apply to adult romantic relationships. Most children develop secure attachment styles, and later in life relate to their close romantic partners without undue anxiety about whether or not their partners will care about them. Those who are insecurely attached in childhood, however, may show a pattern in adulthood of anxious attachment in which they feel they cannot rely on their partner's love and support. Alternatively, insecurely attached adults may show a dismissive or avoidant attachment style in which they fear rejection from others, and therefore try to protect themselves by remaining distant.

An individual's attachment style may also influence how he or she responds to psychotherapy. Across 19 separate studies involving nearly 1,500 clients, researchers found that attachment security was positively related to therapy outcome. Individuals with a secure attachment style, these researchers maintain, are better able

object relations
One's unconscious representations of important people in one's life.

attachment style
The way a person relates to a caregiver figure.

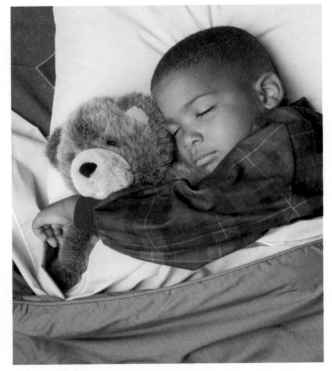

Attachment theorists believe that a child transfers emotional bonding from the primary caregiver to an object, such as a teddy bear, and eventually from this object to people outside the family.

to establish a positive working relationship with their therapists, which, in turn, predicts positive therapy outcomes (Levy, Ellison, Scott, & Bernecker, 2011).

Treatment

The main goal of traditional psychoanalytic treatment as developed by Freud (1913–14/1963) was to bring repressed, unconscious material into conscious awareness. To accomplish this task, he developed the therapeutic method of **free association,** in which the client literally says whatever comes to mind. Freud believed that clients needed to work through their unconscious conflicts, bringing them gradually into conscious awareness.

Current psychodynamic treatment is focused on helping clients explore aspects of the self that are "unconscious" in the sense that the client does not recognize them. Therapists focus in particular on how clients reveal and influence these aspects of the self in their relationship with the therapist. The key elements of psychodynamic therapy involve exploring the client's emotional experiences, use of defense mechanisms, close relationships with others, past experiences, and exploration of fantasy life in dreams, daydreams, and fantasies (Shedler, 2010).

Unlike the stereotyped portrayal that you might see in movies or on television, clinicians need not conduct psychodynamic therapy on a couch, for years at a time, or with a silent therapist. However, given the impracticality of maintaining such a long-term and intense form of treatment, psychotherapists began developing briefer forms of psychodynamic therapy. Instead of attempting to revamp a client's entire psychic structure, psychotherapists using these methods focus their work on a specific symptom or set of symptoms for which the client is seeking help. The number of sessions can vary, but rarely exceeds 25. Unlike traditional psychodynamic therapy, the therapist takes a relatively active approach in maintaining the focus of treatment on the client's presenting problem or issues immediately relevant to that problem (Lewis, Dennerstein, & Gibbs, 2008).

In one version of brief psychodynamic therapy, the clinician identifies the client's "Core Conflictual Relationship Theme (CCRT)." The clinician assesses the client's wishes, expected responses from others, and client responses either to the responses of others or to the wish. Clients describe specific instances in their relationships with others that allow the clinician to make the CCRT assessment. The clinician then works with the clients in a supportive way to help them recognize and eventually work through these patterns (Jarry, 2010).

4.5 Behavioral Perspective

According to the **behavioral perspective,** the individual acquires maladaptive behavior through learning.

Theories

Classical conditioning accounts for the learning of emotional, automatic responses. For example, if you were trapped in a smoke-filled room with no immediate escape, you might experience fear every time you hear a loud buzzing noise that sounds like the fire alarm that blared in the background while you awaited rescue. Much of the classical conditioning that behavioral clinicians focus on involves this type of aversive conditioning in which the individual associates a maladaptive response with a stimulus that could not itself cause harm.

free association
A method used in psychoanalysis in which the client speaks freely, saying whatever comes to mind.

behavioral perspective
A theoretical perspective in which it is assumed that abnormality is caused by faulty learning experiences.

classical conditioning
The learning of a connection between an originally neutral stimulus and a naturally evoking stimulus that produces an automatic reflexive reaction.

Behavioral therapists often use a fear hierarchy to gradually expose an individual to their most feared situations, such as being trapped in a smoke-filled room with no escape.

You Be the Judge

Evidence-Based Practice

As we discussed in Chapter 2, APA adopted principles of evidence-based practice that provide guidelines for clinicians to follow in their provision of psychological treatment. In this chapter, you've learned about the wide range of theoretical models available to clinicians, ranging from psychosurgery at one extreme, to family therapy at another. Given the recommendation that psychologists provide treatment best suited to the client's psychological disorder, the question becomes one of ensuring that each clinician has the ability to provide treatment within each of these theoretical models. However, is this a realistic assumption? Can we expect a clinician literally to be knowledgeable about each theoretical perspective thoroughly enough to be able to give clients the most effective interventions?

As research within clinical psychology and related fields continues to expand by an almost exponential rate, how can each clinician stay on top of all of the latest developments well enough to be comfortable in providing the most recent approaches to each client? According to the APA Ethical Guidelines, clinicians should work within their areas of expertise, and if they must extend outside of this area, then they should seek consultation. Moreover, each state within the United States maintains strict regulations over licensing of psychologists to ensure that they participate in continuing education. As a result, there are many safeguards to give clients protection from receiving outdated or inappropriate intervention methods.

You be the judge: As a consumer of psychology, do you feel that it is more important for potential clients to see a clinician whom they trust based on reputation, prior experience, or recommendations from other people, or should they instead find a specialist who, in the theoretical perspective, most closely matches evidence-based standards? Can a respected "generalist" provide care that is as high quality as another professional who is more narrowly trained? Ultimately, clients have protection against inadequate care by the standards that govern each profession (counseling, psychiatry, psychology, social work). However, it also benefits consumers to stay abreast of the latest developments so that they can make the most informed choices possible.

By contrast, in **operant conditioning** an individual acquires a maladaptive response by learning to pair a behavior with its consequences. The behavior's consequences are its **reinforcement**—the condition that makes the individual more likely to repeat the behavior in the future. Reinforcement can take many forms. For example, through positive reinforcement, your friends may laugh when you express outrageous opinions, making you more likely to express those opinions in the future. You might also learn through negative reinforcement to take an over-the-counter sleep medication if you find that it helps alleviate your insomnia. Both negative and positive reinforcement increase the frequency of the behaviors that precede them. In these examples, the behaviors that increase are speaking outrageous opinions and taking sleep medication.

According to the behavioral perspective, you don't have to directly experience reinforcement in order for it to modify your behavior. Psychologists who study **social learning theory** believe that people can learn by watching others. Through **vicarious reinforcement**, you become more likely to engage in these observed behaviors. You can also develop ideas about your own abilities, or sense of **self-efficacy,** by watching the results of your own actions or those of other people with whom you identify. For example, you may wonder whether you have the ability to overcome your fear of public speaking, but if you see a fellow student present successfully in class, this will build your feelings of self-efficacy, and you do well when it's your turn to get up and speak.

operant conditioning
A learning process in which an individual acquires behaviors through reinforcement.

reinforcement
The "strengthening" of a behavior.

social learning theory
Perspective that focuses on understanding how people develop psychological disorders through their relationships with others and through observation of other people.

vicarious reinforcement
A form of learning in which a new behavior is acquired through the process of watching someone else receive reinforcement for the same behavior.

self-efficacy
The individual's perception of competence in various life situations.

MINI CASE

Panic Disorder with Agoraphobia

Frieda is a 28-year-old former postal worker who sought treatment because of recurrent panic attacks, which have led her to become fearful of driving. She has become so frightened of the prospect of having an attack on the job that she has asked for a medical leave. Although initially she would leave the house when accompanied by her mother, she now is unable to go out under any circumstances, and her family is concerned that she will become a total recluse.

anxiety sensitivity theory
The belief that panic disorder is caused in part by the tendency to interpret cognitive and somatic manifestations of stress and anxiety in a catastrophic manner.

conditioned fear reactions
Acquired associations between an internal or external cue and feelings of intense anxiety.

in increasing a person's likelihood of developing panic disorder due to the role of this neurotransmitter in anxiety (Kalk, Nutt, & Lingford-Hughes, 2011). Furthermore, according to **anxiety sensitivity theory,** people who develop panic disorder have heightened responsiveness to the presence of carbon dioxide in the blood. Hence, they are more likely to panic due to the sensation that they are suffocating (Pérez Benítez et al., 2009).

The most effective antianxiety medications for panic disorder and agoraphobia are benzodiazepines, which increase the availability of GABA, an inhibitory neurotransmitter. However, because they can lead clients to become dependent on them or to abuse them, clinicians may prefer to prescribe SSRIs or SNRIs (Pollack & Simon, 2009).

Psychological Perspectives From a classical conditioning perspective, panic disorder results from **conditioned fear reactions** in which the individual associates unpleasant bodily sensations with memories of the last panic attack, causing a full-blown panic attack to develop even before measurable biological changes have occurred. Building on this notion, the cognitive-behavioral model of anxiety disorders proposes that individuals with panic disorder experience a vicious cycle that begins with the individual's feeling the unpleasant bodily sensations of a panic attack. These sensations in turn lead the person to feel that the panic attack is unpredictable and uncontrollable and that he or she doesn't have the ability to stop the panic attack from occurring (White, Brown, Somers, & Barlow, 2006).

In relaxation therapy, patients learn a variety of techniques that focus on breathing and relaxation in order to overcome the physiological symptoms of anxiety.

Relaxation training is one behavioral technique used to help clients gain control over the bodily reactions involved in panic attacks. After training, the client should be able to relax the entire body when confronting a feared situation. Hyperventilation, a common symptom in panic attacks, is sometimes treated with a form of counterconditioning. In this approach, the client hyperventilates intentionally and then begins slow breathing, a response that is incompatible with hyperventilation. Following this training, the client can begin the slow breathing at the first signs of hyperventilation. Thus, the client learns that it is possible to exert voluntary control over hyperventilation. In the method known as **panic control therapy (PCT),** the therapist combines breathing retraining, psychoeducation, and cognitive restructuring to help individuals recognize and ultimately control the bodily cues associated with panic attacks (Hofmann, Rief, & Spiegel, 2010).

relaxation training
A behavioral technique used in the treatment of anxiety disorders that involves progressive and systematic patterns of muscle tensing and relaxing.

panic control therapy (PCT)
Treatment that consists of cognitive restructuring, exposure to bodily cues associated with panic attacks, and breathing retraining.

5.3 Specific Phobias

A **phobia** is an irrational fear associated with a particular object or situation. It's not unusual for people to be afraid of common objects such as spiders or heights. In a **specific phobia,** however, the fear is marked and intense. People with specific phobia go to great lengths to avoid the object or situation that is the target of their fear. If they can't get away, they endure the situation with great anxiety and distress. As is true for all anxiety disorders, a specific phobia involves significant distress. Moreover, it is not a fleeting condition but must be present for at least six months in order to justify a diagnosis.

Almost any object or situation can form the target of a phobia. People can have phobias for anything from driving to syringes. The four categories of specific phobias include animals, the natural environment (storms, heights, fires), blood-injection-injury (seeing blood, having an invasive medical procedure), and engaging in activities in particular situations (driving, flying, being in an enclosed space). A fifth category of specific phobias includes a variety of miscellaneous stimuli or situations such as a child's fear of clowns or an adult's fear of contracting a particular illness.

Overall, the lifetime prevalence for specific phobia is 12.5 percent (Kessler et al., 2005). The highest lifetime prevalence rates of specific phobias involve fear of natural situations, particularly heights, estimated to be between 3.1 and 5.3 percent. Animal phobia ranges in prevalence from 3.3 to 7 percent. That these are the two most common forms of specific phobia is indicated by the fact that among people with any form of specific phobia, 50 percent have a fear of animals or a fear of heights (LeBeau et al., 2010).

phobia
An irrational fear associated with a particular object or situation.

specific phobia
An irrational and unabating fear of a particular object, activity, or situation.

A common phobia is an excessive fear of spiders.

Theories and Treatment of Specific Phobias

As you have just seen, there are many types of specific phobias, ranging from the common to the relatively obscure. However, the fact that they are grouped together suggests that there is a common theme or element that underlies their cause and, potentially, their treatment. As is true for panic disorder, the primary explanations of specific phobias rely on biological and psychological perspectives. Nevertheless, as is also true for panic disorder, the existence of a specific phobia in an individual can have a significant

MINI CASE

Specific Phobia

Herbert is a 32-year-old lawyer seeking treatment for his irrational fear of thunderstorms. He has had this phobia since age 4, and throughout life he has developed various strategies for coping with his fear. Whenever possible, he avoids going outside when a storm is forecast. Not only will he stay within a building, but he will ensure that he is in a room with no windows and no electrical appliances. As his job has grown in responsibility, Herbert has found that he can no longer afford to take time off because of his fear, which he knows is irrational.

impact on those who are close to that person. Consequently, treatment sometimes involves partners and family members.

Biological Perspectives

Within the biological perspective, researchers believe that the anxiety associated with specific phobias may relate to abnormalities in the anterior insular cortex (Rosso et al., 2010). This area of the brain lies between the temporal and frontal lobes associated with emotion and self-awareness. Interestingly, different specific phobias seem to show different patterns of brain activation (Lueken et al., 2011).

Treatment of specific phobias following from the biological perspective focuses on symptom management. As with panic disorder, clinicians would prescribe anti-anxiety medications such as benzodiazepines. However, unlike panic disorder, specific phobias are more circumscribed in nature and the situations are generally more easily avoided. Thus, clinicians would prescribe medications only when the specific phobia interferes with the individual's ability to carry on everyday activities.

Psychological Perspectives

The behavioral approach to specific phobias emphasizes the conditioning that occurs when the individual learns to associate unpleasant physical sensations to a certain kind of stimulus or situation. Behaviorists assume that there may be some adaptive value to having such reactions because they may truly be ones that should be feared, such as an encounter with a deadly snake. However, the maladaptive nature of the symptoms evolves as individuals begin to generalize this reaction to all stimuli in that category, including harmless ones. There may also be developmental aspects to specific phobias. Young children tend to fear objects or situations they can see; as they get older, the objects become more abstract in nature (such as "the bogeyman") (Davis & Ollendick, 2011). At the other end of the age spectrum, older adults with specific phobias may not report symptoms but instead misattribute their anxiety to a physical condition (Coelho et al., 2010).

According to the cognitive-behavioral view, individuals with specific phobias have overactive "alarm systems" to danger, and they perceive things as dangerous because they misinterpret stimuli. For example, the mistaken perception of an object or a situation as uncontrollable, unpredictable, dangerous, or disgusting is correlated with feelings of vulnerability. These attributions might explain the common phobia of spiders, an insect about which people have many misconceptions and apprehensions. In blood-injury-injection, by contrast, disgust and fear of contamination play a prominent role (de Jong & Peters, 2007). People with phobias also tend to overestimate the likelihood of a dangerous outcome after exposure to the feared stimulus (de Jong & Merckelbach, 2000).

Systematic desensitization is an effective behavioral method for treating specific phobia; in this method the client learns to substitute relaxation for fear through a series of graduated steps. The idea that clients learn to substitute adaptive (relaxation) for maladaptive (fear or anxiety) responses forms the basis for the four types of behavioral treatments involving exposure therapy (see Table 5.1).

In the behavioral technique called **flooding,** the client is totally immersed in the sensation of anxiety, rather than being more gradually acclimated to the feared situation. The clinician may actually take the client to the situation that produces fear such as the top of a tall building for a client who fears heights. A variant of flooding is

flooding
A behavioral technique in which the client is immersed in the sensation of anxiety by being exposed to the feared situation in its entirety.

TABLE 5.1 Methods of Exposure Used in Behavioral Therapy of Phobias

	Graduated Exposure	**Immediate Full Exposure**
Imagery	Systematic desensitization	Imaginal flooding
Live	Graded *in vivo*	*In vivo* flooding

imaginal flooding, in which the clinician virtually exposes the client to the feared situation. Though requiring additional controlled studies, a number of investigations report promising findings about the ability of virtual reality exposure therapy to reduce symptoms (Parsons & Rizzo, 2008).

In vivo flooding is probably the most stressful of any of the treatments described and therefore has a high dropout rate (Choy, Fyer, & Lipsitz, 2007). An alternative is a graded *in vivo* method, involving a graduated exposure to increasingly anxiety-provoking stimuli. In the **graduated exposure** method, clients initially confront situations that cause only minor anxiety and then gradually progress toward those that cause greater anxiety. Often the therapist tries to be encouraging and to model the desired nonanxious response. In treating a client named Tan, who has a fear of enclosed spaces, the therapist could go with him into smaller and smaller rooms. Seeing his therapist showing no signs of fear could lead Tan to model the therapist's response. The therapist could also offer praise, to further reinforce the new response that Tan is learning. As illustrated in Table 5.1, behavioral treatments vary according to the nature of the client's exposure to the phobic stimulus (live or imagined) and the degree of intensity with which the stimulus is confronted (immediate full exposure or exposure in graduated steps).

Positive reinforcement is implicit in all behavioral techniques. The therapist becomes both a guide and a source of support and praise for the client's successes. The therapist may also find it useful to incorporate some techniques from the cognitive perspective into the behavioral treatment, because maladaptive thoughts are often part of the client's difficulties. Cognitive-behavioral treatment focuses on helping the client learn more adaptive ways of thinking about previously threatening situations and objects.

Cognitive restructuring can help the client view the feared situation more rationally by challenging his or her irrational beliefs about the feared stimulus. For example, a therapist may show Victor, who has an elevator phobia, that the disastrous consequences he believes will result from riding in an elevator are unrealistic and exaggerated. Victor can also learn the technique of "talking to himself" while in this situation, telling himself that his fears are ridiculous, that nothing bad will really happen, and that he will soon reach his destination.

In **thought stopping,** the individual learns to stop anxiety-provoking thoughts. In therapy, the client is supposed to alert the therapist when the anxiety-provoking thought is present; at that point, the therapist yells, "Stop!" Outside therapy, the client mentally verbalizes a similar shout each time the anxiety-provoking thought comes to mind.

imaginal flooding
A behavioral technique in which the client is immersed through imagination in the feared situation.

graduated exposure
A procedure in which clients gradually expose themselves to increasingly challenging anxiety-provoking situations.

thought stopping
A cognitive-behavioral method in which the client learns to stop having anxiety-provoking thoughts.

5.4 Social Phobia

The characteristic of **social phobia** is extreme anxiety about being watched by other people. Some people with social phobia experience their symptoms only when they are in a performance situation. But the disorder may also occur for other people when they are in ordinary social settings. Essentially, the anxiety the person with social phobia experiences is centered on a desire to avoid humiliation or embarrassment. Even a simple act such as drinking can provoke symptoms of fear or anxiety.

social phobia
An anxiety disorder characterized by irrational and unabating fear that one's behavior will be scrutinized by others, causing the individual to feel embarrassed and humiliated.

MINI CASE

Social Phobia

Ted is a 19-year-old college student who reports that he is terrified at the prospect of speaking in class. His anxiety about this matter is so intense that he has enrolled in very large lecture classes, where he sits in the back of the room, slouching in his chair to make himself as invisible as possible. On occasion, one of his professors randomly calls on students to answer certain questions. When this occurs, Ted begins to sweat and tremble. Sometimes he rushes from the classroom and frantically runs back to the dormitory for a few hours and tries to calm himself down.

Somatoform Disorders, Psychological Factors Affecting Medical Conditions, and Dissociative Disorders

OUTLINE

Learning Objectives

6.1 Identify the symptoms and treatments of specific disorders in the somatoform disorders category

6.2 Recognize psychological factors affecting medical conditions

6.3 Specify the symptoms of depersonalization disorder and dissociative identity disorder

6.4 Explain the biopsychosocial perspective for somatoform disorders, psychological factors affecting medical conditions, and dissociative disorders

CHAPTER 6

Case Report: Rose Marston

Demographic information: 37-year-old Caucasian female.

Presenting problem: Rose was referred for a psychological evaluation following recovery from a medical hospitalization due to malnutrition. She had reportedly been eating between 400 and 600 calories per day for the past 2 weeks and had lost 20 pounds in the past 2 months.

During this time Rose had also been exercising in her home for 2 to 4 hours per day. In the interview, Rose reported that she had recently lost her job and had been spending most of her time in her apartment. She stated she had started to feel "really bad about myself" following a recent breakup with her boyfriend of two years. She explained that since the breakup three months ago, she has been spending most of her time at home "working on my stomach." Upon further exploration, Rose explained that she especially worried about the size of her abdomen, stating that "it's really huge and juts out way too much," adding "it's disgusting—I just wish I could get it to be flatter. I've tried everything and it's so disappointing that I can't get rid of it. I feel sick when I look at it . . . but a lot of the time I can't stop looking, just to get a good idea of how it looks, and to see if I've made any progress on getting rid of it." Rose stated she was distressed about the amount of time she had spent worrying about her stomach, but also was overwhelmed by feelings of guilt if she did not direct her activities toward trying to reduce her stomach size.

Objectively, Rose appeared underweight, which conflicted with her self-report that her stomach was excessively large. She did not express concerns about any other part of her body, but reported that her exercise and weight-loss efforts were in a direct effort to cut down on her stomach size. She reported that she had always thought her stomach was "too big," but that in the past three months her concerns about this part of her body had become pervasive and intrusive, making it difficult for her to focus in other areas of her life. Until two weeks before her hospitalization, Rose had been working for a publishing company as an assistant editor. She estimated that she had spent about three to four hours of her work day taking trips to the bathroom to look at her stomach in the mirror, and that even when in meetings or when doing work at her desk, would sit in such a way so that she could see her stomach in a window or on her computer screen. Her productivity at work had decreased dramatically and after her boss had given her several opportunities to improve her performance, she was fired. Rose was initially upset by this, but stated part of her was glad so that she could spend more time focusing on her appearance, and trying her best to "fix" her perceived disfigurement. She also stated she was relieved she didn't have to be around others as much, as she often felt that people were looking at her stomach and judging its size.

Rose stated that she had a few good friends, but that she rarely spent time with them, usually preferring to be by herself. Her boyfriend of two years had ended their relationship around the time her concerns about her stomach grew more serious. She stated that she assumed a major reason for their breakup was his "disgust with how I looked," though she said he did not mention this when breaking up with her. She stated that she and her boyfriend did few activities outside of either of their apartments, as she usually felt too uncomfortable to be out in public. This made it difficult for Rose to socialize in general, and since the breakup, Rose spent even less time interacting with others and left her

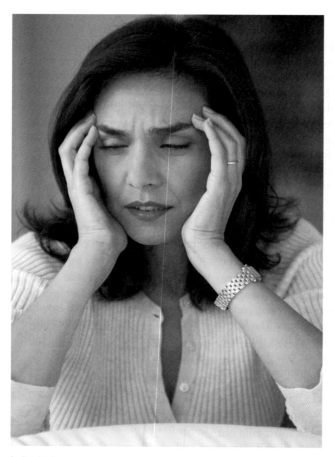

Individuals with somatization disorder suffer from physical ailments that have no medical cause.

somatization disorder

A somatoform disorder in which multiple and recurrent bodily symptoms, which lack a physiological basis, are the expression of psychological issues.

underlying neurological deficit. The problem is exacerbated by the possibility that psychological factors, such as stress, translate into altered brain functioning which, in turn, affects the individual's ability to move the affected body part (Ellenstein, Kranick, & Hallett, 2011). Given the difficulties in diagnosis, clinicians recommend that clients suspected to have conversion disorder receive a thorough neurological examination in addition to follow-up to determine whether the symptoms represent an underlying medical condition (Hurwitz, 2004).

Somatization Disorder and Related Conditions

Like conversion disorder, **somatization disorder** involves the expression of psychological issues through bodily symptoms that any known medical condition cannot explain, or as due to the effects of a substance. The difference between somatization disorder and conversion disorder is that somatization disorder involves multiple and recurrent bodily symptoms, rather than a single physical complaint.

Somatization disorder is relatively rare, but is present with higher than expected frequency among patients seeking treatment for chronic pain (Reme, Tangen, Moe, & Eriksen, 2011). In a small number of cases, the individual does suffer from a diagnosable medical condition, but his or her complaints are far in excess of what we customarily associate with the condition, and the person's impairment level is also much more extreme. Although it may appear that people with this diagnosis are intentionally manufacturing symptoms, they actually are not consciously attuned to the ways in which they express these psychological problems physically.

In **pain disorder,** clients experience pain to such a degree that their lives become consumed by the pursuit of relief. A diagnosable medical condition may exist, but the clinician regards the amount and nature of the pain as not accountable by this condition. There are also clients with pain disorder for whom no diagnosable medical condition exists. As a result of their symptoms, people with pain disorder can

MINI CASE

Somatization Disorder

Helen, a 29-year-old woman, is seeking treatment because her physician said there was nothing more he could do for her. When asked about her physical problems, Helen recited a litany of complaints, including frequent episodes when she could not remember what has happened to her and other times when her vision was so blurred that she could not read the words on a printed page. Helen enjoys cooking and doing things around the house, but she becomes easily fatigued and short of breath for no apparent reason. She often is unable to eat the elaborate meals she prepares, because she becomes nauseated and is prone to vomit any food with even a touch of spice. According to Helen's husband, she has lost all interest in sexual intimacy, and they have intercourse only about once every few months, usually at his insistence. Helen complains of painful cramps during her menstrual periods, and at other times says she feels that her "insides are on fire." Because of additional pain in her back, legs, and chest, Helen wants to stay in bed for much of the day. Helen lives in a large, old Victorian house, from which she ventures only infrequently "because I need to be able to lie down when my legs ache."

find themselves in an endless pursuit of relief, spending considerable time and money looking for a cure, but unable to find one because there is no apparent physical cause.

Hypochondriasis

People with **hypochondriasis** fear or mistakenly believe that normal bodily reactions represent the symptoms of a serious illness. They easily become alarmed about their health and seek unnecessary medical tests and procedures to rule out or treat their exaggerated or imagined illnesses. Their worry is not about the symptoms themselves, but about the possibility that they have a serious disease. In addition to experiencing anxiety over their illness, people with hypochondriasis are preoccupied with their mistaken beliefs about the seriousness of their symptoms.

Conditions Related to Somatoform Disorders

Malingering involves deliberately feigning the symptoms of physical illness or psychological disorder for an ulterior motive such as receiving disability or insurance benefits. Evidence for both feigning and standing to gain from the symptoms must be present for the clinician to give the diagnosis. Although not part of the *DSM* diagnostic procedures, researchers believe that inferring the intent of the client should not be part of the diagnostic process (Berry & Nelson, 2010).

In **factitious disorder,** people show a pattern of falsifying symptoms that are either physical, psychological, or a combination of the two. The individual falsifies these symptoms not to achieve economic gain, but for the purpose of adopting the sick role. In extreme cases, known more informally as **Munchausen's syndrome,** the individual's entire existence becomes consumed with the pursuit of medical care. The individual may also feign the illness of someone else in what we call **factitious disorder by proxy** (or **Munchausen's syndrome by proxy**).

Clinicians assume that clients engage in malingering in order to get a direct benefit, such as paid time off from work, insurance payments, or some other tangible reward. Some of these situations involve what we call **primary gain;** namely the direct benefits of occupying the sick role. The difficult issue that clinicians face in malingering cases is not trying to treat the symptoms, but to detect actual cases.

Factitious disorder presents a different clinical challenge. Clients deliberately feign or exaggerate symptoms, but they are not trying to achieve primary gain. They may be

pain disorder
A somatoform disorder in which the only symptom is pain that has no physiological basis.

hypochondriasis
A somatoform disorder characterized by the misinterpretation of normal bodily functions as signs of serious illness.

malingering
The fabrication of physical or psychological symptoms for some ulterior motive.

factitious disorder
A disorder in which people fake symptoms or disorders not for the purpose of any particular gain, but because of an inner need to maintain a sick role.

Munchausen's syndrome
An extreme form of factitious disorder in which the individual goes to great lengths to maintain a sick role.

factitious disorder by proxy (or Munchausen's syndrome by proxy)
A condition in which a person induces physical symptoms in another person who is under that person's care.

primary gain
The relief from anxiety or responsibility due to the development of physical or psychological symptoms.

MINI CASE
Hypochondriasis

Beth is a 48-year-old mother of two children, both of whom have recently moved away from home. Within the past year, her menstrual periods have become much heavier and more irregular. Seeking an explanation, Beth began to spend days reading everything she could find on uterine cancer. Although medical books specified menstrual disturbance as a common feature of menopause, one newspaper article mentioned the possibility of uterine cancer. She immediately made an appointment with her gynecologist, who tested her and concluded that her symptoms were almost certainly due to menopause. Convinced that her physician was trying to protect her from knowing "the awful truth," Beth visited one gynecologist after another, in search of someone who would properly diagnose what she was certain was a fatal illness. She decided to give up her job as a department store clerk for two reasons. First, she was concerned that long hours of standing at the cash register would aggravate her medical condition. Second, she felt she could not be tied down by a job that was interfering with her medical appointments.

TABLE 6.3 Sleep-Wake Disorders

Although not officially falling into the categories included in this chapter, it's a well-known fact that the sleep quality is intimately tied into our physical and mental health. Many people don't sleep as well when they're stressed, and inability to sleep can lead people to be even more stressed than they otherwise would be. Sleep quality is also affected directly by certain medical disorders. Sleep loss and sleep disorders not only reduce quality of life and a person's productivity but also result in injuries, chronic illness, or death (McKnight-Eily et al., 2008).

Disorder	Predominant Symptom
Insomnia	Dissatisfaction with sleep quantity or quality
Primary hypersomnia	Unexplained excessive sleep and sleepiness
Breathing-related sleep disorders (including sleep apnea)	Symptoms of snoring, snorting, gasping, or pauses in breathing along with daytime sleepiness and fatigue; lack of sufficient ventilation of the lungs during sleep
Circadian rhythm sleep disorder	Disturbance in both sleep and daytime functioning involving disruptions in the normal sleep-wake cycle
Disorder of arousal	Incomplete awakening from sleep, usually during first third of sleep; can involve confusion, sleepwalking, sleep terrors, along with inability to recall the episode after awakening
Nightmare disorder	Recurrent vivid dreams from which a person awakes and has detailed recollection of extended frightening dreams
Rapid eye movement disorder (not present in *DSM-IV*)	Repeated episodes of arousal during sleep associated with speaking and/or motor behaviors that may cause physical injury to self or bed partner
Restless leg syndrome	An urge to move the legs along with uncomfortable and unpleasant sensations; worse at night or present only at night

category of disorders in the *DSM*, sleep disorders are certainly relevant to stress. We show the major categories of sleep disorders in Table 6.3.

There are a number of paradoxical findings from research on stress, immune functioning, and health. Both too much and too little can place the individual at risk for developing poor health outcomes, ranging from heart disease to Alzheimer's disease to some forms of cancer. Additionally, although having a large social network is generally beneficial to immune functioning, if an individual's social network is too large, life stressors may have more of a negative impact on health than they otherwise would. In terms of personality, having a generally optimistic stance toward life is usually beneficial, but in the face of difficult or long-term stressors, then optimism is associated with poorer immune functioning and, ultimately, negative health outcomes (Segerstrom, Roach, Evans, Schipper, & Darville, 2010).

Sociocultural factors also play a role in causing and aggravating stress-related disorders. For example, living in a harsh social environment that threatens a person's safety, interferes with the establishment of social relationships, and involves high levels of conflict, abuse, and violence are conditions related to lower socioeconomic status. Chronic exposure to the stresses of such an environment can lead to a number of changes in hormones that ultimately have deleterious effects on cardiovascular health, interacting with an individual's genetic and physiological risk. Both cardiovascular health and immune system functioning seem to be sensitive to the degree of stress a person experiences as a function of being lower in socioeconomic status. The limbic system, which mediates a person's responses to stress, seems to play a large role in accounting for these connections between social class and health (McEwen & Gianaros, 2010).

Children who are bullied at school may suffer long-term psychological consequences.

Emotional Expression

Coping with stress can help you regulate the emotion of anxiety and hence reduce stress. However, there are times when expressing your emotions can improve your physical and mental well-being. Actively confronting the emotions that arise from an upsetting or traumatic event can have long-term health benefits (Pennebaker, 1997). In one classic study, researchers instructed a group of first-year college students to write about the experience of coming to college. A control group wrote about superficial topics. Those who wrote about coming to college actually reported that they were more homesick than the control subjects. However, they made fewer visits to physicians and by the end of the year, the students who wrote were doing as well as or better than the control subjects in terms of grade point average and the experience of positive moods. The researchers concluded that confronting feelings and thoughts regarding a stressful experience can have long-lasting positive effects, even though the initial impact of such confrontation may be disruptive (Pennebaker, Colder, & Sharp, 1990).

Pennebaker and his colleagues have expanded their findings to a variety of populations. In a meta-analysis of 146 randomized studies, disclosure had a positive and significant effect for people with a wide range of emotional concerns (Frattaroli, 2006). More recently, researchers have even identified positive mental health effects of writing on social media sites, including blogging (Ko & Kuo, 2009).

Personality Style

One of the most thoroughly researched areas investigating the connection between personality and health involves the

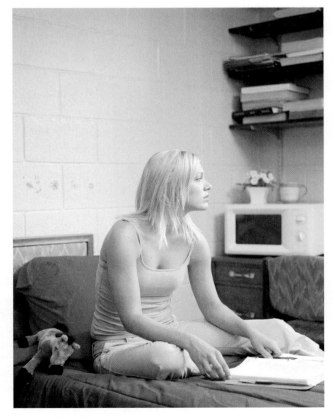

Stressful life events, such as moving away to college, can be damaging to physical health if the individual has difficulty coping with stress she may be experiencing.

Type A behavior pattern
Pattern of behaviors that include being hard-driving, competitive, impatient, cynical, suspicious of and hostile toward others, and easily irritated.

Type D Personality
People who experience emotions that include anxiety, irritation, and depressed mood.

behavioral medicine
An interdisciplinary approach to medical conditions affected by psychological factors that is rooted in learning theory.

Type A behavior pattern, a pattern of behaviors that include being hard-driving, competitive, impatient, cynical, suspicious of and hostile toward others, and easily irritated. Their constantly high levels of emotional arousal keep their blood pressure and sympathetic nervous system on overdrive, placing them at risk for developing heart disease, and at greater risk for heart attacks and stroke. Not only are people with the Type A behavior patterns at high risk because their bodies are placed under stress, but their hard-driving and competitive lifestyles often include high-risk behaviors of smoking, drinking alcohol to excess, and failure to exercise (Mainous et al., 2010).

Another significant personality risk factor for heart disease occurs among people who experience strong depressive affect, but keep their feelings hidden—the so-called **Type D Personality.** Unlike the "A" in Type A, which is not an acronym, the "D" in Type D stands for "Distressed." Type D personalities experience emotions that include anxiety, irritation, and depressed mood. These individuals are at increased risk for heart disease due to their tendency to experience negative emotions while inhibiting the expression of these emotions when they are in social situations. In addition to being at higher risk of becoming ill or dying from heart disease, these individuals have reduced quality of daily life and benefit less from medical treatments. Psychologists think that the link between personality and heart disease for these people is, in part, due to an impaired immune response to stress (Denollet & Pedersen, 2011).

Applications to Behavioral Medicine

Because psychological factors that contribute to a medical condition have such a wide range, clinicians must conduct a careful assessment of how each particular client's health is affected by their behavior. The field of **behavioral medicine** applies the growing body of scientific evidence regarding mind-body relationships to helping improve people's physical health by addressing its relationships to the psychological factors of stress,

---

TABLE 6.4 Are You Type A?

The Jenkins Activity Survey assesses the degree to which a person has a coronary-prone personality and behavior pattern. People with high scores, referred to as Type A, tend to be competitive, impatient, restless, aggressive, and pressured by time and responsibilities. In the items below, you can see which responses would reflect these characteristics.

Do you have trouble finding time to get your hair cut or styled?

Has your spouse or friend ever told you that you eat too fast?

How often do you actually "put words in the person's mouth" in order to speed things up?

Would people you know well agree that you tend to get irritated easily?

How often do you find yourself hurrying to get to places even when there is plenty of time?

At work, do you ever keep two jobs moving forward at the same time by shifting back and forth rapidly from one to the other?

SOURCE: From C. D. Jenkins, S. J. Zyzanski, and R. H. Rosenman, *The Jenkins Activity Survey.* Copyright © 1965, 1966, 1969, 1979 by The Psychological Corporation. © Reprinted by permission of the author.

emotions, behavior patterns, and personality. In addition, clinicians working in behavioral medicine often team up with psychologists and other mental health professionals to help clients adopt strategies to learn and maintain behaviors that will maximize their physical functioning. By improving patient compliance with medical illnesses, these clinicians can help the people with whom they work to achieve better health and avoid further complications.

Psychoeducation is an important component of behavioral medicine. Clients need to understand how their behavior influences the development or worsening of the symptoms of chronic illnesses. Then, the clinician can work with the client to develop specific ways to improve his or her health habits. For example, diet control and exercise are key to preventing and reducing the serious complications of cardiovascular disease. Clinicians can teach clients ways to build these new health habits into their daily regimens. Similarly, clinicians can train people with sleep disorders to improve their sleep habits. People can manage chronic pain, which contributes to depressive symptoms, through strategies such as biofeedback.

Clients can also learn how to manage stress and improve their coping methods. For people who have a personality style that may be contributing to their symptoms, the task becomes more challenging. Psychotherapy provides a useful adjunct to medical care. In the case of people who suffer myocardial infarctions, which often trigger depression, it is crucial for health care personnel to address the client's emotional as well as physical reactions to the experience.

Behavioral medicine is also moving increasingly toward interventions that the profession once considered "alternative" (i.e., alternative to traditional medicine), including mindfulness training, relaxation, and meditation. Clinicians teach clients to monitor without judging their internal bodily states (such as heart rate and breathing), as well as their perceptions, affective states, thoughts, and imagery. By doing so, they can gain the feelings that they can control their body's reactions. With regard to their health, by observing their bodily reactions in this objective fashion, they gain a more differentiated understanding of which aspects of their experiences illness affects and which it does not. They can see their ailments as having natural roles and not impeding their ability to enjoy life in general (Carmody, Reed, Kristeller, & Merriam, 2008).

For example, people with the Type A behavior pattern can benefit from training aimed at improving their awareness of their reactions to stress, methods of coping with stressful situations, and behavioral interventions intended to improve their compliance with medical advice aimed at reducing their cardiovascular risk. Particularly important is a sense of mastery, namely, the belief that you have the ability to cope with or control the problems you encounter in life. People who feel they are in greater control over their life circumstances have a reduced risk of developing cardiovascular and related health problems (Roepke & Grant, 2011). Increasingly, clinicians are finding that efforts to improve people's health by addressing only their medical needs will not have the long-term desired effects unless the clinicians also incorporate these psychological issues into treatment.

6.3 Dissociative Disorders

The human mind seems capable of dissociating, or separating mental functions. You can think intensively about a problem while jogging, perhaps not even realizing that you ran a mile without awareness of your surroundings. In dissociative disorders, the separation of mental functions occurs to a far more extreme degree. Somatoform disorders and psychological factors affecting medical condition raise intriguing questions about the mind-body relationship, but dissociative disorders raise intriguing questions about the ways in which the people's sense of self over time, memory, and sense of reality can become fragmented.

You Be the Judge

Dissociative Identity Disorder

The possibility that an individual may not be responsible for actions committed while one's multiple personalities are in control of the person's behavior leads to fascinating legal questions. Theoretically, of course, it's possible for one alter to commit a crime while the other alters, or even the host, is not aware or in control. Obviously, however, convicting one alter means that the host (along with all the other alters) is also put in prison. At another level, however, the question becomes one related to the legal definition of insanity. Is a person with dissociative identity disorder able to control his or her own mind if part of the mind has split off and is acting independently?

There are three possible approaches to defending a client who legitimately has this diagnosis. In the "alter-in-control" approach, the defendant claims that an alter personality was in control at the time of the offense. In the "each-alter" approach, the prosecution must determine whether each personality met the insanity standard. In the "host-alter" approach, the issue is whether the host personality meets the insanity standard.

Dissociative identity disorder is rarely successful as a legal defense after a public outcry following the ruling in 1974 that serial rapist Billy Milligan was insane due to lack of an integrated personality (*State v Milligan*, 1978). Since that time,

TABLE 6.5 Items from the SCID-D-R

Scale	Items
Amnesia	Have you ever felt as if there were large gaps in your memory?
Depersonalization	Have you ever felt that you were watching yourself from a point outside of your body, as if you were seeing yourself from a distance (or watching a movie of yourself)? Have you ever felt as if a part of your body or your whole being was foreign to you? Have you ever felt as if you were two different people, one going through the motions of life and the other part observing quietly?
Derealization	Have you ever felt as if familiar surroundings or people you knew seemed unfamiliar or unreal? Have you ever felt puzzled as to what is real and what's unreal in your surroundings? Have you ever felt as if your surroundings or other people were fading away?
Identity confusion	Have you ever felt as if there was a struggle going on inside of you? Have you ever felt confused as to who you are?
Identity alteration	Have you ever acted as if you were a completely different person? Have you ever been told by others that you seem like a different person? Have you ever found things in your possession (for instance, shoes) that belong to you, but you could not remember how you got them?

SOURCE: Steinberg, 1994

cases have had a variety of outcomes, ranging from the judgment that multiple personalities do not preclude criminal responsibility (*State v Darnall*, 1980) to the ruling that alter personalities are not an excuse for inability to distinguish right from wrong (*State v Jones*, 1998). The courts threw out two more recent cases in Washington State (*State v Greene*, 1998) and West Virginia (*State v Lockhart*, 2000) on the grounds that lack of scientific evidence and/or adequate reliability standards do not exist in the diagnosis of the disorder (Farrell, 2010). The key issue for forensic psychologists and psychiatrists is determining the difference between malingering and the actual disorder (Farrell, 2011).

There are tools now available for expert clinicians to use in aiding accurate diagnosis. The Structured Clinical Interview for *DSM–IV* Dissociative Disorders–Revised (SCID–D–R) (Steinberg, 1994; see Table 6.5), which the profession has rigorously standardized, includes a careful structuring, presentation, and scoring of questions. The professionals who developed and conducted research on this instrument emphasize that only experienced clinicians and evaluators who understand dissociative diagnosis and treatment issues must administer and score these.

The development of the *DSM-5* is proceeding on the grounds that the diagnosis is a valid one. The precedents created by rulings that the diagnosis is not admissible due to failure to meet scientific standards may, over time, thus be overturned. Nevertheless, the diagnosis is, at best, challenging, and potentially easy to feign, particularly if a clinician inadvertently plants the idea of using the diagnosis as a defense.

Major Forms of Dissociative Disorders

We generally take for granted the idea that each individual has one personality and sense of self. However, in **dissociative identity disorder (DID),** it appears that the individual has developed more than one personality with its associated sense of self. Each separate personality seems to have its own unique characteristic ways of perceiving, relating to, and thinking. By definition, people with DID have at least two distinct identities and when inhabiting the identity of one, are not aware that they also inhabit the other identity. As a result, their experiences lack continuity. They have large gaps in important memories about themselves and their lives. They may

dissociative identity disorder
A dissociative disorder, formerly called multiple personality disorder, in which an individual develops more than one self or personality.

MINI CASE

Dissociative Identity Disorder

Myra is a young single woman who works as a clerk in a large bookstore. She lives by herself, never goes out socially except to see her relatives, and dresses in a conservative manner, which her associates ridicule as prudish. In her early teens, she was involved in an intimate relationship with a middle-aged man who was quite abusive toward her. Although others remind her of this troubled relationship, Myra claims that she has no recollection of that person, and she has even wondered at times whether others have made up the story to annoy her. At age 25, Myra says that she is saving herself sexually for marriage, yet she seems totally uninterested in pursuing any close relationships with men. So far, this describes Myra as her work

acquaintances and family know her. However, alters reside within Myra's body, and they go by other names and behave in ways that are totally incongruous with "Myra's" personality. "Rita" is flamboyant, outgoing, and uninhibited in her sexual passions. She has engaged in numerous love affairs with a variety of unsavory characters she picked up in nightclubs and discotheques. "Rita" is aware of "Myra" and regards her with extreme disdain. A third personality, "Joe," occasionally emerges from Myra's apartment. Dressed in a man's three-piece business suit, "Joe" goes downtown to do some shopping. According to "Joe," "Rita" is nothing but a "slut," who is heading for "big trouble someday." Myra's alters are oblivious to the details of her life.

the local police to find out if there was a report of a missing person. As it turned out, the little girl in the photograph was Norma's daughter. She had been hit by

to recall who she was and the circumstances of the accident, but she remembered nothing of what had happened since.

REAL STORIES

Sexual Disorders

Learning Objectives

7.1 Identify abnormal sexual behavior

7.2 Compare and contrast paraphilic disorders

7.3 Recognize theories and treatments of paraphilic disorders

7.4 Differentiate between disorders involving sexual dysfunction

7.5 Recognize theories and treatments of sexual dysfunctions

7.6 Identify theories and treatments of gender dysphoria

Explain the biopsychosocial perspective for sexual disorders

CHAPTER 7

Case Report: Shaun Boyden

Demographic information: 38-year-old Caucasian male.

Presenting problem: Shaun underwent a court-ordered psychological evaluation after his arrest for kidnapping and sexually molesting a 6-year-old boy. This was Shaun's first encounter with the legal system and his first psychological evaluation. During the evaluation, Shaun admitted that from the time he was 16 years old, he had been stalking young children, sometimes having sex with them. He reported that although his desires to have sex with children never caused any distress, the fantasies, thoughts, and desires were often so intense that he felt driven to act upon them.

At the time of the evaluation, Shaun had been married for 8 years, and stated that his wife was unaware of his abnormal sexual urges. He explained that he and his wife rarely had sex, and when they did he would have to fantasize about children in order to become aroused. He only enjoyed intercourse when it involved children.

Shaun described that while he was growing up, he was rarely very interested in girls, and noticed that when he reached puberty at 16, he began to have sexual fantasies about children and became sexually aroused when he was around them, especially young boys. Eventually his attraction became exclusive to boys. Unsure of whether his peers were experiencing the same feelings, Shaun kept his powerful attraction to children to himself and distracted himself by dating women. However, as he grew older he found it more and more difficult to ignore his strong feelings and urges. Shaun graduated from high school and went on to college, where he received a degree in computer engineering. Throughout college he dated women, but recalls that he was never able to be truly sexually aroused around them. At this point he began to fantasize about young boys in order to achieve arousal and orgasm.

After graduating from college, Shaun began his first serious relationship with a woman, the mother of a 3-year-old boy. His girlfriend often left Shaun to look after her son. Shaun reported that when his girlfriend's son was about 5 years old, he molested him for the first time, no longer able to control the urges he felt when he was alone with the boy. The molestations continued for five years, until Shaun's relationship with the mother ended. During that time, his girlfriend never found out about his behavior with her son. The breakup was very difficult for Shaun because he found he had grown dependent on the satisfaction he achieved from intercourse with the boy and he worried how he would be able to achieve this in the future. Shaun reported that he only worried about the moral implications of his having intercourse with his girlfriend's son a few times over the course of their relationship. He remarked that though he realized it was illegal, it came so naturally to him that he rarely worried about any of the possible consequences. However, due to the demands of his job, it was difficult for Shaun to find time to come into contact with children enough so that he would be able to be alone with them.

Three years after his previous relationship ended, Shaun started dating his future wife, Anne. He gleaned much satisfaction and stability from the relationship with Anne, and found that his urges to have sex with children severely dwindled for the first few years of their marriage. After about five years of marriage, Anne and Shaun began to fight frequently, and Shaun often felt anxious and worried. Anne wanted to have children, but Shaun was staunchly opposed. He knew that he would not be able to resist his urges. As their fighting got worse, Shaun noticed that his fantasies about children returned and he began to think of ways in which he could come into contact with children.

Shaun eventually quit his job at an engineering firm and took a job as an assistant at a day care center, after convincing his wife that he needed to work in a less stressful setting than the company where he had worked for years. He was hesitant to start acting on his urges at his new job right away, although he found his anxiety growing worse the more time he spent around children. He found himself using most of his free time to plan ways in which he could be alone with just one. One day, the day care supervisor assigned Shaun to take a 7-year-old boy home after the parent was unable to retrieve him. Suspicious of a lone car in a dark parking lot, a police officer approached, and luckily, found Shaun just in time to stop him from molesting the young boy. The officer arrested Shaun and charged him with kidnapping and statutory rape.

Relevant history: Shaun had been experiencing his pedophilic urges since the age of 16. He reported that he had been sexually abused "a few times" by his father when he was 5 or 6 years old, although he was unable to recall many details.

Case formulation: As with many individuals diagnosed with pedophilia, Shaun presented as a "normal"

individual with no criminal history or evidence of psychological disturbance. Although he sometimes appeared mildly anxious to other people, his co-workers remarked that they never would have believed that he was a pedophile. Shaun had successfully been keeping his urges and fantasies to himself, and until he was caught by the police officer, he had maintained the cover of a normal life. It was clear from the evaluation, however, that Shaun met all the necessary criteria for pedophilia and had acted on his urges many times. Since his attractions were limited to young boys, his diagnosis specifies this.

Multiaxial assessment:

    Axis I: 302.2 Pedophilia, Sexually Attracted to Males

    Axis II: Deferred

    Axis III: None

    Axis IV: Childhood abuse, marital problems

    Axis V: 50

Treatment plan: Shaun agreed to begin attending weekly psychotherapy sessions targeting his pedophilic urges by using cognitive behavioral techniques. Shaun was also prescribed anti-androgen medication, which aims to reduce sexual urges.

Sarah Tobin, PhD

7.1 What Is Abnormal Sexual Behavior?

When it comes to sexual behavior, the distinction between normal and abnormal becomes even more complicated, perhaps, than in other areas of human behavior. When evaluating the normality of a given sexual behavior, the context is extremely important, as are customs and mores, which change over time. Attitudes and behaviors related to sexuality are continually evolving over time. For example, although not a sexual disorder, addiction to sex over the Internet is becoming progressively prevalent, and clinicians are increasingly seeing clients with Internet-related problems. A survey of over 1500 mental health professionals revealed 11 categories of these problems, with the second most prevalent involving Internet pornography. Infidelity, sexual exploitation, gaming, and role playing were other frequent categories of Internet-related problems (see Figure 7.1).

For decades, there was little scientific research on sexual disorders. In 1886, the Austro-German psychiatrist Richard Freihurr von Krafft-Ebing wrote a comprehensive treatise called *Psychopathia Sexualis* (1886/1950), in which he documented a variety of forms of what he called "sexual perversity," which also linked sexual fantasy and the compulsion to kill.

The three individuals credited with paving the way for contemporary research on human sexuality were Alfred Kinsey, William Masters, and Virginia Johnson. Kinsey was the first to conduct a large-scale survey of sexual behavior in the United States (1948; 1953). Masters and Johnson (1966, 1970) were the first investigators to study sexual behavior in the laboratory.

In the intervening decades, psychologists, along with specialists in the emerging field of sexual medicine, have continued to expand our knowledge of human sexual behavior,

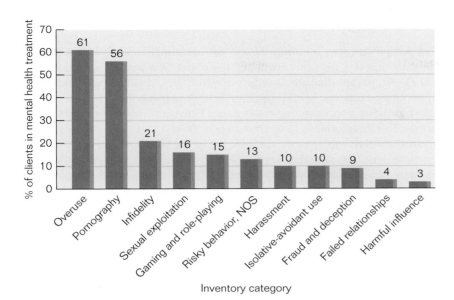

FIGURE 7.1 **Percentage Endorsement of Different Problematic Internet Experiences**

but there is much still for us to learn. However, this is an active area of research in contrast to the disorders that we have covered so far. Because the profession has substantially revised its thinking, we include this rather than cover it separately in the "Toward the *DSM-5*" box. The changes intend to "normalize" variants in sexual behavior that clinicians previously treated as pathological. Consequently, when the authors finalize *DSM-5,* people with these disorders, who already may feel great shame and embarrassment, may feel more comfortable in seeking help.

Alfred Kinsey pioneered a revolutionary study about sexual behaviors that changed the way Americans viewed norms about human sexuality.

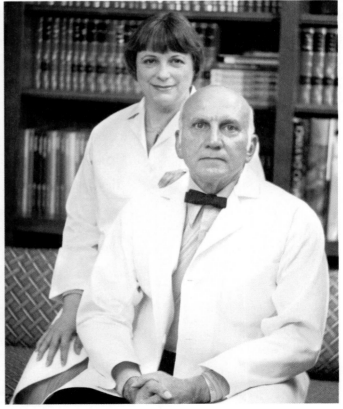

William Masters and Virginia Johnson were among the first researchers to take the study of human sexual behaviors into the lab.

7.2 Paraphilic Disorders

The term *paraphilia* (*para* meaning "faulty" or "abnormal," and *philia* meaning "attraction") literally means a deviation involving the object of a person's sexual attraction. In the *DSM-IV-TR*, **paraphilias** are disorders in which an individual has recurrent, intense sexually arousing fantasies, sexual urges, or behaviors involving (1) nonhuman objects, (2) children or other nonconsenting persons, or (3) the suffering or humiliation of oneself or a partner. This designation is likely to change in *DSM-5* (see box on page 157) when the term paraphilia will not apply to the disorder, but to the behavior of having a powerful and persistent sexual interest other than sexual interest in copulation or foreplay with consenting adult partners (Cantor, Blanchard, & Barbaree, 2009). A clinician will diagnose **paraphilic disorder** when the paraphilia causes intense distress and impairment (see Table 7.1).

It seems worthwhile to incorporate this distinction here because it allows for the possibility that a person's "nonnormative" (i.e., unusual) sexual behavior is not psychopathological. In addition, researchers working on *DSM-5* redefined these disorders somewhat so that they define each as involving "recurrent and intense sexual arousal" as manifested by fantasies, urges, or behaviors. This is an important point as well, because it makes clear the fact that in these disorders, people's fantasies, urges, or behaviors have a sexual arousal component. Previously, the term "sexual arousal" was not included in any of the criteria for the paraphilic disorders.

The essential feature of a paraphilic disorder is that people with one of these disorders are so psychologically dependent on the target of desire that they are unable to experience sexual arousal unless this target is present in some form. The paraphilic disorder may be exacerbated during periods in which the individual feels especially stressed. However, paraphilic disorders are not fleeting whims or daydreams. Each represents a condition that the individual has experienced for at least 6 months.

People with these disorders are recurrently compelled to think about or carry out their unusual behavior. Even if they do not actually fulfill their urges or fantasies, they are obsessed with thoughts about carrying them out. Their attraction can become so strong and compelling that they lose sight of any goals other than achieving sexual fulfillment. By definition, paraphilic disorders cause intense personal distress or impairment in social, work, and other areas of life functioning.

Paraphilic disorders begin in adolescence and tend to be chronic, although they diminish in people who are 60 years or older (Guay, 2009). There are very poor prevalence data of these disorders because people do not voluntarily report that they have them.

paraphilias
A disorder in which an individual has recurrent, intense sexually arousing fantasies, sexual urges, or behaviors involving (1) nonhuman objects, (2) children or other nonconsenting persons, or (3) the suffering or humiliation of self or partner.

paraphilic disorder
Diagnosis in which a paraphilia causes distress and impairment.

TABLE 7.1 Paraphilic Disorders

Disorder	Characteristics
Pedophilic disorder	Sexual arousal for children or adolescents
Exhibitionistic disorder	Derive sexual arousal from exposing their genitals to unsuspecting stranger
Voyeuristic disorder	Derive sexual pleasure from observing nudity or sexual activity of others
Fetishistic disorder and partialism	Fetishism is sexual arousal from an object Partialism is sexual arousal from a part of the body
Frotteuristic disorder	Sexual urges and sexually arousing fantasies of rubbing against or fondling a nonconsenting person
Sexual masochism and sexual sadism	Masochism is aroused by being made to suffer Sadism is aroused by inflicting suffering on another person
Transvestic disorder	Engages in cross-dressing associated with intense distress or impairment

MINI CASE

Pedophilic Disorder

Shortly following his marriage, Kirk began developing an inappropriately close relationship with Amy, his 8-year-old stepdaughter. It seemed to start out innocently, when he took extra time to give her bubble baths and backrubs. But, after only two months of living in the same house, Kirk's behavior went outside the boundary of common parental physical affection. After his wife left for work early each morning, Kirk invited Amy into his bed on the pretext that she could watch cartoons on the television in his bedroom. Kirk would begin stroking Amy's hair and gradually proceed to more sexually explicit behavior, encouraging her to touch his genitals, saying that it would be "good" for her to learn about what "daddies" are like. Confused and frightened, Amy did as she was told. Kirk reinforced compliance to his demands by threatening Amy that, if she told anyone about their secret, he would deny everything and he would severely beat her. This behavior continued for more than two years, until one day Kirk's wife returned home unexpectedly and caught him engaging in this behavior.

Moreover, although having a paraphilic disorder is not illegal, acting on paraphilic urges may be illegal and can result in the individual being subjected to arrest and the requirement, upon release, to register as a sex offender. The large majority of registered sex offenders have committed crimes against individuals under the age of 14 (70%); almost all victims (90%) are 18 or under (Ackerman, Harris, Levenson, & Zgoba, 2011).

We will examine the specific diagnostic criteria along with current literature on the paraphilic disorders; however, there is considerable overlap among them in terms of their association with each other and with other psychological disorders, substance use, and sexual risk taking or novelty seeking. In addition, these disorders are more prevalent in men than women (Långström & Seto, 2006).

Pedophilic Disorder

People diagnosed with pedophilic disorder are sexually aroused by children or adolescents. Clinicians will use this diagnosis for adults who are at least 18 years of age and at least 5 years older than the children to whom they are attracted. Currently, *DSM-IV-TR* divides people with this disorder into two categories based on the age and stage of the individuals they target. The key feature of this disorder is that the individual experiences sexual arousal when with children that may be equal to, if not greater than, that which he or she experiences with individuals who are physically mature.

We do not know the prevalence of pedophilic disorder because people with this disorder rarely step forward to receive treatment given the illegality of their behavior should they act on their urges with underage children. From the data on the prevalence of child sexual abuse cases in the United States, we can get an idea of the prevalence of pedophilic disorder. Among children about whom reports of maltreatment are made, approximately 10 percent involve cases of sexual abuse (U.S. Department of Health and Human Services, 2005). Looked at from a different perspective, approximately two-thirds of all sexual assault victims are children and adolescents. Nearly two-thirds of the victims are females, the vast majority of perpetrators are males, and approximately one-third of the offenders are relatives of the victimized children (Snyder, 2000).

Addiction to Internet sex with children and adolescents and involvement in "chat rooms" is recently coming under scrutiny by mental health professionals. In one study, a police sting operation

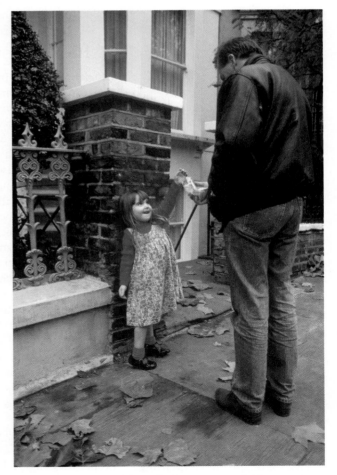

Individuals with pedophilia suffer from uncontrollable urges to engage in sexual activity with young children.

MINI CASE

Exhibitionistic Disorder

Ernie is in jail for the fourth time in the past two years for public exposure. As Ernie explained to the court psychologist who interviewed him, he has "flashed" much more often than he has been apprehended. In each case, he has chosen as his victim an unsuspecting teenage girl, and he jumps out at her from behind a doorway, a tree, or a car parked at the sidewalk. He has never touched any of these girls, instead fleeing the scene after having exposed himself. On some occasions, he masturbates immediately after the exposure, fantasizing that his victim was swept off her feet by his sexual prowess and pleaded for him to make love to her. This time, his latest victim responded by calling the police to track him down. Ernie felt crushed and humiliated by an overwhelming sense of his sexual inadequacy.

caught 51 Internet chat room sex offenders who met the criteria for diagnoses of major depressive disorder, adjustment disorder, and substance use disorders. None were diagnosed with pedophilia. The Internet offenders fell into two groups. Those who were "contact driven" used Internet chat rooms to arrange meetings with the potential victims. The "fantasy driven" offenders engaged their victims in some type of online cybersex intending to achieve sexual climax while online. The majority did not fit the criteria for antisocial personality disorder, and 94% were facing their first encounter with the criminal justice system. The majority were white, had some college education, and had middle-class or higher occupational status (Briggs, Simon, & Simonsen, 2011).

Exhibitionistic Disorder

exhibitionistic disorder
A paraphilic disorder in which a person has intense sexual urges and arousing fantasies involving the exposure of genitals to a stranger.

People who engage in exhibitionism have fantasies, urges, and behaviors suggesting that they derive sexual arousal from exposing their genitals to an unsuspecting stranger. In **exhibitionistic disorder,** these fantasies, urges, and behaviors cause significant distress or impairment. Because people with exhibitionistic disorder may lie about the extent of their behavior, the authors of *DSM-5* are considering adding criteria indicating how often these people have been caught for engaging in exhibitionism.

Exhibitionistic disorder begins early in adulthood and persists throughout life. In one study of a small sample of male outpatients with this disorder (Grant, 2005), researchers found that almost all also had another psychiatric disorder including major depressive disorder and substance abuse. Over half experienced suicidal thoughts. This was one of the few studies in a clinical setting of people with the disorder who were not criminal offenders. In another investigation of men from a police sample, approximately one-quarter also suffered from another psychological disorder (Bader, Schoeneman-Morris, Scalora, & Casady, 2008). The data from these samples are consistent with the findings from the Swedish national sample of nonclinical, noncriminal offenders, whose exhibitionism was also related to the presence of other psychological disorders (Långström & Seto, 2006).

The existence of comorbid conditions such as major depressive disorder and substance abuse, along with the reluctance of people with the disorder to come forward, present numerous challenges both for developing an understanding of the causes of the disorder and for planning its treatment (Murphy & Page, 2008). The most important step in treatment is accurately assessing both the disorder itself and these comorbid conditions (Morin & Levenson, 2008).

Voyeuristic Disorder

voyeuristic disorder
A paraphilia in which the individual has a compulsion to derive sexual gratification from observing the nudity or sexual activity of others.

People who engage in voyeurism derive sexual pleasure from observing the nudity or sexual activity of others who are unaware of being watched. People with **voyeuristic disorder** are sexually aroused by observing an unsuspecting person who is naked, in

This man obtains sexual excitement by engaging in voyeuristic activities, such as looking at unsuspecting victims with binoculars

the process of disrobing, or engaging in sexual activity. Voyeurism, the most frequent paraphilia, is related to exhibitionism, and people with either of these disorders are likely to engage in sado-masochistic behaviors and cross-dressing (Långström, 2010; Långström & Seto, 2006).

Unfortunately, there is very little data on voyeuristic disorder. Unlike exhibitionistic disorder, law officials are unlikely to apprehend individuals with this disorder and these individuals are even less likely to seek treatment.

Fetishistic Disorder

People with **fetishistic disorder** are sexually aroused by an object. In a related disorder, **partialism,** the individual is sexually aroused by the presence of a specific body part. Again, as with all paraphilic disorders, the attraction to objects or body parts must be recurrent, intense, and have lasted at least 6 months. There is a wide range of objects and a number of different body parts that people with fetishistic disorder can develop. However, they do not include articles of clothing associated with cross-dressing or objects such as vibrators that people use in tactile genital stimulation.

In a large-scale Internet study, a team of Swedish researchers investigated the frequency of specific fetishes among 381 "Yahoo! Groups" devoted to the topic (Scorolli, Ghirlanda, Enquist, Zattoni, & Jannini, 2007). They estimated frequency by counting numbers of groups, numbers of members of groups, and numbers of messages within groups. Nearly half of all fetishes counted in this manner involved the feet and toes, and

fetishistic disorder
A paraphilic disorder in which the individual is preoccupied with an object and depends on this object rather than sexual intimacy with a partner for achieving sexual gratification.

partialism
A paraphilia in which the person is interested solely in sexual gratification from a specific body part, such as feet.

MINI CASE

Fetishistic Disorder

For several years, Tom has been breaking into cars and stealing boots or shoes, and he has come close to being caught on several occasions. Tom takes great pleasure in the excitement that he experiences each time he engages in the ritualistic behavior of procuring a shoe or boot and going to a secret place to fondle it and masturbate. In his home, he has a closet filled with dozens of women's shoes, and he chooses from this selection the particular shoe with which he will masturbate. Sometimes he sits in a shoe store and keeps watch for women trying on shoes. After a woman tries on and rejects a particular pair, Tom scoops the pair of shoes from the floor and takes them to the register, explaining to the clerk that the shoes are a gift for his wife. With great eagerness and anticipation, he rushes home to engage once again in his masturbatory ritual.

Individuals with a fetish gain sexual excitement from everyday, nonsexual objects such as feet.

frotteuristic disorder
A paraphilic disorder in which the individual has intense sexual urges and sexually arousing fantasies of rubbing against or fondling an unsuspecting stranger.

sexual masochism disorder
A paraphilia marked by an attraction to achieving sexual gratification by having painful stimulation applied to one's own body.

sexual sadism disorder
A paraphilia in which sexual gratification is derived from activities that harm, or from urges to harm, another person.

of all preferred objects, the most frequent involved objects worn on the legs or feet. In trying to interpret these findings, the study's authors noted that they are consistent with Freud's view that feet are a penis symbol. A preference for feet and foot-related objects may, according to this view, reflect the adult consequences of castration complex associated with the Oedipus phase of development. The simpler behavioral explanation is that the person acquired this fetish through simple conditioning in which the person learned to associate sexual release with the presence of the specific body part or object.

Frotteuristic Disorder

The term "frotteurism" derives from the French word *frotter* (meaning "to rub") and *frotteur* (the person who does the rubbing). The person with **frotteuristic disorder** has recurrent, intense sexual urges and sexually arousing fantasies of rubbing against or fondling a nonconsenting person. Among men diagnosed with paraphilic disorders, approximately 10 to 14 percent have committed acts of frotteurism (Långström, 2010).

Men with frotteuristic disorder seek out crowded places in which they can safely rub up against their unsuspecting victims. Should they be caught, they can pretend that the act was not intentional. There is very little known about the disorder, in part, because the act is difficult to detect. Should someone suspect the individual of having engaged in this behavior, he or she can easily disappear into the crowd before a law official apprehends him or her.

Sexual Masochism and Sexual Sadism Disorders

The term "masochism" refers to seeking pleasure from being in pain. People with **sexual masochism disorder** are sexually aroused by being beaten, bound, or otherwise made to suffer. Conversely, people with **sexual sadism disorder** become sexually aroused from the physical or psychological suffering of another person.

As is true for several of the paraphilic disorders, there is very little in the way of scientific research on sexual masochism and sexual sadism disorders. In addition to the fact that people with these disorders tend not to seek treatment because they feel no need to change, they tend to carry out these behaviors in a great deal of secrecy, and because they often involve consensual behavior.

MINI CASE

Frotteuristic Disorder

Bruce, who works as a delivery messenger in a large city, rides the subway throughout the day. He thrives on the opportunity to ride crowded subways, where he becomes sexually stimulated by rubbing up against unsuspecting women. Having developed some cagey techniques, Bruce is often able to take advantage of women without their comprehending what he is doing. As the day proceeds, his level of sexual excitation grows, so that by the evening rush hour he targets a particularly attractive woman and only at that point in the day allows himself to reach orgasm.

MINI CASE

Sexual Sadism and Sexual Masochism Disorder

For a number of years, Ray has insisted that his wife, Jeanne, submit him to demeaning and abusive sexual behavior. In the early years of their relationship, Ray's requests involved relatively innocent pleas that Jeanne pinch him and bite his chest while they were sexually intimate. Over time, however, his requests for pain increased and the nature of the pain changed. At present, they engage in what they call "special sessions," during which Jeanne handcuffs Ray to the bed and inflicts various forms of torture. Jeanne goes along with Ray's requests that she surprise him with new ways of inflicting pain, so she has developed a repertoire of behaviors, ranging from burning Ray's skin with matches to cutting him with razor blades. Jeanne and Ray have no interest in sexual intimacy other than that involving pain.

Transvestic Disorder

Transvestism, also called "cross-dressing," refers to the behavior of dressing in the clothing of the other sex. The term most commonly refers to men, who are the large majority of individuals who show this behavior. In the *DSM-IV-TR*, **transvestic fetishism** refers to the condition in which the individual engages in cross-dressing, and associated with this behavior, experiences intense distress or impairment. According to this definition, clinicians would consider an individual who engaged in frequent cross-dressing for the purposes of sexual arousal a "transvestite" only if the behavior caused him distress, no matter how often he engaged in cross-dressing and how sexually arousing he found it.

The work group given the task of revising these criteria for the *DSM-5* recommended that, as is true for the paraphilias in general, the name (and the diagnostic concept) change to reflect the fact that a clinician should give a diagnosis of a psychological disorder only if an individual experiences distress or impairment associated with the cross-dressing behavior. According to this logic, then, a clinician would diagnose an individual with **transvestic disorder** only if he showed the symptoms of a paraphilic disorder, namely distress or impairment. Psychologists would consider a man who frequently cross-dresses and derives sexual pleasure from this behavior a transvestite, but they would not diagnose him with a disorder (Blanchard, 2010).

Theories and Treatment of Paraphilic Disorders

As we mentioned at the outset of this section, deciding what is "normal" in the area of sexuality is an issue fraught with difficulty and controversy. Critics of the *DSM* argue against including several of the paraphilic disorders in *DSM* because to do so pathologizes so-called "deviant" (i.e., infrequent) sexual behavior. Moreover, they maintain that breaking the law is not a sufficient basis for determining that an individual engaging in a paraphilic behavior has a psychological disorder. This criticism is particularly leveled at the disorders of exhibitionism, voyeurism, and frotteurism, which don't involve "victims" in the same sense as do the other paraphilic disorders (Hinderliter, 2010).

Researchers and advocates within the field of sexual sadism and sexual masochism are critical of including these disorders in the *DSM* at all, arguing instead that they do not share the qualities of the other paraphilias because they involve consenting adults (Wright, 2010). In any case, researchers argue that clinicians

transvestic fetishism
A paraphilia in which a man has an uncontrollable craving to dress in women's clothing in order to derive sexual gratification.

transvestic disorder
Diagnosis applied to individuals who engage in transvestic behavior and have the symptoms of a paraphilic disorder.

Cross-dressing is considered a psychological disorder only when it causes the individual to feel distress as a result of the cross-dressing behaviors. Cross-dressing is also distinct from transgenderism in that individuals who engage in cross-dressing typically identify with their biological gender.

MINI CASE

Transvestic Disorder

In the evenings, when his wife leaves the house for her part-time job, Phil often goes to a secret hiding place in his workshop. In a locked cabinet, Phil keeps a small wardrobe of women's underwear, stockings, high heels, makeup, a wig, and dresses. Closing all the blinds in the house and taking the phone off the hook, Phil dresses in these clothes and fantasizes that he is being pursued by several men. After about two hours, he usually masturbates to the point of orgasm, as he imagines that a sexual partner is pursuing him. Following this ritual, he secretly packs up the women's clothes and puts them away. Though primarily limiting his cross-dressing activities to the evenings, he thinks about it frequently during the day, which causes him to become sexually excited and to wish that he could get away from work, go home, and put on his special clothes. Knowing that he cannot, he wears women's underwear under his work clothes, and he sneaks off to the men's room to masturbate in response to the sexual stimulation he derives from feeling the silky sensation against his body.

should base decisions about psychiatric diagnoses on empirical evidence rather than on political or moral considerations (Shindel & Moser, 2011).

By redefining the disorders in this area as involving intense distress or impairment, however, the authors of the *DSM-5* hope to avoid the issue of judging on a behavior's normality and instead base the criteria for a disorder on an individual's subjective experience of distress or degree of impairment in everyday life. Yet, there are many challenges facing researchers who attempt to understand the causes of a disorder that enacts so much damage and has so many legal ramifications. Apart from identifying people with the disorder, the problem is made far more difficult because even those who are available for scrutiny by researchers may not represent the population from which they are drawn. For example, most of the people who are available for studying disorders involving criminal acts such as pedophilic disorder are likely to have been arrested. Others who were not arrested are simply not available for study.

Biological Perspectives   Given these qualifications, what do we know about people with paraphilic disorders? The most information in this area is based on research involving people with pedophilic disorder, perhaps because they are most likely to enter the criminal justice system. Clearly, this disorder has unique features, but information about how individuals develop this disorder may be helpful in understanding others.

From a biological perspective, paraphilic disorders involve a combination of influences including genetic, hormonal, and sensory factors in interaction with cognitive, cultural, and contextual influences (Guay, 2009). One theory of pedophilic disorders is that it results from early neurodevelopmental disorders, involving particularly the temporal lobe, which researchers believe is involved in altered sexual arousal. However, these changes could also be the result of early physical abuse or sexual victimization. Researchers have also identified altered serotonin levels in people with this disorder; however, these alterations may also be related to the presence of other psychological disorders in these individuals (Hall, 2007).

Castration as a treatment for men with paraphilic disorder, particularly pedophilic disorder, is intended to destroy the body's production of testosterone through surgical castration (removal of the testes) or chemical castration, in which the individual receives medications that suppress the production of testosterone. The cost of chemical castration is high, ranging from $5000 to $20,000 U.S. dollars per year. Due to the expense of this maintenance treatment, the state of Texas continues to use surgical castration as the only option. Eight other states in the United States can order offenders to submit to chemical or surgical castration. Although castration might seem to be an effective method, one-third of castrated males can continue to engage in intercourse. There are also side effects that may increase the individual's risk of cancer or heart disease (Guay, 2009). There are also significant ethical issues involved that must be balanced against the need to protect the public from sex offenders (Thibaut, De La Barra, Gordon, Cosyns, & Bradford, 2010).

Clinicians treating paraphilic disorders based on the biological perspective may instead use psychotherapeutic medications intended to alter the individual's neurotransmitter levels. Researchers have tested the effectiveness of antidepressants, including fluoxetine, sertraline, phenelzine, and mirtazapine for nearly all of the paraphilic disorders. The other categories of tested psychotherapeutic medications include anticonvulsants, anxiolytics, mood stabilizers, neuroleptics, and opioid antagonists. Other medications that involve GABA or glutamate receptors may work by decreasing the activity of dopamine, a neurotransmitter involved in sexual arousal (Hall, 2007). Unfortunately, most of these studies, including those involving chemical castration, are based on small samples lacking experimental controls. Moreover, many of the participants in these studies had more than one paraphilic disorder and/or another psychiatric diagnosis. However, for individuals who are at moderate or high risk of reoffending, the available data support the use of SSRIs in combination with female hormones that produce a form of chemical castration (Guay, 2009).

The World Federation of Societies of Biological Psychiatry has proposed guidelines for the treatment of people with paraphilic disorder that are staged according to the severity of the individual's symptoms. The aim of treatment is to control sexual fantasies, compulsions, and behavior without impact on the individual's conventional sexual activity and sexual desire. Psychotherapy is the recommended treatment at the first level. If unsuccessful, clinicians add psychotherapeutic medications (SSRIs). At increasing levels of severity defined according to whether treatment is effective or not, clinicians add hormonal treatment starting with antiandrogens, progressing to progesterone, and finally, neurohormones that act on the areas in the pituitary gland that control the release of sex hormones. At this point in treatment, appropriate only for the most severe cases, the goal is complete suppression of sexual desire and activity (Thibaut et al., 2010).

Psychological Perspectives Freud's psychoanalytic understanding of the paraphilias was the dominant psychological perspective throughout the twentieth century. He believed that these disorders were perversions representing both biological and psychological factors in early development (Thibaut et al., 2010). According to John Money (1973/1996), in contrast, paraphilias are the expression of **lovemaps**—the representations of an individual's sexual fantasies and preferred practices. People form lovemaps early in life, during what Money considers a critical period of development: the late childhood years, when an individual first begins to discover and test ideas regarding sexuality. "Misprints" in this process can result in the establishment of sexual

lovemap
The representations of an individual's sexual fantasies and preferred practices.

Toward the DSM-5: The Reorganization of Sexual Disorders

The sexual disorders are undergoing major rethinking in the *DSM-5*, as is evident throughout the chapter. Several of these changes are worth incorporating into the chapter, both because they seem to be empirically supported, and because they involve terminology that avoids some of the unfortunate implications of the *DSM-IV-TR* diagnostic names. The most significant change is declaring that clinicians do not consider paraphilias disorders unless they involve distress or impairment. This change recognizes the continuum along which sexual behavior falls and removes the stigma attached to sexual behaviors that do not cause distress or impairment or harm to others.

Another major change in the paraphilic disorders involves the renaming of pedophilia to pedohebephilic disorder. By making this change, the *DSM-5* authors are acknowledging the fact that erotic preference for prepubescents is similar to erotic preference for pubescents ("hebephilia") because both involve attraction to physically immature individuals.

The sexual dysfunctions are also undergoing significant shifts. Hypoactive sexual desire disorder will be diagnosed only for men; women will receive a diagnosis of hypoactive interest/arousal. The disorders of vaginismus (inability to allow penetration) and dyspareunia (pain with intercourse) will combine into one because they are difficult to distinguish from one another.

We have already discussed other changes including relabeling "premature" ejaculation to "early," and male orgasmic disorder will most likely be relabeled "delayed" ejaculation. Both of these terms reflect a desire, once again, to de-stigmatize a variant on human sexuality.

Finally, the relabeling of "gender identity disorder" in *DSM-IV-TR* to the new proposed term of "Gender Dysphoria," along with other changes within this category, are providing a revamped view of these disorders that not only is more consistent with the research evidence, but will also bring greater understanding to people who experience the emotional distress of a mismatch between their biological sex and their own sense of identity.

Though based on empirical evidence, then, the *DSM-5* changes in the area of sexual disorders will also clarify in important ways the many varieties of "normal" human sexuality. As these changes take hold in the psychological and psychiatric communities, they will provide directions for successful approaches to the treatment of people whose sexuality causes them to experience distress.

The World Federation of Societies of Biological Psychiatry has proposed guidelines for the treatment of people with paraphilic disorder that are staged according to the severity of the individual's symptoms.

habits and practices that deviate from the norm. A paraphilia, according to this view, is due to a lovemap gone awry. The individual is, in a sense, programmed to act out fantasies that are socially unacceptable and potentially harmful.

The majority of the psychological literature on paraphilic disorders focuses on pedophilic disorder. A common theme in this literature is the idea of a "victim-to-abuser cycle" or "abused-abusers phenomena," meaning that abusers were themselves abused at some point in their lives, probably when they were young. Arguing against these explanations is the fact that most abuse victims do not go on to abuse or molest children. On the other hand, some people with pedophilic disorder who were abused as children show an age preference that matches their age when they were abused, suggesting that they are replicating the behaviors that were directed toward them as children.

Treatments within the psychological perspective seem most effective when combining individual with group therapy. The cognitive behavioral perspective is particularly useful in helping clients recognize their distortions and denial. At the same time, these clients benefit from training in empathy, so that they can understand how their victims are feeling. Adding to the equation within the psychological perspective, clinicians may also train clients in learning to control their sexual impulses. Relapse prevention, much as it is used in treating clients with addictive disorders, helps clients accept that even if they slip, this does not mean that they cannot overcome their disorder. Clinicians no longer recommend aversion training, in which they teach clients to associate negative outcomes with sexual attraction toward children and masturbatory reconditioning to change their orientation away from children (Hall, 2007).

Most recently, researchers believe that the most effective treatment involves a combination of hormonal drugs intended to reduce androgen (male sex hormone levels) and psychotherapy (Hughes, 2007). Even so, under the best of circumstances, it appears that the most that we can hope for is that the individuals can manage their urges, but they cannot change their attraction to children (Hall, 2007).

7.3 Sexual Dysfunctions

sexual dysfunction
An abnormality in an individual's sexual responsiveness and reactions.

Sexual arousal leads to a set of physiological changes throughout the body often culminating in orgasm. A **sexual dysfunction** involves a marked divergence of an individual's response in the sexual response cycle along with feelings of significant distress or impairment. To consider it a sexual dysfunction, clinicians must not be able to attribute this divergence to another Axis I disorder, effects of a substance such as a drug of abuse or medication, or a general medical condition (clinicians give separate diagnoses in those cases).

Clinicians rate a person's sexual dysfunction according to whether it is lifelong or acquired, and generalized or situational. An individual with a lifelong dysfunction has experienced it since he or she became sexually active. People with acquired sexual dysfunctions were at some earlier point asymptomatic. Those dysfunctions that are situational occur with only certain types of sexual stimulation, situations, or partners. Generalized dysfunctions affect the individual in all sexual situations.

Masters and Johnson (1966, 1970), based on systematically observing the sexual responses of men and women under controlled laboratory conditions, identified three phases of the sexual response cycle—desire, excitement, and orgasm—with the last stage consisting of resolution (post-orgasm). During the desire (or arousal) stage, the individual's sexual interest heightens, and the body prepares for sexual intercourse (vaginal lubrication in the female, penile erection in the male). Sexual excitement continues to build during the plateau phase, and during the orgasm phase the individual experiences muscular contractions in the genital area that bring intense sensations of pleasure. The resolution phase is a period of return to a physiologically normal state. People differ in their typical patterns of sexual activity, however; some people progress more readily through the phases and others progress at a slower pace. Not every sexual encounter necessarily involves all phases, however, and arousal and desire may arise simultaneously from the processing of sexual stimuli (Basson, 2001).

Physiological factors and chronic health conditions are strongly related to risk of developing sexual disorders. We will outline these where they apply to the specific disorders below, but several risk factors seem to apply generally including diabetes, cardiovascular disease, other genitourinary diseases, psychological disorders, other chronic diseases, and smoking. In the case of some of these conditions, it is the medication and not the condition itself that places the individual at risk, such as anti-hypertensive drugs (Lewis et al., 2010).

There are very few reliable prevalence data on these disorders (Lewis et al., 2010). The reason for this is that the definitions of many of these disorders are highly variable. Only recently are researchers systematically beginning to arrive at measurable criteria based on the unique assessment methods that they require. Fortunately, work toward the *DSM-5* is leading to improved and more rigorous diagnostic procedures that eventually will lead to more reliable data sources.

The Female Sexual Function Index (Rosen et al., 2000) is an empirical measure used in a number of studies to investigate prevalence of sexual dysfunctions in women and as a measure of the efficacy of treatment. You can see sample items from this measure in Table 7.2.

Arousal Disorders

People whose sexual disorders occur during the initial phases of the sexual response cycle have low or no sexual desire, or are unable to achieve physiological arousal. As a result, they may avoid having or be unable to have sexual intercourse.

The individual with **hypoactive sexual desire disorder** has an abnormally low level of sexual activity or may have no interest in sexual activity. In addition, a person with

hypoactive sexual desire disorder
A sexual dysfunction in which the individual has an abnormally low level of interest in sexual activity.

MINI CASE

Hypoactive Sexual Desire Disorder

With the pressures of managing a full-time advertising job and raising 3-year-old twins, Carol says that she has "no time or energy" for sexual relations with her husband, Bob. In fact, they have not been sexually intimate since the birth of their children. Initially, Bob tried to be understanding and to respect the fact that Carol was recovering from a very difficult pregnancy and delivery. As the months went by, however, he became increasingly impatient and critical. The more he pressured Carol for sexual closeness, the more angry and depressed she became. Carol feels that she loves Bob, but she has no interest in sexuality. She does not think about sex and can't imagine ever being sexual again. She is saddened by the effect that this change has had on her marriage, but feels little motivation to try to change.

TABLE 7.2 Scales and Sample Items from the Female Sexual Function Index (FSFI)

Desire scale

Over the past 4 weeks, how **often** did you feel sexual desire or interest?

- Almost always or always
- Most times (more than half the time)
- Sometimes (about half the time)
- A few times (less than half the time)
- Almost never or never

Arousal scale

Over the past 4 weeks, how **often** did you feel sexually aroused ("turned on") during sexual activity or intercourse?

- No sexual activity
- Almost always or always
- Most times (more than half the time)
- Sometimes (about half the time)
- A few times (less than half the time)
- Almost never or never

Lubrication scale

Over the past 4 weeks, how **often** did you become lubricated ("wet") during sexual activity or intercourse?

- No sexual activity
- Almost always or always
- Most times (more than half the time)
- Sometimes (about half the time)
- A few times (less than half the time)
- Almost never or never

Orgasm scale

Over the past 4 weeks, when you had sexual stimulation or intercourse, how **difficult** was it for you to reach orgasm (climax)?

- No sexual activity
- Extremely difficult or impossible
- Very difficult
- Difficult
- Slightly difficult
- Not difficult

Satisfaction scale

Over the past 4 weeks, how **satisfied** have you been with your sexual relationship with your partner?

- Very satisfied
- Moderately satisfied
- About equally satisfied and dissatisfied
- Moderately dissatisfied
- Very dissatisfied

TABLE 7.2 (Continued)

Pain scale

Over the past 4 weeks, how would you rate your **level** (degree) of discomfort or pain during or following vaginal penetration?

- Did not attempt intercourse
- Very high
- High
- Moderate
- Low
- Very low or none at all

SOURCE: (Rosen et al., 2000) http://www.fsfi-questionnaire.com/

this disorder either has relatively few or no sexual fantasies. A woman with **female sexual arousal disorder** is interested in having intercourse, but her body does not physiologically respond during the arousal phase. Clinicians characterize **sexual aversion disorder** by an active dislike and avoidance of genital contact with a sexual partner, which causes personal distress or interpersonal problems. The individual may be interested in sex and may enjoy sexual fantasies, but is repulsed by the notion of sexual activity with another person.

The use of "desire" as a criterion for this disorder presents a challenge when diagnosing women, according to researchers in this field. Some reports indicate that low sexual desire is relatively prevalent among women, with estimates in some samples ranging as high as 55 percent, although the majority of studies from around the world place the prevalence at closer to 40 percent. However, the percent of women who are distressed about having low sex desire is far lower. Thus, the issue for women is that loss of desire might not be the best or only criterion to use in diagnosing a sexual dysfunction. Instead, we may better characterize the disorder as one involving loss of interest, arousal, erotic thoughts, enjoyment of sexual activity, or intensity of sensations during sexual activity (Brotto, 2010).

Men with **erectile disorder** cannot attain or maintain an erection during sexual activity that is sufficient to allow them to initiate or maintain sexual activity. Even if they are able to achieve an erection, they are unable to penetrate or to experience pleasure during a sexual encounter. Although once thought of as either physiologically or

female sexual arousal disorder
A sexual dysfunction characterized by a persistent or recurrent inability to attain or maintain normal physiological and psychological arousal responses during sexual activity.

sexual aversion disorder
A sexual dysfunction characterized by an active dislike of intercourse or related sexual activities.

erectile disorder
Sexual dysfunction in which a man cannot attain or maintain an erection during sexual activity that is sufficient to allow him to initiate or maintain sexual activity.

MINI CASE

Sexual Aversion Disorder

Howard is a 25-year-old law school student who had done very well academically, but worries often about a sexual problem that has plagued him since adolescence. Although he yearns to be in an intimate relationship with a woman, he has steered away from dating because he dreads the prospect of sexual intimacy. Although he jokingly tells others, and himself, that he is asexual, he secretly acknowledges that he is disgusted by the idea of anyone touching his genitals. He feels sexual desire and has no difficulty masturbating to orgasm. Although he feels attracted to women, thoughts of sexual closeness cause him to feel anxious, distressed, and at times even nauseated. Howard dates the origin of his problem to an incident that took place when he was 14 years old when he was by himself in a movie theater. Next to him sat a middle-aged woman who seductively pulled Howard's hand under her dress and rubbed her genitals with it. Shocked and repulsed, Howard ran out of the theater, carrying with him a powerful image and experience that would prove to be a lasting obstacle to sexual closeness.

Sexual pain disorders present a different set of challenges. From a biological perspective, the physical symptoms can come from a variety of sources, including disturbances in the muscle fibers in the

Sexual dysfunctions can be disruptive and frustrating for intimate couples.

REAL STORIES

Sue William Silverman: Sex Addiction

"I can't change all my behaviors in a month. All I can do is keep working on myself, keep moving forward, keep trying."

In *Love Sick: One Woman's Journey Through Sexual Addiction*, author Sue William Silverman tells the story of her battle with sexual addiction, and documents her stay at an intensive, 28-day inpatient hospital treatment program where she begins to battle her addiction for the first time. Sue joined the treatment program only at the urging of her therapist, Ted, who had recognized that her addiction had slowly been destroying every aspect of her life.

The hospital unit that Sue attended was populated with other women struggling with sexual addiction. She describes, "The only other time I was surrounded by women (girls, really) was when I lived in a college dorm. Except I didn't feel surrounded by girls then, either. For my attention was always drawn outside my bay window, to men disturbing the nights of Boston." Sue's interactions with the other women helped her gain a different perspective on her addiction, in seeing how other women were affected by sexual addiction from a more objective point of view.

In the hospital, Sue is required to maintain a rigid, daily schedule that includes group and individual therapy with Ted, regular meal times, and time for personal reflection. Much like Alcoholics Anonymous, she is required to go through a 12-step program toward recovery. As Sue makes her way through the workbook she uses throughout treatment, she reflects on many past sexual encounters with men and how she repeatedly sought out sexual affection in the hope of feeling a sense of genuine fulfillment, though the encounters only left her needing more.

Sue realizes that as a result of her constant need for sexual fulfillment and a propensity to shift her identity based on which man's attention she was seeking, she never took the time to understand her own identity. She describes that rather than her true self, it was a different version of herself—an addict persona, who had sought out all those men. She writes, "When I'm fully in the power of that addict-woman, when I am *most* sick, I am, ironically, totally capable of swimming, going to parties, socializing: *being what appears to be normal.* Yes, all these years I've convinced not only myself, but also others, that my behavior is normal because, in the strength of the addiction, I can *seem* normal. . . . Now, however, when the addiction is receding, when I'm in withdrawal, even though I'm getting better, everything scares me and I appear to be a wreck. Except I'm not; I'm in the process of becoming normal." She is in the process of not only recovering from her addiction, but becoming herself.

In the book, Sue describes how therapy helped her to recognize the danger of her addiction and the consequences of her behaviors. "For months, like a mantra, my therapist has told me, 'These men are killing you.' I don't know if he means emotionally, spiritually, or physically. I don't ask. He explains that I confuse sex with love, compulsively repeating this destructive pattern with one man after another. I do this because as a girl I learned that sex is love from my father, the first dangerous man who sexually misloved me." Sue explains that her father sexually abused her from the time she was a young girl until she left home to go to college in Boston. Once she was in college, Sue found herself spending the majority of her time thinking about and seeking out men for sex. She began a string of sexual affairs that continued until the time she entered the hospital. Each affair began soon after meeting each man, and she would attain an intense feeling of satisfaction during each sexual encounter, followed by feelings of emptiness and then the immediate desire to seek out another sexual encounter.

"The intensity is an addict's 'high,'" my therapist says. "Not love." To numb the shame and fear associated both with the past and with my current sexual behavior, I medicate, paradoxically, by using sex, he explains. "But sometimes that 'high' stops working. Usually after a scary binge."

Sue also suffered from eating disordered behavior, and was dangerously thin when she entered the treatment program. Some of the therapy groups in the treatment program focused on the connection between her body image and her addiction, and she reflects on her thoughts about her body: ". . . But *it* is not *me*—although my body is part of me—the thinner, the better. Less body, less trouble. No body. *No* trouble. If no man is able to see my body, then I won't have to keep having sex."

Throughout the book Sue talks about her marriage, which at the time of her entering treatment had dissolved to the point where she and her husband barely spoke and slept in separate bedrooms. She writes that she married her husband as a way to seek out normalcy and stability. Her husband, Andrew, is not aware of her battles with sexual addiction, and when she comes to the inpatient program she only tells him that she is seeking treatment for depression. Sue visits with her husband briefly while she is in the hospital, and their relationship offers her a sense of security that helps her through the difficulty of becoming, and staying, sober. In the program Sue finds that she longs to achieve a sense of balance and stability in her life. She calls it "a state of nothingness: I won't be drunk; nor will I have to struggle so hard to be sober." Although with her therapist, she comes to realize that stability means more than not giving into her addictive behaviors, but finding out who she is and genuinely being that person.

When she leaves the hospital, Sue continues to attend individual therapy and a weekly Sex Addicts Anonymous group. Through the strength and insight that she attained in the hospital, Sue begins the slow process of recovery. The book ends by describing Sue's first day at home from the hospital. Although she finds herself missing the safety of the unit and the women she came to know, she finds comfort in doing ordinary things like making dinner with her husband and begins to plan for her future. "Now I must learn that love is where I carve out my own life," she writes.

Author Sue William Silverman chronicles her struggle with sexual addiction in *Love Sick: One Woman's Journey Through Sexual Addiction*.

pelvic area (called the "pelvic floor"). When treating these disorders, however, the clinician may be unable to trace the exact cause of the individual's pain. The best approach appears to be multifaceted, including application of corticosteroids and physical therapy to promote muscle relaxation and improved blood circulation. The clinician may also use electrical nerve stimulation to relieve the individual's pain and prescribe pharmacological agents such as amitriptylene and pregabalin (Lyrica®) (Bergeron, Morin, & Lord, 2010).

Psychological Perspectives Recognizing the role of physiological factors, the psychological perspective emphasizes the further contributing effects, if not causal role, of cognitions, emotions, and attitudes toward sexuality. Associations between sexual stimuli and pleasurable feelings also play an important role in sexual excitability. In the case of erectile dysfunction, for example, one team of researchers recently identified as a predisposing factor a man's belief in the "macho myth" of sexual infallibility. Their belief in this myth makes them more prone to developing dysfunctional thoughts (e.g., "I'm incompetent") when they have an unsuccessful sexual experience. Once the man activates these thoughts, they impair his ability to process erotic stimuli and have sexual thoughts and images. By turning his attentional focus away from the encounter and toward his feelings of incompetence and sadness, he then is less able to achieve and maintain an erection during future sexual encounters (Nobre, 2010).

Both men and women may hold negative "sexual self-schemas" such as feeling unloved, inadequate, and unworthy, which they transfer onto sexual situations, causing them to become anxious when they feel that an inability to achieve an orgasm will cause their partner to become tired. The underlying feature that applies both to men and women who have sexual dysfunctions is the belief in their own incompetence in sexual situations (Nobre & Pinto-Gouveia, 2009). In Table 7.3, we have reproduced a portion of the scale that assesses men's responses to unsuccessful sexual situations.

The quality of the relationship may also contribute to sexual dysfunction, particularly for women, whose sexual desire is sensitive to interpersonal factors, including the

TABLE 7.3 Questionnaire of Cognitive Schema Activation in Sexual Context: Male Version

Read carefully each one of the episodes presented below and indicate the extent to which they usually happened to you by circling a number (1-never to 5-often)

I'm alone with my partner. She looks as if she wants to have sex, and she's going to extraordinary lengths to try to arouse me. However, I don't feel like it at all. So instead, I pretend to be tired and change the subject. Yet, she persists. She looks disappointed, and says that I don't love her as much as I used to.

never happened   1   2   3   4   5   happened often

I'm caressing my partner, and she is enjoying it and seems to be ready for intercourse. Upon attempting penetration, I notice that my erection isn't as firm as it normally is and full penetration seems impossible. I try to no avail, and finally quit.

never happened   1   2   3   4   5   happened often

My partner is stimulating me, and I'm becoming very aroused. I'm getting very excited and I immediately try to penetrate her. I feel out of control and reach orgasm very quickly, at which point intercourse stops. She looks very disappointed, as if she expected much more from me.

never happened   1   2   3   4   5   happened often

I'm completely involved in lovemaking and I start to penetrate my partner. In the beginning everything is going fine, but time passes and I can't seem to reach orgasm. She seems to be getting tired. No matter how hard I try, orgasm seems to be farther and farther out of my reach.

never happened   1   2   3   4   5   happened often

Circle all emotions you felt when you imagined the episode that most often happens to you.

Worry Sadness Disillusionment Fear Guilt Shame Anger Hurt Pleasure Satisfaction

SOURCE: Nobre & Pinto-Gouveia, 2009

---

sensate focus
Method of treating sexual dysfunction in which the interaction is not intended to lead to orgasm, but to experience pleasurable sensations during the phases prior to orgasm.

biological sex
The sex determined by a person's chromosomes.

gender identity
A person's inner sense of maleness or femaleness.

gender identity disorder
A condition in which there is a discrepancy between an individual's assigned sex and gender identity, involving a strong and persistent identification with the other gender.

---

frequency of positive interactions (Both et al., 2010). Researchers are also discovering the cognitive factors involved in sexual pain disorders that compound the physical causes, such as catastrophizing about pain and having low levels of self-efficacy.

The core treatment of sexual dysfunctions involving disturbances of arousal and orgasm follows from the principles that Masters and Johnson (1970) established, namely, treating both partners in a couple, reducing anxiety about sexual performance, and the development of specific skills such as **sensate focus,** in which the interaction is not intended to lead to orgasm, but to experience pleasurable sensations during the phases prior to orgasm. This procedure reduces the couple's anxiety levels until eventually they are able to focus not on their feelings of inadequacy but instead on the sexual encounter itself. Clinicians may also teach the partners to masturbate or to incorporate methods of sexual stimulation other than intercourse, such as clitoral stimulation alone.

Expanding on these methods, therapists are increasingly using principles derived from cognitive behavioral therapy that restructure the individual's thoughts that can inhibit sexual arousal and desire. Both partners may also promote their interpersonal communication and have more positive intimate experiences (Both et al., 2010). For sexual pain disorders, cognitive behavioral therapy alone does not seem to be effective, but is most beneficial when integrated with muscle relaxation, biofeedback, and education (Bergeron et al., 2010).

7.4 Gender Dysphoria

We turn now to disorders that involve difficulties that individuals experience due to feeling a mismatch between their **biological sex** (i.e., the sex determined by their chromosomes) and their inner sense of maleness or femaleness, called **gender identity.** In the *DSM-IV-TR,* the term **gender identity disorder** is the term that describes the condition in which a person's gender identity and his or her biological sex do not match. In the current criteria for disorder, the individual experiences identification with the other sex. The feeling that they are "in the wrong body" causes feelings of discomfort and a sense of inappropriateness about their assigned gender. Both of these conditions must be present for a clinician to assign the diagnosis.

Another term that relates to the feeling of cross-gender identification is **transsexualism,** which also refers to this phenomenon in which a person has an inner feeling of belonging to the other sex. Some people with gender identity disorders wish to live as members of the other sex, and they act and dress accordingly. Unlike individuals with transvestic fetishism, these people do not derive sexual gratification from cross-dressing.

The *DSM-5* authors present a strong case for using the term **gender dysphoria** instead of gender identity disorder, specifying whether the individual is a child or post-adolescent. One reason for this proposed change is to take away the stigma attached to the label of the condition as a "disorder." As we did for paraphilic disorders, we are adopting the new terminology because it specifies the condition not as one only involving cross-gender identification, but also involving distress. Having cross-gender identification does not necessarily imply that an individual is distressed or has a "disorder" (Cohen-Kettenis & Pfafflin, 2010). An individual's identification with a sex other than the biologically assigned one need not be a disorder. Only if that person feels dysphoria toward having this sex would a diagnosis be applied. Moreover, although some groups would advocate for the notion of removing gender identity disorder entirely from the diagnostic nomenclature, to do so could potentially preclude individuals who wish to seek sex reassignment surgery from insurance coverage because there would be no "diagnosis" for the clinician to give (Corneil, Eisfeld, & Botzer, 2010).

A small number of individuals with gender identity disorder seek sex reassignment surgery. The procedure is lengthy, expensive, and carries with it a number of stringent conditions, such as requiring that the individual receive a comprehensive psychological assessment and course of psychotherapy prior to acceptance for surgery. However, based on a 5-year follow-up investigation of 42 Swedish adults, the results appear to lead to favorable outcomes, and none of the participants regretted their decision (Johansson, Sundbom, Höjerback, & Bodlund, 2010).

transsexualism
A term sometimes used to refer to gender identity disorder, specifically pertaining to individuals choosing to undergo sex reassignment surgery.

gender dysphoria
Distress associated with feeling that a person has the wrong gender.

MINI CASE

Gender Dysphoria

Dale describes himself as a woman living in a man's body. His memories back to age 4 are of feeling discomfort with his assigned sex. When he was a young child, people often mistook him for a girl, because his mannerisms, style of play, and clothes were stereotypically feminine. He was glad he had an ambiguous name, and throughout adolescence he led others to believe he really was a girl. Schoolmates teased him at times, but this did not bother him, because he took pride in his feminine attributes. Dale's parents became increasingly alarmed, and they sent him to a psychologist when he was 15. The psychologist recognized that Dale had a gender identity disorder, and she explained to Dale that he could not pursue sex reassignment surgery until adulthood, because a surgeon would insist that Dale have the maturity and life experience necessary for making such a dramatic decision. Now, at age 25, Dale is about to follow through on his wish to have the body of a woman and is consulting sex reassignment specialists at a major medical school to prepare for the surgery. After an initial evaluation, the psychologist told Dale that he needed to begin a pre-surgery evaluation process that would last for at least a year and a half. During this time, he would live publicly as a woman. This would involve dressing as a woman and changing all documentation that referred to him as a male (such as voting records, credit card applications, and driver's license). He would have to enter psychotherapy to evaluate his psychological health and readiness for surgery. Dale also had to begin taking hormones that would cause him to develop female secondary sex characteristics. After successfully completing the evaluation process, Dale would be able to enter the next phase of the sex reassignment process, which would start the transformation of his physical characteristics.

Theories and Treatment of Gender Dysphoria

The psychology of the transgendered experience is undergoing radical shifts. Whereas in the past, the profession equated transgenderism with a "disorder," the new terminology is reflecting a theoretical perspective that does not focus specifically on what is "wrong" with people whose self-identification differs from their biological characteristics or social roles. Clinicians who work with transgendered individuals experiencing gender dysphoria take a three-pronged approach to psychotherapy including psychological, hormonal, and potentially sex reassignment surgery. Ideally, according to the World Professional Association for Transgender Health (WPATH), clinicians would provide an assessment of a client's well-being without regard to diagnostic criteria. However, because a clinician must make a diagnosis so that clients can receive insurance, the clinicians take on a "gatekeeper" role, potentially interfering with their ability to establish healthy therapeutic relationships (Corneil et al., 2010).

Given that clinicians will continue to treat individuals with gender dysphoria, however, new approaches are emerging based on transgender theory that emphasizes a more fluid view of gender than the binary male-female dichotomy (Nagoshi & Brzuzy, 2010). Clinicians can challenge this view by using the gender terminology that the client prefers. Rather than assume that people's motivations, behaviors, and attitudes are based on their socially defined identities, clinicians can recognize that these categories are conditional. For example, the clinician can avoid using terms like "real" or "biological" gender. We have summarized the American Psychological Association's Standards of Care for the Treatment of Gender Identity Disorders in Table 7.4.

Even though transgenderism will be "depathologized" if *DSM-5* makes the proposed changes now, clients will, nevertheless, continue to face transphobia, the negative stereotyping and fear of people who are transgendered. Rather than recommend sex reassignment surgery to help clients cope with social pressures to conform to one gender or another, clinicians can instead let their clients create their own gender identities. As a result, transgendered individuals may feel an improved sense of well-being as they are allowed to explore more openly and without bias their multiple, intersecting identities.

After initially coming out as a lesbian and then as transgender, Chaz Bono underwent the process of female-to-male gender conversion between 2008–2010.

7.5 Sexual Disorders: The Biopsychosocial Perspective

The sexual disorders constitute three discrete sets of difficulties involving varying aspects of sexual functioning and behavior. Although there are many unanswered questions concerning their causes, we need a biopsychosocial perspective to understand how individuals acquire and maintain these diverse problems over time. Moreover, researchers and clinicians are increasingly developing models that incorporate integrated treatment. Professionals in the area of sexual medicine are expanding the scope of their work. The growing research base that the team is using to develop *DSM-5*'s sweeping changes reflects not only expansion of the empirical approaches to sexual disorders, but adoption of a broader, more inclusive, and socioculturally sensitive approach to their understanding and treatment.

TABLE 7.4 APA Standards of Care for the Treatment of Gender Identity Disorders

Guidelines for Providers	Mental Health Professional	Physician Prescribing Hormones	Surgeon Performing Sex Reassignment Surgery
Competence	• Master's or doctoral degree • Documented supervised training in psychotherapy • Specialized training in the treatment of sexual disorders • Continuing education in the treatment of gender identity disorders	• Well versed in the relevant medical and psychological aspects of treating patients with gender identity disorders	• Board-certified urologist, gynecologist, plastic or general surgeon competent in urological diagnosis • Documented supervised training in sex reassignment surgery • Continuing education in sex reassignment surgery

Guidelines for Applicants	Eligibility Criteria	Readiness Criteria	
Hormone therapy	• Legal age of majority • Completion of 3 months of real-life experience OR psychotherapy for a duration specified by a mental health professional (usually 3 months) • Demonstrable knowledge of effects and side effects, social benefits, and risks of hormones and documented informed consent	• Further consolidation of gender identity during psychotherapy or the real-life experience • Progress in mastering other identified problems leading to stable mental health • The patient is likely to take hormones in a responsible manner	
Female-to-male chest surgery	• Legal age of majority • Completion of 3 months of real-life experience OR Psychotherapy for a duration specified by a mental health professional (usually 3 months) • Demonstrable knowledge of the potential risks and benefits of chest surgery and documented informed consent	• Further consolidation of gender identity during psychotherapy or the real-life experience • Progress in mastering other identified problems leading to stable mental health	
Male-to-female breast surgery	• Legal age of majority • Completion of 3 months of real-life experience OR Psychotherapy for a duration specified by a mental health professional (usually 3 months) • Hormonal breast development has been achieved (usually after 18 months) • Demonstrable knowledge of the potential risks and benefits of breast surgery and documented informed consent	• Further consolidation of gender identity during psychotherapy or the real-life experience • Progress in mastering other identified problems leading to stable mental health	
Genital reconstructive surgery and surgery affecting the reproductive system	• Legal age of majority • At least 12 months of continuous full-time real-life experience • At least 12 months of continuous hormone therapy • Demonstrable knowledge of the cost, required lengths of hospitalizations, likely complications, and postsurgical rehabilitation requirements of the various surgical approaches and documented informed consent • Awareness of different competent surgeons	• Demonstrable progress in consolidating one's gender identity • Demonstrable progress in dealing with work, family, and interpersonal issues resulting in a significantly better state of mental health	

Return to the Case: Shaun Boyden

As was evident in Shaun's case, individuals with pedophilia often do not feel distressed as a result of their urges. Thus, the first issue to address in psychotherapy was to engage Shaun in therapy by helping him realize the harm he had done to others through his actions; in other words, making his disorder "ego-dystonic." Essentially, the point was to make it difficult for Shaun to continue to deny the problems his pedophilia caused. Some of the consequences addressed were the emotional trauma he had put the children he had molested through, the negative effect on his marriage, and perhaps most salient to Shaun at the time, legal ramifications. Therapy also focused on Shaun's distorted thinking about children, and used empathy training and sexual impulse control training. Further, Anne had decided to stay with Shaun and they began to attend couples therapy to work on their relationship.

Though at first Shaun was hesitant to put forth any effort in therapy, he was eventually able to realize the harm he had done to others with his actions. With that realization, he was able to begin working toward controlling his urges and fantasies about children. In combination with the anti-androgen medication,

therapy began to help Shaun effectively cut down on his frequent fantasies, and he began to experience fewer and fewer urges to have sex with children. Though Shaun began to recognize that he would have to work to control his urges throughout the rest of his life, he was able to accept that his disorder was harmful to others and to his relationship with his wife.

Dr. Tobin's reflections: Shaun's story is similar to that of many other individuals with pedophilia. Though at some level he realized what he was doing to children was morally and legally wrong, his thoughts and actions were not associated with a sense of distress. Like with other pedophiles, Shaun had to develop special plans for getting access to children, and his pedophilic behavior became more intense at times of stress, such as when he and his wife's relationship was going through a difficult period. Shaun's history of sexual abuse from his own father was likely a contributing factor to his disorder, and once Shaun's symptoms have significantly reduced, it may be appropriate to explore the impact of this history.

Sarah Tobin, PhD

SUMMARY

- When it comes to sexual behavior, the distinction between **normal** and **abnormal** becomes even more complicated, perhaps, than in other areas of human behavior. When evaluating the normality of a given sexual behavior, the context is extremely important, as are customs and mores, which change over time.

- The term **paraphilia** (*para* meaning "faulty" or "abnormal," and *philia* meaning "attraction") literally means a deviation involving the object of a person's sexual attraction. In the *DSM-IV-TR*, paraphilias are disorders in which an individual has recurrent, intense sexually arousing fantasies, sexual urges, or behaviors involving (1) nonhuman objects, (2) children or other nonconsenting persons, or (3) the suffering or humiliation of oneself or a partner. The essential feature of a paraphilic disorder is that people with one of these disorders are so psychologically dependent on the target of desire that they are unable to experience sexual arousal unless this target is present in some form.

- Paraphilia disorders include: **pedophilia, exhibitionism, voyeurism, fetishism, frotteurism, sexual masochism, sexual sadism,** and **transvestism.**

- Critics of the *DSM* argue against including several of the paraphilic disorders in *DSM* because to do so pathologizes

so-called **"deviant"** (i.e., infrequent) sexual behavior. By redefining the disorders in this area as involving intense distress or impairment, however, the authors of the *DSM-5* hope to avoid the issue of judging on a behavior's normality and instead base the criteria for a disorder on an individual's subjective experience of distress or degree of impairment in everyday life.

- From a **biological perspective,** paraphilic disorders involve a combination of influences including **genetic, hormonal,** and **sensory factors** in interaction with **cognitive, cultural,** and **contextual influences.** One theory of pedophilic disorders is that it results from early neurodevelopmental disorders, involving particularly the temporal lobe, which researchers believe is involved in altered sexual arousal. However, these changes could also be the result of early physical abuse or sexual victimization. Researchers have also identified altered serotonin levels in people with this disorder; however, these alterations may also be related to the presence of other psychological disorders in these individuals. Clinicians treating paraphilic disorders based on the biological perspective may use psychotherapeutic medications intended to alter the individual's neurotransmitter levels.

- The majority of the psychological literature on **paraphilic disorders** focuses on **pedophilic disorder.** A common theme in this literature is the idea of a "victim-to-abuser cycle" or "abused-abusers phenomena," meaning that abusers were themselves abused at some point in their lives, probably when they were young. Treatments within the psychological perspective seem most effective when combining individual with group therapy. The **cognitive behavioral perspective** is particularly useful in helping clients recognize their distortions and denial. At the same time, these clients benefit from training in empathy, so that they can understand how their victims are feeling. Adding to the equation within the **psychological perspective,** clinicians may also train clients in learning to control their sexual impulses. Most recently, researchers believe that the most effective treatment involves a combination of hormonal drugs intended to reduce androgen (male sex hormone) levels and psychotherapy.

- Sexual arousal leads to a set of physiological changes throughout the body often culminating in orgasm. A **sexual dysfunction** involves a marked divergence of an individual's response in the sexual response cycle along with feelings of significant distress or impairment.

- **Arousal disorders** occur in people who, during the initial phases of the sexual response cycle, have low or no sexual desire, or are unable to achieve physiological arousal. As a result, they may avoid or be unable to have sexual intercourse. These disorders include **hypoactive sexual desire, female sexual arousal, sexual aversion,** and **erectile disorder.**

- There are also disorders involving orgasm. Inability to achieve orgasm, a distressing delay in achieving orgasm, or reduced intensity of orgasm constitutes **female orgasmic disorder.** Men with a marked delay in ejaculation or who rarely, if at all, experience ejaculations have **male orgasmic disorder.**

- Clinicians diagnose sexual pain disorders, which involve the experience of difficulty in sexual relationship due to painful sensations in the genitals from intercourse, as either **dyspareunia** or **vaginismus.** Dyspareunia can affect both males and females.

- We can best view sexual dysfunctions as an interaction of complex **physiological, psychological,** and **sociocultural factors,** which clinicians who work in the field from a **biopsychosocial perspective** understand. In attempting to help a client with a sexual dysfunction, the clinician must first conduct a comprehensive assessment that includes a physical exam and psychological testing, including the client's partner, if appropriate. In addition, the clinician must assess the individual's use of substances including not only drugs and alcohol, but also all medications, including psychotherapeutic ones.

- Disorders that involve difficulties that individuals experience due to feeling a mismatch between their **biological sex** (i.e., the sex determined by their chromosomes), and their inner sense of maleness or femaleness, is called **gender identity.** In the *DSM-IV-TR*, the term **gender identity disorder** is the term that describes the condition in which a person's gender identity and his or her biological sex do not match. In the current criteria for disorder, the individual experiences identification with the other sex. The feeling that they are "in the wrong body" causes feelings of discomfort and a sense of inappropriateness about their assigned gender. Both of these conditions must be present for a clinician to assign the diagnosis. Another term that relates to the feeling of cross-gender identification is **transsexualism,** which also refers to this phenomenon in which a person has an inner feeling of belonging to the other sex.

- The *DSM-5* authors present a strong case for using the term **gender dysphoria** instead of gender identity disorder, specifying whether the individual is a child or post-adolescent. One reason for this proposed change is to take away the stigma attached to the label of the condition as a "disorder." As we did for paraphilic disorders, we are adopting the new terminology because it specifies the condition not as one only involving cross-gender identification, but also as involving distress.

- The psychology of the transgendered experience is undergoing radical shifts. Whereas in the past, the profession equated transgenderism with a "disorder," the new terminology is reflecting a theoretical perspective that does not focus specifically on what is "wrong" with people whose self-identification differs from their biological characteristics or social roles.

- The sexual disorders constitute three discrete sets of difficulties involving varying aspects of sexual functioning and behavior. Although there are many unanswered questions concerning their causes, we need a **biopsychosocial perspective** to understand how individuals acquire and maintain these diverse problems over time.

KEY TERMS

Mood Disorders

Learning Objectives

8.1 Explain the key features of major depressive disorder and dysthymic disorder, including prevalence

8.2 Compare and contrast bipolar I, bipolar II, and cyclothymic disorder

8.3 Understand theories and treatments of depressive and bipolar disorders

8.4 Discuss the relationships among age, gender, and suicide

8.5 Analyze the biopsychosocial model of mood disorders

Case Report: Janice Butterfield

CHAPTER 8

Demographic information: 47-year-old Caucasian female.

Presenting problem: Janice was referred for psychotherapy after a recent hospitalization following a suicide attempt. Janice reported that the precipitant to her suicide attempt was the loss of her job in a real estate company, where she had worked for 25 years. She reported that although she realized her company had downsized due to the economy, she found herself feeling profoundly guilty for the negative impact her unemployment would have on her family. Janice reported she has been married for 27 years and has three daughters, one of whom lives at home. Another is in college, and her youngest will be attending college at the start of the next school year. Janice reported she had felt overwhelmed by the stress about her financial state, as her family mainly relied on her income.

Along with feelings of guilt, Janice reported she had felt so depressed and down that she spent many days in the past 2 weeks in bed, and often found herself thinking of ending her life. She stopped taking pain medication, which was prescribed for her chronic backaches "to save up if I needed them later." One evening when her husband was out of the house, she attempted suicide by taking all of her saved-up medications at once. Janice's husband returned to find her unresponsive and rushed her to the hospital just in time to save her life. She was hospitalized in an inpatient psychiatric unit and given medication until her suicidal thoughts and severe depression decreased enough so that the doctors deemed her no longer a threat to herself. She followed the referral given to her by the psychiatrists on the inpatient unit to attend weekly psychotherapy for follow-up. She had never been in therapy before.

During her first therapy session, Janice reported that she had thought about going to therapy many times before. She explained that her depressions usually lasted about 1 month, but sometimes as long as 3 months. During these periods, she missed a few days of work but she was able to struggle through these periods and go about her normal routine albeit with much difficulty. During these periods, she would go out to her car to cry, because it would be too painful to be around others. "I just didn't want anything to do with life at those points," she recalled. Her depression would eventually improve on its own, as well as her thoughts about getting treatment. She reported that she had occasionally thought about suicide in the past when she was feeling depressed, but had never before made and carried out a plan as she had during the most recent episode.

Janice went on to explain how these depressed moods always caught her "off guard," as they would occur directly after long periods when she felt happy and energetic. She stated these moods usually started after she had made a large real estate sale, and she felt "invincible" after such a sale. During these times, she described that she often needed very little sleep due to the seeming endless amount of energy she possessed, and she would begin to take on many new projects and clients at work—much more than would be expected of her. During these periods she splurged on lavish clothing or jewelry, and during her last energetic period had purchased new cars for herself and her husband. These expenditures were uncharacteristic for Janice, as she described herself as normally financially frugal. Due to her constantly moving thoughts, Janice found it very difficult to concentrate and was so distracted she was rarely able to finish anything she began to take on at work. She would feel disappointed that she had to give up some of her projects, and her joyful feelings would turn to irritability and anger. She reported that her husband usually experienced the brunt of her irritable mood, and this caused major problems in their marriage. Janice further reported that she felt like she ignored her family altogether due to her work habits when she was feeling particularly energetic. She remarked, "When I'm feeling that good, I can only think about myself and what feels good to me. I stop being a mother and a wife." Her extreme spending periods eroded her family's savings, which was especially a concern now that she had lost her job. This also contributed to her guilt about paying for her youngest daughter's college tuition. Janice had never talked with her husband or her children about her vast mood shifts. She stated she worried that if she had told her family about her personal difficulties, they would "see me as a weakling, instead of the head of the household."

Relevant history: Janice had never received psychiatric treatment or therapy in the past, though she reported she had experienced mood swings since she was 19. She estimated that she had severe mood episodes (either manic or depressive) about three to four times per year. When reflecting about the severity of her mood episodes, she stated that she felt her behaviors had been more "extreme" in more recent years than when she was younger. Janice reported that she noticed the patterns in her mood swings always began with an energetic period, directly followed by a depressive episode, and then a period of several months of stability. More recently, though, she noted that the periods of stability had only been lasting 1 or 2 months, and her mood episodes had been lasting longer.

Case formulation: Janice's diagnosis from the psychiatric unit was a Major Depressive Episode, and her current presentation also met this criteria. However, in the initial therapy session she reported also having a history of manic episodes that were followed by periods of depression, which she had not mentioned while she had been hospitalized. The manic symptoms she described caused significant problems for Janice financially, due to her excessive spending sprees. In combination with losing her job, her financial problems caused significant stress for Janice and may have contributed to the severity of her most recent depressive episode, which eventually led to a suicide attempt.

Multiaxial assessment:

Axis I: 296.5x Bipolar I Disorder, Most Recent Episode Depressed
Axis II: Deferred
Axis III: Chronic lower back pain
Axis IV: Loss of employment, financial problems
Axis V: 25

Treatment plan: It is recommended that Janice continue to attend psychotherapy weekly. In therapy, it will be necessary to make a suicide safety plan, given her history of suicidal ideation in the past. Therapy should initially focus on psychoeducation, symptom management, and mood monitoring. She will also be referred to an outpatient psychiatrist for medication reconciliation, as psychotropic medication is highly recommended in the treatment of bipolar disorder.

Sarah Tobin, PhD

---

mood disorder
A disorder that involves a significant disturbance in a person's emotional state.

major depressive disorder
A mood disorder in which the individual experiences acute, but time-limited, episodes of depressive symptoms.

major depressive episode
A period in which the individual experiences intense psychological and physical symptoms related to a dysphoric mood.

A **mood disorder** involves a significant disturbance in a person's emotional state. The two major categories of mood disorders are those that involve depression and those that involve elation. We must combine these core emotional states with other criteria to consider them mood disorders, differentiating them in important ways from ordinary day-to-day highs or lows.

8.1 Depressive Disorders

There are primarily two types of major depressive disorder, which vary in their length and severity. **Major depressive disorder** involves acute, but time-limited, periods of depressive symptoms that are called **major depressive episodes** (see Table 8.1). Dysthymic disorder is a chronic but less severe mood disturbance, in which the individual does not experience a major depressive episode.

TABLE 8.1 Criteria for a Major Depressive Episode

For most of the time during a two-week period, a person experiences at least five of the following criteria. He or she must experience a change from previous functioning (at least one of the first two symptoms must be present), and all but suicidality must be present nearly every day.

- Depressed mood most of the day
- Markedly diminished interest or pleasure in all or most daily activities
- Significant unintended weight loss or unusual increase or decrease in appetite
- Insomnia or hypersomnia
- Psychomotor agitation or retardation observable by others
- Fatigue or loss of energy
- Feelings of worthlessness or excessive or inappropriate guilt
- Difficulty maintaining concentration or making decisions
- Recurrent thoughts of death or having suicidal thoughts, plans, or attempts

The symptoms are not attributable to a medical condition or use of a substance.

The symptoms cause significant distress or impairment.

Major Depressive Disorder

There are two major categories of major depressive disorder: single episode and recurrent. People receive a diagnosis of recurrent major depressive disorder if they have had two or more major depressive episodes with an interval of at least two consecutive months without meeting the criteria for a major depressive episode. Of course, major depressive disorder can be and often is diagnosed with a range of other disorders, including personality disorders, substance abuse disorders, and anxiety disorders, for example. Many conditions can mimic major depressive disorder, including those that are associated with disorders that we will discuss in Chapter 9, which include or are related to schizophrenia. These include schizoaffective disorder, schizophrenia, schizophreniform disorder, delusional disorder, or another psychotic disorder. Therefore, the clinician must rule out these specific disorders before assigning the diagnosis of major depressive disorder to the client.

The lifetime prevalence of major depressive disorder in the United States is 16.6 percent of the adult population (Kessler, Chiu, Demler, Merikangas, & Walters, 2005). Each year, 6.7 percent of the adult population receives a diagnosis of major depressive

MINI CASE

Major Depressive Disorder

Jonathan is a 37-year-old construction worker whose wife took him to a psychiatric facility. Although Jonathan has been functioning normally for the past several years, he suddenly became severely disturbed and depressed. At the time of admission, Jonathan was agitated, dysphoric, and suicidal, even going as far as to purchase a gun to kill himself. He had lost his appetite and had developed insomnia during the preceding 3 weeks. As each day went by, he found himself feeling more and more exhausted, less able to think clearly or to concentrate, and uninterested in anything or anyone. He had become hypersensitive in his dealings with neighbors, co-workers, and family, insisting that others were being too critical of him. This was the second such episode in Jonathan's history, the first having occurred 5 years earlier, following the loss of his job due to a massive layoff in his business.

REAL STORIES

Carrie Fisher: Bipolar Disorder

"I outlasted my problems . . . I am mentally ill. I can say that. I am not ashamed of that. I survived that, I'm still surviving it, but bring it on. Better me than you."

Carrie Fisher is an American actress, screenwriter, novelist, and lecturer who has appeared in 37 films—most notably for her portrayal of Princess Leia Organa in the *Star Wars* trilogy. She has also written four novels, one of which, *Wishful Drinking,* has been turned into a one-woman play performed in venues across the country. In the book, she chronicles her life—from growing up in a Hollywood family, her rise to fame, her struggles with drugs and alcohol, and her battles with bipolar disorder. Carrie talks about her experiences with humor and honesty, revealing the reality of her mental illness.

Born in 1956 in Beverly Hills, California, Carrie is the daughter of actress Debbie Reynolds and singer Eddie Fisher. The product of a Hollywood marriage, Carrie seemed to have been destined to be a Hollywood star from the very beginning. When she was 2 years old, Carrie's father left her mother for Elizabeth Taylor, her mother's best friend. The media highly publicized this story, although in her book, Carrie states that she doesn't believe her childhood experiences affected any of the problems that she encountered later in life. "To complain about my childhood or even a sizeable (?) portion of my life would be as unattractive as it would be inaccurate. I had a very privileged life growing up."

Carrie first began acting at the age of 12, appearing in Las Vegas with her mother, and later dropped out of high school in order to perform on the road with her mother. In 1973, Carrie appeared with her mother in the Broadway musical *Irene,* and 2 years later, after attending drama school in London, made her film debut in the 1975 film *Shampoo* with Burt Reynolds. Two years after that, she instantly became an international celebrity and an icon for her role in the *Star Wars* trilogy. According to Carrie, it was at this point that she began to heavily abuse cocaine and alcohol, having already experimented with marijuana at the age of 13. Looking back on her drug abuse, Carrie recalls that she used drugs as a way to self-medicate her extreme mood episodes: "I used to think I was a drug addict, pure and simple—just someone who could not stop taking drugs willfully . . . and I was that. But it turns out that I am severely manic depressive." She received this diagnosis for the first time when she was 24 years old, although she did not pursue any treatment at that time. As she describes it, ". . . [My psychiatrist] wanted to put me on medication instead of actually treating me. So, I did the only rational thing I could do in the face of such an insult—I stopped talking to the [psychiatrist], flew back to New York, and married Paul Simon a week later."

Carrie was married to singer Paul Simon from 1983 to 1984, although the two dated on and off for a total of 12 years. In 1992, Carrie had a daughter, Billie, with her partner Bryan Lourd.

Despite her chronic battles with substance abuse and bipolar disorder, Carrie continued to appear in films and television shows throughout the 1980s. Her substance abuse led to a hospitalization in the mid 1980s, inspiring her first novel, *Postcards from the Edge,* a semi-autobiographical account of an actress suffering from substance abuse, published in 1987. The book became a successful movie for which she received critical acclaim.

Throughout the 1990s, Carrie continued to appear in films and became well-known in Hollywood for her screenwriting talents. In 1997, she suffered from a psychotic break after she sought out medication to treat her chronic depression. She describes that experience in *Wishful Drinking*: "Now, anyone who has stayed awake for six days knows that there's every chance that they'll wind up psychotic. Anyway, I did, and part of how that manifested was that I thought everything on television was about me . . . I watched CNN, and at the time Versace had just been killed by that man Cunanin, and the police were

After struggling for many years with substance abuse and bipolar disorder, Carrie Fisher is now an activist for destigmatization of mental illness.

frantically scouring the Eastern seaboard for him. So, I was Cunanin, Versace, and the police. Now this is exhausting programming." She was hospitalized for 6 days and then spent 6 months receiving outpatient treatment. Having now accepted her diagnosis of bipolar disorder and finally coming to terms with her need for treatment, Carrie set out to lecture against the stigmatization of mental illness. Since that time she has been an active voice in speaking out about the need for government funding for mental health treatment, and for the need for greater public acceptance of mental illness.

In *Wishful Drinking*, Carrie describes her experiences with switching between mania and depression. "I have two moods . . . One is Roy, rollicking Roy, the wild ride of a mood. And Pam, sediment Pam, who stands on the shore and sobs . . . sometimes the tide is in, sometimes it's out." Carrie also describes some of the various treatments for her illness that she has received, including electroconducive therapy (ECT).

"Why did I feel I needed ECT? Well, it had been recommended by several psychiatrists over the years, to treat my depression. But I couldn't bring myself to consider it as it seemed too barbaric. My only exposure to it was Jack Nicholson in *One Flew Over the Cuckoo's Nest*, which wasn't exactly an enticing example. From the seizures to the biting down on a stick to the convulsions, it looked traumatic, dangerous, and humiliating. I mean, what do we know for certain about it? Aren't there a bunch of risks? What if something goes wrong and my brain blows up?

"But I'd been feeling overwhelmed and pretty defeated. I didn't necessarily feel like *dying*—but I'd been feeling a lot like not being alive. The second reason I decided to get ECT is that I was depressed. Profoundly depressed. Part of this could be attributed to my mood disorder, which was, no doubt, probably the source of the emotional intensity. That's what can take simple sadness and turn it into sadness squared."

"At times," she writes at the end of *Wishful Drinking*, "being bipolar can be an all-consuming challenge, requiring a lot of stamina and even more courage, so if you're living with this illness and functioning at all, it's something to be proud of, not ashamed of."

The *DSM-IV-TR* defines a **manic episode** somewhat differently than will the *DSM-5*. However, the changes seem reasonable because they involve criteria that will allow clinicians to make the diagnosis with greater precision. The *DSM-IV-TR* did not include the phrase "and abnormally and persistently increased activity or energy, lasting at least one week and present most of the day, nearly every day." One important reason for the change has to do with timing. The previous criteria did not include a temporal element other than to say that the disorder had to be present for at least 1 week (unless hospitalization was necessary). By specifying "most of the day, nearly every day," the new criteria will be closer to those for a major depressive episode. Also, by specifying that the individual must be unusually active or excited, the new criteria show clearly that the behavior must be distinctly different from the person's behavior when he or she is not experiencing a manic episode.

manic episode
A period of euphoric mood with symptoms involving abnormally heightened levels of thinking, behavior, and emotionality.

TABLE 8.3 Criteria for a Hypomanic Episode

A distinct period of abnormally and persistently elevated, expansive, or irritable mood and abnormally and persistently increased activity or energy,* lasting at least 4 consecutive days and present most of the day, nearly every day. The episode is not severe enough to require hospitalization.

During the period of mood disturbance and increased energy and activity, three (or more) of the following symptoms have persisted (four if the mood is only irritable), represent a noticeable change from usual behavior, and have been present to a significant degree:

- inflated self-esteem or grandiosity
- decreased need for sleep (e.g., feels rested after only 3 hours of sleep)
- more talkative than usual or pressure to keep talking
- flight of ideas or subjective experience that thoughts are racing
- distractibility (i.e., attention too easily drawn to unimportant or irrelevant external stimuli), as reported or observed
- increase in goal-directed activity (either socially, at work or school, or sexually) or psychomotor agitation
- excessive involvement in pleasurable activities that have a high potential for painful consequences (e.g., the person engages in unrestrained buying sprees, sexual indiscretions, or foolish business investments)

*The increase in activity or energy is *DSM-5*.

FIGURE 8.2 **Range of Moods Present in People with Bipolar Disorder**

severe depression, moderate depression, and mild low mood

normal or balanced mood

hypomania and severe mania

hypomanic episode
A period of elated mood not as extreme as a manic episode.

The two major categories of bipolar disorder are Bipolar I and Bipolar II. A diagnosis of Bipolar I disorder describes a clinical course in which the individual experiences one or more manic episodes with the possibility, although not the necessity, of experiencing one or more major depressive episodes. In contrast, a diagnosis of Bipolar II disorder means that the individual has had one or more major depressive episodes and at least one that we call a **hypomanic episode.** The criteria for a hypomanic episode are similar to those of a manic episode, but involve a shorter duration (4 days instead of 1 week).

Individuals who are in a manic, hypomanic, or major depressive episode may show features of the opposite pole, but not to an extreme enough degree to meet diagnostic criteria. For example, people in a manic episode may report feeling sad or empty, fatigued, or suicidal. *DSM-IV-TR* included criteria for a "mixed episode" (i.e., mixed depressive and manic episode), but *DSM-5* will use a specifier of "mixed features" to apply to such situations. The existence of this additional "mixed" category accounts for those people whose symptoms may, either simultaneously with or close in time to, show the opposite mood symptoms.

Bipolar disorder has a lifetime prevalence rate of 3.9 percent in the U.S. population (Kessler, Berglund, et al., 2005) and a 12-month prevalence of 2.6 percent (Kessler, Chiu, et al., 2005). Of those diagnosed with bipolar disorder in a given year, nearly 83 percent (2.2 percent of adult population) have cases classified as "severe." At least half of all cases begin before a person reaches the age of 25 (Kessler, Chiu, et al., 2005). Nevertheless, approximately 60 percent of all individuals with bipolar disorder can live symptom-free if they receive adequate treatment (Perlis et al., 2006).

Of all psychological disorders, we most likely associate bipolar disorder with substance abuse. People with bipolar and substance abuse disorders have an earlier onset of bipolar disorder, more frequent episodes, greater chances of having anxiety- and stress-related disorders, aggressive behavior, problems with the law, and risk of suicide (Swann, 2010). As you can see in Figure 8.2, bipolar disorder can cause people to experience a range of moods.

rapid cycling form of bipolar disorder
Individuals with bipolar disorder who have four to eight mood episodes within the course of a year.

Clinicians diagnose people who have four or more episodes of major depression, mania, hypomania, or mixed symptoms with the **rapid-cycling form of bipolar disorder.** In some individuals, the cycling may occur within 1 week or even 1 day. The factors that predict rapid cycling include earlier onset, higher depression scores, higher mania scores,

MINI CASE

Cyclothymic Disorder

Larry is a 32-year-old bank cashier who has sought treatment for his mood variations, which date back to age 26. For several years, co-workers, family, and friends have repeatedly told him that he is very moody. He acknowledges that his mood never feels quite stable, although at times others tell him he seems more calm and pleasant than usual. Unfortunately, these intervals are quite brief, lasting for a few weeks and usually ending abruptly. Without warning, he may experience either a depressed mood or a period of elation. During his depressive periods, his confidence,

energy, and motivation are very low. During his hypomanic periods, he willingly volunteers to extend his workday and to undertake unrealistic challenges at work. On weekends, he acts in promiscuous and provocative ways, often sitting outside his apartment building, making seductive comments and gestures to women walking by. Larry disregards the urging of his family members to get professional help, insisting that it is his nature to be a bit unpredictable. He also states that he doesn't want some shrink to steal away the periods during which he feels fantastic.

and lower global assessment of functioning. A history of rapid cycling in the previous year and use of antidepressants also predict rapid cycling (Schneck et al., 2008). Medical conditions such as hypothyroidism, disturbances in sleep-wake cycles, and use of anti-depressant medications can also contribute to the development of rapid cycling (Papad-imitriou, Calabrese, Dikeos, & Christodoulou, 2005).

Cyclothymic Disorder

Cyclothymic disorder symptoms are more chronic and less severe than those of bipolar disorder. People with this disorder have met the criteria for a hypomanic episode many times over a span of at least 2 years (1 year in children and adolescents) and also have numerous periods of depressive symptoms, but never meet the criteria for a major depressive episode. During their respective timeframes, adults, children, or adolescents have never been without these symptoms for more than 2 months at a time.

cyclothymic disorder
A mood disorder with symptoms that are more chronic and less severe than those of bipolar disorder.

8.3 Theories and Treatments of Mood Disorders

Biological Perspectives

Long aware of the tendency for mood disorders to occur more frequently among bio-logically related family members, researchers working within the biological perspective are attempting to pinpoint genetic contributors to these disorders. However, there are most likely multiple genes that interact in complex ways with environmental risk factors, complicating tremendously their work (Kamali & McInnis, 2011).

Researchers estimate that first-degree relatives are 15 to 25 percent more likely to have major depressive disorder than nonrelatives, or two to four times the rates of nonrelatives. However, children of depressed parents are more likely to have major depressive disorder than are parents of depressed children. However, recall from Chapter 4 that family inheri-tance studies cannot separate genetic from environmental factors. Children of depressed parents grow up in households that we might imagine are different in important ways from those with children whose parents do not have major depressive disorders. Twin studies comparing identical or monozygotic (MZ) with fraternal or dizygotic (DZ) twins provide stronger evidence in favor of a genetic interpretation. Based on numerous studies involving these comparisons, researchers estimate that genetic influences on major depressive disor-der are in the range of 30 to 40 percent. However, genetic predisposition interacts with environmental factors including stress, social support, and life events (Lau & Eley, 2010).

Altered serotonin functioning seems to play an important role in causing genetically predisposed individuals to develop major depressive disorder. The best evidence for sero-tonin's role comes from studies in which individuals are experimentally deprived of tryptophan, an amino acid that aids the body in manufacturing serotonin (Cowen, 2008). A second research area on biochemical abnormalities in people with major depressive disorder involves brain-derived neurotrophic factor (BDNF), a protein involved in keeping neurons alive and able to adapt and change in response to experi-ence. Researchers are finding that people with major depressive disorder seem to have inherited a version of a gene that codes BDNF, resulting in lower levels in areas of the brain regions involved in controlling mood (Lau & Eley, 2010).

Compared to major depressive disorder, bipolar disorder has an even stronger pattern of genetic inheritance with an estimated heritability of 60 percent. In a comprehensive analysis of 367 genes possibly involved in bipolar disorder, a team of researchers from the National Institute of Mental Health narrowed the search to a defect in the "PCLO" gene (called the "piccolo" gene). This gene seems to play a role in synaptic transmission (Choi et al., 2011). Brain scan and neuropsychological testing of individuals with bipolar disorder suggest that they have difficulties in attention, memory, and executive function consistent with abnormalities in the primary visual cortex, the frontal lobes, the temporal

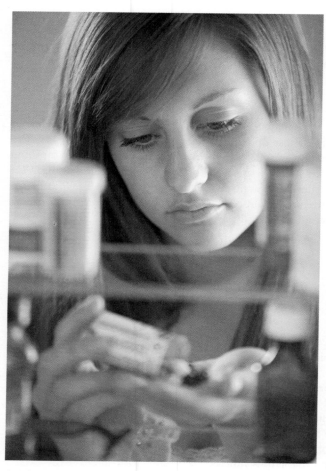

Antidepressant medication is commonly prescribed to individuals who suffer from Major Depressive Disorder.

lobes, and the cingulate cortex (Benabarre et al., 2005). Further research suggests that the inability to inhibit responses that may have a genetic component may, consequently, serve as an endophenotype for bipolar disorder (Schulze et al., 2011).

Antidepressant medication is the most common form of biologically based treatment for people with major depressive disorder. As we discussed in Chapter 4, clinicians diagnose antidepressants from four major categories of selective serotonin reuptake inhibitors (SSRIs), serotonin and norepinephrine reuptake inhibitors (SNRIs), tricyclic antidepressants, and monoamine oxidase inhibitors (MAOIs).

SSRIs block the uptake of serotonin, enabling more availabilty of this neurotransmitter for action at the receptor sites. These medications include fluoxetine (Prozac), citalopram (Celexa), escitalopram (Lexapro), paroxetine (Paxil), and sertraline (Zoloft). Compared to other antidepressants, SSRIs have fewer unpleasant side effects such as sedation, weight gain, constipation, blood pressure changes, and dry mouth. However, SSRIs are not without side effects. The most commonly reported complaints are nausea, agitation, and sexual dysfunction. SNRIs increase both norepinephrine and serotonin levels by blocking their reuptake. They include duloxetine (Cymbalta), venlafaxine (Effexor), and desvenlaxafine (Pristiq).

Compared to SSRIs, the SNRIs seem to be statistically but not clinically more efficacious, and they have a greater chance of adverse reactions (Machado & Einarson, 2010) including suicidal thoughts or attempts as well as allergic symptoms, gastrointestinal disturbances, weakness, nausea, vomiting, confusion, memory loss, irritability, and panic attacks, among other unpleasant reactions. In 2010, the manufacturer of Cymbalta (Eli Lilly) also achieved approval from the Federal Drug Administration to market the medication for chronic lower back pain, and it began extensive marketing for this purpose.

Tricyclic antidepressants (TCAs) derive their name from the fact that they have a three-ring chemical structure. These medications, such as amitriptyline (Elavil, Endep), desipramine (Norpramin), imipramine (Tofranil), and nortriptyline (Aventyl, Pamelor), are particularly effective in alleviating depression in people who have some of the more common biological symptoms, such as disturbed appetite and sleep. Although the exact process by which tricyclic antidepressants work still remains unclear, we do know that they block the premature reuptake of biogenic amines back into the presynaptic neurons, thus increasing their excitatory effects on the postsynaptic neurons.

Clinicians believe that the antidepressant effects of MAOIs, such as phenelzine (Nardil) and tranylcypromine (Parnate), occur because the medications inhibit the enzyme monoamine oxidase, which converts the biogenic amines, such as norepinephrine and serotonin, into inert substances, so that they cannot excite the postsynaptic neurons. MAOIs prolong the life of neurotransmitters, thus increasing neuronal flow. These medications are particularly effective in treating depression in people with chronic depression that dates back many years, and who have not responded to the tricyclics. However, clinicians do not prescribe MAOIs as commonly as the other two medication types, because their interactions with other substances can cause serious complications. Specifically, people taking MAOIs are not able to take certain allergy medications or to ingest foods or beverages containing a substance called tyramine (for example, beer, cheese, and chocolate), because the combination can bring on a hypertensive crisis in which the person's blood pressure rises dramatically and dangerously.

Antidepressant medications take time to work—from 2 to 6 weeks before a client's symptoms begin to lift. Once the depression has subsided, the clinician usually urges him or her to remain on the medication for 4 or 5 additional months, and much longer for clients with a history of recurrent, severe depressive episodes. Because of medication side

Psychotropic medication offers relief to many individuals who suffer from mood disorders and are often used in combination with other modes of treatment, such as psychotherapy, to help patients manage their symptoms.

effects and client concerns, clinicians have found it helpful to develop therapeutic programs that involve regular visits early in treatment, expanded efforts to educate clients about the medications, and continued monitoring of treatment compliance.

Studies on antidepressant effectiveness suffer from the "file drawer problem" phenomenon—the fact that we are likely to file away and not even submit for publication consideration studies that fail to establish significant benefits of an intervention such as a medication. In one analysis of 74 FDA-registered studies on antidepressants, 31 percent of them, accounting for 3,349 study participants, were not published. Of the published studies, 94 percent of the medication trials reported positive findings. This bias toward publishing only positive results severely limits our ability to evaluate the efficacy of antidepressants because we are only seeing a slice of the actual data (Turner, Matthews, Linardatos, Tell, & Rosenthal, 2008). Adding further complications, some researchers have questioned whether people with less than severe depression might have experienced positive results because of their expectation of benefit, otherwise known as the placebo effect (Kirsch et al., 2008).

Although there have been media reports about the higher suicide risk that occurs with the SSRI medication category, an investigation of all suicides in the years between 1996 and 1998 revealed a lower rate of suicide among individuals who are receiving treatment with these medications compared to other forms of antidepressants. In part, this was due to the generally better medical care in facilities that prescribe SSRIs compared to the older and less effective tricyclic antidepressants (Gibbons, Hur, Bhaumik, & Mann, 2005).

The traditional treatment for bipolar disorder is lithium carbonate, referred to as lithium, a naturally occurring salt (found in small amounts in drinking water) that, when used medically, replaces sodium in the body. The medication's psychopharmacological effect decreases the catecholamine levels in the nervous system, which, in terms of behavior, calms the individual experiencing a manic episode. Researchers have examined the efficacy of lithium in numerous studies over the past three decades, and the conclusion seems clear

Toward the DSM-5: Mood Disorders

Modifications to the category of Mood Disorders in *DSM-5* will allow greater precision in the diagnosis by refining the criteria for major depressive episode, manic episode, and hypomanic episode. Our description of these episodes partially reflects these anticipated changes, because the American Psychiatric Association is very likely to adopt them. One of the major problems in the *DSM-IV-TR* was a failure to differentiate these episodes from a person's typical level of activity, sadness, or disturbance. The difficulty in particular led to a failure to distinguish bipolar disorder from attention-deficit hyperactivity disorder, which, in turn, may have led to overdiagnosis of children and adolescents with bipolar disorder. Thus, these changes represent a slight, but important, improvement and will lead to greater specificity.

Another important and useful change is the addition of chronic depressive disorder and the removal of "dysthymic disorder." The term "chronic depressive" seems much more understandable; however, in this regard, it is interesting that the *DSM-5* authors are (so far, at least) retaining the parallel term "cyclothymic." However, not only are they changing the terminology, but also the rationale for having chronic depressive disorder as a diagnosis. The researchers involved in writing *DSM-5* argue that clinicians could not reliably distinguish dysthymic disorder from chronic nonbipolar major depression. By combining these two diagnoses, both reliability and validity should improve in the future.

Other changes in the *DSM-5* may be more controversial, for example, a new disorder called pre-menstrual dysphoric disorder (PMDD). This disorder was previously in the Appendix (i.e., not a diagnosable condition) in *DSM-IV-TR*. By making this disorder part of the standard psychiatric nomenclature, the *DSM-5* authors believe that better diagnosis and treatment can result for women who truly experience a highly exaggerated mood disturbance prior to their monthly menstrual cycle. Rather than pathologizing women, as critics argue this does, the change would make it clear that the majority of women do not experience severe mood alterations on a monthly basis.

The *DSM-5* authors also proposed making changes in the handling of bereavement. In the previous *DSMs*, bereavement was an exclusion from the criteria for a major depressive episode. This meant that clinicians do not diagnose major depressive disorder within the first 2 months after loss of a loved one. After an outcry from the public and mental health professionals, the *DSM-5* authors decided to retain this exclusion. Had they not, people who are experiencing symptoms of major depression, even if recently bereaved, would have received a psychiatric diagnosis. In addition, clinicians would not consider the normal reactions that accompany divorce or job loss to be symptomatic of major depressive disorder.

The authors are proposing a new disorder, disruptive mood dysregulation disorder, which is characterized by severe and recurrent temper outbursts in response to common stressors with an onset in children between 6 and 10 years of age. Critics may argue that this disorder is pathologizing the "normal" experience in children of having temper tantrums. The rationale for proposing this new diagnosis is that it would reduce the frequency of diagnosing bipolar disorder in children. By separating severe chronic irritability from bipolar disorder, the authors argue that children will not be misdiagnosed.

Finally, the authors considered a new category called "Mixed Anxiety-Depression." This diagnosis was present in the *DSM-IV-TR* Appendix (i.e., was not a diagnosis) and is included in the ICD-10. The authors of *DSM-5* believed that by including this diagnosis, they would acknowledge the high proportion of individuals with depressive symptoms who also have significant anxiety symptoms as well as maintain consistency with the ICD-10. However, upon further review, the *DSM-5* authors decided that there was insufficient evidence to support this diagnosis. One complaint was that it would have labeled many people with moderate symptoms as having a psychiatric disorder.

that lithium is effective in treating acute mania symptoms and in preventing the recurrence of manic episodes (Shastry, 2005).

Clinicians advise people who have frequent manic episodes (i.e., two or more a year) to remain on lithium continuously as a preventive measure. The drawback is that, even though lithium is a natural substance in the body, it can have side effects, such as mild central nervous system disturbances, gastrointestinal upsets, and more serious cardiac effects. Because of these side effects, some people who experience manic episodes are reluctant or even unwilling to take lithium continuously. Furthermore, lithium interferes with the euphoria that can accompany, at least, the beginnings of a manic episode. Consequently, people with this disorder who enjoy those pleasurable feelings may resist taking the medication. Unfortunately, by the time their euphoria escalates into a full-blown episode, it's too late because their judgment is clouded by their manic symptoms of grandiosity and elation. To help overcome this dilemma, clinicians may advise their clients to participate in lithium groups, in which members who use the medication on a regular basis provide support to each other regarding the importance of staying on the medication.

Because of the variable nature of bipolar disorder, additional medication is often beneficial in treating some symptoms. For example, people in a depressive episode may need to take an antidepressant medication in addition to the lithium for the duration of the episode. However, this can be problematic for a person who is prone to developing mania, because an antidepressant might provoke hypomania or mania. Those who have psychotic symptoms may benefit from taking antipsychotic medication until these disturbing symptoms subside. People who experience rapid cycling present a challenge for clinicians because of the sudden changes that take place in their emotions and behavior.

Psychopharmacologists report that rapid cyclers, especially those for whom lithium has not been sufficient, seem to respond positively to prescriptions of anticonvulsant medication, such as carbamazepine (Tegretol) or valproate (Depakote), although these alone are not as effective as lithium (Kessing, Hellmund, Geddes, Goodwin, & Andersen, 2011).

For some clients with mood disorders, medication is either ineffective or slow in alleviating symptoms that are severe and possibly life-threatening. Even with the best of treatment, between 60 and 70 percent of individuals with major depressive disorder do not achieve symptom relief (Rush et al., 2006). A combination of genetic, physiological, and environmental factors are involved in determining response to medication. Researchers hope to improve the efficacy of medications through **pharmacogenetics,** the use of genetic testing to determine who will and will not improve with a particular medication including antidepressants (Crisafulli et al., 2011) and lithium (McCarthy, Leckband, & Kelsoe, 2010).

pharmacogenetics
The use of genetic testing to determine who will and will not improve with a particular medication.

Clinicians, at present, have several somatic alternatives to medication for treatment-resistant depression. As we discussed in Chapter 4, one alternative is electroconvulsive therapy (ECT) (Lisanby, 2007). Clinicians and clients are not sure exactly how ECT works, but most current hypotheses center on ECT-induced changes in neurotransmitter receptors and in the body's natural opiates. As we discussed in Chapter 4, deep brain stimulation (DBS) is another somatic treatment that clinicians use to target major depressive disorder (as well as obsessive-compulsive disorder and movement disorders).

Circadian rhythms are the daily variations that regulate biological patterns such as sleep-wake cycles. Based on the hypothesis that at least some mood disorders reflect a disruption in circadian rhythms, researchers are proposing the use of treatments that "reset" the individual's bodily clock. Such treatments include light therapy, in which the individual is seated in front of a bright light for a period of time, such as 30 minutes in the morning. One distinct advantage of light therapy is that its side effects are minimal and are almost entirely gone after the reduced dosage or discontinued treatment (Pail et al., 2011). Researchers also believe that lithium may work on at least some individuals with bipolar disorder by resetting their circadian rhythms (McClung, 2007).

Although somatic interventions provide effective and sometimes lifesaving help for many people, most therapists regard these treatments as insufficient by themselves. Consequently, clinicians typically recommend individual, family, or group psychotherapy as an adjunct to help the individual understand both the etiology of the disorder and the strategies for preventing recurrences. Let's turn now to the contributions of the various perspectives that address these psychological issues.

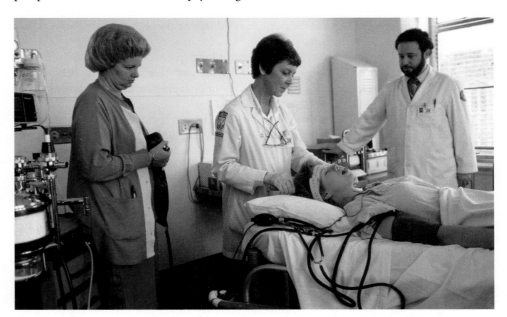

Once a risky and controversial procedure, electroconvulsive therapy is now a highly regulated and safe procedure available for individuals with severe depression who have not responded to other treatment options.

Psychological Perspectives

Psychodynamic Approaches Early psychoanalytic theories of mood disorders proposed that people with depressive disorders had suffered a loss early in their lives that affected them at a deep, intrapsychic level (Abraham, 1911/1968). Attachment theory focuses on the individual's feelings of security or insecurity toward the way that their caregivers reared them in childhood. Bowlby proposed that people with an insecure attachment style have a greater risk for developing a depressive disorder in adulthood (Bowlby, 1980). Following up on Bowlby's ideas, Bemporad (1985) proposed that insecurely attached children become preoccupied with the need to be loved by others. As adults, they form relationships in which they overvalue the support of their partners. When such relationships end, they become overwhelmed with feelings of inadequacy and loss.

Psychoanalytic explanations of bipolar disorder propose that manic episodes are defensive responses through which individuals stave off feelings of inadequacy, loss, and helplessness. They develop feelings of grandiosity and elation or become hyperenergetic as an unconscious defense against sinking into a state of gloom and despair. In one investigation, the level of use of denial and narcissistic defense mechanisms was related to extent of manic symptoms (Sharma & Sinha, 2010).

Models of treatment for depression are increasingly moving toward the application of cognitive-behavioral techniques; however, there is also evidence of the beneficial effects of psychodynamically based therapy. Contemporary approaches within the psychodynamic perspective involve short (8- or 10-session) and focused treatments. A review of eight studies comparing short-term psychodynamic therapy to other methods showed this method to be as least as effective as CBT in the treatment of major depressive disorder (Lewis, Dennerstein, & Gibbs, 2008).

Behavioral and Cognitive Behavioral Approaches One of the earliest behavioral formulations of theories of depression regards the symptoms of depression symptoms as resulting from lack of positive reinforcement (Lazarus, 1968; Skinner, 1953). According to this view, depressed people withdraw from life because they no longer have incentives to be active. Contemporary behaviorists base their approach on Lewinsohn's (1974) model. He maintained that depressed people have a low rate of what he termed "response contingent positive reinforcement behaviors" that increase in frequency as the result of performing actions that produce pleasure. According to the behaviorist point of view, the lack of positive reinforcement elicits the symptoms of low self-esteem, guilt, and pessimism.

behavioral activation
Behavioral therapy for depression in which the clinician helps the client identify activities associated with positive mood.

In the method known as **behavioral activation** for depression, based on these behaviorist principles, the clinician helps the client identify activities associated with positive mood. The client keeps a record of the frequency of engaging in these rewarding activities and sets weekly, small goals that gradually increase the frequency and duration of these activities. These activities are preferably ones that are consistent with the client's core values. Some clients may prefer to spend time exploring the arts, and others to spend time in physical activity. Behavioral activation seems particularly well-suited for clients who are not "psychologically minded," for group therapy, and for settings such as hospitals, nursing homes, and substance-abuse treatment centers (Sturmey, 2009).

Clinicians increasingly are integrating behavioral with cognitive approaches that focus on the role of dysfunctional thoughts as causes, or at least contributors to mood disorders. Recall that the cognitive perspective is based on the idea that people's thoughts lead to their emotions. People with depressive disorders think in repetitively negative ways that maintain chronically their negative emotions. Beck (1967) defined these thoughts as the cognitive triad: a negative view of the self, the world, and the future. A sense of loss profoundly lowers their self-esteem, which causes them to feel that they cannot have what they need to feel good about themselves. They assume that they are worthless and helpless and that their efforts to improve their lives are doomed to fail. In the course of their daily experiences, they make faulty interpretations that perpetuate the cycle of negative thoughts and emotions (Beck, Rush, Shaw, & Emery, 1979; Beck & Weishaar, 1989). These faulty

TABLE 8.4 Examples of Cognitive Distortions

Type of Distortion	Definition	Example
Overgeneralizing	If it's true in one case, it applies to any case that is even slightly similar.	"I failed my first English exam, so I'm probably going to fail all of them."
Selective abstraction	The only events that the person takes seriously are those that represent failures, deprivation, loss, or frustration.	"Even though I won the election for the student senate, I'm not really popular because not everyone voted for me."
Excessive responsibility	I am responsible for all bad things that happen to me or others to whom I am close.	"It's my fault that my friend didn't get the internship—I should've warned her about how hard the interview would be."
Assuming temporal causality	If it has been true in the past, then it's always going to be true.	"My last date was a wipeout, my next date will probably hate me too."
Making excessive self-references	I am the center of everyone else's attention, and they can all see when I mess up.	"When I tripped over the branch in the sidewalk, everyone could see how clumsy I am."
Catastrophizing	Always thinking the worst and being certain that it will happen.	"Because I failed my accounting exam, I will never make it in the business world."
Dichotomous thinking	Seeing everything as either one extreme or another rather than as mixed or in between.	"I can't stand people who are liars because I can never trust them."

SOURCE: Adapted from A. T. Beck, A. J. Bush, B. F. Shaw, & G. Emery in *Cognitive Therapy of Depression*. Copyright ©1979 Guilford Publications, Inc. Reprinted by permission.

interpretations include making arbitrary inferences, incorrectly jumping to conclusions, mistakenly overgeneralizing from their experiences, and taking details out of context which they then misinterpret (see Table 8.2).

Clinicians who conduct behavioral therapy with clients who have depressive disorders follow the general principles that we outlined in Chapter 4. They begin with a careful assessment of the frequency, quality, and range of activities and social interactions in their client's life, focusing on sources of positive and negative reinforcement. Based on this analysis, behaviorally oriented clinicians help their clients make changes in their environments and teach them necessary social skills. These clinicians also encourage them to increase their involvement in activities that they find positively rewarding.

Behaviorally oriented clinicians also believe that education is an essential component of therapy. Individuals with depressive disorders perpetuate their negative emotions by setting unrealistic goals, which they are then unable to achieve. Clinicians assign homework exercises that encourage clients to make gradual behavioral changes, which will increase the probability that they can achieve their goals, and thus feel rewarded. Another technique involves behavioral contracting combined with self-reinforcement. For example, the clinician and client may agree that a client would benefit from meeting new people or going out with old friends. They would then set up a schedule of rewards in which they pair the social activity with something the client identifies as a desirable reward. Other methods the behaviorally oriented clinician would use include more extensive instruction, modeling, coaching, role playing, and rehearsal, and perhaps working with the client in a real-world setting.

Clinicians who practice cognitively based therapy (CBT), also called cognitive therapy (CT), work with their clients to try to change the nature of their thought processes so that they will be less depressed. Like behaviorally oriented therapy, CBT involves an active collaboration between the client and the clinician. In contrast to behaviorally oriented therapy, however, CBT focuses additionally on the client's dysfunctional thoughts and how to change them through cognitive restructuring. Research comparing

CBT and CT to either other psychological forms of therapy or medication supports its greater effectiveness both in the short- and long-term, particularly for moderate or mild depressive disorders. Moreover, CBT can also be an effective intervention for clients with bipolar disorder to help them cope with the periods in which their symptoms are beginning to emerge, but before they are full-blown (Driessen & Hollon, 2010).

Clinicians treating people with bipolar disorder customarily turn first to pharmacological interventions. However, they are also likely to incorporate psychological interventions designed to help clients develop better coping strategies in an effort to minimize the likelihood of relapse (Bowden, 2005). Psychoeducation is an especially important aspect of treating people with bipolar disorder in order to help clients with this condition understand its nature, as well as the ways in which medication is so important in controlling symptoms. Many people who have experienced a manic episode are tempted to forgo taking their medication in the hope that they might once again experience the exciting highs of a manic episode. If they can develop insight into the risks involved in noncompliance, as well as an improved understanding of medications such as lithium, they are more likely to adhere to the treatment program.

interpersonal therapy (IPT)
A time-limited form of psychotherapy for treating people with major depressive disorder, based on the assumption that interpersonal stress induces an episode of depression in a person who is genetically vulnerable to this disorder.

Interpersonal Approaches   Researchers originally developed **interpersonal therapy** as a brief intervention, lasting between 12 and 16 weeks, which emerged from interpersonal theory. This approach adheres to a set of guidelines derived from research data. Although interpersonal therapy involves many of the techniques that most therapists use spontaneously, it frames these techniques in a systematic approach, including manuals to guide them in applying the method.

We can divide interpersonal therapy into three broad phases. The first phase involves assessing the magnitude and nature of the individual's depression using quantitative assessment measures. Interview methods also determine the factors that precipitated the current episode. At that point, depending on the type of depressive symptoms that the individual shows, the therapist considers treatment with antidepressant medications.

In the second phase, the therapist and the client collaborate in formulating a treatment plan that focuses on the primary problem. Typically, these problems are related to grief, interpersonal disputes, role transitions, and problems in interpersonal relationships stemming from inadequate social skills. The therapist then carries out the treatment plan in the third phase, with the methods varying according to the precise nature of the client's primary problem. In general, the therapist uses a combination of techniques, such as encouraging self-exploration, providing support, educating the client in the nature of depression, and providing feedback on the client's ineffective social skills. Therapy focuses on the here and now, rather than on past childhood or developmental issues. A large-scale analysis of studies conducted over 30 years on interpersonal therapy showed that, compared to cognitive-behavioral therapy and medications, interpersonal therapy was significantly more effective (Bowden, 2005).

For clients who cannot take antidepressant medications or where it is impractical to use medications, IPT is an especially valuable intervention in that nonmedical personnel can administer it or clients, with instruction, can learn it themselves (Weissman, 2007). In addition, for clients with personality disorders, IPT may be less effective than CBT, which is more structured and also focuses less on interpersonal difficulties (Carter et al., 2011).

Interpersonal and social rhythm therapy (IPSRT) (Frank, 2007) is a biopsychosocial approach to treating people with bipolar disorder that proposes that relapses can result from the experience of stressful life events, disturbances in circadian rhythms (e.g., sleep-wake cycles, appetite, energy), and problems in personal relationships. According to the IPSRT model, mood episodes are likely to emerge from medication nonadherence, stressful life events, and disruptions in social rhythms. Clinicians who are using this approach focus on educating clients about medication adherence, giving them a forum to explore their feelings about the disorder, and helping them develop insight about the ways in which the disorder has altered their lives. Clinicians work with clients in paying careful attention to the regularity of daily routines (including the timing of events and the stimulation that occurs with

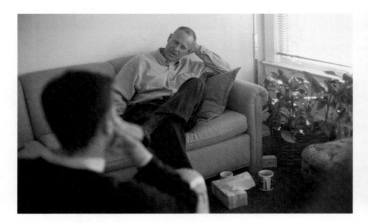

An interpersonal therapist carefully collaborates with each client to generate a unique treatment plan, based on the client's symptoms and particular areas of concern.

Interpersonal and social rhythm therapy incorporates biological approaches to treatment such as light therapy to regulate an individual's circadian rhythms.

these events), and the extent to which life events, positive as well as negative, influence daily routines. The goal of IPSRT is to increase stability in a client's social rhythms.

Clinicians who adhere to the IPSRT model believe that the reduction of interpersonal stress in clients with bipolar disorder is important for several reasons. First, stressful life events affect circadian rhythm because an individual feels a sense of heightened arousal of the autonomic nervous system. Second, many life events, both stressful and nonstressful, do cause changes in daily routines. Third, major life stressors affect a person's mood and also lead to significant changes in social rhythms (Frank, 2007). Clinicians help the client stabilize social rhythms or routines while improving their interpersonal relationships. Researchers employing IPSRT have found that this form of intensive psychosocial treatment enhances relationship functioning and life satisfaction among people with bipolar disorder, particularly when combined with pharmacological interventions (Frank, Maggi, Miniati, & Benvenuti, 2009).

In reviewing the results of virtually all published studies on interventions for mood disorders, Hollon and Ponniah (2010) concluded that cognitive behavioral and behavioral therapy have received the strongest support, particularly for individuals with less severe or chronic depression. Individuals with more severe depressive or bipolar disorders also benefit from cognitive behavioral, interpersonal, and behaviorally oriented therapy above and beyond the effects of pharmacotherapy, and perhaps even instead as a first-line of approach, such as therapists currently implement in England.

Sociocultural Perspectives

According to the sociocultural perspective, individuals develop depressive disorders in response to stressful life circumstances. These circumstances can involve specific events such as sexual victimization, chronic stress such as poverty and single parenting, or episodic stress such as bereavement or job loss. Women are more likely to be exposed to these stressors than are men, a fact that may account, at least in part, for the higher frequency in the diagnosis of depressive disorders in women (Hammen, 2005).

However, acute and chronic stressors seem to play a differential role in predisposing an individual to experiencing depressive symptoms. Exposure to an acute stress such as the death of a loved one or an automobile accident could precipitate a major depressive episode. However, exposure to chronic strains from poor working conditions, health problems, interpersonal problems, and financial adversities can interact with genetic predisposition and personality to lead to more persistent feelings of hopelessness. Moreover, once activated, an individual's feelings of depression and hopelessness can exacerbate exposure to stressful environments which, in turn, can increase further the individual's feelings of chronic strain (Brown & Rosellini, 2011).

Do-Not-Resuscitate Orders for Suicidal Patients

Medical professionals encourage (or sometimes require) patients, whether they are terminally ill or not, to direct them on how they wish to be treated should they require life support. Often, for such an "Advance Directive," also known as a "Living Will," patients specify whether or not they wish to have artificial life support should they be unable to survive on their own.

The issue of whether physicians should assist patients in ending their own lives, a process known as "Physician-Assisted Suicide," came to public attention in the 1990s when Dr. Jack Kevorkian, a Michigan physician, began providing terminally ill patients with the means to end their lives through pharmacological injections. Kevorkian's very public involvement in what he saw as a righteous campaign to alleviate people's suffering and allow them to "die with dignity" soon received national attention. He was imprisoned for 8 years following the televised assisted suicide that he performed on a man with amyloid lateral sclerosis (ALS), a terminal nervous system disease.

The purpose of a DNR is not to bring about a patient's death, but to make the patient's wishes clear regarding life support. As such, medical personnel respect the DNR when they must make life-and-death decisions. In contrast, when individuals who have psychological disorders and wish to end their lives embark upon the same plans as a medical patient with a life-threatening illness, clinicians treat them to prevent them from committing suicide. The treatment may include involuntary hospitalization.

The obligation to respect end-of-life wishes may present an ethical conflict for mental health professionals when treating suicidal individuals who complete a DNR stating that they do not wish to obtain life support. The question is whether having a serious psychological disorder that is incapacitating, resistant to treatment, and debilitating is any different from having a similarly untreatable and painful medical illness. Does the individual's right to autonomy, respected with a DNR, differ in this type of case (Cook, Pan, Silverman, & Soltys, 2010)?

On the positive side, strong religious beliefs and spirituality may combine with the social support that membership in a religious community provides to lower an individual's chances of developing depression even in those with high risk. Among the adult children of individuals with major depressive disorder, those with the strongest beliefs were less likely to experience a recurrence over a 10-year period.

8.4 Suicide

Although not a diagnosable disorder, suicidality is one potential diagnostic feature of a major depressive episode. We define suicide as a "fatal self-inflicted destructive act with explicit or inferred intent to die" (Goldsmith, Pellman, Kleinman, & Bunney, 2002) (p. 27). Suicidal behavior runs from a continuum of thinking about ending one's life ("suicidal ideation") to developing a plan, to nonfatal suicidal behavior ("suicide attempt"), to the actual ending of one's life ("suicide") (Centers for Disease Control and Prevention, 2011c).

The rates of completed suicide in the United States are far lower than other reported causes of death, amounting to nearly 35,000 in the year 2007 (Xu, Kochanek, Murphy, & Tejada-Vera, 2010). However, underreporting is likely due to the difficulty of establishing cause of death as intentional rather than unintentional harm. The highest suicide rates by age are for people 45 to 54 years old (17.7 per 100,000). Individuals 75 to 84 years old have the next highest rates (16.3) and also the highest rates for suicide by discharge of firearms (12.2). However, the absolute numbers of suicides is almost twice as high in younger adults (approximately 9,400) than in the 55- to 64-year-old age group (5,069). Within the United States, white men are much more likely than are non-white men to commit suicide.

Around the world, there are approximately one million suicides each year with a global mortality rate of 16 per 100,000. The highest suicide rates around the world are for males in Ukraine (52.1 per 100,000) and for females in Sri Lanka (16.8 per 100,000),

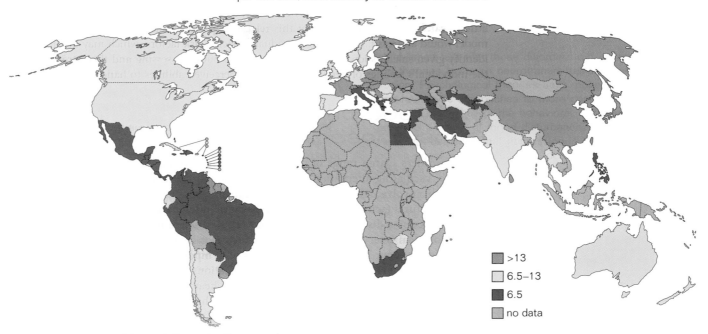

Map of suicide rates
(per 100 000; most recent year available as of 2011)

>13
6.5–13
6.5
no data

FIGURE 8.3   Map of Suicide Rates

and the lowest rates (near 0) for several Latin American and Caribbean countries, Jordan, and Iran (see Figure 8.3). In one-third of countries, young adults are at highest risk of suicide, reflecting worldwide increases in this age group compared to older adults. In Europe and North America, depression and alcohol-use disorders are a major risk factor for suicide with over 90 percent of suicides (in the United States) associated with a psychological disorder (Goldsmith, et al., 2002). In contrast, impulsiveness plays a higher role in the suicides of people from Asian countries (World Health Organization, 2011).

The biopsychosocial perspective is particularly appropriate for understanding why people commit suicide and in many ways parallels the understanding provided from an integrative framework for major depressive disorders. Biological theories emphasize the genetic and physiological contributions that also contribute to the causes of mood disorders. Psychological theories focus on distorted cognitive processes and extreme feelings of hopelessless that characterize suicide victims. From a sociocultural perspective, the variations from country to country and within countries suggest that there are contributions relating to an individual's religious beliefs and values as well as to the degree to which the individual is exposed to life stresses.

The perspective of positive psychology provides a framework for understanding why individuals who are at high risk for the above reasons nevertheless do not commit suicide. The buffering hypothesis of suicidality (Johnson, Wood, Gooding, Taylor, & Tarrier, 2011) describes three aspects of resilience. First, we can distinguish resilience as a separate dimension from risk. You may be at risk of committing suicide, but if you are high on resilience, you are unlikely to do so. Second, we can view both risk and resilience as bipolar dimensions: you can be high on one, both, or neither. Third, resilience is a psychological construct such as the belief that you have the ability to overcome adversity. Resilience is not a statistical correlate of suicidality such as living in a nonstressful environment. An individual can live in a highly stressful environment (high risk), but feel that he or she can cope successfully with these circumstances (high resilience).

The factors that seem to comprise high resilience include the ability to make positive assessments of one's life circumstances and to feel in control over these circumstances. On the negative side, low resilience occurs with high levels of perfectionism and hopelessness. Also, the ability to solve problems, high levels of self-esteem, confidence in one's

larly unkempt, which was unusual as he normally took very good care of himself. Upon approaching David, Mark also noticed that he was smiling and laughing to himself. Mark assumed that he was doing so because he was in a particularly good mood, though David's

not been attending his classes. She decided to write to David's professors, asking for an incomplete grade as it was clear that David was unable to successfully complete his classes in his current state. David stayed with Ann for the next three weeks,

Schizophrenia and

Case Report *continued*

during which time he continued to display bizarre behavior. Ann had hoped that he was going to recover at any given time, but it was becoming clear that he was not improving. When Ann would return home from work, she would find dirty laundry, dishes, pizza boxes, and cigarette ashes all around the house. Often David would stay in his room all day long, coming out only to use the bathroom or eat a meal. When Ann did see him she noticed that he appeared rather sad and withdrawn, barely speaking to her. Normally they had a very close relationship and enjoyed spending time together around the house. Though she worried about her son, she wasn't sure what she could do to help him.

By the time the next school year was about to start, Ann felt that David seemed to have made a great improvement—he was engaging more with her at home and was less messy and the content of his speech was less bizarre. He did seem much more withdrawn in general than he once had been, and was engaging in a minimal amount of activities. He was able to hold a part-time job for about one month in the spring at a gas station, but was fired due to excessively showing up late for work. Otherwise, he mostly stayed in his room listening to music and writing. He spent time with Mark occasionally, though David often cancelled their plans stating that he simply didn't feel like being around people.

David and Ann decided that he should re-enroll at the university, and at David's urging, he was sent to once again live in the dormitories. Two weeks later, David again disappeared. Ann again got a phone call one evening from David, who said he was in Manhattan. She reported that David said he had owed his landlord some money for needing a new set of keys. Ann had been unaware that David even went to New York or that he was living there. David asked for her credit card information over the phone and said that if he didn't come up with the money the landlord was threatening violence against him. When Ann asked where he was exactly, David hung up the phone, and Ann did not hear from him until he showed up at her house three days later, completely disheveled and visibly filthy. He told Ann that he was afraid his roommate was going to burn all of his belongings. While he was telling the story he was laughing. It appeared to Ann that David was once again acting bizarrely and after the previous experience she knew that this time something had to be done. Unsure of where to turn, Ann brought David to the closest general hospital, where he was admitted to the psychiatric ward.

Relevant history: David has no previous history of psychiatric treatment. His mother reported that he had experi-

enced some mild depression earlier in his teenage years. She recalled that David had always been "somewhat different" from his peers, noting that he had only a few close friends throughout his childhood and adolescence.

In terms of family history, Ann reported that David's paternal grandfather had been diagnosed with schizophrenia though there was no other noted family history of mental illness.

Case formulation: It was clear from the presenting story that David had experienced two psychotic episodes over the past few months. His first psychotic break occurred after a major stressor—moving away from home for the first time. This is a typical stressor that occurs around the developmental period when psychotic symptoms may first begin to fully emerge, due to the high base rate of major life events that occur during this time. By Ann's report, David had perhaps displayed some prodromal symptoms as an adolescent, which is also typical in the case of individuals with schizophrenia. David meets diagnostic criteria for schizophrenia, disorganized type, as his symptoms lasted for longer than six months, and included over one month of active symptoms. Further, his general level of functioning was greatly reduced following the first psychotic episode; he was unable to hold a job and remained withdrawn from his interpersonal relationships.

David's delusion about making a deal with a publishing company in New York for a book of poetry did not carry over into his next psychotic episode, which centralized from a different theme. This is typical for individuals suffering from disorganized type of schizophrenia.

Assessment:

Axis I: 295.10 Schizophrenia, Disorganized Type

Axis II: None

Axis III: None

Axis IV: Change in living situation, academic stress

Axis V: 20 (Current), 60 (Highest in past year)

Treatment plan: David will be stabilized on antipsychotic medication while in the hospital, and his psychiatrists will aim to find a suitable maintenance dose for once he is discharged back home. He will be set up with an outpatient psychiatric facility to provide him medication and weekly psychotherapy. It is also recommended that David attain a case manager to help him with vocational activities and to decide whether continuing to pursue a higher educational degree is a possibility, given his past vulnerabilities when enrolled in college.

Sarah Tobin, PhD

9.1 Characteristics of Schizophrenia

The broad category of **schizophrenia** includes a set of disorders in which individuals experience distorted perception of reality and impairment in thinking, behavior, affect, and motivation. Schizophrenia is a serious mental illness, given its potentially broad impact on an individual's ability to live a productive and fulfilling life. Although a significant number of people with schizophrenia eventually manage to live symptom-free lives, many must find ways to adapt their lives to the reality of the illness. In economic terms, schizophrenia also exacts a heavy burden with an annual estimated cost in the United States (in 2002 dollars) of $62.7 billion, which includes direct costs of care and indirect costs of loss of productivity (McEvoy, 2007).

Table 9.1 contains schizophrenia's six diagnostic criteria. The symptoms in Criterion A refer to the **active phase** of the disorder, that is, the period during which the individual's symptoms are most prominent. The symptoms the individual experiences during the active phase fall into two categories: positive symptoms and negative symptoms. **Positive symptoms** are exaggerations or distortions of normal thoughts, emotions, and

schizophrenia
A disorder with a range of symptoms involving disturbances in content of thought, form of thought, perception, affect, sense of self, motivation, behavior, and interpersonal functioning.

active phase
A period in the course of schizophrenia in which psychotic symptoms are present.

positive symptoms
The symptoms of schizophrenia, including delusions, hallucinations, disturbed speech, and disturbed behavior, that are exaggerations or distortions of normal thoughts, emotions, and behavior.

TABLE 9.1 Diagnostic Features of Schizophrenia

For an individual to be diagnosed with schizophrenia, he or she must meet all of the criteria listed in A–F.

A. Two of the following symptoms must be present for a significant portion of time during a one-month period (although this can be less if the individual is successfully treated). At least one symptom must be from the first three categories.

1. Delusions

2. Hallucinations

3. Disorganized speech

4. Grossly abnormal psychomotor behavior

5. Negative symptoms such as restricted affect, avolition, and asociality.

B. Occupational dysfunction

For a significant portion of the time since the onset of the disturbance, one or more major areas of functioning such as work, interpersonal relations, or self-care are markedly below the level achieved prior to the onset (or when the onset is in childhood or adolescence, the person fails to achieve expected level of interpersonal, academic, or occupational achievement).

C. Duration of at least six months

Signs of the disturbance must persist for at least six months. During at least one of these six months, the person must show the active-phase symptoms from Criterion A (or less if the person was successfully treated). The six months may include periods during which the individual had symptoms leading up to (prodromal) or following (residual) an active phase. During these periods, the person must show only negative symptoms or two or more of the active-phase symptoms but in attenuated form.

D. No evidence of schizoaffective or mood disorder

E. Symptoms must not be due to substance abuse disorder or general medical condition

F. Relationship to a Pervasive Developmental Disorder: If there is a history of Autistic Disorder or another Pervasive Developmental Disorder or other communication disorder of childhood onset, the additional diagnosis of schizophrenia is made only if prominent delusions or hallucinations are also present for at least a month (or less if successfully treated).

delusion
Deeply entrenched false belief not consistent with the client's intelligence or cultural background.

hallucination
A false perception not corresponding to the objective stimuli present in the environment.

incoherent
Language that is incomprehensible.

behavior. Referring to Table 9.1, symptoms numbered 1 through 4 under Criterion A fit into this category.

A **delusion** is a deeply entrenched false belief not consistent with the client's intelligence or cultural background. For example, a delusion of persecution is the false belief that someone or something is out to harm you (Table 9.2). A **hallucination** is a false perception not corresponding to the objective stimuli present in the environment. Disorganized speech refers to language that is **incoherent**, meaning that it is incomprehensible. The thought process underlying this type of speech reflects **loosening of associations**; namely, a flow of thoughts that is vague, unfocused, and illogical.

TABLE 9.2 Types and Examples of Delusions

Grandeur

A grossly exaggerated conception of the individual's own importance. Such delusions range from beliefs that the person has an important role in society to the belief that the person is actually Christ, Napoleon, or Hitler.

Control

The feeling that one is being controlled by others, or even by machines or appliances. For example, a man may believe that his actions are being controlled by the radio, which is "forcing" him to perform certain actions against his will.

Reference

The belief that the behavior of others or certain objects or events are personally referring to oneself. For example, a woman believes that a soap opera is really telling the story of her life, or a man believes that the sale items at a local food market are targeted at his own particular dietary deficiencies.

Persecution

The belief that another person or persons are trying to inflict harm on the individual or on that individual's family or social group. For example, a woman feels that an organized group of politically liberal individuals is attempting to destroy the right-wing political organization to which she belongs.

Self-blame

Feelings of remorse without justification. A man holds himself responsible for a famine in Africa because of certain unkind or sinful actions that he believes he has committed.

Somatic

Inappropriate concerns about one's body, typically related to a disease. For example, without any justification, a woman believes she has brain cancer. Adding an even more bizarre note, she believes that ants have invaded her head and are eating away at her brain.

Infidelity

A false belief usually associated with pathological jealousy involving the notion that one's lover is being unfaithful. A man lashes out in violent rage at his wife, insisting that she is having an affair with the mailman because of her eagerness for the mail to arrive each day.

Thought broadcasting

The idea that one's thoughts are being broadcast to others. A man believes that everyone else in the room can hear what he is thinking, or possibly that his thoughts are actually being carried over the airwaves on television or radio.

Thought insertion

The belief that outside forces are inserting thoughts into one's mind. For example, a woman concludes that her thoughts are not her own, but that they are being placed there to control her or upset her.

MINI CASE

Schizophrenia, Catatonic Type

Maria is a 21-year-old college junior who has been psychiatrically hospitalized for a month. The resident assistant in Maria's dormitory brought her to the hospital in December, because she had grown increasingly concerned about Maria's deteriorating behavior over the course of the semester. When Maria returned to college in September, her roommate told others, including the resident assistant, that Maria was acting oddly. For example, she had an annoying habit of repeating other people's words, she stared listlessly out the window, and she ignored her personal hygiene. As the semester's end approached, Maria retreated more and more into her own world, until her behavior reached a point such that she was completely unresponsive to others. In the hospital, she maintains rigid posturing of her body, while staring at the ceiling and spending most of the day in a trancelike state that seems impenetrable. The staff members treating her are in a quandary about what intervention to use for Maria because of her hypersensitivity to most medications.

The symptoms in #5 under Criterion A are **negative symptoms,** meaning that they involve functioning below the normal level of behavior. **Restricted affect,** as the term implies, refers to a narrowing of the range of outward expressions of emotions. **Avolition** is a lack of initiative, either not wanting to take any action or lacking the energy and will to take action. **Asociality** refers to a lack of interest in social relationships, including an inability to empathize and form close relationships with others.

Criterion B is consistent with other *DSM* criteria for psychological disorders involving significant impairment. However, for schizophrenia, the degree of impairment is more far-reaching. Criterion C, indicating the period of disturbance, is also carefully delineated to ensure that individuals receive this diagnosis only if they show a substantial duration of symptoms. Criteria D and E refer to other disorders that should not be present in people diagnosed with schizophrenia. In the case of Criterion D, schizoaffective disorder, which we discuss below, is particularly important to rule out.

Currently, clinicians diagnose an individual with schizophrenia into one of five subtypes based on which symptoms are most prominent: catatonic, disorganized, paranoid, undifferentiated, and residual. It is likely that these subtypes will disappear in *DSM-5* because the members of the schizophrenia task force believe that they are not supported by empirical evidence. Instead, the *DSM-5* authors will most likely recommend conceptualizing schizophrenia as a spectrum or set of related disorders characterized by dimensions.

Clinicians use the diagnosis of **catatonic type** schizophrenia for individuals whose symptoms include a set of extreme motor disturbances that have no direct physiological cause, known as **catatonia.** In one form of catatonia, the afflicted individuals are unable to speak, move, or respond and may hold themselves in the same pose for a considerable length of time ranging from days to weeks. They may stare blankly into space, seeming unaware of the people or objects around them. The poses they hold may be odd and uncomfortable (such as standing on one leg for an extended period of time). In some cases, they may allow others to reposition their bodies and they will then hold that pose for an extended period of time. Alternatively, people showing symptoms of catatonia may instead engage in highly agitated and purposeless motor activity such as running, jumping, or fidgeting, that has no connection with what is going on around them. One option that the *DSM-5* task force is considering is to specify catatonia when it occurs with either a medical condition or in conjunction with disorders other than schizophrenia.

The symptoms that people display with the **disorganized type** of schizophrenia include severe thought disturbance. Their speech may be almost completely indecipherable and rambling, containing **neologisms,** which are invented ("new") words. Unlike words that eventually may become accepted words in a particular language (such as

loosening of associations
Flow of thoughts that is vague, unfocused, and illogical.

negative symptoms
The symptoms of schizophrenia, including affective flattening, alogia, avolition, and anhedonia, that involve functioning below the level of normal behavior.

restricted affect
Narrowing of the range of outward expressions of emotions.

avolition
A lack of initiative, either not wanting to take any action or lacking the energy and will to take action.

asociality
Lack of interest in social relationships.

schizophrenia, catatonic type
A type of schizophrenia characterized by a variety of bodily movement abnormalities.

catatonia
Extreme motor disturbances in a psychotic disorder not attributable to physiological causes

schizophrenia, disorganized type
A type of schizophrenia characterized by a combination of symptoms, including disorganized speech and behavior and flat or inappropriate affect. Even delusions and hallucinations lack a coherent theme.

neologisms
Invented ("new") words.

MINI CASE

Schizophrenia, Disorganized Type

Joshua is a 43-year-old man who stands daily near the steps of a local bank on a busy street corner. Every day, he wears a Red Sox baseball cap, a yellow T-shirt, worn-out hiking shorts, and orange sneakers. Rain or shine, day in and day out, Joshua maintains his post at the bank. Sometimes he is conversing with imaginary people. Without provocation, he sobs miserably. Sometimes he explodes in shrieks of laughter. Police and social workers keep taking him to shelters for the homeless, but Joshua manages to get back on the street before he can receive treatment. He has repeatedly insisted that these people have no right to keep bothering him.

Individuals with schizophrenia present with a wide range of symptoms, based on subtype. Those with the paranoid type typically maintain delusions that they are in danger.

inappropriate affect
The extent to which a person's emotional expressiveness fails to correspond to the content of what is being discussed.

"google"), these words have highly idiosyncratic meanings that are used only by the individual. The behavior of the person with this type of schizophrenia is, as the term implies, highly disorganized and they may be unable to complete such basic tasks of everyday life as bathing. Another characteristic symptom is **inappropriate affect,** meaning that the person's emotional response does not match the social cues present in a situation, such as laughing after hearing a sad story.

Paranoia, the irrational belief or perception that others wish to cause you harm, is the primary symptom of people who have the diagnosis of paranoid schizophrenia. People diagnosed with the **paranoid type** of schizophrenia are preoccupied with one or more bizarre delusions or have auditory hallucinations related to a theme that somebody is persecuting or harassing them. They do not, however, have symptoms of disorganized speech or disturbed behavior.

Clinicians diagnose people with schizophrenia who do not have one predominant symptom as having the **undifferentiated type.** They may fluctuate among the other three types, but do not show a consistent enough pattern to be diagnosed with one of those types. Clinicians use the final type, called **residual,** to diagnose people whose symptoms are mild and do not include prominent symptoms in any of the other categories.

French physician Benedict Morel (1809–1873) first identified schizophrenia as a disease which he coined *démence precocé* (brain dementia of the young). German psychiatrist Emil Kraepelin (1856–1926) renamed the condition *dementia praecox.* He included in the definition a group of nine different clinical forms that shared a similar course in which the afflicted individuals ultimately experienced severe behavioral and cognitive decline. Underlying the different symptoms, Kraepelin believed, was one underlying disease process causing the "weakening" of mental processes.

MINI CASE

Schizophrenia, Paranoid Type

Esther is a 31-year-old unmarried woman who lives with her elderly mother. A belief that the outside air is filled with radio waves that will insert evil thoughts into her head keeps Esther from leaving the house. The windows in her bedroom are "protected" with aluminum foil that "deflect the radio waves." She often hears voices that comment on these radio signals. For example, one comment is the slow, deep voice of an elderly man, who angrily states, "We're going to get these thoughts into your head. Give up your fight!"

MINI CASE

Schizophrenia, Undifferentiated Type

Almost everyone who meets Bruce, a 24-year-old maintenance worker, considers him peculiar. He has a strange look in his eyes, and he often mumbles to himself, as if he were holding a conversation with someone. The words he uses sometimes sound like those of a foreign language, but no one else can understand them. At times, he stares out the window for hours, and he barks angrily at anyone who disturbs him. It seems as though he is lost in a world of fantasy, but he nevertheless manages to keep up with his custodial duties.

Swiss psychologist Eugen Bleuler (1857–1939) proposed a dramatic change in both the name and the understanding of the disorder. According to Bleuler (1911), the disorder was not one, but instead, a set of diseases which he labeled the *schizophrenias*. The term *schizophrenia* is not a splitting of personalities (as in dissociative identity disorder), but a splitting of (schiz) the functions of the mind. Unlike Kraepelin, Bleuler thought it was possible for people with schizophrenia to recover from the disorder.

Clinicians still refer to fundamental features of the disorder that he identified as Bleuler's "Four A's," meaning that it includes:

1. Thought disorder, as might be evident through rambling and incoherent speech ("Association")

2. Disorder of the experience and expression of emotion ("Affect")

3. Inability to make or follow through on decisions ("Ambivalence")

4. Withdrawal from reality ("Autism")

In the decades following Bleuler's work, clinicians in Europe and the United States proposed further distinctions within the schizophrenia grouping. One notable contributor to the debate was the German psychiatrist, Kurt Schneider (1887–1967), who believed that clinicians should only diagnose schizophrenia when an individual has certain "first-rank symptoms." People with these symptoms believe, for example, that someone else is controlling their impulses and feelings. *DSM-III* and the ICD-10 included the first-rank symptoms as part of clinicians' attempts to develop a more precise set of diagnostic criteria than those present in earlier editions of these systems. However, evidence emerged from family inheritance studies showing that relatives of people with schizophrenia developed not only schizophrenia, but also schizophrenia-like disorders. Researchers began to speak of the "schizophrenia spectrum" rather than a single disease entity, leading to new diagnostic categories that included, for example, personality and affective disorders.

paranoia
The irrational belief or perception that others wish to cause you harm.

schizophrenia, paranoid type
A type of schizophrenia characterized by preoccupation with one or more bizarre delusions or with auditory hallucinations that are related to a particular theme of being persecuted or harassed.

schizophrenia, undifferentiated type
A type of schizophrenia characterized by a complex of schizophrenic symptoms, such as delusions, hallucinations, incoherence, or disorganized behavior, that does not meet the criteria for other types of schizophrenia.

schizophrenia, residual type
A type of schizophrenia in which people who have previously been diagnosed as having schizophrenia may no longer have prominent psychotic symptoms but still show some lingering signs of the disorder, such as emotional dullness, social withdrawal, eccentric behavior, or illogical thinking.

MINI CASE

Schizophrenia, Residual Type

Three years after her third hospitalization for schizophrenia, Joyce's condition seems to have stabilized. She has a set routine for taking her antipsychotic medications, for checking in regularly at the Center for Independent Living (which supervises her work placement in a glove factory), and for visiting with her sister and family. At 45, Joyce shows only occasional signs of the illness that, at one time, had totally incapacitated her. She still sometimes becomes preoccupied with the idea that her former mother-in-law is sending her poisoned envelopes in the mail. At other times, she cannot stop herself from pacing the floor. These symptoms never last very long, though, and she is soon able to resume her daily schedule without undue distress.

Toward the DSM-5: Schizophrenia Dimensions

The *DSM*-5 authors are suggesting a major change in their approach to diagnosing schizophrenia. As we mentioned at the beginning of the chapter, it is likely that they will eliminate the types of schizophrenia. Instead, clinicians will assign a diagnosis of schizophrenia to which they will add a rating of the individual's symptoms along a set of dimensions, as Table 9.3 shows.

Using this system, then, clinicians will rate each individual whom they diagnose with schizophrenia on each dimension. A rating of two or higher will be sufficient to determine that the individual fits a Criterion A diagnostic indicator. Clinicians will base their ratings on the individual's behavior within the past month. As of now, the diagnostic criteria for schizophrenia will not change other than to remove the stipulation that a client needs only one symptom from Category A if the delusions are bizarre or hallucinations consist of a voice keeping up a running commentary or two or more voices talking with each other.

By eliminating the subtypes of schizophrenia, the *DSM*-5 authors are hoping to improve both the diagnostic reliability and validity of the system, but also allow researchers and clinicians to have a more quantifiable basis for research on the disorder's causes as well as for treatment planning. For example, a clinician evaluating the results of cognitive behavioral therapy could use the ratings of hallucination and delusion severity to determine whether the intervention is reducing the specific symptoms toward which they are targeting treatment.

The *DSM*-5 authors also decided to include cognitive impairment as a dimension, given the importance of cognitive deficits in current understandings of the individual's ability to carry out social and occupational activities and to carry out the tasks involved in everyday living. Recognizing the importance of cognitive symptoms as central to the disorder, the *DSM*-5 authors are considering whether or not to require that clinicians conduct a neuropsychological assessment as part of the diagnostic process (Reichenberg, 2010).

The *DSM*-5 authors also plan to include ratings of depression and mania for all psychotic disorders. Schizoaffective disorder as a separate entity will most likely eventually disappear as a diagnosis, because evidence continues to accumulate showing that it should not be a separate category.

Although not there yet, the *DSM*-5 authors believe that clinicians will eventually diagnose schizophrenia as a "spectrum" disorder. This would mean, potentially, that even diagnoses long in use in psychiatry would disappear, including schizophreniform disorder, schizoaffective disorder, and the two personality disorders associated with schizophrenic-like symptoms. As we mentioned in the chapter, the *DSM*-5 authors will almost certainly decide to diagnose catatonia not as a type of schizophrenia, but as an associated condition with other psychiatric disorders and/or general medical conditions. They also will be eliminating shared psychotic disorder in the interests of reducing the number of different disorders within the overall category.

If carried out, these changes in the *DSM*-5 will represent a hybrid between the old categorization system and the newer, dimensional approach. By including severity ratings rather than subtypes, they are making it possible for clinicians and researchers to track individuals over time in a quantifiable fashion.

Along with the changing conceptualizations of schizophrenia, researchers and clinicians began to distinguish between the so-called "positive" symptoms of delusions and hallucinations and "negative" symptoms that included social withdrawal, loss of volition, affective flattening, and empty or meaningless speech. Researchers proposed that positive symptoms reflected activated dopamine levels in the nervous system and negative symptoms reflected abnormalities in brain structure (Jablensky, 2010). Increasingly, investigators are beginning to recognize that cognitive impairment plays an important role in this disorder (Reichenberg, 2010). Instead of focusing on the positive symptoms only, they are redefining cognitive deficits as core features of the disorder (Gur & Gur, 2010). We will talk more about these later in the chapter, under psychological perspectives.

Clinicians thought for many years that the lifetime prevalence of schizophrenia was 1 per 100, but several large-scale relatively recent reviews provide a lower estimated lifetime prevalence of 7 per 1,000 (i.e., 0.7 per 1000). People with schizophrenia are two to three times more likely to die compared to others within their age group. The disparities in mortality risk between people with and without schizophrenia are significant. This is in part because the medications that clinicians use to treat people with schizophrenia may contribute to weight gain, which in turn increases the risk of life-threatening diseases. The sex ratio is tilted slightly in the direction of males. For every three men who develop schizophrenia over the course of their lives, two women are affected with the disorder.

Although the prevalence of schizophrenia is relatively low compared to other psychological disorders, a surprisingly high percentage of adults report experiencing minor psychotic symptoms. Reviewing a large number of studies on psychotic symptoms, one group of researchers estimate the lifetime prevalence as about 5% and the prevalence at any one time of about 3% (van Os, Linscott, Myin-Germeys, Delespaul, & Krabbendam, 2009).

remission
Term used to refer to the situation when the individual's symptoms no longer interfere with his or her behavior and are below those required for a *DSM* diagnosis.

Course of Schizophrenia

Schizophrenia may take one of several courses. In the most serious, the individual does not recover and continues to experience continuous positive symptoms. Clinicians define **remission** as occurring when the individual's symptoms no longer interfere with

TABLE 9.3 Dimensional Ratings of Symptoms in Schizophrenia

	Halluci-nations	Delusions	Disorganiza-tion	Abnormal Psycho-motor Behavior	Restricted Emotional Expression	Avolition	Impaired Cognition	Depression	Mania
0	Not Present	Not Present	Not Present	Not Present	Not Present	Not Present	Not Present	Not Present	Not Present
1	Equivocal (severity or duration not sufficient to be considered psychosis)	Equivocal (severity or duration not sufficient to be considered psychosis)	Equivocal (severity or duration not sufficient to be considered disorganiza-tion)	Equivocal (severity or duration not sufficient to be considered abnormal psy-chomotor behavior)	Equivocal decrease in facial expres-sivity, pros-ody, or gestures	Equivocal decrease in self-initiated behavior	Equivocal (cog-nitive function not clearly out-side the range expected for age or SES, i.e., within 1 SD of mean)	Equivocal (some depressed mood, but insufficient symptoms, duration or severity to meet diagnos-tic criteria)	Equivocal (some inflated or irritable mood, but insufficient symptoms, duration, or severity to meet diagnos-tic criteria)
2	Present, but mild (little pressure to act upon voices, not very bothered by voices)	Present, but mild (delusions are not bizarre, or lit-tle pressure to act upon delu-sional beliefs, not very both-ered by beliefs)	Present, but mild (some difficulty fol-lowing speech and/or occa-sional bizarre behavior)	Present, but mild (occa-sional abnor-mal motor behavior)	Present, but mild decrease in facial expressivity, prosody, or gestures	Present, but mild in self-initiated behavior	Present, but mild (some reduction in cognitive func-tion below expected for age and SES, b/w 1 and 2 SD from mean)	Present, but mild (meets criteria for Major Depres-sion, with mini-mum number of symptoms, duration, and severity)	Present, but mild (meets criteria for Mania with minimum num-ber of symp-toms, dura-tion, and severity)
3	Present and moderate (some pres-sure to respond to voices, or is somewhat bothered by voices)	Present and moderate (some pres-sure to act upon beliefs, or is some-what bothered by beliefs)	Present and moderate (speech often difficult to fol-low and/or frequent bizarre behavior)	Present and moderate (fre-quent abnor-mal motor behavior)	Present and moderate decrease in facial expres-sivity, pros-ody, or gestures	Present and moderate in self-initiated behavior	Present and moderate (clear reduction in cognitive function below expected for age and SES, b/w 2 and 3 SD from mean)	Present and moderate (meets criteria for Major Depression with somewhat more than the minimum num-ber of symp-toms, duration, and/or severity	Present and moderate (meets criteria for Mania with somewhat more than the minimum num-ber of symp-toms, duration, and/or severity)
4	Present and severe (severe pressure to respond to voices, or is very bothered by voices)	Present and severe (severe pressure to act upon beliefs, or is very bothered by beliefs)	Present and severe (speech almost impos-sible to follow and/or behav-ior almost always bizarre)	Present and severe (abnor-mal motor behavior almost constant)	Present and severe decrease in facial expres-sivity, pros-ody, or gestures	Present and severe in self-initiated behavior	Present and severe (severe reduction in cognitive func-tion below expected for age and SES, > 3 SD from mean)	Present and severe (meets criteria for Major Depres-sion with many more than the minimum num-ber of symp-toms and/or severity)	Present and severe (meets criteria for Mania with many more than the mini-mum number of symptoms and/or severity)

his or her behavior and are below those required for a *DSM* diagnosis (Lambert, Karow, Leucht, Schimmelmann, & Naber, 2010).

Researchers have long attempted to chart the long-term outcome of schizophrenia and, in particular, how to quantify the phases of the disorder. They are also concerned with how to provide consistent criteria for "recovery." How long and how well does an individual have to be in order to be completely symptom-free? An international team of scientists, the Remission in Schizophrenia Working Group, published a consensus statement in 2005 in which they defined remission according to a combination of symptoms (e.g., delusions, hallucinations, disorganized speech) and time course (a minimum of six months) (Lambert et al., 2010).

The Working Group proposed that clinicians use the remission definition as an abso-lute threshold, meaning that rather than comparing an individual to himself or herself at an earlier point, the clinicians would evaluate the individual according to which

Schizophrenia Diagnosis

As we discussed in the chapter, the outcome of schizophrenia is not necessarily positive. Although many people do achieve recovery, particularly if they were treated early in the course of the disorder, people with schizophrenia nevertheless face substantial risks of relapse over the rest of their lives. Therefore, when a mental health professional provides a diagnosis to an individual with schizophrenia, this is serious news that could lead the individual to experience great distress, much as a person with cancer might feel at receiving that diagnosis.

There are other ethical issues that practitioners face when working with people diagnosed with schizophrenia (Howe, 2008). Not only must mental health professionals attempt to determine whether or not to provide a diagnosis of this serious disorder, but they also face specific questions relevant to the individual's particular symptoms. For example, the clinician may consider it more acceptable to inform clients with delusional disorder that they are receiving medication for anxiety, stress, or dysphoria rather than for having delusions. To inform the client about the actual nature of his or her symptoms might interfere with the ability to form a therapeutic alliance, which could interfere with the ultimate success of the treatment.

To overcome this obstacle, a clinician may decide to share a "partial" truth. Specifically, the clinician may reframe a client's symptoms as strengths. Rather than seeing a client's attachments to inanimate objects as a symptom, for example, the clinician may reframe the behavior as proving the client's exceptional capacity for caring.

A second ethical dilemma involves balancing a client's desire to succeed in life with the reality that due to the disorder, he or she may be unable to realize these ambitions. The stress of, for example, a competitive career might push the client over the edge into a relapse. Should the clinician try to protect the client from undertaking this venture or respect the client's autonomy to make his or her own decisions?

As if these two challenges were not enough, consider the situation in which a clinician wishes to involve the client's family in treatment. As we observed in the chapter, overinvolved and critical family members can exacerbate a client's symptoms. Should the clinician try to persuade the client to make the family part of treatment, knowing that this could potentially be helpful to the client's overall chances of recovery? Or would such persuasion be unethical, again, violating the client's autonomy?

Finally, given that people with a family history of schizophrenia have increased risk of developing the disorder, how much should clinicians warn high-risk adolescents or young adults? On the one hand, telling people who are asymptomatic that they may develop this serious illness could in and of itself provoke an episode. On the other hand, by not telling those at genetic risk about the possibility of their developing schizophrenia may mean that they don't take preventive steps.

Howe (2008) suggests that mental health professionals can navigate these ethical dilemmas by using an "ethical sliding scale." They can base their ethical decisions by taking into account the client's ability to achieve insight, the strength of their relationship with the client, and the nature of and strength of the client's relationship with family. Although respecting the client's autonomy should be the primary guiding principle, clinicians should balance this principle against the client's decision-making abilities.

symptoms he or she displays and for how long. These criteria would help to reduce the variation in the way various individuals, including the client, define remission. For example, people with schizophrenia tend to judge their own remission by how well they are feeling. Psychiatrists base their judgments on whether or not the individual continues to meet *DSM-IV* criteria.

Compared to other psychological disorders, the course and outcome are poorer for people with schizophrenia (Jobe & Harrow, 2010). During the first 10 to 15 years, people with schizophrenia have more recurrent episodes and their chances of completely recovering, even after the first 10 years, are worse than those of people with other disorders. Most people continue to experience psychotic symptoms and disordered thinking, as well as negative symptoms. They are less able to obtain or keep a job. On the positive side, however, if they receive current treatment during their acute phase, over 40% can recover (i.e., have no symptoms or hospitalizations and at least part-time work) for one or more years at a time. Some people with schizophrenia can even show complete recovery for the remainder of their lives.

Researchers who follow people with schizophrenia for extended periods of time propose a model in which 25 to 35 percent show chronic psychotic symptoms. However, even when they are symptom-free, they may still be impaired in their functioning and adjustment. The factors that contribute to poorer prognosis include poorer cognitive skills, a longer period of time without treatment, substance abuse, a poorer course of early development, higher vulnerability to anxiety, and negative life events. In addition, overinvolvement of family members in the individual's life, as we discuss later in the chapter, also predicts poorer outcome (Jobe & Harrow, 2010).

Single men seem to be at particularly high risk if they possess these additional characteristics (Gómez-de-Regil et al., 2010). Men also are more likely to experience negative symptoms, to have poorer social support networks, and to have poorer functioning over time than females (Willhite et al., 2008). The prognosis for individuals from developing (agricultural-based) countries is better than that for individuals from developed (industrial) nations due to greater resources for treating affected individuals (Hopper, Harrison, Janca, & Sartorius, 2007).

9.2 Other Psychotic Disorders

For many years, up through the early 1980s, with no comprehensive diagnostic criteria at their disposal, psychiatrists used schizophrenia as a catchall term applied to the majority of people requiring institutionalization for psychotic symptoms. Unfortunately, this meant that even for people experiencing a brief episode or a disorder other than schizophrenia, the diagnosis might remain with them for years in a so-called "residual" phase. Making the situation worse was the fact that psychiatrists would prescribe their clients antipsychotic medication for life to prevent their symptoms from recurring. This situation began to change during the 1970s as researchers and clinicians developed a better understanding of the nature of psychotic disorders.

Currently, the *DSM* includes a set of so-called "psychotic" disorders that share three features: (1) each is a form of psychosis representing a serious break with reality, (2) the condition is not caused by a known cognitive impairment, and (3) there is no mood disturbance as a primary symptom.

Brief Psychotic Disorder

As the term implies, **brief psychotic disorder** is a diagnosis that clinicians use when an individual develops symptoms of psychosis that do not persist past a short period of time. To receive this diagnosis, an individual must experience one of four symptoms, which include delusions, hallucinations, disorganized speech, and grossly disorganized or catatonic behavior. The diagnosis requires that the individual experience symptoms for more than a day, but recover in less than a month.

In assigning this diagnosis, the clinician must take into account the client's cultural background. As we discussed in Chapter 2,

brief psychotic disorder
A disorder characterized by the sudden onset of psychotic symptoms that are limited to a period of less than a month.

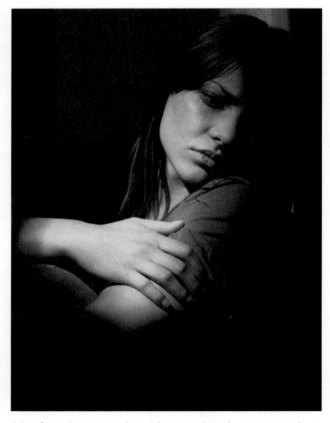

A brief psychotic episode can last anywhere between one day and one month.

MINI CASE

Brief Psychotic Disorder

Anthony is a 22-year-old senior at a prestigious small college. His family has traditionally held high standards for Anthony, and his father had every expectation that his son would go on to enroll at Harvard Law School. Anthony felt intensely pressured as he worked day and night to maintain a high grade-point average, while diligently preparing for the national examination for admission to law schools. His social life became devoid of any meaningful contact. He even began skipping meals, because he did not want to take time away from studying. When Anthony received his scores for the law school admission exam, he was devastated, because he knew that they were too low to allow him to get into any of the better law schools. He began crying uncontrollably, wandering around the dormitory hallways, screaming obscenities, and telling people that there was a plot on the part of the college dean to keep him from getting into law school. After two days of this behavior, Anthony's resident adviser convinced him to go to the infirmary, where clinicians diagnosed and treated his condition. After a week of rest and some medication, Anthony returned to normal functioning and was able to assess his academic situation more rationally.

cultures vary in what the members of that culture consider an appropriate response pattern. The clinician also must take note of whether the client has experienced a recent stressor, such as a flood, the loss of a close relative, or an automobile accident. Clinicians also note if a woman develops this disorder within four weeks of giving birth.

Schizophreniform Disorder

schizophreniform disorder
A disorder characterized by psychotic symptoms that are essentially the same as those found in schizophrenia, except for the duration and chronic nature of the symptoms; specifically, symptoms usually last from 1 to 6 months.

People receive a diagnosis of **schizophreniform disorder** if they experience Criteria A, D, and E of schizophrenic disorder for a period of from one to six months. If they have their symptoms for longer than six months, the clinician would conduct an evaluation to determine whether they should receive a diagnosis of schizophrenia. People have good chances of recovering, and not developing schizophrenia, when they show a rapid development of symptoms (within a span of 4 weeks), confusion or perplexity while in the peak of the episode, and good social and personal functioning prior to the episode. They are also likely to have a good prognosis if they do not show the negative symptoms of apathy, withdrawal, and asociality.

MINI CASE

Schizophreniform Disorder

At the time that Edward developed a psychological disorder, he was 26 years old and worked for a convenience store chain. Although family and friends always regarded Edward as unusual, he had not experienced psychotic symptoms. This all changed as he grew more and more disturbed over the course of several months. His mother thought that he was just "stressed out" because of his financial problems, but Edward did not seem concerned about such matters. He gradually developed paranoid delusions and became preoccupied with reading the Bible. What brought his disturbance to the attention of his supervisors was the fact that he had submitted an order to the district office for 6,000 loaves of bread. He had scribbled at the bottom of the order form, "Jesus will multiply the loaves." When his supervisors questioned this inappropriate order, Edward became enraged and insisted that they were plotting to prevent him from fighting world hunger. Paranoid themes and bizarre behaviors also surfaced in Edward's dealings with his wife and children. Following two months of increasingly disturbed behavior, Edward's boss urged him to see a psychiatrist. With rest and relatively low doses of antipsychotic medication, Edward returned to normal functioning after a few weeks of hospitalization.

MINI CASE

Schizoaffective Disorder

At the time of her admission to a psychiatric hospital, Hazel was a 42-year-old mother of three children. She had a 20-year history of schizophrenia-like symptoms, and she experienced periodic episodes of mania. Her schizophrenia-like symptoms included delusions, hallucinations, and thought disorder. These symptoms were fairly well controlled by antipsychotic medications, which she received by injection every two weeks. She was also treated with lithium to control her manic episodes; however, she often skipped her daily dose because she liked "feeling high." On several occasions following extended periods of abstinence from the lithium, Hazel became manic. Accelerated speech and bodily activity, sleepless nights, and erratic behavior characterized these episodes. At the insistence of her husband and her therapist, Hazel would resume taking her lithium, and shortly thereafter her manic symptoms would subside, although her schizophrenia-like symptoms were still somewhat evident.

Schizoaffective Disorder

In **schizoaffective disorder** individuals with a mood disorder (depressive or bipolar) also have delusions and/or hallucinations. The diagnosis is made more complicated by the fact that individuals must have at least a two-week period in which they have no mood disorder symptoms, but do have psychotic symptoms. However, for the majority of the duration of their illness, they must have a major mood disorder as well as symptoms of schizophrenia. In other words, they must have both a mood and a psychotic disorder, but at least two weeks during which their delusions and/or hallucinations are the only symptoms that they show.

schizoaffective disorder
A psychotic disorder involving the experience of a major depressive episode, a manic episode, or a mixed episode while also meeting the diagnostic criteria for schizophrenia.

Delusional Disorders

People with delusional disorders have as their only symptom delusions that have lasted for at least one month. They receive this diagnosis if they have no other symptoms of schizophrenia and have never met the criteria for schizophrenia. In fact, these individuals can function very well and they do not seem odd to others except when they talk about their particular delusion.

Based on which delusional theme is prominent, clinicians diagnose individuals with delusional disorders into one of five types. People with the **erotomanic type** of delusional disorder falsely believe that another person is in love with them. The target of their delusion is usually a person of higher status than they are. For example, a woman may be certain that a famous singer is in love with her and that he communicates secret love

erotomanic type
Delusional disorder in which individuals falsely believe that another person is in love with them.

MINI CASE

Delusional Disorder

Paul is a 28-year-old man who has recently experienced tremendous stress at his job. Although he has avoided dwelling on his job problems, he has begun to develop irrational beliefs about his lover, Elizabeth. Despite Elizabeth's repeated vows that she is consistently faithful in the relationship, Paul has become obsessed with the belief that Elizabeth is sexually involved with another person. Paul is suspicious of everyone with whom Elizabeth interacts, questioning her about every insignificant encounter. He searches her closet and drawers for mysterious items, looks for unexplained charges on the charge card bills, listens in on Elizabeth's phone calls, and has contacted a private investigator to follow Elizabeth. Paul is now insisting that they move to another state.

MINI CASE

Shared Psychotic Disorder

Julio and Carmen, both in their thirties, had been dating for six months. Having met at the accounting office where they both worked, they kept their intimate relationship a secret from co-workers at the insistence of Julio, the dominant partner in the relationship. Carmen submitted, and the couple kept exclusive company with each other. Most of their conversation centered on Julio's unwavering belief, which Carmen had come to share, that other people at their office did not like them and that several people wanted them fired. The two of them often stayed after work to search the desks and files of co-workers for evidence that would support Julio's notion. They construed the slightest comment directed toward either of them as evidence of this plot. On the rare occasions when they talked to co-workers, they immediately recorded the conversation in a secret log book. They refused to use the office computer, because they were convinced that it was programmed to keep tabs on them. Eventually, both lost their jobs, but not for the reasons they had constructed. Their odd behaviors aroused so much suspicion that the office routine was disrupted, and they had to be let go.

grandiose type
An exaggerated view of oneself as possessing special and extremely favorable personal qualities and abilities.

jealous type
Delusional disorder in which individuals falsely believe that their romantic partner is unfaithful to them.

messages to her in his songs. Convinced that they are extremely important, in contrast, characterizes people who have the **grandiose type** of delusional disorder. For example, a man may believe that he is the Messiah waiting for a sign from heaven to begin his active ministry. In the **jealous type** of delusional disorder, individuals are certain that their romantic partner is unfaithful to them. They may even construct a plan to entrap their partner to prove the partner's infidelity. People with the **persecutory type** of delusional disorder believe that someone or someone close to them is treating them in a malevolent manner. They may, for example, become convinced that their neighbors are deliberately poisoning their water. People with the **somatic type** of delusional disorder believe that they have a medical condition. Unlike people with an anxiety disorder, people with a delusional disorder have these beliefs, but they are not anxiety based.

The *DSM-IV* also lists **shared psychotic disorder** as a diagnosis for clinicians to use in cases when one or more people develop a delusional system as a result of a close

Shared psychotic disorder, also referred to as "folie à deux" involves at least two people who engage in the same delusion.

relationship with a psychotic person who is delusional. When two people are involved in this disorder, clinicians apply the term *folie à deux* (folly of two) to the pair. Occasionally, three or more people or the members of an entire family are involved. Because this disorder is very rare, and would be covered by the category of delusional disorder, the *DSM-5* authors recommended dropping it as a separate diagnosis. There is very little research on the disorder, and when it does exist, clinicians can indicate the fact that a delusion is shared on Axis IV.

9.3 Theories and Treatment of Schizophrenia

Theories accounting for the origin of schizophrenia have traditionally fallen into two categories: biological and psychological. In the first part of this century, a debate raged between proponents of both sides. However, it's now clear that both biology and experience interact in the determination of schizophrenia and have built complex theoretical models that incorporate multiple factors (McGuffin, 2004). Researchers base these models on the concept of vulnerability, proposing that individuals have a biologically determined predisposition to developing schizophrenia, but that the disorder develops only when certain environmental conditions are in place. As we look at each of the contributions to a vulnerability model, keep in mind that no single theory contains the entire explanation.

Biological Perspectives

Theories Biological explanations of schizophrenia have their origins in the writings of Kraepelin, who thought of schizophrenia as a disease caused by a degeneration of brain tissue. Kraepelin's ideas paved the way for the later investigation of such factors as brain structure and genetics, which are now recognized as contributing to an individual's biological vulnerability to schizophrenia.

Scientists first became interested in possible brain abnormalities in people with schizophrenia in the nineteenth century. The methods available to these researchers were not up to the task, however. Instead of the sophisticated brain imaging techniques that researchers now can use, early investigators could only examine the brains from autopsied individuals. Not only were the autopsy-based measures imprecise, but researchers could not draw connections between the individual's behavior and brain abnormalities. The technologies of computerized tomography (CT, or CAT, scan) and magnetic resonance imaging (MRI) are enabling researchers in schizophrenia to take pictures of the living brain and analyze those pictures quantitatively, and in real time.

One of the earliest discoveries to emerge from neuroimaging methods were that the brains of people with schizophrenia have enlarged ventricles, which are the cavities within the brain that hold cerebrospinal fluid. This condition, called ventricular enlargement, often occurs in people with schizophrenia alongside cortical atrophy, a wasting away of brain tissue. The loss of brain volume is particularly pronounced in the prefrontal lobes, the area of the brain responsible for planning as well as for inhibiting thoughts and behaviors (Molina, Sanz, Sarramea, Benito, & Palomo, 2005). The prefrontal lobe also shows abnormal fluctuations in people who are in the early stages of the disorder (Huang et al., 2010). Over the course of the illness, the cortex shows pronounced thinning throughout the brain, but particularly in the frontal lobes and the temporal lobes, the parts of the brain that process auditory information (van Haren et al., 2011).

Neuroimaging studies using CT scans, fMRIs, and PET scans show widespread, though subtle, changes in brain structures that may affect the individual's thinking by interfering with the integration of neural and cognitive functioning (Shenton, Whitford, & Kubicki, 2010). Specifically, through fMRI studies, people with schizophrenia have a

persecutory type
Delusional disorder in which individuals falsely believe that someone or someone close to them is treating them in a malevolent manner.

somatic type
Delusional disorder in which individuals falsely believe that they have a medical condition.

shared psychotic disorder
Delusional disorder in which one or more people develop a delusional system as a result of a close relationship with a psychotic person who is delusional.

REAL STORIES

Elyn Saks: Schizophrenia

"If you are a person with mental illness, the challenge is to find the life that's right for you. But in truth, isn't that the challenge for all of us, mentally ill or no? My good fortune is not that I've recovered from mental illness. I have not, nor will I ever. My good fortune lies in having found my life."

In her memoir, *The Center Cannot Hold: My Journey through Madness*, UCLA professor Elyn Saks tells the moving story of her lifelong struggle with schizophrenia. Her story provides a unique perspective on one of the most debilitating psychological disorders, and offers a firsthand account of the experience of psychosis. Elyn begins the book by describing the first signs of her illness as a child growing up in an upper-middle class family in Miami, Florida.

"When I was about eight, I suddenly needed to do things a little differently than my parents would have wished me to do them. I developed, for loss of a better word, a few little quirks. For instance, I couldn't leave my room unless my shoes were all lined up in my closet. Or beside my bed. Some nights, I couldn't shut off my bedroom light until the books on my shelves were organized just so." Elyn also recalls early dissociative experiences that began around this same time. These experiences of "disorganization" as she refers to them initially elicited fear. This was partially because she was unable to express what was happening to her with her family who were otherwise supportive and caring.

Throughout her formative years, Elyn continued to experience what she now recognizes as prodromal symptoms of schizophrenia. At the time her experiences caused her to feel paranoid around others, afraid that they would find out her secret. She attended college at Vanderbilt University, and at first greatly enjoyed her newfound independence. However, within the first two weeks of school, away from the protective clutches of her family and all the comforts that came along with being taken care of, as she puts it "everything slowly began to unravel." Her inability to perform self-care activities such as bathing signaled the start of her illness, and Elyn had several, very brief psychotic episodes, which resolved without intervention. In the book, she describes the insidious nature of her illness when it began to manifest itself.

"Schizophrenia rolls in like a slow fog, becoming imperceptibly thicker as time goes on. At first, the day is bright enough, the sky is clear, the sunlight warms your shoulders. But soon, you notice a haze beginning to gather around you, and the air feels not quite so warm . . . For me (and for many of us), the first evidence of that fog is a gradual deterioration of basic common-sense hygiene . . . Once away from my parents' watchful eyes, I grew inconsistent about asking myself the taken-for-granted questions."

After returning home from her freshman year, Elyn continued to experience paranoia and occasional hallucinations though now in addition to those symptoms she was feeling depressed and lethargic. Her parents took her to see a psychiatrist whose only insight to her condition was that she "needed help." Once Elyn returned to Vanderbilt for her sophomore year, her symptoms subsided as she found comfort in her studies and with a close-knit group of friends. With strong social support, Elyn was able to remain in a relatively stable condition for the rest of her time in college. However, that comfort quickly turned to fear as graduation approached and she felt the fragile structure that kept her content was about to be shaken.

Elyn won a highly prestigious Marshall scholarship to study philosophy at Oxford University in England. She was terrified of living in a new country, so far away from everything she knew, and particularly of being away from her routine and friends at college. Indeed, after just a few weeks at Oxford, Elyn's still unnamed illness again began to take hold, and her fear of

Elyn Saks has enjoyed a successful law career despite suffering from schizophrenia

her illness turned into suicidal ideation. At the urging of a friend, she saw a psychiatrist and admitted that she had thoughts of ending her life. She entered a day treatment program at a psychiatric hospital though she had no idea just how ill she was. "This was like a bad cold, or a bout of the flu. Something had gone wrong; it was simply a matter of finding out what that something was and fixing it," she writes of her perspective on her symptoms at the time.

At the hospital, Elyn received intensive psychotherapy and spent the rest of her time working on her studies. Her program did not require her to attend classes, and so she was able to isolate herself in her apartment while she worked, which made it difficult for her to realize the extent of her psychological difficulties. She was not taking any medication at the time, and her ability to attain a firm grasp on reality slowly deteriorated. When she reported to her psychiatrist that her suicidal ideation had worsened, she was urged to become a full-time patient at the hospital where she remained for two weeks. After beginning a course of psychotropic medication, Elyn eventually felt well enough to return to her studies though she soon began to decompensate. She returned to the hospital where she languished in psychosis and depression for several months. Once she was stabilized, her psychiatrist recommended that she enter psychoanalysis. Determined to finish her degree at Oxford, Elyn continued

at her studies while seeing a psychoanalyst for five days per week. Even after finishing her studies, which ended up taking 4 years instead of 2, Elyn felt that her relationship with her analyst was helping her so much so that she decided to stay in England to continue their work together for 2 more years. In the book, Elyn describes her experience of living with her illness during this time in her life. "Completely delusional, I still understood essential aspects of how the world worked. For example, I was getting my schoolwork done, and I vaguely understood the rule that in a social setting, even with the people I most trusted, I could not ramble on about my psychotic thoughts. To talk about killing children, or burning whole worlds, or being able to destroy cities with my mind was not part of polite conversation . . . At times, though, I was so psychotic that I could barely contain myself. The delusions expanded into full-blown hallucinations, in which I could clearly hear people whispering. I could hear my name being called when no one was physically around—in a corner of the library, or late at night, in my bedroom where I slept alone. Sometimes, the noise I heard was so overwhelming it drowned out almost all other sound."

After leaving England, Elyn decided to attend law school at Yale University, where she continued to struggle with psychotic episodes that resulted in several lengthy hospitalizations though she was eventually able to finish her de-

gree. She had discovered a passion for helping psychiatric patients after working in a mental health law clinic, fueled by her intimate understanding of the experience of herself being a psychiatric patient. Throughout her career she has worked toward creating a high legal standard of care for psychiatric patients in the United States.

Elyn eventually took a position at the law school at UCLA where she continues to work as a tenured faculty member. Over the years she has worked hard to keep her psychotic symptoms at bay with help from a combination of talk therapy, medication, and social support from her husband and close friends. Though Elyn struggled for many years to accept the reality of her illness, she now accepts her diagnosis and all that it entails. At the end of the book, Elyn writes that she feels grateful to be one of the lucky few able to successfully live with schizophrenia. She dispels the idea that she has had a better life because of schizophrenia, but instead states that she has been able to live her life despite it. Often throughout her career in discussing legal aspects of mental health treatment she noticed others stigmatizing those with mental illness, not believing that they could lead normal lives or even be trusted to not be violent. When explaining why she decided to write the book and "out" herself as mentally ill, she describes that she decided to write the book because "I want to bring hope to those who suffer from schizophrenia, and understanding to those who do not."

wide range of deficits including poor performance on motor tasks, difficulties in working memory, poorer attention, reduced word fluency, deficient processing of emotional information, and impaired decision making (Gur & Gur, 2010). Researchers are also using **diffusion tensor imaging (DTI),** a method to investigate abnormalities in the white matter of the brain. This method tracks the activity of water molecules as they diffuse along the length of axons, making it possible to investigate abnormalities in neural pathways (Figure 9.1). The results of DTI studies show that in addition to its association with changes in brain structures, schizophrenia is related to loss of connectivity among brain regions caused by changes in neural pathways (Coyle, Balu, Benneyworth, Basu, & Roseman, 2010).

diffusion tensor imaging (DTI) A method to investigate abnormalities in the white matter of the brain.

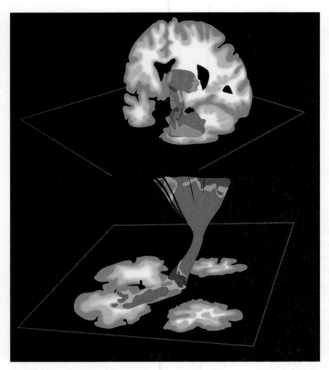

FIGURE 9.1 DTI Scan of Brain of Individual with Schizophrenia

Diffusion tensor imaging (DTI) yields images of nerve fiber tracts. Different colors indicate the organization of the nerve fibers. Here, a tract originating at the cerebellum is superimposed on a structural-MRI image of a cross section of the brain.

neurodevelopmental hypothesis
Theory proposing that schizophrenia is a disorder of development that arises during the years of adolescence or early adulthood due to alterations in the genetic control of brain maturation.

extrapyramidal symptoms (EPS)
Motor disorders involving rigid muscles, tremors, shuffling movement, restlessness, and muscle spasms affecting their posture.

Structural changes alone, as important as they may be, cannot entirely explain what happens to the brain to increase the individual's susceptibility to developing schizophrenia. Based on the observation that a drug to relax surgical patients seemed to have calming effects, French physicians began to experiment with its use on patients with psychotic disorders. Physicians believed that the drug, chlorpromazine, had its effect by blocking dopamine receptors, giving rise to the dopamine hypothesis of schizophrenia (Carlsson, 1988). More specifically, the D2 receptor seems to be the one involved in schizophrenia (Hirvonen et al., 2005). Gamma-aminobutyric acid (GABA), an inhibitory neurotransmitter, also appears to be involved in schizophrenia. Changes in the N-methyl-D-aspartate (NMDA) receptors, which are GABA receptors, also seem to play a role. NMDA receptors help to promote new learning in the brain by helping to build synapses. These alterations may, in turn, be related to changes in the neurons that make them less capable of supporting memory and learning. Symptoms of schizophrenia related to increased excitation, decreased inhibition, and altered cognitive functioning would thus correspond to these changes in the neurotransmitters (Coyle et al., 2010).

Research on patterns of family inheritance supports the idea that schizophrenia is, at least in part, a genetically caused disorder with heritability estimates ranging from 64 to 81 percent (Lichtenstein et al., 2009; Sullivan, Kendler, & Neale, 2003). Having established that there is a high heritability to schizophrenia, researchers have since moved on to attempting to locate the specific genes involved and to understanding the factors that increase the genetically vulnerable person's chances of actually developing the disorder. The combination of neuroimaging and genomics shows, further, that siblings show fMRI abnormalities less severe than those that appear in the brains of affected individuals (Gur & Gur, 2010).

At present, researchers have identified at least 19 possible genes dispersed over chromosomes 1, 2, 5, 6, 8, 11, 13, 14, 19, and 22. Some of the functions served by these genes involve the neurotransmitters we've already discussed, including dopamine and GABA, as well as serotonin and glutamate. These genetic abnormalities could also affect brain development, synaptic transmission, immune functioning, and the manufacturing of important proteins involved in neurotransmission (Tiwari, Zai, Muller, & Kennedy, 2010). For example, some individuals with schizophrenia have a particular allele in the gene for the enzyme catechol-O-methyltransferase (COMT) that could be responsible for decreased activity in the prefrontal area of the cortex. People who have inherited this allele from both of their parents are less likely to engage the prefrontal cortex and hippocampus when performing memory tasks in the lab (Gur & Gur, 2010).

However, in contrast to disorders such as dementia, which cause a progressive loss of neural tissue in adulthood, researchers believe that the changes in the brains of people with schizophrenia represent an evolution over time, beginning early in life and proceeding throughout the course of the disorder.

According to the **neurodevelopmental hypothesis** (Andreasen, 2010), schizophrenia is a disorder of development that arises during the years of adolescence or early adulthood due to alterations in the genetic control of brain maturation. Individuals with schizophrenia may have a genetic vulnerability, which becomes evident if they are exposed to certain risks during early brain development. These risks can occur during the prenatal period in the form of viral infections, malnutrition, or exposure to toxins. They may also occur during or shortly after birth if they are exposed to injuries or viral infections, or if their mothers suffer birth complications. The harm to their developing brains may show up early in life in the form of decreased head size, motor impairments, and impairments in cognition and social functioning. Support for the neurodevelopmental hypothesis also comes from the fact that individuals having their first psychotic episodes have a number of inexplicable brain abnormalities as the result of the illness. As their illness proceeds, they may show continued deleterious changes through a process of "neuroprogression" in which the effects of schizophrenia interact with brain changes caused by normal aging.

Treatments   The primary biological treatment for schizophrenia is antipsychotic medication. As we discussed in Chapter 4, psychiatrists prescribe two categories of antipsychotic medication, also called neuroleptics (derived from the Greek words meaning "to seize the nerve"). In addition to their sedating qualities, neuroleptics reduce the frequency and severity of the individual's psychotic symptoms. The two main categories of neuroleptics are the so-called "typical" or "first generation" and "atypical" or "second generation" antipsychotics.

As we discussed in Chapter 4, the first medication that doctors used in treating schizophrenia was the typical antipsychotic chlorpromazine (Thorazine), a sedative developed by Paul Charpentier, a French chemist. Haloperidol (Haldol) is another typical antipsychotic medication that was in widespread use. These neuroleptics seem to have their effect on reducing symptoms primarily by acting on the dopamine receptor system in areas of the brain associated with delusions, hallucinations, and other positive symptoms.

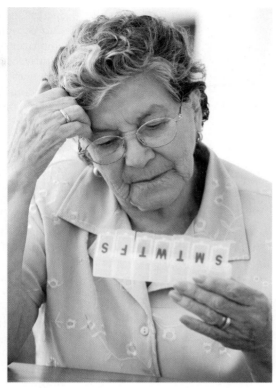

Dementia often causes secondary physical problems when those who suffer from it are unable to take the correct dosages of their medication.

In addition to being highly sedating, causing a person to feel fatigued and listless, the typical antipsychotics also have serious undesirable consequences. These include **extrapyramidal symptoms (EPS),** which are motor disorders involving rigid muscles, tremors, shuffling movement, restlessness, and muscle spasms affecting their posture. After several years, they can also develop **tardive dyskinesia,** another motor disorder, which consists of involuntary movements of their mouth, arms, and trunk of the body.

The distressing side effects and failure of typical antipsychotics to treat negative symptoms of schizophrenia led psychiatric researchers on a search to alternatives that would both be more effective and not cause tardive dyskinesia. The atypical (second generation) antipsychotics operate on both serotonin and dopamine neurotransmitters and hence, are also called serotonin-dopamine antagonists. Clinicians thought that these later medications resulted in fewer side effects and helped in treating negative symptoms. However, doctors discovered that one of the first atypical antipsychotics, clozapine (Clozaril), had potentially lethal side effects by causing agranulocytosis, a condition that affects the functioning of the white blood cells. Clinicians now recommend it only under very controlled conditions and only when other medications do not work. Instead, clinicians can now prescribe one of a number of safer atypical antipsychotics, including risperidone (Risperdal), olanzapine (Zyprexa), and quetiapine (Seroquel).

tardive dyskinesia
Motor disorder that consists of involuntary movements of the mouth, arms, and trunk of the body.

Unfortunately, even medications in the newer group of atypical antipsychotics are not without potentially serious side effects. They can cause metabolic disturbances, particularly weight gain, increases in blood cholesterol, and greater insulin resistance, placing them at greater risk of diabetes and cardiovascular disease.

Because of the many complexities in the biological treatment of individuals with schizophrenia, researchers and clinicians

Psychiatrists strive to find an appropriate regimen of medication in order to prevent individuals with psychotic disorders from experiencing highly disruptive psychotic symptoms.

increasingly recognize the need to take the individual's medical and psychiatric profile into account. For treatment-resistant clients, clozapine is the only approach that has empirical support. In other instances, clinicians may attempt to find a combination of antipsychotics or a combination of antipsychotics with other classes of medications. The next question becomes one of determining how long to maintain a client on medications balancing the value of continued treatment against the risk of relapse and possible health hazards that occur with their use over time (Kane & Correll, 2010).

Psychological Perspectives

Theories   With increasing evidence suggesting specific genetic and neuro-physiological abnormalities in the brains of people with schizophrenia, researchers are becoming increasingly interested in finding out more about the role of cognitive deficits in causing the disorder. As we mentioned earlier, delusions and hallucinations are obviously disruptive to a person's life and critically important to the diagnosis of the disorder. However, these symptoms, as surprising as it may seem, may not be at the core of the disorder. Instead, cognitive functions affected by schizophrenia may be more fundamental to understanding the disorder's central features.

Figure 9.2 shows the average impairment of people with schizophrenia on a variety of neuropsychological tests. They have lower than average intellectual ability, but also deficits in the specific areas of attention, declarative memory (long-term recall of information), and processing speed. Although it is possible that these abnormalities are the result of other factors that can influence how people with schizophrenia perform on these tests, such as age, educational background, use of medication, or severity or length of illness. However, people who are experiencing positive symptoms (delusions and hallucinations) perform inconsistently on these tasks. Overall, estimates of how many people with schizophrenia are cognitively impaired vary from 55 to between 70 and 80 percent (Reichenberg, 2010).

People with schizophrenia also show deficits in the area of social cognition, meaning that they have difficulty perceiving the emotions of others. This deficit in social cognition is particularly problematic when they are given the task of recognizing the emotions of fear, anger, and disgust. People with schizophrenia are, however, better at identifying

FIGURE 9.2 Neuropsychological Performance Profile of Schizophrenia

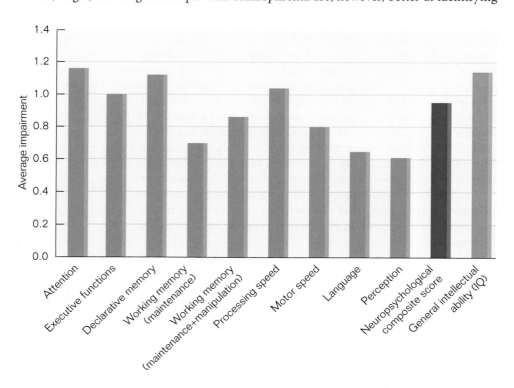

mild happiness in the facial expressions of other people. Not only do they have difficulty recognizing emotions from a person's face, but their brains become less activated when given a social cognition task (Gur & Gur, 2010).

These impairments in cognitive functioning can lead to many problems in the individual's daily life, setting up a vicious cycle. Their problems in memory, planning, and processing speed, for example, interfere with their ability to hold down mentally challenging jobs. The limitations they have in social cognition make it difficult for them to work in people-oriented jobs. With an inability to maintain consistent employment, they can slip into poverty which, as we will see in the next section, further stresses their abilities to lead productive lives. Moreover, living in high-poverty areas places them at risk for becoming involved in substance abuse, which can contribute to the symptoms they experience as a result of their disorder.

Treatments For many years, the most common psychological interventions for people with schizophrenia involved behavioral treatments intended to lower the frequency of an individual's maladaptive behaviors that interfere with social adjustment and functioning. These interventions typically employed a **token economy** (Ayllon & Azrin, 1965), in which institutionalized individuals received rewards for acting in socially appropriate ways. The expectation was that, over time, the new behaviors would become habitual and not dependent on reinforcement by tokens. However, this form of intervention is no longer practical given that most individuals with schizophrenia receive treatment in the community. In addition, there is little data on its effectiveness, and with clinicians focusing on evidence-based treatment, the profession cannot justify its use (Dickerson, Tenhula, & Green-Paden, 2005).

token economy
A form of contingency management in which a client who performs desired activities earns chips or tokens that can later be exchanged for tangible benefits.

More promising is cognitive-behavioral therapy when clinicians use it as an adjunct to pharmacological treatments (Wykes, Steel, Everitt, & Tarrier, 2008). Clinicians using cognitive-behavioral therapy to treat individuals with symptoms of psychosis (CBTp) do not try to change their delusions or eliminate their hallucinations, but instead try to reduce their distress and preoccupation with these symptoms. In addition, cognitive-behavioral therapists attempt to teach their clients coping skills so that they can improve their ability to live independently. Clinicians might assign homework of having their clients keep a diary of their experiences of hearing voices or a "reality check" of their delusional beliefs. CBTp was initially developed in the United Kingdom, perhaps because service providers were more interested in developing nonmedical approaches to treating the symptoms of psychosis than is true in the United States. However, the method is gaining more widespread acceptance in the United States, based on studies showing its effectiveness, particularly in conjunction with atypical antipsychotics (Pinninti, Rissmiller, & Steer, 2010).

Researchers are also developing interventions to help address the cognitive deficits of individuals with schizophrenia, particularly those who suffer from primarily negative symptoms (see Figure 9.4). Like physical fitness training, people with schizophrenia receive cognitive training that builds on their current level of functioning to restore or enhance their performance. Cognitive training is guided by the findings from neuroscience showing that people with schizophrenia have deficits in memory and sensory processing. One promising cognitive training approach involves training in speech recognition and auditory perception. By improving their memory and sensory skills, individuals with schizophrenia are then better able to take advantage of other psychologically based interventions as well as to participate more successfully in vocational rehabilitation programs. These studies are also showing that people with schizophrenia can actually show neural "plasticity," meaning that their brains undergo positive adaptive changes during training (Genevsky, Garrett, Alexander, & Vinogradov, 2010).

Sociocultural Perspectives

Theories In some of the earliest formulations about schizophrenia's causes, psychological theorists proposed that disturbed patterns of communication in a child's

FIGURE 9.3 Change in Cognitive Performance in Patients with Schizophrenia after 50 Hours of Computerized Auditory Training

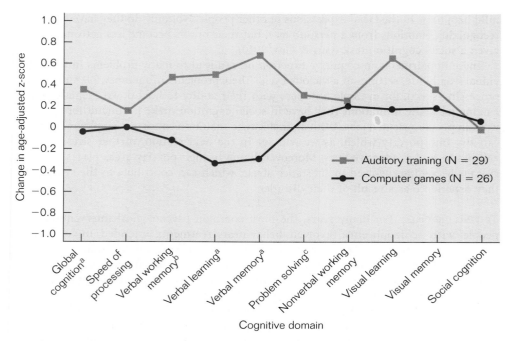

[a]Significant difference between groups (P < 0.01, repeated-measure ANOVA)
[b]Significant difference between groups (P < 0.05, repeated-measure ANOVA)
[c]Nonsignificant difference between groups (P = 0.10, repeated-measure ANOVA)

family environment could precipitate the development of schizophrenia. In studies on modes of communication and behavior within families with a schizophrenic member, researchers attempted to document deviant patterns of communication and inappropriate ways that parents interacted with their children. Clinicians thought that these disturbances in family relationships led to the development of defective emotional responsiveness and cognitive distortions fundamental to the psychological symptoms of schizophrenia.

Contemporary researchers have approached the issue by trying to predict outcome or recovery in adults hospitalized for schizophrenia. Instead of regarding a disturbed family as the cause of schizophrenia, these researchers view the family as a potential source of stress in the environment of the person who is trying to recover from a schizophrenic episode. The index of expressed emotion (EE) reflects the stress that family members create. This provides a measure of the degree to which family members speak in ways that reflect criticism, hostile feelings, and emotional overinvolvement or overconcern. Supporting the concept of EE as a source of stress, researchers found that people living in families high in EE are more likely to suffer a relapse, particularly if they are exposed to high levels of criticism (Marom, Munitz, Jones, Weizman, & Hermesh, 2005). One fMRI study showed that people with schizophrenia have higher activation of brain regions involved in self-reflection and sensitivity to social situations when hearing speech high in EE compared to neutral speech (Rylands, McKie, Elliott, Deakin, & Tarrier, 2011).

It goes without saying that research on EE could never employ an experimental design. Consequently, researchers can never draw causal links between EE and schizophrenia, even in people whose schizophrenia may have reflected genetic or neurodevelopmental vulnerability. It is also very likely that the presence of an individual with schizophrenia creates stress within the family, even if the family member is not living at home. The individual's disorder can impact parents, siblings, and even grandparents, particularly when the symptoms first begin to emerge in an individual's early adult years.

Moving beyond the family environment, researchers have also studied broader social factors, such as social class and income, in relationship to schizophrenia. In perhaps the first epidemiological study of mental illness in the United States, Hollingshead and

Redlich (1958) observed that schizophrenia was far more prevalent in the lowest socio-economic classes. A number of researchers have since replicated the finding that more individuals with schizophrenia live in the poorer sections of urban areas in the United States and Europe. One possible interpretation of this finding is that people with schizophrenia experience "downward drift," meaning that their disorder drives them into poverty, which interferes with their ability to work and earn a living. The other possibility is that the stress of living in isolation and poverty in urban areas contributes to the risk of developing schizophrenia. However, the rates of schizophrenia are higher in individuals who were born or raised in urban areas, not just those who moved there as adults (Stilo & Murray, 2010).

People who were born in a country other than the one in which they are currently living (i.e., those who have "migrant" status) also have higher rates of schizophrenia. The individuals most at risk for schizophrenia are those who migrate to lower-status jobs and urban areas where they are more likely to suffer from exposure to environmental pollutants, stress, and overcrowding (McGrath, Saha, Chant, & Welham, 2008). However, as the rates of ethnic minorities in a neighborhood increases, the rates of schizophrenia are lower, suggesting that these individuals benefit from less exposure to discrimination and more opportunities for social support in their immediate environments (Veling et al., 2007).

Other risk factors for schizophrenia, or at least symptoms of psychosis related to an individual's sociocultural background, include adversity in childhood including parental loss or separation, abuse, and a target of bullying. In adulthood, individuals more vulnerable to first or subsequent episodes of psychosis include people who have experienced severely stressful life events, including being a victim of assault (Stilo & Murray, 2010). Individuals with high genetic risk who are exposed to environmental stressors are more likely than others who experience mild psychotic symptoms to develop a full-blown disorder (van Os et al., 2009). People who use cannabis (marijuana) also show an elevated risk of developing schizophrenia. Although researchers were long aware of the cannabis-schizophrenia link, they believed that people with schizophrenia used the drug to alleviate their symptoms. Long-term follow-up studies show, instead, that people develop the disorder after continued use of cannabis. The more they use the drug, the greater their chances of having schizophrenia (McGrath et al., 2010).

Recognizing that the causes of schizophrenia are multifaceted and develop over time, Stilo and Murray (2010) proposed a "developmental cascade" hypothesis that integrates genetic vulnerabilities, damage occurring in the prenatal and early childhood periods, adversity, and drug abuse as leading, ultimately, to changes in dopamine expressed in psychosis (see Figure 9.3).

FIGURE 9.4 Developmental Cascade toward Schizophrenia

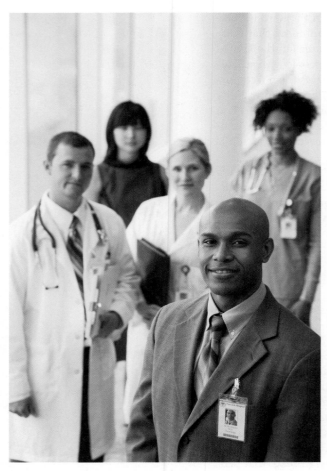

Assertive Community Treatment involves a highly skilled and collaborative team of psychiatrists, nurses, social workers, and other mental health care professionals.

Assertive Community Treatment (ACT)
Where a team of professionals from psychiatry, psychology, nursing, and social work reach out to clients in their homes and workplaces.

Treatments The coordination of services is especially important in programs geared toward helping people with schizophrenia. One approach to integrating various services is **Assertive Community Treatment (ACT),** in which a team of professionals from psychiatry, psychology, nursing, and social work reach out to clients in their homes and workplaces. ACT's focus is on engendering empowerment and self-determination on its "consumers," the term they use to refer to their clients. Typically, a team of about a dozen professionals work together to help approximately 100 consumers with issues such as complying with medical recommendations, managing their finances, obtaining adequate health care, and dealing with crises when they arise. This approach involves bringing care to the clients, rather than waiting for them to come to a facility for help, a journey that may be too overwhelming for seriously impaired people. Although approaches such as ACT are expensive, the benefits are impressive. Researchers have conducted dozens of studies on the effectiveness of ACT and have concluded that ACT has had significant positive impact on reducing hospitalizations, stabilizing housing in the community, and lowering overall treatment costs (Bond, Drake, Mueser, & Latimer, 2001).

As effective as it can be, critics charge that ACT is not provided in a manner consistent with its goal of empowering consumers and instead is coercive and paternalistic. To address this charge, ACT researchers are investigating the possibility of combining ACT with another program, called Illness Management and Recovery (IMR). In IMR, consumers receive training in effective ways to manage their illnesses and pursue their goals for recovery. Resting on the principle of self-determination, IMR is based on the premise that consumers should be given the resources they need to make informed choices. IMR uses peers and clinicians to deliver structured, curriculum-based interventions. Although an initial investigation of ACT-IMR revealed that the providers experienced a number of difficulties in implementing the program, it appeared to reduce hospitalization rates. Moreover, even after the funding for the study ran out, the teams continued to provide services (Salyers et al., 2010).

9.4 Schizophrenia: The Biopsychosocial Perspective

Definitions and diagnostic approaches to schizophrenia are undergoing significant revisions, but throughout the past decade, researchers have gained a great deal of understanding about its many possible causes. Perhaps most exciting is the evolution of an integrated approach to theories that focus on underlying brain mechanisms as expressed in cognitive deficits. Treatment is moving beyond the provision of medication to greater use of evidence-based psychological interventions. Finally, researchers appear to be gaining greater appreciation of the role of sociocultural influences. Together, these advances are increasing the chances that individuals with these disorders will receive integrated care, maximizing their chances of recovery (Sungur et al., 2011).

Clinicians, also, increasingly understand schizophrenia from a life-span perspective. The needs and concerns of individuals with this disorder vary over the years of adulthood. In addition to the fact that many actually do recover, researchers and mental health practitioners are recognizing that part of their job involves providing ways to help people with long-term schizophrenia adapt both to changes involved in the aging process, as well as changes involved in the evolution of the disease. The idea that schizophrenia is a neurodevelopmental disorder highlights this important new focus and provides a basis for interventions that take into account individual changes over time.

Return to the Case: David Marshall

David was eventually able to return to school part-time, living at home with Ann. Though he struggled with the change in his level of functioning, he was able to use therapy and case management to understand his limitations. By doing so, the aim is to avoid future stressors from occurring and from inducing psychotic episodes. It is difficult to completely avoid any instances of psychosis from occurring with a disorder as severe as schizophrenia. However, with the proper contingencies and social support the impact of his symptoms will be easier for David to tolerate.

Dr. Tobin's reflections: David's move into the dorms presented as a first major life stressor. Though he had already been attending college for one year, living with his mother seems to have provided a feeling of safety that was shattered once he moved away. It was difficult though, as

David certainly wished he could attain independence and wanted to be able to. Though he was not at his same level of functioning as before, David and Ann had assumed that whatever David had been going through was finished. Returning to the dormitories however proved too great a stressor and so David's symptoms were brought on once again.

Luckily for David, Ann was able to take action to help David after it had become clear that he was suffering from something very serious that neither of them had quite understood. Having "caught" the disorder early on, and entering a treatment program, is beneficial as it decreases the likelihood that his life will be complicated by the fallout from future psychotic episodes. However, prevention of future episodes is contingent upon his participation in therapy and his medication compliance.

SUMMARY

- **Schizophrenia** is a serious mental illness, given its potentially broad impact on an individual's ability to live a productive and fulfilling life. Although a significant number of people with schizophrenia eventually manage to live symptom-free lives, many must find ways to adapt their lives to the reality of the illness.

- There are six diagnostic criteria for schizophrenia (see Table 9.1) Currently, clinicians diagnose an individual with schizophrenia into one of five subtypes based on which symptoms are most prominent: **catatonic, disorganized, paranoid, undifferentiated,** and **residual.** It is likely that these subtypes will disappear in *DSM-5* because the members of the schizophrenia task force believe that they are not supported by empirical evidence. Instead, the

DSM-5 authors will most likely recommend conceptualizing schizophrenia as a spectrum or set of related disorders characterized by dimensions.

- Characteristic symptoms of **disorganized schizophrenia** include **neologisms, inappropriate affect,** and **paranoia.** Clinicians diagnose people with schizophrenia who do not have one predominant symptom as having the **undifferentiated** type. They may fluctuate among the other three types, but do not show a consistent enough pattern to be diagnosed with one of those types. Clinicians use the final type, called **residual,** to diagnose people whose symptoms are mild and do not include prominent symptoms in any of the other categories.

- First identified as a disease in the 1800s by Benedict Morel, researchers, including physicians, psychiatrists, and psychologists, have been studying schizophrenia, theorizing its origin, and identifying symptoms and categories. As the years unfold, researchers attempt to develop a more precise set of diagnostic criteria.

- Schizophrenia may take one of several courses. When symptoms no longer interfere with a patient's behavior, he or she is in **remission.** Compared to other psychological disorders, the course and outcome are poorer for people with schizophrenia

- For many years, up through the early 1980s, with no comprehensive diagnostic criteria at their disposal, psychiatrists used schizophrenia as a catchall term applied to the majority of people requiring institutionalization for psychotic symptoms. Currently, the *DSM* includes a set of so-called "psychotic" disorders that share three features: (1) each is a form of psychosis representing a serious break with reality, (2) the condition is not caused by a known cognitive impairment, and (3) there is no mood disturbance as a primary symptom. These include **brief psychotic disorder, schizophreniform disorder, delusional disorders (erotomanic, grandiose, jealous, persecutory,** and **somatic types**), and **shared psychotic disorder.**

- Theories accounting for the origin of schizophrenia have traditionally fallen into two categories: **biological** and **psychological.** In the first part of this century, a debate raged between proponents of both sides. More recently, researchers have begun to accept that both biology and experience interact in the determination of schizophrenia and have begun to build complex theoretical models that incorporate multiple factors. This includes the **neurodevelopmental hypothesis,** which states that schizophrenia is a disorder of development that arises during the years of adolescence or early adulthood due to alterations in the genetic control of brain maturation.

- The primary biological treatment for schizophrenia is **antipsychotic medication,** or **neuroleptics.** The two main categories of **neuroleptics** are the so-called "typical" or "first generation" and "atypical" or "second generation" antipsychotics. The distressing side effects and failure of typical antipsychotics to treat negative symptoms of schizophrenia have led psychiatric researchers on a search to alternatives that would both be more effective and not cause **tardive dyskinesia,** a motor disorder that consists of involuntary movements of their mouth, arms, and trunk of the body. Because of the many complexities in the biological treatment of individuals with schizophrenia, researchers and clinicians increasingly recognize the need to take the individual's medical and psychiatric profile into account.

- From a psychological perspective, with increasing evidence suggesting specific genetic and neurophysiological abnormalities in the brains of people with schizophrenia, researchers are becoming increasingly interested in finding out more about the role of cognitive deficits in causing the disorder. However, these symptoms may not be at the core of the disorder. Instead, cognitive functions affected by schizophrenia may be more fundamental to understanding the disorder's central features.

- For many years, the most common psychological interventions for people with schizophrenia involved behavioral treatments intended to lower the frequency of an individual's maladaptive behaviors that interfere with social adjustment and functioning. However, this form of intervention is no longer practical given that most individuals with schizophrenia receive treatment in the community. In addition, there is little data on its effectiveness and with clinicians focusing on evidence-based treatment, the profession cannot justify its use. More promising is cognitive-behavioral therapy when clinicians use it as an adjunct to pharmacological treatments. Clinicians using cognitive-behavioral therapy to treat individuals with symptoms of psychosis (CBTp) do not try to change their delusions or eliminate their hallucinations, but instead try to reduce their distress and preoccupation with these symptoms. Researchers are also developing interventions to help address the cognitive deficits of individuals with schizophrenia, particularly those who suffer from primarily negative symptoms.

- There have been many theories regarding schizophrenia from a sociocultural perspective. Contemporary researchers have approached the issue by trying to predict the outcome or recovery of adults hospitalized for schizophrenia. The index of expressed emotion (EE) provides a measure of degree to which family members speak in ways that reflect criticisms, hostile feelings, and emotional overinvolvement or overconcern. Moving beyond the family environment, researchers have also studied broader social factors, such as social class and income, in relationship to schizophrenia. Other risk factors for schizophrenia, or at least symptoms of psychosis related to an individual's sociocultural background, include adversity in childhood including parental loss or separation, abuse, and a target of bullying.

- The coordination of services is especially important in programs geared toward helping people with schizophrenia.

- From a biopsychosocial perspective, an exciting development is the evolution of an integrated approach to theories that focus on underlying brain mechanisms as expressed in cognitive deficits. Treatment is moving beyond the provision of medication to greater use of evidence-based psychological interventions. Finally, researchers appear to be gaining greater appreciation of the role of sociocultural influences. Together, these advances are increasing the chances that individuals with these disorders will receive integrated care, maximizing their chances of recovery. Clinicians, also, increasingly understand schizophrenia from a life-span perspective. The idea that schizophrenia is a neurodevelopmental disorder highlights this important new focus and provides a basis for interventions that take into account individual changes over time.

KEY TERMS

Personality Disorders

Learning Objectives

10.1 Identify the characteristics of personality disorders

10.2 Explain characteristics, theories and treatments of antisocial personality disorder

10.3 Describe avoidant personality disorder

10.4 Explain characteristics, theories, and treatments of borderline personality disorder

10.5 Describe narcissistic personality disorder

10.6 Describe obsessive-compulsive personality disorder

10.7 Describe schizotypal personality disorder

10.8 Identify the dropped personality disorders from *DSM-IV*

10.9 Analyze the biopsychosocial model of personality disorders

CHAPTER 10

Case Report: Harold Morrill

Demographic information: Harold is a 21-year-old Caucasian male.

Presenting problem: Harold presented for an emergency intake evaluation at his university's counseling center due to self-reported suicidal ideation. He reported to the intake counselor that he had a strong, pervasive desire to kill himself. He presented as angry and emotionally distraught, and he grew easily frustrated with the counselor several times throughout the interview. Harold reported that this was not the first time he had wanted to kill himself, and without being prompted showed the counselor a large, vertical scar down his left forearm indicating a previous suicide attempt. He stated that he was 17 at the time he slit his wrist, and that he had been under the influence of alcohol and cocaine at the time. He remarked that he barely remembered the incident. Following this suicide attempt, Harold had been admitted to an inpatient psychiatric unit and was stabilized on medication, though he discontinued his medication on his own once he was discharged, against the recommendations of his doctors.

Harold became highly agitated when asked questions about his past during the evaluation, at one point yelling at the counselor and threatening to storm out of the room. Once the counselor was able to calm him down, he tearfully stated, "I'm just so sick of feeling this way," and agreed to continue with the evaluation. This was in contrast to his initial presentation as pleasant and polite, even as he described his thoughts about ending his life.

Harold reported having few close interpersonal relationships. He stated that he didn't have any close friends at school and had switched dormitories four times during his freshman year alone. He was vague in describing the reasoning behind this, remarking only that "all my roommates have been total jerks." Harold went on to discuss his various romantic relationships during the past four years, when he began dating. He stated that each relationship lasted a few weeks, the longest lasting for two months. When describing the relationships, he reported that they usually ended due to "blow out" arguments. When asked about the nature of the arguments, he stated in each case he had accused the woman of infidelity and would immediately end the relationship. Harold elaborated that he felt "no one could ever make me happy. I don't know why I even try. Nothing that I ever do makes me feel better, so I keep trying new things and looking for new people. But none of it works." He related this to his recurrent thoughts of suicide and past suicide attempts. When asked about his family, Harold reported that he was "disgusted" with them and how they treated him as a child (see Relevant history, below).

Harold reported that he frequently abuses alcohol—as many as seven days per week—and that he typically drinks to the point of blacking out. He described that he mostly enjoys going to bars and did so with a "fake ID" before he turned 21. He explained that he enjoyed meeting new people, and that drinking "helps me to not be so bored all of the time." Harold also reported a history of drug abuse including marijuana, cocaine, and ecstasy since the age of 13. Harold stated that he had been caught with substances by the police on campus, though he had avoided being arrested. He was arrested for a DUI during his freshman year and had attended alcohol education classes, which he called "a complete waste of my time." Following the arrest, Harold lost his driver's license which greatly upset him, as he typically enjoyed driving to the bars in town or other towns nearby when he was feeling tired of his own town. He regained his license and had been frequenting bars and drinking heavily until three weeks prior to the current intake evaluation.

Harold stated that for the past three weeks he had been spending most of his time alone in his room, saying, "why would anyone want to spend time with such a lousy person. That's why I wanted to die." He had also quit his part-time job at a grocery store and was attending only a few classes per week. He was unable to recall a specific event that brought on his current depression. While being asked about his current depression, Harold burst into tears and pleaded with the evaluator for help. "I just know I'm going to kill myself." He showed the evaluator burn marks on his legs that appeared to be recently inflicted. The evaluator asked Harold about his current suicidal ideology, and he was able to contract for safety, meaning he agreed not to hurt himself and that if his thoughts about death grew stronger he would call the emergency room or the counseling center. Following this, Harold asked the evaluator if she could be his therapist. The evaluator described the counseling center's policy, that the intake evaluator could not see clients being evaluated for psychotherapy. "Just like a typical woman," he retorted. "You don't want to be with me. I think you're terrible at your job, anyway."

Relevant history: Harold stated that he had attended psychotherapy sessions in the past, but that he "hated every single one of them," referring to his therapists, when describing why he never stayed in therapy long. He had seen about five different therapists since the age of 14, but described the experiences as "uncomfortable and just weird. They didn't get me." When the counselor asked Harold why he had gone to therapy as an adolescent, he stated, "I think my mom thought I was messed up. I didn't think I needed it." He described his childhood as "a disaster" and his father as a severe alcoholic, who was often emotionally abusive and sometimes physically abusive. He reported that his mother worked two jobs to

support the family, and so he spent much of his time alone as a child.

Case formulation: Harold's behaviors and reported history during the evaluation match with criteria for a Personality Disorder as defined by the *DSM-IV-TR,* and his symptoms meet criteria for Borderline Personality Disorder. Although he often abused substances, Harold's personality disorder was not a result of substance use, and instead is a reflection of his impulsivity and inability to cope with strong emotions that is typical of Borderline individuals.

His symptoms of depression for the past three weeks meet criteria for a Major Depressive Episode, though it is unknown whether these have been recurrent for Harold or whether this was a singular intense episode. It might be that it is recurrent, given his prior suicide attempts, though these may be related to the instability that is a feature of his Borderline symptoms, therefore Major Depressive Disorder was added as a rule-out on Axis I.

Multiaxial assessment:

Axis I: Major Depressive Episode, single episode-R/O Major Depressive Disorder, Polysubstance abuse, current

Axis II: Borderline personality disorder

Axis III: None

Axis IV: Abusive father, invalidating home environment

Axis V: 40- Current

Treatment plan: Dialectical Behavior Therapy or DBT is currently the preferred treatment for Borderline Personality Disorder. Once Harold made a safety plan with the counselor, he was referred to a private DBT outpatient program two miles from his college campus. Harold was also referred to the psychiatrist on campus for a medication consultation.

Sarah Tobin, PhD

personality trait
An enduring pattern of perceiving, relating to, and thinking about the environment and others.

In this chapter, our focus shifts from examining the Axis I clinical syndromes to the set of disorders on Axis II that represent long-standing patterns of impairments in an individual's self-understanding, ways of relating to others, and personality traits. As we discussed in Chapter 4, a **personality trait** is an enduring pattern of perceiving, relating to, and thinking about the environment and others, a pattern that characterizes the majority of a person's interactions and experiences. Most people are able to draw upon their personality traits in a flexible manner, adjusting their responses to the needs of the situation. However, when people become rigidly fixed on one particular trait or set of traits, they may place themselves at risk for developing a personality disorder.

10.1 The Nature of Personality Disorders

When does a personality trait become a disorder? What may be a characteristic way of responding can develop into a fixed pattern that impairs a person's ability to function satisfactorily. Perhaps you're the type of person who likes to have your room look "just so." If someone moves your books around or changes the arrangement of your clothes on the hanger, you feel a little bothered. At what point does your unhappiness with a change in the order of your possessions become so problematic that you have crossed over from a little finicky to having a personality disorder involving extreme rigidity? Should this behavioral pattern place you into a diagnostic category with a distinct set of criteria that separates you from people with other personality traits and related behaviors?

As conceptualized in the *DSM-IV-TR,* the **personality disorders** represent a collection of distinguishable sets of behavior, falling into 11 distinct categories. The types of behavior that these disorders represent can involve, for example, excessive dependency, overwhelming fear of intimacy, intense worry, exploitative behavior, or uncontrollable rage. With their current definitions, these behavior patterns, to fit the diagnostic criteria, must manifest themselves in at least two of these four areas: (1) cognition, (2) affectivity, (3) interpersonal functioning, and (4) impulse control. As a result of these behaviors, the individual experiences distress or impairment.

The *DSM-IV-TR* groups the 11 diagnoses into three clusters based on shared characteristics. Cluster A includes paranoid, schizoid, and schizotypal personality disorders, which share the features of odd and eccentric behavior. Cluster B includes antisocial, borderline, histrionic, and narcissistic personality disorders, which share overdramatic, emotional, and erratic or unpredictable attitudes and behaviors. Cluster C includes avoidant, dependent, and obsessive-compulsive personality disorders, which share anxious and fearful behaviors.

Because the personality disorders fall into separate categories, clinicians evaluating individuals for a possible diagnosis must decide how many of the criteria a client meets within each category and assign a diagnosis on that basis. Either the client has the disorder or not. The clinician may start by trying to match the most prominent symptoms that the individual shows with the diagnostic criteria. If the client does not fit the

Toward the DSM-5: Dimensionalizing the Personality Disorders

The area of personality disorders is receiving, perhaps, the greatest attention from clinicians and researchers as they wait for the unveiling of the final revisions to the *DSM-5.* As we mentioned at the beginning of the chapter, clinicians began to challenge the categorization system in the early *DSM*s even when the American Psychiatric Association was developing the *DSM-IV.* The presently proposed system retains some of the previous categorical disorders, but disposes almost half of the previous set present in the *DSM-IV-TR.* At the same time, the *DSM-5* authors propose adding a dimensional rating system of pathological personality traits that will address the criticism that we cannot easily divide personality into separate and discrete chunks.

DSM-5 supporters and critics are already discussing a *DSM-6* that will eliminate all categories entirely and instead use a dimensional system that allows clinicians to rate the personality traits of all their clients. The disorders may explicitly appear as clusters of particular traits rather than, as the authors currently propose, constituting an additional dimension beyond the categories.

For the present, by reducing the number of discrete categories, the *DSM-5* authors hope to improve the system's reliability and validity by eliminating imprecisely defined low-prevalence disorders. This is not to say that the new system will be without its detractors. For example, one critic argues that clinicians will have trouble differentiating among the remaining six disorders. The currently proposed criteria still do not seem precise enough to allow clinicians or researchers to make clear-cut diagnoses. Worse, clinicians may still have in their heads the old system and therefore find it difficult to make the transition to the new, partially dimensional, one.

The history of personality disorders, which are not so much "illnesses" as characteristics of an individual's core ways of relating to others and experiencing the self, further complicates these diagnostic issues. How do you summarize the many complex facets of personality into a discrete set of units? Unlike mood and anxiety disorders, which people may "overcome," the personality disorders are by definition (in the minds of many psychologists) enduring features of the individual. Personality traits can, and do, change over time. However, clinicians are used to thinking of these disorders as deeply seeded, and many of the disorders were framed within a psychoanalytic perspective with long clinical histories. It is convenient for clinicians to describe their "borderline" clients rather than to list all the personality traits that particular individuals display.

The tension between the categorical and dimensional approaches to disorders will most likely persist for the upcoming decade, at least. Meanwhile, by revising Axis II so dramatically, researchers are hopeful that they can provide a system that will have diagnostic and empirical utility, ultimately improving the nature of treatment that they can offer clients with these forms of psychopathology.

personality disorder
Ingrained patterns of relating to other people, situations, and events with a rigid and maladaptive pattern of inner experience and behavior, dating back to adolescence or early adulthood.

TABLE 10.1 *DSM-5* Personality Disorder Framework

	Personality Functioning		Interpersonal Functioning		Personality traits
	Identity	**Self-direction**	**Empathy**	**Intimacy**	
Antisocial	Egocentrism; self-esteem derived from personal gain, power, or pleasure.	Goal-setting based on personal gratification; absence of prosocial internal standards associated with failure to conform to lawful or culturally normative ethical behavior.	Lack of concern for feelings, needs, or suffering of others; lack of remorse after hurting or mistreating another.	Incapacity for mutually intimate relationships, as exploitation is a primary means of relating to others, including by deceit and coercion; use of dominance or intimidation to control others.	**Antagonism:** Manipulativeness Deceitfulness Callousness Hostility **Disinhibition:** Irresponsibility Impulsivity Risk taking
Avoidant	Low self-esteem associated with self-appraisal as socially inept, personally unappealing, or inferior; excessive feelings of shame or inadequacy.	Unrealistic standards for behavior associated with reluctance to pursue goals, take personal risks, or engage in new activities involving interpersonal contact.	Preoccupation with, and sensitivity to, criticism or rejection, associated with distorted inference of others' perspectives as negative.	Reluctance to get involved with people unless certain of being liked; diminished mutuality within intimate relationships because of fear of others shaming or ridiculing.	**Detachment** Withdrawal Intimacy Avoidance Anhedonia **Negative affectivity** Anxiousness
Borderline	Markedly impoverished, poorly developed, or unstable self-image, often associated with excessive self-criticism; chronic feelings of emptiness; dissociative states under stress.	Instability in goals, aspirations, values, or career plans.	Compromised ability to recognize the feelings and needs of others associated with interpersonal hypersensitivity (i.e., prone to feel slighted or insulted); perceptions of others selectively biased toward negative attributes or vulnerabilities.	Intense, unstable, and conflicted close relationships, marked by mistrust, neediness, and anxious preoccupation with real or imagined abandonment; close relationships often viewed in extremes of idealization and devaluation and alternating between over involvement and withdrawal.	**Negative affectivity** Emotional lability Anxiousness Separation Hostility Depressivity **Disinhibition** Impulsivity Risk taking **Antagonism** Hostility
Narcissistic	Excessive reference to others for self-definition and self-esteem regulation; exaggerated self-appraisal may be inflated or deflated, or vacillate between extremes; emotional regulation mirrors fluctuations in self-esteem.	Goal-setting is based on gaining approval from others; personal standards are unreasonably high in order to see oneself as exceptional, or too low based on a sense of entitlement; often unaware of own motivations.	Impaired ability to recognize or identify with the feelings and needs of others; excessively attuned to reactions of others, but only if perceived as relevant to self; over- or underestimate own effect on others.	Relationships largely superficial and exist to serve self-esteem regulation; mutuality constrained by little genuine interest in others' experiences and predominance of a need for personal gain.	**Antagonism** Grandiosity Attention seeking

TABLE 10.1 *DSM-5* Personality Disorder Framework (*Continued*)

Obsessive-Compulsive Personality Disorder	Sense of self derived predominantly from work or productivity; constricted experience and expression of strong emotions.	Difficulty completing tasks and realizing goals associated with rigid and unreasonably high and inflexible internal standards of behavior; overly conscientious and moralistic attitudes.	Difficulty understanding and appreciating the ideas, feelings, or behaviors of others.	Relationships seen as secondary to work and productivity; rigidity and stubbornness negatively affect relationships with others.	**Compulsivity** Rigid perfectionism **Negative affectivity** Perseveration
Schizotypal Personality Disorder	Confused boundaries between self and others; distorted self-concept; emotional expression often not congruent with context or internal experience.	Unrealistic or incoherent goals; no clear set of internal standards.	Pronounced difficulty understanding impact of own behaviors on others; frequent misinterpretations of others' motivations and behaviors.	Marked impairments in developing close relationships associated with mistrust and anxiety.	**Psychoticism** Eccentricity Cognitive and perceptual dysregulation Unusual beliefs and experiences **Detachment** Restricted affectivity Withdrawal **Negative affectivity** Suspiciousness

criteria for that disorder, the clinician may either move to another disorder or decide that the client has a personality disorder "not otherwise specified."

Even as the authors were writing *DSM-IV*, a number of prominent researchers went on record as stating that the categorical diagnostic system was flawed. They maintained that there were too many fine distinctions that the diagnoses required. These distinctions, they maintained, were not sufficiently clear and there were many overlapping criteria. Consequently, clinicians could not empirically justify the diagnoses. Clinicians found that they were using most commonly the less than precise diagnosis of "personality disorder not otherwise specified" (Widiger & Trull, 2007). A second major flaw with the categorical rating system is that it did not allow for the possibility of a client's "somewhat" antisocial or narcissistic behavior. Clients either did or did not fit into a diagnostic category.

In the process of revising the *DSM-IV-TR,* the personality disorders panels developed a number of alternative models to get away from the categorical diagnostic system. At one time, researchers even proposed eliminating the categories entirely and replacing them with dimensional ratings, such as scales based on the Five Factor Model. Nevertheless, the categories seemed to hold worth and, as long as the researchers could delineate distinct empirically based criteria, the *DSM-5* authors proposed an acceptable compromise. They revamped the original 12 personality disorders (11 categories plus "not otherwise specified") into 6 (plus an additional category for individuals who did not fit into the 6). Within each personality disorder, the authors set empirically based criteria (Livesley, 2011) along the dimensions of self and interpersonal relationships. In addition, in this framework, clinicians would evaluate all clients on a consistent set of five personality traits. Table 10.1 shows the complete diagnostic system.

Clinicians will make their diagnoses on the basis of three sets of criteria. The first two reflect personality "functioning," meaning how the individual expresses personality in his or her identity and self-direction. The second two reflect the individual's personality as reflected in relationships with other people in terms of the ability to understand other people's perspectives and form close relationships. Clinicians rate individuals from mild to extreme in these domains. The third set of criteria involves ratings of the individual's specific personality trait. A person must have significant impairment in both areas of personality functioning to receive a diagnosis of personality disorder. With respect to the personality traits, the individual must have pathological traits in at least one of five trait domains: antagonism, disinhibition, detachment, negative affectivity, and compulsivity. Clinicians can rate all clients on these personality traits if such an assessment is conceptually helpful. The new diagnostic system reduces the set of 79 criteria in *DSM-IV-TR* to 25 core criteria. Clinicians use the remaining category of "personality disorder trait specified" for people who show significant impairment in personality functioning, but who rate at the maladaptive end of one or more personality traits.

With this background, you can now understand the logic behind the general criteria for a personality disorder in *DSM-5* as Table 10.2 shows. Behavioral indicators specifiy each level of personality functioning. For example, an individual with moderate impairment in sense of self needs the approval of others to feel adequate or complete. A person with extreme impairment in interpersonal relationships has little or no interest in the feelings of others.

Each of the five trait domains also have explicit definitions as Table 10.3 shows. This trait model is not the same as the Five Factor Model as it is oriented toward abnormal, not normal, personality. For example, detachment in the *DSM-5* system is a pathological variant of introversion (or low extraversion). In developing these factors for the *DSM-5* reformulation of the personality disorders, the authors made clear that although these are bipolar (i.e., two-way) dimensions, people with one of these disorders would score at the maladaptive end of the domains of detachment, antagonism, disinhibition, and negative affectivity. However, the fifth trait in the Five Factor Model, openness to experience, does not fit into this framework because it is not a feature of any of the personality disorders. Instead, authors have introduced the dimension of psychoticism into the *DSM-5* that they associate with schizotypal personality disorder.

Clinicians base prevalence statistics for the personality disorders on the current system of the *DSM-IV-TR*, but this will almost certainly change once *DSM-5* is available due to the changes in the diagnostic criteria as well as the number of disorders. Currently, studies comparing the United States and the United Kingdom yield an overall prevalence among nationally representative samples of 9 to 10 percent. Personality disorders are highly comorbid with drug dependence. For example, among people with antisocial personality disorder, the lifetime prevalence rate of alcohol dependence is 27 percent and 59 percent for nicotine dependence (Trull, Jahng, Tomko, Wood, & Sher, 2010).

TABLE 10.2 Criteria for a Personality Disorder

The essential features of a personality disorder are impairments in **identity and sense of self** and in the capacity for effective **interpersonal functioning.**
To diagnose a personality disorder, the impairments must meet *all* of the following criteria:

A. A rating of mild impairment or greater in **self** and **interpersonal** functioning on the **Levels of Personality Functioning.**

B. Associated with a "good match" or "very good match" to a **personality disorder type** *or* with a rating of "quite a bit like the trait" or "extremely like the trait" on one or more personality **trait domains.**

C. Relatively stable across time and consistent across situations.

D. Not better understood as a norm within an individual's dominant culture.

E. Not solely due to the direct physiological effects of a substance (e.g., a drug of abuse, medication) or a general medical condition (e.g., severe head trauma).

TABLE 10.3 Personality Domains in the DSM-5

Negative Affectivity involves experiencing negative emotions frequently and intensely.

Trait facets: Emotional lability, anxiousness, separation insecurity, perseveration, submissiveness, hostility, depressivity, suspiciousness, restricted affectivity (−).

Detachment involves withdrawal from other people and from social interactions.

Trait facets: Restricted affectivity, depressivity, suspiciousness, withdrawal, anhedonia, intimacy avoidance.

Antagonism involves behaviors that put the person at odds with other people.

Trait facets: Manipulativeness, deceitfulness, grandiosity, attention seeking, callousness, hostility.

Disinhibition involves engaging in behaviors on impulse, without reflecting on potential future consequences. Compulsivity is the opposite pole of this domain.

Trait facets: Irresponsibility, impulsivity, distractibility, risk taking, rigid perfectionism (−).

Psychoticism involves unusual and bizarre experiences.

Trait facets: Unusual beliefs & experiences, eccentricity, cognitive & perceptual dysregulation.

10.2 Antisocial Personality Disorder

Synonymous in the past with "psychopaths" or "sociopaths," the *DSM-IV-TR* defined people who receive the diagnosis of **antisocial personality disorder** as highly impulsive and lacking in the capacity for regret over their actions. Television depicts serial killers as having these qualities, and then some. However, we can find people with antisocial personality operating in much more mundane situations. The phenomenon of the "psychopath in the boardroom" describes corporate executives who ruthlessly exploit investors and employees alike, seeking their own gain at the expense of the bank accounts and livelihood of their victims (Jonson, 2011). Such individuals also commit acts of bullying in the workplace, increasing the risk of unfair supervision (Boddy, 2011).

antisocial personality disorder
A personality disorder characterized by a lack of regard for society's moral or legal standards.

Characteristics of Antisocial Personality Disorder

The diagnosis of antisocial behavior has its origins in the work of Hervey Cleckley, whose 1941 book, *The Mask of Sanity*, represented the first scientific attempt to list and categorize the behaviors of the "psychopathic" personality. Cleckley (1976) developed a set of criteria

MINI CASE

Antisocial Personality Disorder

Tommy was the leader of a teenage street gang that had the reputation as the most vicious in the neighborhood. He grew up in a chaotic home atmosphere, his mother having lived with a series of violent men who were heavily involved in drug dealing and prostitution. At age 18, Tommy was jailed for brutally mugging and stabbing an older woman. This was the first in a long series of arrests for offenses ranging from drug trafficking to car thefts to counterfeiting. At one point, between jail terms, he met a woman at a bar and married her the next day. Two weeks later, he beat her when she complained about his incessant drinking and involvement with shady characters. Tommy left her when she became pregnant, and he refused to pay child support. From his vantage point now as a drug trafficker and leader of a child prostitution ring, Tommy shows no regret for what he has done, claiming that life has "sure given me a bum steer."

psychopathy

A personality type characterized by a cluster of traits that constitutes the core of what is now called *antisocial personality disorder.*

for **psychopathy,** a cluster of traits that includes lack of remorse or shame for harmful acts committed to others; poor judgment and failure to learn from experience; extreme egocentricity and incapacity for love; lack of emotional responsiveness to others; impulsivity; absence of "nervousness"; and unreliability, untruthfulness, and insincerity. Cleckley used the term "semantic dementia" to capture the psychopath's inability to react appropriately to expressions of emotionality. Other people may find it difficult to see the psychopath's true colors because they are able to disguise their egocentric and impulsive behaviors beneath a veneer of superficial charm and seeming intelligence.

Cleckley's notion of psychopathy remains a key concept in descriptions of antisocial personality disorder. Building on Cleckley's work, Canadian psychologist Robert D. Hare developed the Psychopathy Checklist–Revised (PCL-R) (Hare, 1997), an assessment instrument whose two factors are the core psychopathic personality traits and an antisocial lifestyle (Table 20.4). The core personality traits include glibness and superficial charm, a grandiose sense of self-worth, pathological lying, a lack of empathy for others,

TABLE 10.4 Items and Factors in the PCL-R Scales

PCL-R	PCL:YV	PCL:SV
F1		**P1**
Interpersonal	**Interpersonal**	**Interpersonal**
1. Glibness–superficial charm	1. Impression management	1. Superficial
2. Grandiose sense of self-worth	2. Grandiose sense of self-worth	2. Grandiose
4. Pathological lying	4. Pathological lying	3. Deceitful
5. Conning–manipulative	5. Manipulation for personal gain	
Affective	**Affective**	**Affective**
6. Lack of remorse or guilt	6. Lack of remorse	4. Lacks remorse
7. Shallow affect	7. Shallow affect	5. Lacks empathy
8. Callous–lack of empathy	8. Callous–lack of empathy	6. Does not accept responsibility
16. Failure to accept responsibility	16. Failure to accept responsibility	
F2		**P2**
Lifestyle	**Behavioural**	**Lifestyle**
3. Need for stimulation	3. Stimulation seeking	7. Impulsive
9. Parasitic lifestyle	9. Parasitic orientation	9. Lacks goals
13. Lack of realistic, long-term goals	13. Lack of goals	10. Irresponsibility
14. Impulsivity	14. Impulsivity	
15. Irresponsibility	15. Irresponsibility	
Antisocial	**Antisocial**	**Antisocial**
10. Poor behavioural controls	10. Poor anger control	8. Poor behavioural controls
12. Early behavioural problems	12. Early behaviour problems	11. Adolescent antisocial behaviour
18. Juvenile delinquency	18. Serious criminal behaviour	12. Adult antisocial behaviour
19. Revocation of conditional release	19. Serious violations of release	
20. Criminal versatility	20. Criminal versatility	

The PCL-R, PCL:YV, and PCL:SV items are from Hare,[14,20] Forth et al,[24] and Hart et al,[23] respectively. Reprinted by permission of the copyright holders, RD Hare and Multi-Health Systems. Note that the item titles cannot be scored without reference to the formal criteria contained in the published manuals. PCL-R items 11, Promiscuous sexual behaviour and 17, Many short-term marital relationships, contribute to the total score but do not load on any factors. PCL:YV items 11, Impersonal sexual behaviour, and 17, Unstable interpersonal relationships, contribute to the total score but do not load on any factor. F1 and F2 are the original PCL-R factors, but with be addition of item 20. Parts 1 and 2 (P1 and P2) are described in the PCL:SV manual[23]

SOURCE: Hare & Neumann, 2009.

lack of remorse or guilt, and an unwillingness to accept responsibility for one's actions. The antisocial-lifestyle trait revolves around impulsivity, a characteristic that can lead to behaviors expressed in an unstable lifestyle, juvenile delinquency, early behavioral problems, lack of realistic long-term goals, and a need for constant stimulation (Hare & Neumann, 2005).

The diagnostic criteria in the *DSM-IV-TR* require that an individual show a pervasive pattern of three out of seven possible behaviors including failure to conform to social norms, deceitfulness, impulsivity, aggressiveness, disregard for safety of self or others, irresponsibility, and lack of remorse. Although they do not actually experience feelings of remorse, they may feign their regret for harming others in order to get themselves out of a difficult situation when they get caught. These individuals also try hard to present themselves in as favorable a light as possible. You might think of them as the "smooth talkers" who can con anyone out of anything, such as asking someone for money or favors that they have no intention of repaying.

The changes in *DSM-5*'s diagnostic system for personality disorders will result in organizing the seven *DSM-IV-TR* criteria into the categories of personality functioning, interpersonal functioning, and personality traits. These criteria conform more to those in the PCL-R because they include grandiosity or egocentrism and lack of ability to enter into close relationships, criteria that were not in the *DSM-IV-TR*. In addition, each of the three major components of the diagnosis will involve clinician ratings of the severity of the individual's symptoms rather than a simple count of the number of behaviors the individual exhibits.

There is a difference between antisocial personality disorder and antisocial behavior. Stealing, lying, and cheating are examples of antisocial behavior. There is also a difference between antisocial and criminal behavior. The term "criminal" has meaning in the legal system, but is not a psychological concept. Still, many individuals who land in prison meet the psychological criteria for antisocial personality disorder. At the same time, not all individuals with antisocial personality disorder engage in explicitly criminal behavior, but instead their disorder may manifest itself in behaviors such as job problems, promiscuity, and aggressiveness.

Antisocial personality disorder seems to emerge in childhood, both in terms of the development of psychopathic traits and rates of breaking the law. We may consider

Typical antisocial behaviors include lying, cheating and stealing.

a certain degree of antisocial behavior normative in teenagers; however, this behavior can have lifelong consequences if it leads teenagers to drop out of school, accumulate a criminal record and incarceration, and develop an addiction to drugs (Salekin, 2008).

Over the course of their adult years, people with antisocial personality disorder seem to become less likely to commit criminal acts (Moran, 1999). The rate of homicide offenses for people over the age of 35 is lower than for people under the age of 34 and even lower for people 50 and older (Bureau of Justice Statistics, 2011). Overall, the rates for violent crime drop from approximately 1,000 per 100,000 for people aged 35 to 39 to 93 per 100,000 for people 60 and older (Federal Bureau of Investigation, 2004). Less than 1 percent of all prisoners, federal and state, are over 65 and 5 percent are 55 to 64 (Glaze, 2011). The components of psychopathy involving impulsivity, social deviance, and antisocial behavior are less prominent in prison inmates who are in their mid-forties and older (Harpur & Hare, 1994). Perhaps antisocial individuals experience burnout or have become more adept at avoiding detection, or perhaps some of the more extreme cases are eliminated from the population, because these people are killed or arrested in the course of their criminal activities.

Another possibility is that aging brings with it a reduction of the acting-out and impulsive behaviors that we associate with antisocial, as well as with histrionic and borderline personality disorders. The **"maturation hypothesis"** suggests that older individuals are better able to manage their high-risk tendencies (Segal, Coolidge, & Rosowsky, 2000). A longitudinal study of men from adolescence to middle adulthood supports this hypothesis. Personality traits related to antisocial behavior decreased in a large majority of men in midlife (Morizot & Le Blanc, 2005).

maturation hypothesis
The proposition that people with antisocial personality and the other Cluster B disorders become better able to manage their behaviors as they age.

Theories of Antisocial Personality Disorder

As you have seen, antisocial personality disorder represents a deeply entrenched pattern of behavior, with wide-ranging effects on both the individual and the people with whom the individual comes into contact. In this section, we will consider the most compelling explanations for the development of this personality disorder. It is important to remember that some of these investigations pertain to criminals, who may or may not have been diagnosed specifically with antisocial personality disorder.

Biological Perspectives Family inheritance studies provide strong evidence in favor of genetic explanations of antisocial personality disorder, the personality trait of psychopathy, and antisocial behavior with heritability estimates as high as 80 percent. To explain this genetic variation, their attention is focused on genes related to the activity of serotonin and dopamine. One in particular is monoamine oxidase A, an enzyme coded by the MAOA gene. A mutation in this gene results in insufficient amounts of monoamine oxidase in the nervous system, which results in abnormally high levels of dopamine, serotonin, and norepinephrine. High levels of these neurotransmitters are linked to greater impulsivity. Researchers also believe that dependence of the mother during pregnancy can lead to epigenetic influences through DNA methylation (Gunter, Vaughn, & Philibert, 2010). Malnutrition in early life may serve as another risk factor for the development of antisocial personality disorder. In a study of children tested from ages 3 to 17, those who experienced poor nutrition at age 3 showed more aggressiveness and motor activity as they grew up. By age 17 they had a higher likelihood of conduct disorder, a precursor to antisocial personality disorder (Liu, Raine, Venables, & Mednick, 2004).

The hippocampus, the brain structure involved in short-term memory processing, seems to function abnormally in individuals with psychopathy. Although the volume of the hippocampus does not seem to differ between psychopath and nonpsychopath samples, these brain structures seem to have abnormal shapes in people with psychopathy (Boccardi et al., 2010). Neuroimaging studies also suggest that people high in psychopathy have deficits in frontal lobe functioning, meaning that they are less able to inhibit

Antisocial Personality Disorder and Moral Culpability

If antisocial personality disorder is a psychological disorder, should people who meet the diagnosis be held responsible for criminal acts that they may commit? What about people who have the personality trait of psychopathy? Are they somehow more or less culpable? The question of criminal responsibility permeates the ethical literature on ASPD and the related personality trait of psychopathy. According to Robert Hare, when the judicial system applies the term "psychopathy" rather than "antisocial personality disorder" to an offender, that offender is likely to receive a harsher sentence because the court perceives the person (usually a male) as lacking any redeeming qualities. Canadian philosopher Ishtiyaque Haji challenges the idea that people high in psychopathy are mentally healthy and thus, responsible for their crimes (Haji, 2010). He suggests that these individuals have less moral responsibility for their crimes than do people who are not high on the psychopathy trait. According to Haji, the emotional insensitivity that is a hallmark of psychopathy makes an individual less able to appreciate the moral consequences of his or her actions.

Carrying this argument further, consider the factors that may lead an individual to develop high levels of the trait of psychopathy. Perhaps their lack of emotional sensitivity relates to an abnormality of brain development, as some researchers suggest. If they truly cannot experience empathy, how can they relate to the harm that they may be causing a victim? Similarly, if they lack the neurological basis for learning fear, and thus are less likely to avoid the negative consequences of criminal activity, is this flaw of brain development a fact that makes them similar to people who have a physical illness? Without the ability to appreciate the punishment that may follow a crime, people high in psychopathy cannot learn from their experiences and seem doomed to continue to become "emotionally depraved" (in Haji's words).

The question of whether people high in psychopathy have a true impairment that prevents them from recognizing the moral implications of their actions will, no doubt, continue. Each case of a serial murderer committed by an individual with antisocial personality disorder or one who is high on psychopathy seems to raise the issue all over again. With increasingly sophisticated evidence on the neurodevelopmental factors that predispose individuals to developing this disorder, we may eventually understand the issue with greater clarity.

input from subcortical areas of the brain that are involved in aggression (Pridmore, Chambers, & McArthur, 2005).

Psychological Perspectives   Closely related to the biological perspective is the hypothesis that antisocial personality disorder causes neuropsychological deficits reflected in abnormal patterns of learning and attention. Recall that Cleckley believed that psychopathic individuals lack emotional reactivity. David Lykken (1957) took this idea into the lab and demonstrated that psychopathic individuals exposed to aversive stimuli indeed failed to show the normal fear response. Consequently, they do not learn from their negative experiences. We call this deficit of classical conditioning passive avoidance, meaning that the correct responses involve learning to avoid responding to a previously punished stimulus. Poor passive avoidance learning in people high in the personality trait of psychopathy may be related to deficits in the activation of limbic system circuits responsible for emotional processing (Birbaumer et al., 2005).

People high in psychopathy also have difficulty processing negative emotional stimuli such as sad facial expressions (Sommer et al., 2006). Researchers believe that this emotional processing deficit could relate to the inability that these individuals have to develop a sense of morality. Since they can't empathize with their victims, they do not feel remorse over harming them.

REAL STORIES

Ted Bundy: Antisocial Personality Disorder

". . . the most cold-hearted son of a bitch you'll ever meet."

Infamous serial killer Ted Bundy was born in 1946 in Burlington, Vermont. Although the identity of his father is unknown, various sources have suspected that it may be his grandfather who was abusive and violent toward Ted's mother. This caused Ted to harbor a lifelong resentment toward his mother for never revealing who his father was. In turn, Ted looked up to his grandfather who was known for his bigotry and propensity toward violence. As a child, Ted's mother recalls him engaging in strange behaviors, including placing knives around his mother's bed while she slept, waking to find him standing over her and smiling.

Ted and his mother moved to Washington State, where his mother married Johnny Bundy, who formally adopted him. The couple had four children of their own and although they made a point to include Ted in all of their activities, Ted preferred to stay out of the family's affairs and kept mostly to himself. Ted described varying accounts of his early life to biographers, although in general it appears that he presented himself as a charming, outgoing young man. However, on the inside he felt no desire to make any connection with others and had difficulty keeping friends and romantic partners.

After dropping out of college, Ted began working at a suicide hotline and enrolled in a community college where he studied psychology. Eventually, he went to law school at the University of Utah, although by the end of his first year he had stopped attending classes. He moved back to the Pacific Northwest and worked on political campaigns, and around this time, young women had begun disappearing. Profilers on the cases of the murdered women had Ted on their suspect list, although they had difficulty believing that such

an engaging and motivated young man could be capable of such crimes. Between the years of 1974 and 1978, Ted was responsible for the grisly murders of at least 30 women in Utah, Washington, Oregon, Idaho, and Florida. The details of these murders are gruesome. In his book *The Bundy Murders*, Kevin M. Sullivan describes that "The planning, hunting, taking, and subsequent killing of his victims (not to mention his penchant for necrophilia) would prove to be a time-consuming process." Ted would reportedly approach his young female victims in public places, often in broad daylight, and pretend to either be an authority figure, or to be injured before taking them to a more secluded area where he would molest, assault, and eventually murder them.

Ted escaped from prison following his first arrest. He was finally convicted for the murder of Kimberly Leach. In his book *The Bundy Murders,* Kevin M. Sullivan describes this murder: "He was intoxicated, but not with alcohol. His intoxication was the deep and vicious craving to which he had surrendered himself long ago. This craving, which had so utterly taken control and superseded every other aspect of his life, would never stop seeking victims as long as he was alive."

After his conviction, Bundy was sentenced to death by electrocution in the state of Florida in 1989. *The Bundy Murders* described how Ted gained a very high profile status in the media during his trial and subsequent time spent on death row. During his trial, Ted attempted to use his law school experience to argue his way out of a guilty conviction.

Dr. Emmanuel Tanay, a professor of psychiatry at Wayne State University conducted a

clinical interview with Ted with an aim to find Ted not guilty by reason of insanity. A report of the interview goes as follows:

"Bundy is a 32-year-old, handsome-looking man, dressed with the casual elegance of a young college professor. He was meticulously groomed with well-cared-for fingernails to freshly washed hair. He was in total command of the situation. The deputy sheriffs appeared more like a part of his entourage than policemen guarding a prisoner . . . At the outset of the interview, Mr. Bundy commented on the security precautions, saying that they were the result of 'the Bundy mystique,' which has developed as a result of news media activities. This was presented in the manner of a complaint; it was however my impression that Mr. Bundy was taking pride in his

Executed in 1989 for murder, Ted Bundy admitted to being responsible for the deaths of at least 30 people.

celebrity status. In the nearly three hours which I spent with Mr. Bundy, I found him to be in a cheerful even jovial mood; he was witty but not flippant, he spoke freely; however, meaningful communication was never established. He was asked about his apparent lack of concern so out of keeping with the charges facing him. He acknowledged that he is facing a possible death sentence, however, 'I will cross that bridge when I get to it.' Mr. Bundy has an incapacity to recognize the significance of evidence held against him. It would be simplistic to characterize this as merely lying inasmuch as he acts as if his perception of the significance of evidence was real . . . In his decision-making process, Mr. Bundy is guided by his emotional needs, sometimes to the detriment of his legal interests. The pathological need of Mr. Bundy to defy authority, to manipulate his associates and adversaries, supplies him with 'thrills' to the detriment of his ability to cooperate with his counsel."

In the end, Ted decided not to plead insanity. As Sullivan writes, "In Bundy's mind, everything he'd ever done was apparently outside the realm of 'insanity.' The removal and sequestering of his victims' heads and having sex with the dead did not, in his mind, constitute mental aberration. He would refer to this sort of thing only as 'my problem.' Committing murder, Ted Bundy once told a writer, was nothing more than 'acting out.'"

After the court rejected his final appeal, Ted Bundy was executed by electric chair on the morning of January 24, 1989. Of his execution, Sullivan writes, "Apparently, Bundy was free of any feelings of animosity towards those who helped put him there as he had conciliatory body gestures (head notes, etc.) for others entering the room. But when it came to his last statement, he spoke only of giving his 'love to my family and friends,' leaving the living victims of Bundy's homicidal rage little more than a final slap in the face."

The response modulation hypothesis attempts to explain the failure of individuals high in psychopathy to learn from negative experience and to process emotional information (Glass & Newman, 2009). According to this explanation, people have a dominant and nondominant focus of their attention in any given situation. For example, you may be focusing your attention now on your reading, but at the same time, in the background, you are surrounded by noises such as music, other students talking, or the sound of traffic. Although your primary responses right now are to try to understand what you are reading, you might switch over to the secondary cues if something changes to require your attention, such as another student talking directly to you. You need to pay enough attention to those secondary cues to switch if necessary, but not so much that you are unable to carry out your primary task.

According to the response modulation hypothesis, individuals high on the trait of psychopathy are unable to pay enough attention to secondary cues to switch (i.e., modulate) their attention when necessary. Therefore, in a passive avoidance task, they pay attention only to the trials in which they will receive a reward and do not learn from trials in which they incur punishment. In their behavior in the outside world, this pattern would translate into a tendency to focus only on what they can get from a situation (money, power, or other desired goals) and not consider that if they pursue these rewards that punishment might result. Similarly, they focus on their own pleasure, but not on the pain that they may cause the people that they hurt.

The majority of research on psychopathy is focused on men and, in fact, researchers primarily developed and tested the response modulation hypothesis on male populations. Interestingly, when researchers examined both emotion processing and passive avoidance learning in women, they did not find differences between women high and low in psychopathy. It is possible that women are better able to attend to nondominant responses compared to men (Vitale, MacCoon, & Newman, 2011).

Early life experiences can also serve as important influences on whether an individual develops antisocial personality disorder. The parents of individuals with this disorder are more likely to have been overburdened, lack parenting skills, and themselves exhibit antisocial behaviors (Lykken, 2000).

Individuals with antisocial personality disorder may engage in manipulative behaviors due to a lack of remorse about hurting other people.

relationships. Therapists, regardless of orientation, must be extremely patient in their attempts to build a therapeutic relationship. The very nature of the avoidant condition makes the treatment prognosis poor, primarily because these clients tend to be intensely sensitive to the possibility of any form of negative evaluation (Millon, Davis, Millon, Escovar, & Meagher, 2000).

10.4 Borderline Personality Disorder

The term "borderline" in this personality disorder relates to its origins in the 1930s as a condition on the "border" between neurotic and psychotic forms of psychopathology, on the edge of schizophrenia. The criteria are very different now than they were at the time, reflecting continuing revisions of the criteria of this disorder, but the terminology remains with us today.

Characteristics of Borderline Personality Disorder (BPD)

borderline personality disorder (BPD)
A personality disorder characterized by a pervasive pattern of poor impulse control and instability in mood, interpersonal relationships, and self-image.

In *DSM-IV-TR,* the diagnosis of **borderline personality disorder (BPD)** rests on the individual's demonstration of at least five out of a possible nine behaviors, including frantic efforts to avoid abandonment, unstable and intense relationships, identity disturbance, impulsivity in areas such as sexuality, spending, or reckless driving, recurrent suicidal behavior, affective instability, chronic feelings of emptiness, difficulty controlling anger, and occasional feelings of paranoia or dissociative symptoms. As you can see from Table 10.1, instability will remain one of the hallmark features of the diagnostic criteria for BPD in *DSM-5,* but the authors organize the nine possible symptoms into four categories, plus the personality traits of negative affectivity, disinhibition, and antagonism. With the new system, clinicians will evaluate individuals along the dimensions of personality and interpersonal functioning, as well as on the extent to which they show negative personality traits. The system will result in a less arbitrary basis to help a clinician determine whether an individual has this disorder (i.e., meeting perhaps four instead of five criteria).

Men who suffer from borderline personality disorder are more likely to present with antisocial symptoms than women.

MINI CASE

Borderline Personality Disorder

Lisa is a 28-year-old account executive with a long history of interpersonal problems. At the office, her co-workers view her as intensely moody and unpredictable. On some days, she is pleasant and high-spirited, but on others she exhibits uncontrollable anger. People are often struck by her inconsistent attitudes toward her supervisors. She vacillates between idealizing them and devaluing them. For example, she may boast about the brilliance of her supervisor one day, only to deliver a burning criticism the next day. Her co-workers keep their distance from her, because they have become annoyed with her constant demands for attention. She has also gained a reputation in the office for her promiscuous involvements with a variety of people, male and female. On several occasions, colleagues have reprimanded her for becoming inappropriately involved in the personal lives of her clients. One day, after losing one of her accounts, she became so distraught that she slashed her wrists. This incident prompted her supervisor to insist that Lisa obtain professional help.

DSM-5 will still retain the BPD's central feature, which is that of instability. In their self-definition, people with this disorder go beyond insecure. They literally rely on other people to help them feel "whole." Even after they have passed through the customary time of identity questioning in adolescence, they remain unsure and conflicted about their life's goals. Their chronic feelings of emptiness also lead individuals with BPD almost to morph their identities into those of the people to whom they are close. Unfortunately for them, the more that they seek the reassurance and closeness of others, the more they drive these people away. As a result, their disturbed feelings only become more intense, and they become more and more demanding, moody, and reckless. In this way, the symptoms of the disorder become cyclical and self-perpetuating, often escalating to the point at which the individual requires hospitalization.

A term that the profession often uses to describe the way that people with BPD relate to others is "**splitting.**" This means that their preoccupation with feelings of love for the object of their desire and attention can readily turn to extreme rage and hatred when that love object rejects them. They may apply this all-good vs. all-bad dichotomy to other experiences and people as well. The intense despair into which they can become thrust may also lead them to perform suicidal gestures, either as a way to gain attention, or to derive feelings of reality from the physical pain that this action causes. These so-called "parasuicides" may lead to hospitalization, where clinicians detect that the act was, in fact, a gesture and not a true desire to die.

splitting

A defense, common in people with borderline personality disorder, in which individuals perceive others, or themselves, as being all good or all bad, usually resulting in disturbed interpersonal relationships.

Individuals who have BPD improve over time, at least in terms of the severity of their symptoms. In a 10-year longitudinal study of 175 individuals with this disorder, a team of leading researchers in the field found that 85 percent no longer had symptoms, although they improved at slower rates than did people with either major depressive disorder or other personality disorders. However, their overall social functioning and Global Assessment of Functioning (GAF) scores remained lower over time than those of individuals with other personality disorders. Thus, although people may experience improved functioning in terms of their psychiatric disorder, they remain challenged when it comes to their employment and interpersonal relationships (Gunderson et al., 2011).

BPD's lifetime prevalence in the United States is 7 percent. The prevalence is much higher (15 to 20 percent) in psychiatric hospitals and outpatient community settings (Gunderson, 2011). At one time, researchers believed that women were more likely to have BPD than were men, but they consider the prevalence equal between the genders. However, there are gender differences in specific symptoms and in other disorders that occur in conjunction with a diagnosis of BPD. Men with BPD are more likely to have substance abuse disorder and antisocial personality characteristics. Women have higher rates of mood and anxiety disorders, eating disorders, and post-traumatic stress disorder. These differences in the nature of their associated disorders may account for the previous estimates of higher rates of the disorder in women, who clinicians more likely encountered in mental health settings. In contrast, clinicians are more likely to see men in substance abuse programs (Sansone, Dittoe, Hahn, & Wiederman, 2011).

Theories and Treatment of BPD

BPD symptoms are tied to a number of biological factors, including high heritability (42 to 68 percent) and abnormalities in the amygdala and prefrontal cortex, areas of the brain involved in emotional processing and regulation. People with BPD may also have abnormalities in neurotransmitters and hormones involved in regulating emotional responses and sensitivity to pain (Gunderson, 2011). Although biological factors may certainly create a vulnerability to developing BPD, the psychological perspective is more prominent in the approach taken by clinicians who provide treatment. Disturbances in emotional functioning form an important component of the diagnosis of BPD and correspondingly, researchers have focused their efforts on identifying the specific psychological processes that contribute to these emotional disturbances. People with BPD seem to have an inability to regulate emotions (**emotional dysregulation**), limitations in ability to withstand distress (distress tolerance), and avoidance of emotionally uncomfortable situations and feelings (experiential avoidance).

You might be able to imagine how these difficulties can translate into the symptoms of people with BPD in their everyday lives when they encounter stressful situations. More so than other people, they dislike emotionally tense situations, feel uncomfortable when distressed, and have great difficulty handling their anger when something does go wrong. Researchers investigating the relationships among these three types of emotional disturbance in a sample of young adult outpatients found that, after controlling for depressive symptoms, it was experiential avoidance that had the highest relationship to BPD symptoms (Iverson, Follette, Pistorello, & Fruzzetti, 2011).

Early childhood experiences play an important role in the development of BPD. These include childhood neglect or traumatic experiences, and marital or psychiatric difficulties in the home. Additionally, children who were insecurely attached are more likely to develop into adults with BPD (Gunderson, 2011).

As we pointed out earlier, people with BPD experience significant challenges in social functioning, but they can achieve significant relief of their symptoms. The treatment with the greatest demonstrated effectiveness is **dialectical behavior therapy (DBT)**, a form of psychotherapy. Psychologist Marsha Linehan developed this type of behavior therapy specifically to treat individuals with BPD (Linehan, Cochran, & Kehrer, 2001). In DBT, the clinician integrates supportive and cognitive behavioral treatments with the goal of reducing the frequency of the client's self-destructive acts and to increase his or her ability to handle emotional distress.

The term "dialectical" in DBT refers to the back-and-forth process in which the clinician accepts clients as they are, but also confronts them about their problematic behavior, moving them slowly toward greater control over their feelings and behaviors. Therapists working from this perspective help their clients find new ways to analyze their problems and to develop healthier solutions. Clinicians help clients regulate their emotions, develop greater effectiveness in handling social relationships, tolerate emotional distress, and develop self-management skills. Using a process called core mindfulness, DBT clinicians teach their clients to balance their emotions, reason, and intuition as they approach life's problems.

Another evidence-based treatment for BPD, transference-focused psychotherapy, uses the client-clinician relationships as the framework for helping clients achieve greater understanding of their unconscious feelings and motives (Levy et al., 2006). Psychiatrically based management incorporates psychodynamic therapy as developed for BPD treatment, along with family interventions and pharmacologic treatment (Gunderson & Links, 2008).

Regardless of the specific treatment approach that they use, clinicians have the greatest success if they follow a set of basic principles (Table 10.5). These principles set the

---

emotional dysregulation
Lack of awareness, understanding, or acceptance of emotions; inability to control the intensity or duration of emotions; unwillingness to experience emotional distress as an aspect of pursuing goals; and inability to engage in goal-directed behaviors when experiencing distress.

Dialectical behavior therapy (DBT)
Treatment approach for people with borderline personality disorder that integrates supportive and cognitive-behavioral treatments to reduce the frequency of self-destructive acts and to improve the client's ability to handle disturbing emotions, such as anger and dependency.

Table 10.5 Needs Involved in Basic Principles of Effective Treatment for Clients with BPD

Need for Clinicians to:	Explanation
Take over a primary role in treatment	One clinician discusses diagnosis, assesses progress, monitors safety, and oversees communication with other practitioners and family.
Provide a therapeutic structure	The clinician establishes and maintains goals and roles, particularly outlining limits on his or her availability and a plan to manage the client's possible suicidal impulses or other emergencies.
Support the client	The clinician validates the client's emotions of distress and desperation, providing hopeful statements that change is possible.
Involve the client in the therapeutic process	The clinician recognizes that progress depends on the client's active efforts to take control over his or her behavior.
Take an active role in treatment	The clinician is active in therapy, focuses on situations in the here-and-now, and helps the client connect his or her feelings to events in the past.
Deal with the client's suicidal threats or self-harming acts	The clinician expresses concern about and listens patiently to threats, but behaves judiciously (i.e., not always recommending hospitalization).
Be self-aware and ready to consult with colleagues	The clinician may require consultation when the client-clinician relationship becomes problematic.

SOURCE: Adapted from Gunderson, 2011.

stage for the clinician to help the client because they focus on providing key features that can be therapeutic for people with this specific disorder. Although many of these principles could generalize beyond clients with BPD, the need to establish clear boundaries, expectations, structure, and support are particularly important for individuals with this diagnosis. The last principle encourages clinicians to seek support themselves when the client's symptoms lead to difficulties within therapy. For example, the symptom of splitting shown by individuals with BPD may lead them alternatively to devalue and idealize the clinician. In these cases, the clinician may experience complicated reactions and would benefit from obtaining the outside perspective of a supervisor or consultant.

10.5 Narcissistic Personality Disorder

As you can see from Table 10.2, people who meet the criteria for the diagnosis of **narcissistic personality disorder (NPD)** base their self-esteem excessively on the views of other people. They see themselves as exceptional and have a strong sense of entitlement. Because they see themselves as exceptional, they may set their personal standards as unrealistically high. Conversely, they may regard themselves as entitled to whatever they want and therefore set their personal standards far too low. Their impairments in goal setting also include a constant attempt to gain approval from other people.

In terms of their own sense of identity, people with NPD derive their self-definition and self-esteem from the way that they believe other people view them. However, although sensitive to others' opinions, they are unable to empathize with other people. They entirely direct whatever concern they have for others toward determining whether people like them or not. In their special personal relationships, they cannot establish true closeness with an intimate partner because they are so focused on themselves, their feelings, and how people perceive them. Their sense of entitlement translates into personality traits of grandiosity, and their desire for admiration leads them to seek out recognition whenever possible.

narcissistic personality disorder (NPD)
A personality disorder primarily characterized by an unrealistic, inflated sense of self-importance and a lack of sensitivity to the needs of other people.

MINI CASE

Narcissistic Personality Disorder

Chad is a 26-year-old man who has been desperately trying to succeed as an actor. However, he has had only minor acting jobs and has been forced to support himself by working as a waiter. Despite his lack of success, he brags to others about all the roles he rejects because they aren't good enough for him. Trying to break into acting, he has been selfishly exploitive of any person whom he sees as a possible connection. He has intense resentment for acquaintances who have obtained acting roles and devalues their achievements by commenting that they are just lucky, yet, if anyone tries to give him constructive criticism,

Chad reacts with outrage, refusing to talk to the person for weeks. Because of what he regards as his terrific looks, he thinks he deserves special treatment from everyone. At the restaurant, Chad has recurrent arguments with his supervisor, because he insists that he is a "professional" and that he should not have to demean himself by clearing dirty dishes from the tables. He annoys others because he always seeks compliments on his clothes, hair, intelligence, and wit. He is so caught up in himself that he barely notices other people and is grossly insensitive to their needs and problems.

histrionic personality disorder

A personality disorder characterized by exaggerated emotional reactions, approaching theatricality, in everyday behavior.

Although people with NPD may appear to think of themselves as better than others, this grandiosity may mask an underlying vulnerability in their sense of self. Some individuals with NPD may have a truly inflated and grandiose sense of self; hence, clinicians refer to them as high on grandiose narcissism. However, clinicians more accurately characterize others as high on vulnerable narcissism. These are the individuals who rely excessively on other people to confirm their worth. Those high on vulnerable narcissism are more sensitive to rejection, more likely to feel a sense of shame, and are less able to bolster their fragile sense of self by making up grandiose fantasies. They may appear shy and even empathic. When they feel that they have not lived up to their standards, they are more likely to become socially withdrawn. People who are higher on grandiose narcissism are more threatened by failure in the realm of personal accomplishments. Those high on vulnerable narcissism, by contrast, react more negatively when they feel that someone who is important to them is humiliating or betraying them (Besser & Priel, 2010). The *DSM-5* does not explicitly make this distinction, but clinicians and researchers maintain that it is an important differentiation (Pincus, 2011).

The *DSM-IV-TR* gave the diagnosis of **histrionic personality disorder** to people whose behavior reflected many of these behaviors and traits, particularly the personality trait of attention seeking. However, *DSM-5* will remove histrionic personality disorder as a unique diagnosis. Instead, the *DSM-5*'s reformulation of narcissistic personality disorder includes attention-seeking as one of the pathological personality traits. Researchers found that clinicians rarely diagnosed histrionic personality disorder diagnosis in actual practice, with a prevalence of 0.4 percent. Moreover, when people did receive this diagnosis, they also fit the criteria for other personality disorders, particularly borderline, narcissistic, and dependent (Bakkevig & Karterud, 2010). Therefore, the *DSM-5* task force recommended its exclusion as a diagnostic entity in *DSM-5*.

Prevalence studies reveal a wide variation in estimates of NPD's prevalence in the population. Averaging across these studies, researchers believe that NPD may occur in approximately one percent of the population. However, the rates are far higher in populations of individuals seeking clinical treatment, with those estimates ranging from 2 to as high as 36 percent (Dhawan, Kunik, Oldham, & Coverdale, 2010).

The authors of *DSM-5* almost deleted NPD due to overlap with other diagnoses, but they retrieved it, in part, because the theoretical significance of the concept of narcissism is so intense that it reaches pathological levels (Pincus, 2011). The traditional Freudian psychoanalytic approach regards narcissism as the individual's failure to progress beyond the early, highly self-focused stages of psychosexual development. Theorists operating within the object relations framework regard the narcissistic individual as having failed

Individuals with narcissistic personality disorder often devote their lives to seeking approval from others despite having very little concern for the well-being of other people.

to form a cohesive, integrated, sense of self. The narcissistic individual expresses insecurity, paradoxically, in an inflated sense of self-importance as he or she tries to make up for early parental support (Kohut, 1966, 1971). Lacking a firm foundation of a healthy self, these individuals develop a false self that they precariously base on grandiose and unrealistic notions about their competence and desirability (Masterson, 1981). We can understand narcissistic personality disorder, then, as the adult's expression of this childhood insecurity and need for attention.

Clinicians who work within the psychodynamic perspective attempt to provide a corrective developmental experience, using empathy to support the client's search for recognition and admiration. At the same time, the clinician attempts to guide the client toward a more realistic appreciation that no one is flawless. As clients feel that their therapists increasingly support them, they become less grandiose and self-centered (Kohut, 1971).

Cognitive-behavioral theorists focus on the maladaptive ideas that their clients hold, including the view that they are exceptional people who deserve far better treatment than ordinary humans. These beliefs hamper their ability to perceive their experiences realistically, and they encounter problems when their grandiose ideas about themselves clash with their experiences of failure in the real world. Correspondingly, clinicians working in the cognitive-behavioral perspective structure interventions that work with, rather than against, the client's self-aggrandizing and egocentric tendencies. For example, rather than try to convince the client to act less selfishly, the therapist might try to show that there are better ways to reach important personal goals. At the same time, the therapist avoids capitulating to the client's demands for special favors and attention. When the therapist establishes and follows an agenda with clear treatment goals, the client may learn how to set limits in other areas of life (Beck, Freeman, & Davis, 2004).

Cutting across these theoretical perspectives, the most effective approach that clinicians can use in treating people with NPD is to provide reassurance while at the same time encouraging them to develop a more realistic view of themselves and other people. Unfortunately, people with NPD are difficult to treat because they tend not to have insight into their disorder. Moreover, the therapists who treat them may experience strong negative reactions to them due to the very nature of their symptoms of grandiosity and entitlement, making them critical and demeaning of their therapists (Dhawan et al., 2010). Their extreme perfectionism can also obstruct treatment. They have filled their lives with success and accomplishments that preserve their self-esteem and ward off their insecurities. As a result, it is particularly difficult for them to confront their anxieties and inner securities (Ronningstam, 2011).

10.6 Obsessive-Compulsive Personality Disorder

People with **obsessive-compulsive personality disorder (OCPD)** define their sense of self and self-worth in terms of their work productivity. We have just seen that people with NPD may also become excessively oriented toward work accomplishments to bolster their sense of self. People with OCPD are not looking for approval from their work accomplishments, but instead throw themselves into their work to the exclusion of their social relationships. Unfortunately, the extreme perfectionism that people with OCPD have about their work makes it difficult for them to complete a task because they can always see a flaw in what they have done. Their work products are never good enough to meet their unrealistic standards. They can also be overly moralistic because they stick to overly conscientious standards that almost anyone would find difficult to meet.

As you can see from Table 10.1, people with OCPD have a great deal of difficulty understanding how other people feel, particularly when those feelings differ from their own. Other people, in turn, perceive them as rigid and stubborn. Because they have such high standards for themselves, people with OCPD are very critical of other people who they see as not matching their own expectations.

The pathological personality trait of compulsivity that people with OCPD have to an excessive degree reflects this rigid perfectionism. Things must be "just so," or they are miserable. They also experience a great deal of negative affect and tend to go back over and over what they've done, looking for flaws. This is the quality of perseveration.

The words "obsessive" and "compulsive" as applied to the OCPD personality disorder have a different meaning than in the context of obsessive-compulsive disorder. People with OCPD do not experience obsessions and compulsions. The hyphenated term in OCPD refers to this rigidly compulsive (i.e., fixated on certain routines) personality tendency and also obsessive concern with perfectionism. This may seem like splitting hairs, but it is an important distinction for you to keep in mind. Moreover, OCPD is a disturbance of personality, not a disturbance involving anxiety or even out-of-control behaviors, as reflected in the *DSM-5* authors' proposal to remove OCD from the anxiety disorders.

It is important to keep in mind that there is a difference between the hard-working, well-organized person with high standards and a concern about getting a job done right and the person with an obsessive-compulsive personality disorder. People with this disorder are unproductive, and their pursuit of perfection becomes self-defeating rather than constructive.

MINI CASE

Obsessive-Compulsive Personality Disorder

For as long as he can remember, Trevor has been preoccupied with neatness and order. As a child, his room was meticulously clean. Friends and relatives chided him for excessive organization. For example, he insisted on arranging the toys in his toy closet according to color and category. In college, his rigid housekeeping regimens both amazed and annoyed his roommates. He was tyrannical in his insistence on keeping the room orderly and free from clutter. Trevor has continued this pattern into his adult life. He is unhappy that he has not found a woman who shares his personal habits, but consoles himself by becoming immersed in his collection of rare record albums featuring music of the 1940s.

Trevor, a file clerk, prides himself on never having missed a day of work, regardless of health problems and family crises. However, his boss will not offer Trevor a promotion because she feels he is overly attentive to details, thus slowing up the work of the office as he checks and rechecks everything he does. He enhances his sense of self-importance by looking for opportunities in the office to take control. For example, when his co-workers are planning a party, Trevor tends to slow down matters because of his annoying concerns about every detail of the event. More often than not, his co-workers try to avoid letting him get involved because they object to his rigidity, even in such trivial matters.

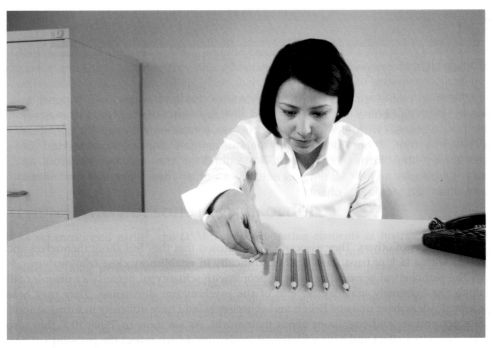

A woman with obsessive-compulsive personality disorder is so highly driven for order and perfection that she is unable to tolerate the anxiety she feels when objects in her vicinity are disorganized.

From a psychodynamic standpoint, Freud believed that people with an obsessive-compulsive style have not progressed from, or are constantly returning to, the anal stage of psychosexual development. Psychodynamic theorists no longer focus entirely on psychosexual stages, but instead give more attention to cognitive factors and prior learning experiences as central to the development of OCPD.

From the standpoint of cognitive-behavioral theory, people with this disorder have unrealistic expectations about being perfect and avoiding mistakes (Beck et al., 2004). Their feelings of self-worth depend on their behaving in ways that conform to an abstract ideal of perfectionism. If they fail to achieve that ideal (which, inevitably, they must), they regard themselves as worthless. In this framework, obsessive-compulsive personality disorder is based on a problematic way of viewing the self.

Clinicians using cognitive-behavioral treatment for clients with OCPD face challenges due to characteristic features of this personality disorder. The person with OCPD tends to intellectualize, to ruminate over past actions, and to worry about making mistakes. Cognitive-behavioral therapy, with its focus on examining the client's thought processes, may reinforce this ruminative tendency. Consequently, therapists may use more traditional behavioral techniques, such as thought stopping with the intention of having the client "stop" when he or she is overtaken by ruminative worry (Millon et al., 2000). Clinicians might also find it useful to use metacognitive interpersonal therapy, a procedure that causes patients to "think about their thinking." In this procedure, clinicians help their clients take a step back and learn to identify their problematic ruminative thinking patterns in the context of a building a supportive therapeutic alliance (Dimaggio et al., 2011).

10.7 Schizotypal Personality Disorder

Confusions and distortions in the individual's basic sense of self are a core feature of **schizotypal personality disorder.** Similarly, they lack a clear sense of direction or motivation, and do not have a clear set of standards against which to measure their behavior. Not only do they have difficulty understanding their own sense of self and motivation, but people with schizotypal personality disorder also have difficulty understanding the motives

schizotypal personality disorder
A personality disorder that primarily involves peculiarities and eccentricities of thought, behavior, appearance, and interpersonal style. People with this disorder may have peculiar ideas, such as magical thinking and beliefs in psychic phenomena.

Autistic savants often excel in one specific skill, such as playing an entire song on the piano from memory after hearing it only one time.

In a multi-site surveillance study in 14 states using records from educational and health settings, the Centers for Disease Control and Prevention reported an estimated prevalence rate averaging 0.66 percent or one out of approximately 150 children, a large increase from previously reported rates (Centers for Disease Control and Prevention, 2007). The publication of this report drew a great deal of media attention to what the authors regarded as a public health crisis. In the wake of this report, researchers have been trying to understand the reasons for the apparent increase in prevalence. Several possibilities stand out. One is that there have been changes in the way in which clinicians interpret the diagnostic criteria. Another pertains to the overlap between mental retardation and autistic disorder. Previously, the Centers for Disease Control and Prevention estimated that 75 percent of individuals with autistic disorder were also mentally retarded; however, in the CDC study, the percentage ranged from 33 percent to 64 percent. This change reflects the fact that clinicians evaluate children with a certain constellation of dysfunctional communication behaviors under current systems of categorization differently than in previous decades. Another possible reason for the increase in estimated prevalence is that, although researchers used *DSM* criteria in identifying autistic individuals, they conducted evaluations using case records rather than in-person evaluations. It is possible that individuals might interpret case records differently than face-to-face evaluations.

An unusual variant of this disorder, called autistic savant syndrome, occurs in people with autism who possess an extraordinary skill, such as the ability to perform extremely complicated numerical operations—for example, correctly naming the day of the week on which a date thousands of years away would fall (Thioux, Stark, Klaiman, & Schultz, 2006). The autistic savant syndrome typically appears at an early age, when the young child with autistic disorder appears to have exceptional musical skills, artistic talent, or the ability to solve extremely challenging puzzles. It is perhaps due to their tendency to focus intensely on the physical attributes of objects rather than the implications of these attributes: seeing the trees, but not the forest. However, memory for areas outside of their own areas of expertise appears to be no better than that of autistic people without special memory skills (Neumann et al., 2010).

Biological Perspective   Evidence pointing to patterns of familial heritance supports the theory that autistic disorder is biologically caused. Based on these investigations, researchers estimate the heritability of autistic disorder at approximately 90 percent, with genetic abnormalities suspected to exist on chromosomes 7, 2, and 15. No clear evidence exists regarding specific deficits in brain structure, but researchers have focused on the cerebellum, frontal cortex, hippocampus, and amygdala. In addition, people with autistic disorder appear to have deficits in the association areas of the cortex (Minshew & Williams, 2007). There is some evidence that overall brain size is increased in some individuals with autistic disorder (Santangelo & Tsatsanis, 2005).

Abnormalities exist in the neural circuitry of people with autistic disorder, as reflected by their particular difficulty in processing facial stimuli (Batty, Meaux, Wittemeyer, Rogé, & Taylor, 2011; Dalton et al., 2005). These brain alterations may account for the fact that people with autistic disorder are less likely to gaze into other people's eyes when communicating with them and less able to use emotional cues when processing information from other people's facial expressions (Bayliss & Tipper, 2005; Dawson et al., 2004).

Behavioral Perspective   Given the strong evidence favoring neurobiological abnormalities in individuals with autistic disorder, the behavioral perspective is most relevant to treatment. Clinicians treating children with autistic disorder from a

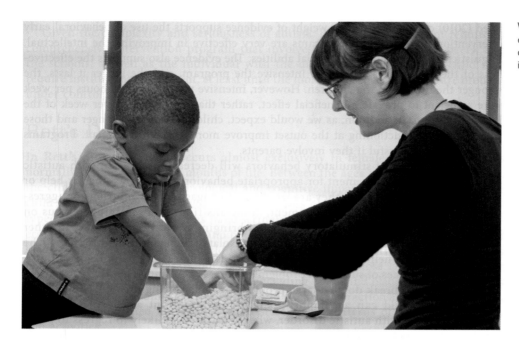

With early therapeutic intervention, children who are diagnosed with autism can experience significant symptom improvement.

behavioral perspective base their methods on the early intervention programs devised by UCLA psychologist Ivar Lovaas in the late 1980s (Lovaas, 1987). In the original report on the program, Lovaas and his associates randomly assigned 38 children ages 3 to 4 diagnosed with autistic disorder to two treatment groups. One group received intervention for at least 40 hours per week for 2 or more years. Children in the second group received treatment with the same intervention for less than 10 hours per week. Another group of children received treatment outside of the Lovaas clinic. Using IQ scores as dependent variables, nearly half (9) of the 19 children who received intensive treatment increased by over 20 points; by age 13, 8 of the children had maintained their IQ gains. By contrast, only one child in the less intensive treatment showed these IQ improvements. The Lovaas studies, as impressive as they were, received criticism from other researchers because the study never assessed the intervention's effects on social and communication skills.

The Lovaas treatment rests on principles of operant conditioning, practiced both by student therapists and parents. The behavioral aspects of the intervention consisted of ignoring the child's aggressive and self-stimulatory behaviors, using time-outs when children were disruptive, and positively attending to the children only when they engaged in socially appropriate behavior, using shaping to increase the performance of the targeted behaviors. As a last resort, when children engaged in undesirable behavior, they were given a loud "no" or a slap on the thigh.

In the first year, the treatment focused on reducing self-stimulatory and aggressive behaviors, shaping the children to comply with simple verbal requests, using imitation learning, establishing the beginnings of play with toys, and extending the treatment into the family home. In the second year of the intervention, the children learned how to use language in an expressive and abstract manner. They also learned how to play interactively with their peers. In the third year, the children learned how to express emotions appropriately, academic tasks to prepare them for school, and observational learning in which they learned by watching other children learn. The clinicians attempted to place the children in mainstream classes rather than special education classes with the idea that others would not label them as "autistic" or as a "difficult child." Children who did not recover received an additional six years of training. The others remained in contact with the project team for occasional consultation.

In the years following the Lovaas study, a number of researchers attempted to replicate his findings. Reviewing 14 of the best-controlled of these studies, Makyrgianni and situations. Behavioral techniques that clinicians use for treating fears and anxieties in children include systematic desensitization, prolonged exposure, and modeling. Contingency management and self-management are also useful in teaching the child to react more positively and competently to a fear-provoking situation. The clinicians may apply behavioral techniques either individually or in combinations. For example, a child with separation anxiety disorder may learn relaxation techniques along with cognitive strategies for thinking more positively about separation (Jurbergs & Ledley, 2005).

Cognitive behavioral therapy (CBT) seems to hold the most promise for treating children with this disorder. Researchers investigating the effectiveness of this approach have developed a form of CBT that clinicians can administer in an intensive and time-limited manner, so that children do not have to commit to weeks or months of therapy. In one version of time-limited CBT, girls with social anxiety disorder attended a 1-week camp where they received intensive CBT in a group setting (Santucci, Ehrenreich, Trosper, Bennett, & Pincus, 2009) (Table 11.6).

TABLE 11.6 Summer Treatment for Girls with Social Anxiety Disorder Program Schedule of Events

Day	Group Content	Separation	Exposure Activities
Monday 10am to 3pm	Children and Parent(s): psychoeducation; interaction between thoughts, feelings, behaviors; exposure rationale ("riding the wave" of anxiety; Subjective Units of Distress), rewards, begin cognitive restructuring (identify anxious thought; generate coping thought). Break-out Parent Group (11:30 to 12:30): differential reinforcement skills (active ignoring, creating reward system) tolerating distress in child and self, structuring of in-vivo exposures.	Parents walk participants to store; separation occurs after 15 minutes of choosing beads (approx. 1:15pm)	Jewelry making (1–3pm)
Tuesday 10am to 3pm	Child and Parent(s): continue cognitive restructuring (identify thinking trap, evaluate evidence for worried thought) Break-out Parent Group (11am–noon): problem solving surrounding implementation of exposure or reward system, autonomy granting	At clinic, prior to departure for activity (approx. noon)	Pottery painting; Eat lunch and use public transportation without parent(s)
Wednesday 10am to 3pm	Child Group: interoceptive exposure, including identification of somatic symptoms and repeated practice eliciting and habituating to relevant symptoms. No Parent Group	At clinic, following homework review (approx. 10.15am)	Bowling (noon to 3pm); Lunch at bowling alley
Thursday 10am to 3pm	Child Group (10am to noon): Progressive Muscle Relaxation, including measuring SUD's before and after practice and when to use PMR. Parent–Group (2–3pm, while participants off-site at exposure activity): review of CBT skills taught to children, problem solving surrounding evening activity and sleepover, planning exposure after treatment ends.	Immediately	Tour of city; Lunch on way to activity; "Bravery Bingo"
Friday 6pm to 9pm	n/a	Immediately	Movie night
Saturday 6pm–morning	n/a	Immediately	Sleepover
Sunday 8am to 9am	Children and Parent(s): awards ceremony, goal setting for upcoming weeks, relapse prevention (e.g. lapse vs. relapse)	n/a	n/a

(Santucci, et al., 2009)

Pilot testing of the summer camp program on five girls, ages 8 to 11, provided encouraging results in that four out of the five girls no longer met the diagnostic criteria for the disorder following treatment, and the fifth showed substantive improvement. The advantages of such an intensive program are that the camp immerses children in the treatment context, the therapy takes place in a time-limited fashion, and parents are involved in the treatment.

In the past, SSRIs such as fluoxetine were the psychopharmacological treatment of choice for children with separation anxiety disorder. However, clinicians are less likely to prescribe these medications following reports of extreme impulsive reactions, including suicidal attempts, among a small number of children taking SSRIs (Ramchandani, 2004). There are few controlled studies on children compared to adults (Ravindran & Stein, 2011). In contrast, behavioral and cognitive behavioral treatments do not carry these adverse effects and therefore appear to be a far more effective approach.

11.7 Other Disorders That Originate in Childhood

Children may develop one of a set of relatively rare but serious disorders, which range from movement abnormalities to specific forms of eating and anxiety disorders. Even though many children do overcome these disorders by the time they reach adulthood, the effects may linger and continue to impair their ability to function in everyday life.

Childhood Eating Disorders

Children with **pica** eat inedible substances, such as paint, string, hair, animal droppings, and paper. This is a serious disorder because even one incidence can cause the child to experience significant medical consequences due to lead poisoning or injury to the gastrointestinal tract. Pica is the most serious cause of self-injury to occur in people with intellectual developmental disabilities. Clinicians treating pica must use not only a behavioral treatment strategy to reduce the individual's injurious behaviors, but must institute prevention by ridding the home of potentially dangerous substances (Williams, Kirkpatrick-Sanchez, Enzinna, Dunn, & Borden-Karasack, 2009).

Two other eating disorders that can affect children specifically are **feeding disorder of infancy or early childhood** and **rumination disorder**. In feeding disorder, the child persistently fails to eat and consequently loses or fails to gain adequate weight. In rumination disorder, the infant or child regurgitates and rechews food after swallowing it.

Researchers investigating feeding and rumination disorder have identified five common disturbances in these children, including (1) delayed or absent development of feeding and eating skills, (2) difficulty managing or tolerating food or drink, (3) reluctance to eat food based on taste, texture, and other sensory factors, (4) lack of appetite or interest in food, and (5) using feeding behaviors to comfort, self-soothe, or self-stimulate. Twenty-five to 45 percent of developmentally normal children, and 80 percent of those who are intellectually disabled, have feeding problems to varying degrees. However, there are many variations in the way clinicians report these disturbances and therefore, epidemiologists do not have exact estimates of their prevalence. Further complicating the clinical picture is the fact that many different factors can contribute to eating problems in children, ranging from a choking experience to medical background, temperament, and physiological abnormalities that create eating problems (Bryant-Waugh, Markham, Kreipe, & Walsh, 2010).

The authors of *DSM-5* have already targeted eating disorders of infancy and childhood for change, which will bring them in line with similar disorders in adolescents

pica
A condition in which a person eats inedible substances, such as dirt or feces; commonly associated with mental retardation.

feeding disorder of infancy or early childhood
A disorder involving the persistent failure to eat, leading to a loss of weight or failure to gain weight.

rumination disorder
An eating disorder in which the infant or child regurgitates food after it has been swallowed and then either spits it out or reswallows it.

the role of biological rather than psychological factors as the source of the disorders that strike children early in life and appear to affect their behavioral functioning by creating brain abnormalities.

- Intellectual disability disorder refers to intellectual and adaptive deficits that are first evident in children. Genetic abnormalities are a significant case. The three most important genetic causes are Down syndrome, phenylketonuria, and fragile X syndrome. Another genetic disorder is Tay-Sachs disease.

- Environmental hazards during prenatal developing are the second category of causes of intellectual developmental disabilities. These hazards, called "teratogens," include drugs or toxic channels, maternal malnutrition, and infections in the mother during critical phases of fetal development. Consumption of alcohol during pregnancy can lead to Fetal Alchohol Syndrome (FAS).

- People with intellectual developmental disabilities can benefit from early intervention aimed at providing them with training in motor coordination, language use, and social skills. Educators can combine mainstreaming, which integrates them into ordinary school classrooms, with special education that provides them with assistance geared to their particular needs.

- Autism is another intellectual development disorder that incorporates a range of serious disturbances in the ways that individuals interact with and communicate with others, as well as in behaviors that can include a person's interest and activity patterns. The *DSM-5* authors are proposing to replace this category with "autism spectrum disorder" to provide a more reliable and valid distinction between children who clearly show "typical development" and those who demonstrate the range of deficits in communication and social behaviors that *DSM-IV-TR* attempts to differentiate.

- Evidence pointing to patterns of familiar heritance supports the theory that autistic disorder is biologically caused. Although it is evident that neurological differences exist between people with and without autistic disorder, the basis for these differences and their implications are not clear.

- Given the strong evidence favoring neurobiological abnormalities in individuals with autistic disorder, the behavioral perspective is the most relevant to treatment. UCLA psychologist Ivar Lovaas developed treatment that rests on principles of operant conditioning practiced by student therapists and parents. Disruptive and self-stimulatory behaviors will decrease if children with autistic disorder receive reinforcement for appropriate behaviors, such as asking for help or feedback. In such instances, they are less likely to engage in self-injurious or aggressive behaviors.

- Other disorders include Rett's and Asperger's. Attention-Deficit/Hyperactivity (ADHD) is the most commonly

recognized disorder and there are many theories and treatments. These include biological heritability as high as 76 percent. Although researchers have found fundamental and structural abnormalities in the brains of people with ADHD, most agree that genetic vulnerability interacts with environmental exposure. Social-cultural influences also play a role in the aggravation of the ADHD symptom picture.

- Other disorders include conduct disorder and oppositional defiant disorder. There are also learning disorders such as dyslexia (reading disorder), mathematical skills disorder, and written expression disorder. Communication disorders include expressive language disorder, receptive-expressive language disorder, phonological disorder, and stuttering. The primary form of motor skill disorder is developmental coordination disorder. The most widely accepted explanation of the learning, communication, and motor skills disorders proposes that they are due to neurological dysfunction.

- Practitioners believe that the best approach to identifying children with learning disorders uses the "Response to Intervention" (RTI) approach in which they institute a set of evidence-based procedures that follow a series of steps.

- Additional disorders include separation anxiety disorder, childhood eating disorders, including pica, feeding disorder of infancy, or early childhood and rumination disorder.

- Tic disorders involve a rapid, recurring involuntary movement or vocalization. This includes Tourette's syndrome.

- The *DSM-IV-TR* defines two elimination disorders that can affect children and adolescents: enuresis and encopresis.

- Children with reactive attachment disorder have severe disturbances in the way they relate to others. There are two types: indiscriminately social/disinhibited and emotionally withdrawn/inhibited.

- Stereotypic movement disorder is representative of children who engage in repetitive, seemingly driven behaviors that interfere with their normal functioning and cause bodily injury.

- Refusing to talk in specific situations is the core feature of selective mutism.

- The disorders covered in this chapter include a range of conditions that reflect, to differing degrees, combinations of biological, psychological, and sociocultural influences. Genetic influences on many of these disorders are clearly evident, but even so, interactions with social context play an important role. Moreover, because these disorders by definition begin early in life, they have the potential to exert profound psychological effects on an individual's life.

KEY TERMS

Aging-Related and Cognitive Disorders

Learning Objectives

12.1 Describe characteristics of aging-related and cognitive
disorders

12.2 Explain delirium

12.3 Describe amnestic disorders

12.4 Identify traumatic brain injury

12.5 Identify dementia

12.6 Explain Alzheimer's disease, including its diagnosis, theories,
and treatments

12.7 Analyze the biopsychosocial model of aging-related and
cognitive disorders

CHAPTER 12

Case Report: Irene Heller

Demographic information: Irene is a 76-year-old Caucasian female.

Presenting problem: Irene was referred for neuropsychological testing from her primary care physician, who noted a significant decline in her memory and motor functioning from the previous year. During a routine physical evaluation, Irene's doctor reported that she displayed cognitive impairments and abnormal reflexes. She was referred for neuropsychological testing to a private specialty practice.

During the initial interview before neuropsychological testing was conducted, Irene was asked about her cognitive functioning. Her daughter Jillian accompanied her to the appointment. Irene had difficulty answering some of the questions in the interview, and thus Jillian provided most of the information for the interview. Jillian reported that her mother's visit to the doctor was not the first sign of any recent abnormalities in her behavior, and that over the past month both she and her other siblings noticed that their mother was acting strangely. Irene currently lives by herself in the town where her two grown children live. On two separate occasions Irene's neighbors had reportedly found her in the parking lot of the apartment complex where she lives late at night in her nightgown looking "totally out of it." The neighbors had brought her back into her home, though Irene did not recall these incidents occurring.

When asked about any physical changes she had noticed recently, Irene stated that was having difficulty writing because she was unable to grasp pens or other writing instruments. As a result she stated she hadn't been able to pay her bills and sometimes had trouble preparing food for herself. In fact, she noted that she had lost about 10 pounds over the past two months because of this.

Jillian also reported that she had noticed her mother was having significant walking difficulties recently. Irene preferred to stay at home as a result and had begun to miss out on many activities that she had previously enjoyed, including spending time with her family and weekly bridge games.

Jillian added that Irene typically called either her or her brother at least once per day, and that they had family meals together once or twice every week. Jillian reported that during the past two months when she or her brother called their mother on the phone, her speech was sometimes difficult to understand, and that Irene would forget to whom she was speaking in the middle of the conversation. All of this was very troubling to Jillian, though Irene wasn't able to acknowledge much of what Jillian was reporting. "I guess I sometimes have a hard time paying my bills or calling my children. I guess I just don't feel like it these days."

Jillian stated that she and her brother thought that perhaps Irene's behavior was due to medical reasons. Irene has been diagnosed with Type II Diabetes and according to Jillian, had forgotten to check her blood sugar and take insulin for two days in a row. Since Jillian and her brother Steve hadn't been talking to their mother, they were unaware that this was occurring. When they didn't hear from their mother, Jillian and Steve went to Irene's house to check on her, finding her nearly unconscious in her living room. After giving her insulin, the siblings made an appointment with Irene's primary care physician for the next day.

After the clinical interview, Irene completed neuropsychological testing, which consisted of a battery of cognitive tests aimed at measuring her overall cognitive functioning.

Relevant history: Irene reported that she has remained relatively healthy throughout her life and that she has never experienced any major medical, emotional, or cognitive problems. Two years prior to the interview, Jillian stated that her mother was diagnosed with Type II Diabetes and has been taking insulin to regulate her blood sugar. Jillian reported that until her recent decline, Irene had remained quite active and participated in many social activities and was able to carry out all of her activities of daily living without difficulty.

Case formulation: The rather sudden onset of Irene's symptoms is typical of Vascular Dementia. Though the onset varies, typically it occurs suddenly due to the nature of the etiology. Since Irene had stopped taking her medication, she was putting herself at significant medical risk. Further, as with diagnostic criteria, Irene's functioning was significantly impaired—she had ceased her previous activities and had even stopped paying her bills due to her motor difficulties.

The results of the neuropsychological testing indicated that Irene indeed was experiencing a significant impairment in her short-term memory and her ability to speak fluently and

coherently, and also evidenced difficulties in her executive functioning, including organizing and sequencing information that was presented to her. Taken together with the physical examination from her doctor, Irene is given a diagnosis of Vascular Dementia, although until she has an MRI to confirm the existence of brain lesions, the diagnosis will be tentative.

Multiaxial assessment:

Axis I: 29.40 Vascular Dementia, with Behavioral Disturbance
Axis II: None
Axis III: Diabetes type II
Axis IV: Memory and cognitive difficulties interfering with ability to perform activities of daily living.
Axis V: Current: 35; highest in the past year: 85

Treatment plan: Irene will be referred for an MRI in order to confirm her diagnosis, upon which she will be given a referral for medication and follow-up home care, if needed.

Sarah Tobin, PhD

12.1 Characteristics of Aging-Related and Cognitive Disorders

The brain's functioning affects our abilities to think, remember, and pay attention. The disorders that we will discuss in this chapter share the common feature of involving damage to the brain, which in turn affects these cognitive abilities. There are many sources of insults or injuries to the brain including trauma, disease, or exposure to toxic substances, including drugs. The *DSM-IV-TR* provides descriptions to help clinicians diagnose people with disorders that reflect clear brain injury or disease as having a delirium, dementia, amnestic, or other cognitive disorders. For the sake of brevity, we will use the term "cognitive disorders" as a comprehensive label.

As the seat of all thoughts, actions, motivations, and memories, the brain, when damaged, can cause a variety of symptoms. Some of these symptoms may mimic schizophrenia, mood disorders, and personality disorders. People can develop delusions, hallucinations, mood disturbances, and extreme personality changes due to brain changes resulting from disease, reactions to medication, and exposure to toxic substances. Although we may think of these symptoms as "psychological," they must, by necessity, have a physiological basis. In the cognitive disorders, we can clearly identify this physiological basis.

Clinicians use neuropsychological testing and neuroimaging techniques, as well as an individual's medical history, to decide whether an individual's symptoms fall into the category of a cognitive disorder. Neuropsychological testing helps clinicians identify specific patterns of responses that fit known disease profiles. They combine this knowledge with their client's medical histories to see if a specific event triggered the symptoms. In addition, neuroimaging provides clinicians with an inside look at the brain to help them connect symptoms with specific illnesses or injuries.

12.2 Delirium

People who experience **delirium** temporarily lose their conscious awareness and are unable to focus, maintain, or shift their attention. The symptoms tend to appear abruptly and fluctuate over the course of the time that they have the disorder. *DSM-IV-TR* defines delirium in terms of a disturbance of "consciousness," but *DSM-5* will most likely change this definition to be disturbance in level of "awareness" given the vague nature of the term consciousness. Regardless of what it is called, the core of the disorder involves an acute state of confusion, impairment in cognitive processing that affects memory, orientation, executive functioning, ability to use language, visual perception, and learning. To receive a diagnosis of delirium, the individual must show these changes in consciousness or awareness over a very short period of time, on the order of hours or days, and tending to fluctuate over the course of the day. Finally, a general medical condition must cause the disturbance, which the clinician must specify in the diagnosis along with a rating on Axis III.

Delirium can develop for a variety of reasons, including substance intoxication or withdrawal, head injury, high fever, and vitamin deficiency. People of any age can experience delirium, but it is more common among medically or psychiatrically hospitalized older adult patients, particularly among surgical patients with pre-existing cognitive impairment and depressive symptoms (Minden et al., 2005). In addition to age, the risk factors for delirium include a previous history of stroke, dementia, sensory impairment, and use of multiple prescription medications ("polypharmacy"). People at risk may develop delirium following infections, urinary retention or use of catheters, dehydration, loss of mobility, and disorders involving heart rate. Changes in neurotransmitters may be involved in delirium. People who develop delirium following a stroke may do so due to loss of neuron oxygenation in the brain (Dahl, Rønning, & Thommessen, 2010). Increases in immune system inflammatory responses may also contribute to delirium (Simone & Tan, 2011).

Infection is another precipitating factor in at-risk individuals. In a survey of nearly 1.3 million patients studied over the years 1998 to 2005, researchers found that the most frequent causes were infections, including respiratory infections, cellulitis, and urinary tract and kidney infections. The next largest cause of delirium consisted of some type of central nervous system disorder, including cancer, dementia, strokes, and seizures. The third most frequent cause of delirium included metabolic disorders, cardiovascular disease, and orthopedic procedures. However, over the course of the study, drug-induced delirium increased in prevalence among older adults, suggesting that either hospital workers became more attuned to this diagnosis or that people in this age group are becoming more and more likely to receive delirium-inducing medications. Making health professionals aware of adverse drug effects may ultimately help to reduce the prevalence of delirium in high-risk individuals (Lin, Heacock, & Fogel, 2010).

Apart from the cognitive symptoms of inattention and memory loss, individuals experiencing delirium may also have hallucinations, delusions, abnormalities in sleep-wake cycles, changes in mood, and movement abnormalities (Jain, Chakrabarti, & Kulhara, 2011). Once

delirium
A temporary state in which individuals experience a clouding of consciousness in which they are unaware of what is happening around them and are unable to focus or pay attention.

Delirium is a temporary condition that can have a wide range of physiological causes. Individuals who experience this condition suffer from several sensory disturbances simultaneously.

TABLE 12.1 Delirium Rating Scale—Revised—98 (DRS-R-98)

1. Sleep-wake cycle disturbance

    0. Not present
    1. Mild sleep continuity disturbance at night or occasional drowsiness during the day
    2. Moderate disorganization of sleep-wake cycle (e.g., falling asleep during conversations, napping during the day, or several brief awakenings during the night with confusion/behavioral changes or very little nighttime sleep)
    3. Severe disruption of sleep-wake cycle (e.g., day-night reversal of sleep-wake cycle or severe circadian fragmentation with multiple periods of sleep and wakefulness or severe sleeplessness)

2. Perceptual disturbances and hallucinations

    0. Not present
    1. Mild perceptual disturbances (e.g., feelings of derealization or depersonalization; or patient may not be able to discriminate dreams from reality)
    2. Illusions present
    3. Hallucinations present

3. Delusions

    0. Not present
    1. Mildly suspicious, hypervigilant, or preoccupied
    2. Unusual or overvalued ideation that does not reach delusional proportions or could be plausible
    3. Delusional

4. Lability of affect (outward presentation of emotions)

    0. Not present
    1. Affect somewhat altered or incongruent to situation; changes over the course of hours; emotions are mostly under self-control
    2. Affect is often inappropriate to the situation and intermittently changes over the course of minutes; emotions are not consistently under self-control, although they respond to redirection by others
    3. Severe and consistent disinhibition of emotions; affect changes rapidly, is inappropriate to context, and does not respond to redirection by others

5. Language

    0. Normal language
    1. Mild impairment including word-finding difficulty or problems with naming or fluency
    2. Moderate impairment including comprehension difficulties or deficits in meaningful communication (semantic content)
    3. Severe impairment including nonsensical semantic content, word salad, muteness, or severely reduced comprehension

6. Thought process abnormalities

    0. Normal thought processes
    1. Tangential or circumstantial
    2. Associations loosely connected occasionally, but largely comprehensible
    3. Associations loosely connected most of the time

7. Motor agitation

    0. No restlessness or agitation
    1. Mild restlessness of gross motor movements or mild fidgeting
    2. Moderate motor agitation including dramatic movements of the extremities, pacing, fidgeting, removing intravenous lines, etc.
    3. Severe motor agitation, such as combativeness or a need for restraints or seclusion

they experience this condition, people who had delirium are more likely to experience medical complications that can cause rehospitalization and a higher risk of mortality (Marcantonio et al., 2005). People who experience delirium following a stroke also have higher rates of developing dementia within 2 years (van Rijsbergen et al., 2011).

There are several specialized tests to assess delirium. The Delirium Rating Scale-Revised (DRS-R-98) (Trzepacz et al., 2001) is a widely used measure that has been translated into several languages (Table 12.1) and has well-established validity and reliability (Grover, Chakrabarti, Shah, & Kumar, 2011). The advantage of using this scale is that although

TABLE 12.1 Delirium Rating Scale—Revised—98 (DRS-R-98) (continued)

8. Motor retardation

    0. No slowness of voluntary movements
    1. Mildly reduced frequency, spontaneity or speed of motor movements, to the degree that may interfere somewhat with the assessment.
    2. Moderately reduced frequency, spontaneity, or speed of motor movements to the degree that it interferes with participation in activities or self-care
    3. Severe motor retardation with few spontaneous movements

9. Orientation

    0. Oriented to person, place, and time
    1. Disoriented to time (e.g., by more than 2 days or wrong month or wrong year) or to place (e.g., name of building, city, state), but not both
    2. Disoriented to time and place
    3. Disoriented to person

10. Attention

    0. Alert and attentive
    1. Mildly distractible or mild difficulty sustaining attention, but able to refocus with cueing. On formal testing makes only minor errors and is not significantly slow in responses
    2. Moderate inattention with difficulty focusing and sustaining attention. On formal testing, makes numerous errors and requires prodding either to focus or to finish the task
    3. Severe difficulty focusing and/or sustaining attention, with many incorrect or incomplete responses or inability to follow instructions. Distractible by other noises or events in the environment

11. Short-term memory (Defined as recall of information [e.g., 3 items presented either verbally or visually] after a delay of about 2 to 3 minutes.)

    0. Short-term memory intact
    1. Recalls 2/3 items; may be able to recall third item after category cueing
    2. Recalls 1/3 items; may be able to recall other items after category cueing
    3. Recalls 0/3 items

12. Long-term memory

    0. No significant long-term memory deficits
    1. Recalls 2/3 items and/or has minor difficulty recalling details of other long-term information
    2. Recalls 1/3 items and/or has moderate difficulty recalling other long-term information
    3. Recalls 0/3 items and/or has severe difficulty recalling other long-term information

13. Visuospatial ability

Assess informally and formally. Consider patient's difficulty navigating one's way around living areas or environment (e.g., getting lost). Test formally by drawing or copying a design, by arranging puzzle pieces, or by drawing a map and identifying major cities, etc. Take into account any visual impairments that may affect performance.

    0. No impairment
    1. Mild impairment such that overall design and most details or pieces are correct; and/or little difficulty navigating in his/her surroundings
    2. Moderate impairment with distorted appreciation of overall design and/or several errors of details or pieces; and/or needing repeated redirection to keep from getting lost in a newer environment despite trouble locating familiar objects in immediate environment
    3. Severe impairment on formal testing; and/or repeated wandering or getting lost in environment

SOURCE: Trzepacz et al., 2001

designed for psychiatrists, other professionals (physicians, nurses, psychologists) and researchers can also use it. When completing the instrument, the clinician can use information gathered from family members, visitors, hospital staff, physicians, medical charts, and even hospital roommates.

To treat delirium, clinicians may use a pharmacological approach in which they administer antipsychotics. The standard approach involves using haloperidol, but clinicians may use "off-label" antipsychotics such as respiridone. This combination

vascular dementia
A form of dementia resulting from a vascular disease that causes deprivation of the blood supply to the brain.

multi-infarct dementia (MID)
A form of dementia caused by transient attacks in which blood flow to the brain is interrupted by a clogged or burst artery.

Another possible cause of dementia is cardiovascular disease affecting the supply of blood to the brain. As we pointed out earlier, this condition, called **vascular dementia,** is highly prevalent and researchers link it to a variety of cardiovascular risk factors. Dementia can follow a stroke, in which case we call it acute onset vascular dementia, but the most common form of vascular dementia is **multi-infarct dementia (MID),** caused by transient attacks in which blood flow to the brain is interrupted by a clogged or burst artery. The damage to the artery deprives the surrounding neurons of blood and oxygen, which causes the neurons to die. Although each infarct is too small to be noticed at first, over time the progressive damage caused by the infarcts leads the individual to lose cognitive abilities.

Vascular dementia resembles the dementia due to Alzheimer's disease in some ways. People with vascular dementia experience memory impairment, as well as one of the following: aphasia, apraxia, agnosia, or disturbance in executive functioning. However, there are some significant differences between these two forms of dementia. People with vascular dementia show a particular set of physical abnormalities, such as walking difficulties and weakness in the arms and legs. Furthermore, people with vascular dementia show a pattern of cognitive functioning that is distinctly different from that in people with Alzheimer's. In the typical clinical picture of vascular dementia, certain cognitive functions remain intact and others show significant loss, a pattern that we call patchy deterioration. Another unique feature of vascular dementia is that it shows a stepwise deterioration in cognitive functioning: a function that was relatively unimpaired is suddenly lost or severely deteriorates. This is in contrast to the gradual pattern of deterioration in Alzheimer's disease.

As is true for Alzheimer's disease, there is no treatment to reverse the cognitive losses in MID. However, individuals can take preventive actions throughout adulthood to protect themselves from the subsequent onset of vascular dementia. Reducing the risk of hypertension and diabetes is one important way to lower the chances of developing cognitive disorders in later life (Papademetriou, 2005).

Depression Adding to the complexity of separating the causes of dementia in disorders other than Alzheimer's is the fact that depression can lead to symptoms that are similar to those apparent in the early stages of Alzheimer's disease. Depression may also co-exist with Alzheimer's disease, particularly during the early to middle phases, when the individual is still cognitively intact enough to be aware of the onset of the disorder and to foresee the deterioration that lies ahead. Although depressive symptoms are distinct from Alzheimer's disease, these symptoms may serve to heighten the risk of developing Alzheimer's disease, particularly among men. In a 40-year longitudinal study of nearly 1,400 older adults, men who were depressed had twice the risk of developing Alzheimer's disease as men who were not depressed (Dal Forno et al., 2005). Interestingly, the brain autopsies of 90 of the participants who died during the course of the study did not show the characteristic brain changes that occur with Alzheimer's disease (Wilson et al., 2007). A study linking loneliness to the development of Alzheimer's disease in both men and women showed similar findings. Such findings strengthen the notion that loneliness can trigger depression, which in time may lead to brain deterioration and symptoms of dementia similar to those in people with diagnosable Alzheimer's disease.

pseudodementia
Literally, false dementia, or a set of symptoms caused by depression that mimic those apparent in the early stages of Alzheimer's disease.

In assessing dementia-like symptoms, clinicians must be aware of the condition **pseudodementia,** or false dementia, a severe form of depression. Distinguishing between these conditions is important because one can successfully treat depression.

Several indicators can help the clinician differentiate depression from dementia. For example, depressed individuals are more keenly aware of their impaired cognition and frequently complain about their faulty memory. In contrast, individuals with Alzheimer's usually try to hide or minimize the extent of impairment or to explain it away when they cannot conceal the loss. As the disorder progresses, people with Alzheimer's disease lose awareness of the extent of their cognitive deficits and may even report improvement as they lose their capacity for critical self-awareness.

The order of symptom development also differs between Alzheimer's disease and depression. In depressed elderly people, mood changes precede memory loss. The reverse is true for people with Alzheimer's disease. People with depression are anxious, have difficulty sleeping, show disturbed appetite patterns, and experience suicidal thoughts, low self-esteem, guilt, and lack of motivation. People with dementia, in contrast, experience unsociability, uncooperativeness, hostility, emotional instability, confusion, disorientation, and reduced alertness. People with pseudodementia also are likely to have a history of prior depressive episodes that may have been undiagnosed. Their memory problems and other cognitive complaints have a very abrupt onset, compared with those of people with dementia, who experience a more slowly developing downward course. Another clue that can help clinicians distinguish between Alzheimer's and pseudodementia is to explore the individual's recent past to determine whether a stressful event has occurred that may have precipitated the onset of depression. Sensitive tests of memory also may enable the clinician to distinguish pseudodementia from Alzheimer's disease. People with pseudodementia are likely to not respond when they are unsure of the correct answer. In contrast, individuals with Alzheimer's adopt a fairly liberal criterion for making responses and, as a result, give many incorrect answers.

Diagnosis of Alzheimer's Disease

Because of the importance of early diagnosis to rule out treatable dementias, researchers and clinicians devote significant energy and attention to the development of behavioral tests for diagnosing Alzheimer's disease in its initial stages. An erroneous diagnosis would be a fatal mistake if the person had a dementia that would have been reversible if the clinician had applied proper treatment when the symptoms first became evident. Similarly, if the individual had a disorder with a nonorganic basis, the clinician would have missed a crucial opportunity to intervene. Unfortunately, the early symptoms of Alzheimer's do not provide a sufficient basis for diagnosis.

Only an autopsy can make a definitive diagnosis of Alzheimer's disease by studying microscopic changes in brain tissue, leaving clinicians with the only option of conducting diagnosis by exclusion. However, in the later stages of the disease, there are diagnostic guidelines that the clinician can apply that have 85 to 90 percent accuracy. A joint commission of the National Institute of Neurological and Communicative Disorders and Stroke and the Alzheimer's Disease and Related Diseases Association developed these guidelines in 1984. We refer to them as the NINCDS/ADRDA Guidelines (McKhann et al., 1984). The diagnosis of Alzheimer's disease, which at present is based on the NINCDS/ADRDA criteria, involves thorough medical and neuropsychological screenings. Even with these very stringent and complete guidelines, the diagnoses to which they lead is at best one of "probable" Alzheimer's disease, again reflecting the fact that only through an autopsy can we obtain a certain diagnosis.

Clinicians are using brain imaging techniques increasingly for diagnosing Alzheimer's disease. The continued improvement of MRI has resulted in a virtual explosion of studies on the diagnosis of Alzheimer's disease through brain imaging. In addition to using brain imaging, clinicians are investigating the feasibility of diagnosing the disease from the amount of amyloid in spinal fluid.

Many psychologists, nevertheless, remain firm that accurate diagnosis of Alzheimer's disease must ultimately rest upon neuropsychological testing. They cite the expense, invasiveness, and lack of clear-cut connections to behavior of these biologically based diagnostic methods. Some argue that until there are effective treatments, early diagnosis does not help clients or their families, but only increases their anxiety.

In 2011, a group of researchers and clinicians convened to revise the 1984 NINCDS/ADRDA Guidelines, taking into account improved knowledge of the clinical manifestations and biological changes involved in Alzheimer's disease (McKhann et al., 2011). They also believed that it is important to acknowledge the fact that memory changes may or may not occur in individuals whose brains show signs of the disease. Their goal was to develop diagnostic criteria not dependent on the expensive and potentially invasive brain scans used in research. The group recognized that there is still no infallible way of diagnosing the disorder in a living individual, proposing that clinicians diagnose an individual

TABLE 12.5 Mechanism of Action and Side Effects of Alzheimer's Medications

Drug Name	Drug Type and Use	How It Works	Common Side Effects
Namenda® **(memantine)**	N-methyl D-aspartate (NMDA) antagonist prescribed to treat symptoms of moderate to severe AD	Blocks the toxic effects associated with excess glutamate and regulates glutamate activation	Dizziness, headache, constipation, confusion
Razadyne® **(galantamine)**	Cholinesterase inhibitor prescribed to treat symptoms of mild to moderate AD	Prevents the breakdown of acetylcholine and stimulates nicotinic receptors to release more acetylcholine in the brain	Nausea, vomiting, diarrhea, weight loss, loss of appetite
Exelon® **(rivastigmine)**	Cholinesterase inhibitor prescribed to treat symptoms of mild to moderate AD	Prevents the breakdown of acetylcholine and butyryl-choline (a brain chemical similar to acetylcholine) in the brain	Nausea, vomiting, diarrhea, weight loss, loss of appetite, muscle weakness
Aricept® **(donepezil)**	Cholinesterase inhibitor prescribed to treat symptoms of mild to moderate, and moderate to severe AD	Prevents the breakdown of acetylcholine in the brain	Nausea, vomiting, diarrhea

its release into the synaptic cleft. Because these slow the breakdown of acetylcholine, they allow higher levels to remain in the brain, thus facilitating memory. All have significant side effects. Memantine falls into a separate category of FDA-approved medications for treatment of Alzheimer's disease in the moderate to severe stages. An NMDA antagonist, memantine regulates glutamate, which, in excessive amounts, may destroy neurons.

The side effects that Table 12.5 shows include those that clinicians consider mild and therefore tolerable. However, the anticholinesterases can have serious side effects that include fainting, depression, anxiety, severe allergic reactions, seizures, slow or irregular heartbeat, fever, and tremor. Memantine's side effects can include hallucinations, seizures, speech changes, sudden and severe headache, aggressiveness, depression, or anxiety. When prescribing these medications, clinicians must weigh any benefits against these side effects, which themselves may interact with other medications that the individual is receiving for other health conditions, such as aspirin and nonsteroidal anti-inflammatory drugs (NSAIDs), Tagamet (used to treat heartburn), certain antibiotics, anti-depressants, and medications that improve breathing. In addition, none of these medications are available in generic form, and can cost nearly $200 per month.

The benefits of the current medications to treat Alzheimer's disease symptoms are short-lived. Memantine, prescribed for moderate to severe Alzheimer's disease, shows positive effects for up to 12 weeks (Schulza et al., 2011). Although donepezil may reduce

MINI CASE

Dementia of the Alzheimer's Type

Ellen is a 69-year-old woman whose husband took her to her family physician as he was becoming increasingly concerned by her failing memory and strange behavior. Ellen's husband had first become concerned a few months earlier when Ellen couldn't remember the names of basic household items, such as spoon and dishwasher. Her day-to-day forgetfulness became so problematic that she would repeatedly forget to feed or walk the dog. As the weeks went by, Ellen seemed to get worse. She would leave food burning on the stove and water overflowing the bathtub. A review of Ellen's medical history found no physical problems that could account for her deterioration, nor could her physician or a neurologist determine any current medical basis for her behavior.

symptoms by as much as 39 to 63 percent (Lopez et al., 2010), past the first 12 weeks of treatment its benefits begin to diminish. After 3 years, individuals on any of the three anticholinesterases show poorer performance on the MMSE than they did at the beginning of treatment (Figure 12.7). Administering higher levels of anticholinesterases may slow the progression somewhat, but does not prevent deterioration in cognitive functioning over 3 years of treatment (Wattmo, Wallin, Londos, & Minthon, 2011). Done-pezil may reduce the perception by caregivers of their burden and of the other symptoms shown by the patients they care for, but these effects have not been studied past 12 weeks of treatment (Carrasco, Aguera, Gil, Morinigo, & Leon, 2011). Another medication, galantamine (Razadyne), acts as an anticholinesterase and may have positive effects for up to 3 years, but also has a higher

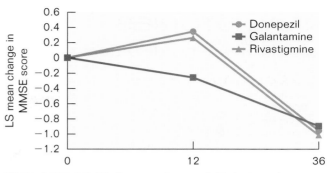

FIGURE 12.7 Comparison of Alzheimer's Medications

death rate associated with its use (Scarpini et al., 2011). Medications that address the deleterious changes in tau are being developed, but at present are not suitable for use in humans (Navarrete, Pérez, Morales, & Maccioni, 2011).

Other approaches to treating Alzheimer's disease target the free radicals, which are molecules that form when beta amyloid breaks into fragments. Free radicals most likely damage neurons in the surrounding brain tissue. Antioxidants can disarm free radicals and, therefore, may be another treatment for Alzheimer's disease. Bioflavonoid, a substance that occurs naturally in wine, tea, fruits, and vegetables, is one such antioxidant. Researchers view naturally occurring bioflavonoids (in, for example, blueberries) as having important preventive roles in reducing the extent of memory loss in later adulthood (Joseph, Shukitt-Hale, & Casadesus, 2005). A longitudinal study of over 1,300 French people found that bioflavonoids were beneficial in reducing the risk of Alzheimer's disease (Commenges et al., 2000).

Given that no medical treatments exist to cure the disease, behavioral psychologists are developing strategies to maximize the daily functioning of people with Alzheimer's disease. They often target these efforts at the caregivers, who are the people (usually family members) primarily responsible for caring for the person with the disease. Caregivers often suffer adverse effects from the constant demands placed on them, effects that we call caregiver burden (Table 12.6). However, we can teach caregivers behavioral strategies that can promote the patient's independence and reduce his or her distressing behaviors. Support groups can also provide a forum in which caregivers learn ways to manage the emotional stress that occurs with their role.

Table 12.6 APA Caregivers Briefcase

In 2011, the American Psychological Association launched the Caregivers Initiative under the leadership of then-president Carol Goodheart. The Caregivers Briefcase summarizes resources, facts, and tips for caregivers: http://www.apa.org/pi/about/publications/caregivers/index.aspx

This summary of five tips suggests helpful strategies for family caregivers, whether parents are caring for children, partners for partners, or children for parents:

1. **Recognize how widespread caregiving situations are.** Although everyone's situation is unique, you're not alone in experiencing burden.

2. **Take advantage of support services.** Sharing your experiences with others can give you both practical and emotional help.

3. **Focus on positive coping strategies.** Adapt the self-statements and coping strategies mentioned above until you find the ones that work for you.

4. **Take care of your own needs.** You need to focus on your health, both mental and physical, if you're going to be an effective caregiver. You'll also feel better.

5. **Ask for help when you need it.** You don't have to be a martyr. Reaching out to others will alleviate your stress. You may be surprised at the willingness of others to offer you assistance.

SOURCE: Whitbourne, S. K. (March, 2011). Family caregiving across the generations. *Psychology Today*, http://www.psychologytoday.com/blog/fulfillment-any-age/201103/family-caregiving-across-the-generations.

REAL STORIES

Ronald Reagan: Alzheimer's Disease

"I didn't know then to what degree Alzheimer's would be a slow prelude to dying, a blurring of everything that was uniquely, essentially my father."

—Patti Reagan Davis

Born in 1911, Ronald Reagan was the oldest American president to take the oath of office, at 70 years old. He served two terms between 1981 and 1989, and is remembered as one of the most popular presidents of recent history. His political and economic policies changed the face of the nation and as president he helped, in part, to end the Cold War between the United States and the former Soviet Union. In 1994, four years after leaving office, Reagan publicly disclosed that he had been diagnosed with Alzheimer's disease. He passed away in 2004, after spending the final 3 years of his life confined to a hospital bed in his California home.

A native of Illinois, Reagan attended college in Eureka before moving to Iowa to begin his career in radio broadcasting. He soon moved to Los Angeles and launched his acting career, starring in many popular films and television shows. Following a turn as a spokesman for General Electric, Reagan became involved in politics. He served as governor of California for 10 years before he was elected president in 1980, having run unsuccessfully twice before and beating out the incumbent President Jimmy Carter.

A *New York Times* article from 1997 described Reagan's life just a few short years after coming forward with his diagnosis. At the time of the article, Reagan appeared unchanged, although he was on the verge of showing some of the more severe signs of Alzheimer's. The article stated, "If, at the age of 86, the old movie actor still looks the image of vigorous good health, the truth is that the man behind the firm handshake and barely gray hair is steadily, surely ebbing away." Although the signs were becoming clear, Reagan was still able to perform activities of daily living such as dressing himself and he continued to partake in his regular routine, which involved playing golf, exercising, and making occasional public appearances. Despite his healthy exterior and extensive support network, at this point Reagan's condition began to deteriorate.

During his presidency, Ronald Reagan notoriously struggled with his memory, particularly when it came to remembering people's names. By 1997, this difficulty was much more pronounced and the only person he was able to remember on a consistent basis was his wife, Nancy. Following the revelation of his diagnosis, there was much controversy as to whether or not he had symptoms of Alzheimer's disease during his presidency. The *New York Times* article cites Reagan's doctor who confirmed that he did not actually start showing any symptoms until at least 3 years following the end of his final term.

"Alzheimer's is often said to involve a family of victims," the article states. "As it inexorably shuts off communication, the disease breeds loneliness, frustration and confusion not just for the patient, but for the spouse, relatives and friends. Many longtime friends and aides say they find it too painful to compare the Ronald Reagan afflicted with Alzheimer's with his former self."

In 2001, 4 years after the article appeared, Reagan suffered a fall in his home and broke his hip. Although his hip was repaired, he became homebound as his condition had greatly deteriorated. In her book, *The Long Goodbye*, Reagan's daughter Patti Davis recalls that doctors had given him just months to live. In the end, he lived another 4 years. Her book poignantly depicts the heartache and struggle that haunts not only the patients, but the families of those dying from Alzheimer's disease. Patti highlights that the most painful aspect of the process of watching a loved one suffer from Alzheimer's is the length of the process of physical and mental deterioration and the psychological effect this has on the family.

"I am a daughter who lived her life missing her father." Patti describes her father as a man who had little time to be involved in the lives of his children as he spent 8 years of his life as leader of a powerful nation. The turmoil of watching their father's long and slow death was made all the more excruciating due to Reagan's guarded personal disposition. As Patti describes in the book, "Even my mother has admitted there was a part of him—a core—that she could never touch."

The book started as a collection of diary entries that Patti had written about her experiences watching her father succumb to his disease. The second youngest of Reagan's five children, Patti was often at odds with her father's social and political views. In the book she writes about how

Ronald Reagan began to show pronounced signs of Alzheimer's disease just a few short years after completing two consecutive terms as President of the United States.

their relationship changed as the years went on and as she stuck by his side throughout the progression of his illness. Not only did her father's relationship with her change with the course of his disease, but the entire family dynamic shifted as the differences between them drifted away in light of their desire to be together through this difficult time. This is not uncommon as families come together to cope with the slow loss of a loved one to Alzheimer's.

"Alzheimer's disease locks all the doors and exits. There is no reprieve, no escape. Time becomes the enemy, and it seemed to stretch out in front of us like miles of fallow land." Patti goes on to describe the insidious nature of the disease and its slow progression throughout the years as she witnessed in her father. Alongside observations of her father as he grew older and as Alzheimer's increasingly took its toll, Patti recalls the memories of him throughout her life—giving a speech on her wedding day, swimming with her in the ocean, singing together in church. These memories were important in helping the family cope with the pain of slowly losing their father. "You breathe life into your own memories because right there, in front of you, sitting in the chair he always goes to, or walking down the hall, or gazing out the window, is a reminder of the hollowness that's left when memories are erased. So you welcome it when images come back, or bits of conversations. You seize them, dust them off, and pray they'll stay as bright."

In her book, Patti describes the process that her mother endured as she slowly lost her husband of over 40 years. "My mother speaks of the loneliness of her life now. He's here, but in so many ways he's not. She feels the loneliness in small ways— he used to put lotion on her back; now he doesn't. And in the huge, overwhelming ways—a future that will be spent missing him."

Patti also addresses the issue of Nancy Reagan's decision to keep the details of her husband's suffering private from the watchful eye of the media. "My mother has called it a long goodbye—the way Alzheimer's slowly steals a person away. It's been one of her only public comments; upon agreement, we have chosen the cloak of respectful silence when it comes to the subject of my father's condition. It's a heartbreaking phrase, and she's told me she won't say it again because it ushers in tears." Even on the day that her father passed away on June 5, 2004, Patti recalls a reporter hovering around the home, as rumors that he was nearing the end of his life had surfaced to the public. As the family gathered around Reagan's bed during his final moments of life, Patti remembers hearing news reports in the next room that his condition was grave and how more reporters began calling and coming to the house. In the end, the family was prepared for their father to pass away, although this did not erase the pain that they shared when his battle with Alzheimer's finally ended.

"There will be times," Patti writes of their reaction to his death, "when we are lifted up on the back of memories, and other times when sorrow drives us to our knees. Especially my mother, who will have moments of wondering why he had to leave first. We will wait for him to enter our dreams. We will look for him in every breeze that drifts through every open window. We will breathe deep and wait for his whisper to stream into us—tell us secrets and make us smile."

Behavioral strategies aimed at increasing the patient's independence include giving prompts, cues, and guidance in the steps involved in self-maintenance. For example, the clinician can encourage the patient to relearn the steps involved in getting dressed and then positively reward him or her with praise and attention for having completed those steps. Through modeling, the patient relearns previous skills through imitation. We can also teach the caregiver time management, which involves following a strict daily schedule. As a result, the patient is more likely to fall into a regular routine of everyday activities. All of these methods benefit both the patient and the caregiver. The patient regains some measure of independence, which reduces the caregiver's burden to the extent that the patient can engage in self-care tasks (see Table 12.6).

Behavioral strategies can also eliminate, or at least reduce the frequency of, wandering and aggression in an Alzheimer's patient. One possible approach, which is not always practical, involves extinction. The caregiver ignores certain disruptive behaviors, with the intention of eliminating the reinforcement that has helped maintain them. However, extinction is not practical for behaviors that may lead to harm to the patient, such as wandering if it involves leaving the house and walking into the street. One possibility is to give the patient positive reinforcement for staying within certain boundaries. However, this may not be sufficient, and, at that point, the caregiver needs to install protective barriers. Another possible approach is for the caregiver to identify situations that are particularly problematic for the patient, such as in the bathtub or at the table. The caretaker can then use behavioral methods in these circumstances. For example, if the problem occurs while eating, it may be that the caretaker can encourage the patient to relearn how to use a knife and fork, rather than feeding him or her. Again, such an intervention can reduce caregiver burden, as well as increase the patient's functional skills (Callahan et al., 2006).

The caregiver can implement behavioral interventions through individual therapy or in a support group. The support group facilitator can teach these methods to participants. Furthermore, caregivers can share strategies among themselves based on their experiences. The emotional support that caregivers can provide for each other can be just as valuable as the actual instruction that they receive. Ultimately, the Alzheimer's patient receives better quality care when caregiver burden is minimized.

You can see, then, that although the prospect of Alzheimer's is frightening and painful for all individuals involved, a number of interventions are available. However, until researchers find a cure for the disorder, clinicians must be content to measure their gains less as progress toward a cure and more as success in prolonging the period of maximum functioning for the individual and the individual's family.

12.7 Cognitive Disorders: The Biopsychosocial Perspective

We can best understand the cognitive impairments that occur with the disorders that we discussed in this chapter, by definition, from a biological perspective. However, the biological perspective has not yet produced a viable treatment for one of the most devastating of these disorders, Alzheimer's disease. Until researchers find a cure, individuals and their families whose lives are touched by the disease must be willing to try a variety of approaches to alleviate the suffering. Many research programs are currently underway to explore strategies for reducing the stress placed on caregivers. Some of these strategies involve innovative, high-technology methods, such as computer networks. Others take the more traditional approach of providing emotional support to individuals with Alzheimer's disease and their families. The application of cognitive-behavioral and other methods of therapy to help people cope with Alzheimer's is another useful approach. It seems that the bottom line in all this research on understanding and treating those affected by Alzheimer's disease is that it is not necessary for psychologists to wait until biomedical researchers discover a cure. They can do quite a bit to improve the quality of life for people with Alzheimer's and to help them maintain their functioning and their dignity as long as possible.

Return to the Case: Irene Heller

Irene's MRI showed multiple vascular legions on her cerebral cortex and the subcortical structures of her brain, confirming her diagnosis of Vascular Dementia. The qualifier of "with behavioral disturbance" was added to her diagnosis due to her history of wandering spells that had occurred with the onset of her symptoms.

Following her diagnosis, Irene was immediately started on medication, and after a few weeks she and her family began noticing that she had returned to her "premorbid" (previous) level of functioning. Upon a recommendation made by the neuropsychologist she saw for testing, Irene began to attend a support group for those who have been diagnosed with Vascular Dementia offered in a community center in her town. Irene avidly attends every week and has reported benefiting due to the social support aspect of the group as well as learning more about the disease and how it affects each

person differently. The support group has also educated Irene to be mindful of any changes in her cognition or motor movements, and to seek consultation immediately with her physician should any new difficulties arise. Due to her improved memory, Irene's health remained stable as she was remembering to take her insulin as prescribed. Irene enjoyed taking part in her regular activities again and spending time with her family, no longer burdened by motor difficulties. Irene will undergo a brief battery of neuropsychological testing every 6 months to monitor for any further deterioration in her cognition and to assess efficacy of her treatment regimen.

Dr. Tobin's reflections: Vascular Dementia can result from a stroke. Due to the patchy and irregular deterioration of Irene's symptoms it is more likely that her dementia resulted from a more gradual process of cerebrovascular disease. In many cases, adults live for some time with mild symptoms of dementia. Irene was fortunate to have attentive children who noticed her symptoms relatively soon after they arose and she was able to seek treatment that I hope will slow the development of this disorder. She was also fortunate that her diagnosis was based on careful consideration of multiple sources of testing, as many older adults with Vascular Dementia are incorrectly diagnosed with Alzheimer's disease, which is irreversible and requires a different course of treatment and case planning.

SUMMARY

- Cognitive disorders (formally called "delirium, dementia, amnestic, and other cognitive disorders") are those in which the central characteristic is cognitive impairment that results from causes such as brain trauma, disease, or exposure to toxic substances.

- Delirium is a temporary state in which individuals experience a clouding of consciousness in which they are unaware of what is happening and are unable to focus or pay attention. They experience cognitive changes in which their memory is foggy and they are disoriented, and they may have various other symptoms, such as rambling speech, delusions, hallucinations, and emotional disturbances. Delirium, which is caused by a change in the brain's metabolism, can result from various factors, including substance intoxication or withdrawal, head injury, high fever, and vitamin deficiency. The onset is generally rapid and the duration brief.

- Amnestic disorders are conditions in which people are unable to recall previously learned information or to register new memories. These disorders are due either to the use of substances or to medical conditions such as head trauma, loss of oxygen, and herpes simplex.

- Researchers are increasingly recognizing traumatic brain injury (TBI) as an important cause of mental and physical dysfunction. Symptoms include headaches, sleep disturbances, sensitivity to light and noise, and diminished cognitive performance on tests of attention, memory, language, and reaction time. These individuals may also suffer depression, anxiety, emotional outbursts, mood changes, or inappropriate affect.

- Dementia is a form of cognitive impairment involving generalized progressive deficits in a person's memory and learning of new information, ability to communicate, judgment, and motor coordination. In addition to experiencing cognitive changes, individuals with this condition undergo changes in their personality and emotional state. Dementia results from profuse and progressive brain damage that occurs with physical conditions, such as vascular diseases, AIDS, head trauma, psychoactive substances, and various neurological disorders.

- The best-known form of dementia is Alzheimer's disease, a condition that occurs with severe cerebral atrophy as well as with characteristic microscopic changes in the brain. Clinicians specify Alzheimer's disease according to subtypes: with delirium, with delusions, with depressed mood, or uncomplicated. The diagnosis of Alzheimer's is challenging for several reasons. Some conditions, such as vascular dementia, have symptoms similar to those of Alzheimer's. Other conditions, such as depression, can lead to symptoms that mimic those in the early stages of Alzheimer's. All theories regarding the cause of Alzheimer's disease focus on biological abnormalities involving the nervous system—specifically, two types of brain changes. The first is the formation of neurofibrillary tangles, in which the cellular material within the cell bodies of neurons becomes replaced by densely packed, twisted microfibrils, or tiny strands, of protein. The second change involves the development of amyloid plaques, which are clusters of dead or dying neurons mixed with fragments of protein molecules. In addition to biological explanations, researchers have also focused on environmental contributors to Alzheimer's, as well as the role of certain behaviors in preventing the development of the disease. Although there is no cure for this disease, researchers are attempting to find medications, such as anticholinesterase agents, that alleviate its symptoms. At the same time, experts have focused their attention on refining behavioral techniques for managing symptoms and have given particular attention to strategies for alleviating caregiver burden.

KEY TERMS

Substance-Related Disorders

Learning Objectives

13.1 Explain the difference between substance abuse and substance dependence

13.2 Explain alcohol use/abuse and theories and treatments of alcohol dependence

13.3 Differentiate among other drugs of abuse and describe theories and treatments for them

13.4 Analyze the biopsychosocial model of substance-related disorders

Case Report: Carl Wadsworth

Demographic information: Carl is a 32-year-old African American male.

Presenting problem: Carl's sister Janice made an appointment for him to see a therapist at a local outpatient therapy clinic following an arrest for public intoxication. Janice stated that the family was "sick of being worried" about him. She reported that Carl had been drinking much more frequently over the past few years than ever before, culminating in his recent arrest for public intoxication. Janice also reported that Carl has bipolar disorder, although he is not on medication currently, about which she and the family were concerned.

During the intake session, the therapist noticed that Carl appeared intoxicated. She decided not to confront him about this during the appointment. When he presented for the next appointment intoxicated again, the therapist asked him directly if he had been drinking prior to the session, as she was concerned that his alcohol usage would interfere with therapy. Carl's reply was, "Maybe . . . just a little." The therapist asked Carl to refrain from drinking before their next appointment, to which he agreed. When he showed up to the third appointment intoxicated yet again, the therapist decided that she needed to address his alcohol use before he could make any progress in therapy. Carl had expressed that he was ashamed of his alcohol use, but that he found himself unable to cut down on his drinking. He described symptoms of withdrawal such as shaking and feeling nauseous if he did not have a drink within the first few hours of waking up in the morning. Carl stated that he had been working in a liquor store for the past 4 years, and it was difficult for him to refrain from drinking when he could so easily access alcohol. He agreed with the therapist that it would be important to address his issues with alcohol before beginning psychotherapy.

Janice called the therapist the following week to tell her that Carl had been in a car accident and was arrested for driving while under the influence of alcohol. Carl had driven into a lamppost near her home and reportedly had a blood alcohol level over three times the legal limit at the time of the accident. Janice reported that Carl sustained only a minor concussion and a few scratches. While he was in the hospital for observation, he told Janice that he was ready to quit drinking for good and wanted to go to therapy. Janice explained that Carl had lost his job after his first arrest for public intoxication, and he and the family were "willing to try anything" to help him quit drinking. The therapist agreed to see Carl, and he attended the following session sober.

Carl told his therapist about his experiences with bipolar disorder and with Lithium, a medication that clinicians typically prescribe to treat the disorder. Carl described that he preferred drinking to taking medication because he did not experience side effects, and he found weekly blood testing while on Lithium "annoying." Carl stated that he had never really drunk much alcohol, as his parents are both former alcoholics and he worried that he might be susceptible to alcoholism. His drinking began 4 years prior when he began working at a liquor store. At the time, he was stable on medication and had not experienced any significant psychological impairment for several years. "I wasn't planning on drinking at work ever, but my boss sure liked to, so we started getting drunk together after closing up for the night," Carl reported. Since he found it difficult to drink heavily while on Lithium, he decided to stop taking his medication so that he could drink with his boss, who would taunt Carl to drink if he declined his offer. Since Carl was drinking mostly at night and

Toward the DSM-5

Combining Abuse and Dependence

DSM-5's authors are proposing a radical departure from *DSM-IV-TR*'s approach to the classification of substance-related disorders. Instead of the two separate sets of disorders for "abuse" and "dependence," they would combine abuse and dependence into a single dimensional rating. Individuals would receive a diagnosis based on meeting only two criteria, but would be rated according to the degree of severity of their symptoms. Critics believe that the revised system would result in too many individuals with mild symptoms who do not have an "addiction" to receive a diagnosis of a substance-related disorder (Martin, Steinley, Vergés, & Sher, 2011). A second major change in *DSM-5* is the transition of caffeine withdrawal from a research-only to a clinical diagnosis. The *DSM-5* authors argue that there is now sufficient evidence from large enough populations to warrant recognition of this condition as a psychiatric diagnosis. They believe, furthermore, that by placing a diagnosis on the condition, clinicians will be more likely to recognize, and then correctly treat, individuals who have these symptoms. They believe that many caffeine users who suffer from caffeine withdrawal attribute their symptoms to other disorders, leading to unnecessary health care utilization and associated costs.

intravenous or smokable drugs into the bloodstream is likely to lead to a more intense kind of intoxication than are drugs taken in pill form.

Clinicians might also assign diagnoses that refer to a particular syndrome, such as dementia, in association with a person's chronic use of particular substances. For example, cognitive disorders can include substance-induced delirium, persisting dementia, and persisting amnestic disorder. Other disorders can also be associated with substance abuse including psychotic disorder, mood disorder, anxiety disorder, sexual dysfunction, and sleep disorder. People may also show comorbidity of the substance-related disorder with another condition, such as an anxiety disorder or a mood disorder.

13.2 Disorders Associated with Specific Substances

Alcohol

Patterns of Use and Abuse Statistics based on the United States show that alcohol is a commonly used substance. More than half (51.8 percent) of Americans over age 12 reported that they had had at least one drink in the month prior to being surveyed. Nearly one-quarter (23.1 percent) of Americans 12 and older reported that they engaged in binge drinking, meaning that they had had five drinks on one occasion in the past 30 days. Heavy drinking, defined as consuming five or more drinks on the same occasion on at least 5 days in the month, was found in 6.7 percent of Americans 12 and older. Variables associated with higher rates of alcohol consumption were as follows: being male, white, married, a smoker, employed, and having a higher educational level and a higher income (Moore et al., 2005).

MINI CASE

Substance Dependence (Alcohol)

Rhona is a 55-year-old homemaker married to a successful builder. Every afternoon, she makes herself the first in a series of daiquiris. On many evenings, she passes out on the couch by the time her husband arrives home from work. Rhona lost her driver's license a year ago after being arrested three times on charges of driving while intoxicated. Although Rhona's family has urged her to obtain treatment for her disorder, she denies that she has a problem because she can "control" her drinking. The mother of three grown children, Rhona began to drink around age 45, when her youngest child left for college. Prior to this time, Rhona kept herself extremely busy through her children's extracurricular activities. When she found herself alone every afternoon, she took solace in having an early cocktail. Over a period of several years, the cocktail developed into a series of five or six strong drinks. Rhona's oldest daughter has begun lately to insist that something be done for her mother. She does not want to see Rhona develop the fatal alcohol-related illness that caused the premature death of her grandmother.

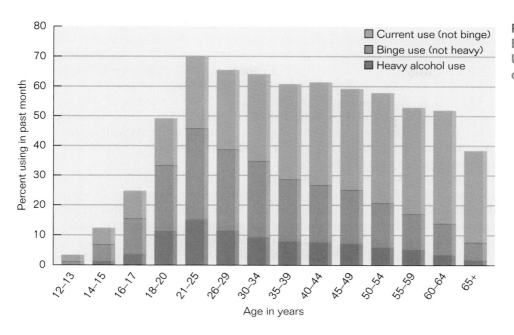

FIGURE 13.1 Current, Binge, and Heavy Alcohol Use among Persons Aged 12 or Older, by Age: 2010

Patterns of alcohol use are also associated with age (Figure 13.1). Young adults ages 18 to 25 have the highest rates of binge drinking and heavy drinking. Of that group, adults ages 21 to 25 have the highest rates of drinking, with 45.5 percent engaging in binge drinking. The rates of binge and heavy drinking decline sharply throughout adulthood; among people 65 and older, 7.6 percent engage in binge drinking and 1.6 percent in heavy drinking.

The decline in binge and heavy drinking are part of a larger picture of "maturing out," similar to the maturation hypothesis of age and personality disorders. However, the pattern of age-related changes in drinking patterns is not that clear-cut. Longitudinal studies show that, although people are less likely to start drinking after the young adult years, many people continue to persist in their previously established patterns of alcohol dependence throughout adulthood. Certain life transitions are associated, however, with decreases in alcohol dependence. For men, parenthood is associated with lower rates of alcohol use after the age of 38; women show the opposite pattern. Men who lose their jobs have the highest rates of alcohol use after age 38; for women, there are no relationships between job status and alcohol-use persistence. These findings suggest that the relationships among alcohol use, life transitions, and gender are complex so that maturation alone is not sufficient for understanding age-related changes in alcohol dependence (Vergés et al., 2011).

Effects of Alcohol Use

Clinicians classify alcohol as a nervous system **depressant.** Its effects vary by the amount that the drinker ingests. In small amounts, alcohol has sedating effects, leading users to feel relaxed. As people ingest more alcohol, they may begin to feel more outgoing, self-confident, and uninhibited. As people drink beyond that point, the depressant effects become apparent, leading users to experience sleepiness, lack of physical coordination, dysphoria, and irritability. Continuing past this point, excessive drinking can be fatal as the individual's vital functions completely shut down. More severe effects also occur when the individual mixes alcohol with other drugs, a situation referred to as **potentiation,** meaning that the effects of two drugs taken together are greater than the effect of either substance alone. Combining alcohol with another depressant, for example, can be a fatal outcome of such potentiation.

The rate at which alcohol absorption occurs in the bloodstream depends in part on a number of factors, including how much a person consumes, over what time period,

depressant
A psychoactive substance that causes the depression of central nervous system activity.

potentiation
The combination of the effects of two or more psychoactive substances such that the total effect is greater than the effect of either substance alone.

and whether the person has food present in the digestive system. Another factor is the drinker's metabolic rate (the rate at which the body converts food substances to energy). The average person metabolizes alcohol at a rate of one-third of an ounce of 100 percent alcohol per hour, which is equivalent to an ounce of whiskey per hour. Following a bout of extensive intake of alcohol, a person is likely to experience an abstinence syndrome, or the phenomenon commonly called a "hangover." The symptoms of abstinence syndrome include a range of phenomena including nausea and vomiting, tremors, extreme thirst, headache, tiredness, irritability, depression, and dizziness. As with alcohol absorption, the extent of abstinence syndrome reflects the amount and rate of alcohol consumption and the individual's metabolic rate.

Alcohol affects almost every organ system in the body, either directly or indirectly. Long-term use of alcohol can lead to permanent brain damage, with symptoms of dementia, blackouts, seizures, hallucinations, and damage to the peripheral parts of the nervous system. Two forms of dementia are associated with long-term, heavy alcohol use: **Wernicke's disease** and **Korsakoff's syndrome.**

Wernicke's disease is an acute and potentially reversible condition involving delirium, eye movement disturbances, difficulties in movement and balance, and deterioration of the peripheral nerves, to the hands and feet. It is not the alcohol but a deficiency of thiamine (Vitamin B_1) that causes Wernicke's disease. Long-term heavy use of alcohol has deleterious effects on the body's ability to metabolize nutrients, and such alcohol users often have an overall pattern of poor nutrition. Adequate thiamine intake can reverse Wernicke's disease.

Korsakoff's syndrome is a permanent form of dementia in which the individual develops **retrograde amnesia,** an inability to remember past events, and **anterograde amnesia,** the inability to remember new information. The chances of a person recovering from Korsakoff's syndrome are less than one in four, and about another one in four people who have this disorder require permanent institutionalization.

Chronic heavy alcohol consumption also causes a number of harmful changes in the liver, gastrointestinal system, bone density, muscles, and immune system. When people abruptly stop ingesting alcohol after periods of chronic usage, they can experience sleep disturbances, profound anxiety, tremors, hyperactivity of the sympathetic nervous system, psychosis, seizures, or death.

Theories and Treatment of Alcohol Dependence

Clinicians who design interventions targeting individuals who have alcohol dependence begin by conducting an assessment of the alcohol use patterns of their clients. The "AUDIT," or Alcohol Use Disorders Identification Test, shown in Table 13.1, is one such instrument (National Institute on Alcohol Abuse and Alcoholism, 2007).

Biological Perspectives Twin, family, and adoption studies consistently point to the importance of genetic factors as contributors to alcohol-related disorders, with an estimated heritability of 50 to 60 percent. However, trying to pinpoint the genes involved in alcohol-related disorders is a great challenge to researchers, particularly for those who want to find genes that control the amount of alcohol consumption (Heath et al., 2011). The greatest success in studying the genetics of alcohol-related disorders comes from studies examining associations with genes involved in alcohol metabolism and neural transmission. Researchers are attempting to connect variations in some of these genes not only with patterns of alcohol use, but also with psychological factors, such as personality traits, and physiological factors, such as alcohol-related organ damage (Kimura & Higuchi, 2011). Large-scale analyses using genome-wide association studies are beginning to identify a large number of potential genes associated with alcohol dependence that may pave the way toward understanding how the disorder develops (Wang et al., 2011). Using these new discoveries, researchers have already identified a relatively large number of genes, suggesting that alcohol dependence will not show a simple pattern of genetic transmission (Frank et al., 2012).

Wernicke's disease
A form of aphasia in which the individual is able to produce language but has lost the ability to comprehend, so that these verbal productions have no meaning.

Korsakoff's syndrome
A permanent form of dementia associated with long-term alcohol use in which the individual develops retrograde and anterograde amnesia, leading to an inability to remember recent events or learn new information.

retrograde amnesia
Amnesia involving loss of memory for past events.

anterograde amnesia
Amnesia involving the inability to remember new information.

TABLE 13.1 The Alcohol Use Disorders Identification Test ("AUDIT")

Scoring the AUDIT

Record the score for each response in the blank box at the end of each line, then total these numbers. The maximum possible total is 40.

Total scores of 8 or more for men up to age 60 or 4 or more for women, adolescents, and men over 60 are considered positive screens. For patients with totals near the cut-points, clinicians may wish to examine individual responses to questions and clarify them during the clinical examination.

PATIENT: Because alcohol use can affect your health and can interfere with certain medications and treatments, it is important that we ask some questions about your use of alcohol. Your answers will remain confidential, so please be honest.

Place an X in one box that best describes your answer to each question.

Questions	0	1	2	3	4	
1. How often do you have a drink containing alcohol?	Never	Monthly or less	2 to 4 times a month	2 to 3 times a week	4 or more times a week	☐
2. How many drinks containing alcohol do you have on a typical day when you are drinking?	1 or 2	3 or 4	5 or 6	7 to 9	10 or more	☐
3. How often do you have 5 or more drinks on one occasion?	Never	Less than monthly	Monthly	Weekly	Daily or almost daily	☐
4. How often during the last year have you found that you were not able to stop drinking once you had started?	Never	Less than monthly	Monthly	Weekly	Daily or almost daily	☐
5. How often during the last year have you failed to do what was normally expected of you because of drinking?	Never	Less than monthly	Monthly	Weekly	Daily or almost daily	☐
6. How often during the last year have you needed a first drink in the morning to get yourself going after a heavy drinking session?	Never	Less than monthly	Monthly	Weekly	Daily or almost daily	☐
7. How often during the last year have you had a feeling of guilt or remorse after drinking?	Never	Less than monthly	Monthly	Weekly	Daily or almost daily	☐
8. How often during the last year have you been unable to remember what happened the night before because of your drinking?	Never	Less than monthly	Monthly	Weekly	Daily or almost daily	☐
9. Have you or someone else been injured because of your drinking?	No		Yes, but not in the last year		Yes, during the last year	☐
10. Has a relative, friend, doctor, or other health care worker been concerned about your drinking or suggested you cut down?	No		Yes, but not in the last year		Yes, during the last year	☐
					Total	

SOURCE: National Institute on Alcohol Abuse and Alcoholism, 2007

Note: This questionnaire (the AUDIT) is reprinted with permission from the World Health Organization. To reflect standard drink sizes in the United States, the number of drinks in question 3 was changed from 6 to 5. A free AUDIT manual with guidelines for use in primary care settings is available online at www.who.org.

Physicians prescribe medications increasingly as biological treatment for alcohol dependence if not as the sole form of treatment, then in conjunction with psychologically based therapies. A large number of well-controlled studies support the use of naltrexone as an aid in preventing relapse among people with alcohol dependence. As an opioid receptor antagonist, it blocks the effects of the body's production of alcohol-induced opioids, perhaps through involving dopamine (Hillemacher, Heberlein, Muschler, Bleich, & Frieling, 2011). The individual who takes naltrexone is less likely to experience pleasurable effects of alcohol and even less likely to feel pleasure thinking about alcohol. As a result, people taking naltrexone feel less of an urge to drink and therefore will be less likely to suffer a relapse in which they engage in heavy drinking. An injectable form of naltrexone called nalmefene seems to be effective in promoting total abstinence (Garbutt et al., 2005).

Disulfiram is a medication that operates by the principles of aversion therapy. An individual taking disulfiram who consumes alcohol within a two-week period will experience a variety of unpleasant physical reactions, including flushing, palpitations, increased heart rate, lowered blood pressure, nausea and vomiting, sweating, and dizziness. Disulfiram works primarily by inhibiting the action of an enzyme that normally breaks down acetaldehyde, a toxic product involved in ethanol metabolism. Although not as effective as naltrexone, highly motivated individuals, particularly those treated in supervised settings who are also older, have a longer drinking history, and participate in Alcoholics Anonymous meetings, have used Disulfiram effectively (Arias & Kranzler, 2008).

The third medication shown to be effective in treating alcohol abuse is acamprosate, an amino acid derivative. Acamprosate reduces the risk of relapse by reducing the individual's urge to drink and thereby reducing the drive to use alcohol as a way of reducing anxiety and other negative psychological states. Acamprosate appears to work by modulating glutamate receptors and other reactions within the cell. Individuals who seem to benefit the most from acamprosate are those who are older when they become dependent on alcohol, have physiological signs of higher dependence, and have higher levels of anxiety, although in general, the evidence in favor of acamprosate is positive (Arias & Kranzler, 2008). People who are more highly motivated to become fully abstinent at the start of treatment are more likely to comply with remaining on the medication and therefore more likely to improve (Koeter, van den Brink, & Lehert, 2010).

Researchers consider other medications used in the treatment of alcohol dependence as less effective based on the available evidence. These include anticonvulsant medications, SSRIs, Lithium, and baclofen, which works on GABA receptors (Arias & Kranzler, 2008).

disulfiram
Known popularly as Antabuse, a medication used in the treatment of alcoholism that inhibits aldehyde dehydrogenase (ALDH) and causes severe physical reactions when combined with alcohol.

dual-process theory
A theory regarding alcohol use proposing there are automatic processes that generate an impulse to drink alcohol and controlled, effortful processing that regulates these automatic impulses.

Anticonvulsant medications, such as Midazolam, can help treat individuals with alcohol use disorders.

Psychological Perspectives Current psychological approaches to alcohol dependence focus on the cognitive systems that guide people's drinking behavior. According to **dual-process theory,** one system involves fast, automatic processes that generate an impulse to drink alcohol. The more positive the associations that people have to alcohol, the more likely they are to consume it. The second system involves the controlled, effortful processing that regulates these automatic impulses. The more the individual can inhibit the automatic impulse, the less likely the individual is to consume excessive amounts of alcohol (Bechara, Noel, & Crone, 2006). Dual-process theory predicts that as individuals become better able to inhibit the automatic impulse to consume alcohol, they should also reduce their drinking behavior. Although the results show promise, researchers have only applied this theory in an experimental setting (Houben, Nederkoorn, Wiers, & Jansen, 2011).

In general, alcohol expectancies involve an "if–then" set of contingencies: if I consume alcohol, then I can expect certain behaviors and effects to follow. Individuals develop alcohol expectancies early in life, even before they first taste alcohol. These expectancies can include the potential for alcohol to reduce tension, cope with social challenges, feel better, feel sexier, and become more mentally alert. Based on the notion of self-efficacy, expectancies about alcohol can also include people's beliefs in their ability to resist or control their drinking (Young, Connor, & Feeney, 2011).

Cognitive factors also can influence what happens when a person consumes alcohol, particularly whether he or she engages in impulsive and potentially harmful behaviors, such as high-risk sexual activities. The high prevalence of binge drinking on college campuses presents a particular concern for this reason. According to **alcohol myopia theory,** as individuals consume greater amounts of alcohol, they are more likely to make risky choices because the immediate temptation of the moment (such as risky sex) overcomes the long-term consequences of the behavior (such as developing a sexually transmitted disease) (Griffin, Umstattd, & Usdan, 2010).

There are several well-tested psychological approaches to treating alcohol dependence. The most successful approaches involve cognitive-behavioral interventions, motivational approaches, and expectancy manipulation (Arias & Kranzler, 2008). Part of effective treatment for alcohol dependence also involves **relapse prevention,** in which the clinician essentially builds "failure" into treatment. If the client recognizes that occasional slips from abstinence are bound to occur, then he or she will be less likely to give up on therapy altogether after suffering a temporary setback.

The COMBINE project developed the most comprehensive protocol for psychological treatment as part of a project funded by the National Institute on Alcohol Abuse and Alcoholism (NIAAA). In this treatment, known as Combined Behavioral Intervention (CBI) (Miller, 2002), participants receive up to 20 sessions, according to their needs, beginning semiweekly and then eventually biweekly or less, for up to 16 weeks. The primary emphasis of CBI is on enhancing reinforcement and social support for abstinence. Clinicians assign motivational enhancement therapy at the outset, meaning that the clinician attempts to draw out the client's own motivation to change. The clinical style used in CBI follows from the motivational interviewing perspective (Table 13.2), in which the clinician uses a client-centered but directive style.

Clinicians expect and encourage families and significant others to participate throughout treatment, and they also encourage mutual help and involvement among clients including participation in Alcoholics Anonymous (AA). CBI includes content modules focusing on coping skills (e.g., coping with cravings and urges), refusing drinks and avoiding social pressure to drink, communication skills, assertiveness skills, management of moods, social and recreational counseling, social support for sobriety, and job-seeking skills. As needed, clinicians may also monitor sobriety, provide telephone consultation, and provide crisis intervention. They also put procedures in place to work with clients who resume drinking during treatment. Toward the end of the treatment period, clients enter a maintenance phase and then complete treatment in a termination session.

The COMBINE study evaluated the efficacy of naltrexone and acamprosate alone and in combination with CBI using placebos and medical management as control conditions. Although CBI alone was not as effective in producing abstinent days as was CBI plus medication and management immediately after treatment, 1 year after treatment ended, the CBI-only group did not differ significantly from those receiving medication (Anton et al., 2006).

Sociocultural Perspective Researchers and theorists working within the sociocultural perspective regard stressors in the family, community, and culture as factors that, when combined with genetic vulnerability, lead the individual to develop alcohol dependence. Researchers gave support to the sociocultural perspective in a

alcohol myopia theory
Proposes that as individuals consume greater amounts of alcohol, they are more likely to make risky choices because the immediate temptation of the moment overcomes the long-term consequences of the behavior.

relapse prevention
A treatment method based on the expectancy model, in which individuals are encouraged not to view lapses from abstinence as signs of certain failure.

Eating Disorders and Impulse-Control Disorders

Learning Objectives

14.1 Differentiate characteristics, theories, and treatments of eating disorders

14.2 Differentiate between impulse-control disorders

14.3 Analyze the biopsychosocial model of eating disorders and impulse-control disorders

CHAPTER 14

Case Report: Rosa Nomirez

Demographic information: Rosa is a 25-year-old Hispanic female.

Presenting problem: Rosa self-referred to a community mental health center for feelings of depression. During the intake evaluation, Rosa stated that she had been feeling down and depressed for several months, and since her depression had not remitted on its own, she decided to seek treatment. She stated this was not an easy decision for her, as she usually was able to handle difficult emotions on her own. Rosa also reported that those close to her were worried about her health and had been urging her for some time to seek treatment, although she stated that she couldn't understand why they were concerned. The clinician noted that Rosa appeared severely underweight and frail. Rosa stated she was feeling depressed, mainly because as she described, "I feel like a fat monster all of the time." Rosa estimated that these feelings originated while she was pregnant with her daughter, now 14 months old. She had stopped working after giving birth in order to focus on raising her daughter, while her husband provided for the family. Rosa stated that she had a difficult time returning to her normal weight after giving birth, and that she believed that she still appeared to look pregnant. She remarked that "all I can see in the mirror is my stomach and how enormous it makes me look all over." She reported that she did not know her current weight and that she was afraid to weigh herself for fear that she was continuing to gain weight. She exclaimed, "I feel so ashamed that I am so fat still. I feel like I'll never look normal again."

Rosa reported that she followed a diet consisting of about 300 to 400 calories per day, and that she had been "working her way down" in terms of daily caloric consumption ever since her concerns about her weight began. At that time, Rosa had searched diet tips on an Internet search engine. She discovered an online community devoted to supporting women who wanted to lose weight and stay thin. These "pro-ana" sites as she described them offered her support from other users, as well as helpful tips for not only how to restrict her caloric intake, but how to hide it from others whose concern she saw as bothersome and interfering with her goals of losing weight. She had been using the sites daily for about 6 months. Her husband discovered the sites on the computer, and recognizing the danger they posed, pleaded with Rosa to stop using them. She stated that she didn't understand why he didn't want her using the sites, as maintaining a low body weight was so important to her, and the thought of gaining weight caused her intense feelings of anxiety.

Although she stated that she rarely felt interested in sex and had not gotten her menstrual period for about 4 months, Rosa explained that she and her husband had been trying to have another child for about 6 months. The clinician asked about any other physiological changes that she had noticed. Rosa stated she felt tired much of the time, but beyond that, she denied any difficulties. "I usually just think about my daughter and about staying thin. There isn't really time to worry about much else." She further stated that while out in public, she often compares her body to others. This had become a source of overwhelming anxiety and so she typically preferred to stay home so she didn't feel "judged for being fat" as she explained.

According to Rosa, her family had been "constantly bothering" her about her weight. "They just don't understand how I feel. They try to force me to eat and it just makes me feel so uncomfortable and depressed. It feels like they are mocking because they know how disgusting I am, so I

MINI CASE

Pathological Gambling

Wayne is a 22-year-old auto mechanic, a father of two, married to a factory worker. Two years ago, he went to the local racetrack with a friend, who showed him how to bet on horses. To his surprise, Wayne made some good bets and came home with a $50 profit. Buoyed by his success, he made repeated trips to the track and, in time, began taking days off from work to bet on the races. On one of these occasions, Wayne won $5,000. This made him feel extremely proud of his betting expertise and convinced him that he had special skills at picking the right horse. Even though he was losing many of his bets, he now felt certain that his winnings would more than compensate. He had a feeling of self-confidence that, for once in his life, he was a success. To keep up his image, Wayne started to make larger and larger bets on long shots that failed to pay off. As his losses accumulated into the tens of thousands of dollars, he grew panicky and felt driven to bet even more.

gambling in *DSM-IV-TR* includes a set of criteria also seen in other impulse-control disorders and others that are unique to this disorder. The unique features of pathological gambling include behaviors seen when people engage in chasing a bad bet, lying about how much they have lost, seeking financial bailouts, and committing crimes to support their gambling.

As venues for gambling continue to become available on a more widespread basis, including online gambling, the incidence of pathological gambling appears to be on the increase. Among countries with legalized gambling, lifetime prevalence estimates range from about 0.5 to as high as 3.5 percent of the adult population (Stucki & Rihs-Middel, 2007). In the United States, although the large majority of adults have gambled at some point in their lives, pathological gambling was estimated to be diagnosable in 0.6 percent. Moreover, the greater the number of occasions on which people gambled, the higher their chances of developing pathological gambling—with the highest prevalence occurring after people had gambled 1,000 times in their lives.

Individuals with gambling disorders often experience severe financial problems due to their inability to stop betting money, no matter how much they try to stop.

Like other impulse control disorders, pathological gambling often co-occurs with other psychological disorders. The highest risk of developing pathological gambling occurs among people who engage in gambling on games involving mental skill (such as cards), followed by sports betting, gambling machines, and horse races or cock/dog fights (Kessler et al., 2008). Pathological gamblers who bet on sports tend to be young men who have substance disorders. Those who bet on slot machines are more likely to be older women who have higher rates of other psychological disorders and begin gambling at a later age (Petry, 2003). In general, women are less likely than men to engage in the type of gambling that depends on strategy, such as poker (Odlaug, Marsh, Kim, & Grant, 2011).

People with pathological gambling also have high rates of other disorders, particularly nicotine dependence (60 percent), dependence on other substances (58 percent), mood disorder (38 percent), and anxiety disorder (37 percent). Mood and anxiety disorders are more likely to precede, rather than follow, the onset of pathological gambling (Lorains, Cowlishaw, & Thomas, 2011). Unfortunately, the likelihood of an individual always having symptoms of pathological gambling continues to predict gambling behavior. A follow-up of Vietnam War veterans showed that even after controlling for family genetics, education, substance dependence, and other disorders, the men most likely to have symptoms were the ones who showed symptoms 10 years earlier (Scherrer et al., 2007).

As is true for kleptomania, pathological gambling seems to involve abnormalities in multiple neurotransmitters including dopamine, serotonin, noradrenaline, and opioid. The repetitive behaviors characteristic of this disorder may be viewed as resulting from an imbalance between two competing and relatively separate neurobiological mechanisms—those that are involved in urges and those that are involved in cognitive control (Grant, Chamberlain, Odlaug, Potenza, & Kim, 2010). There may also be genetic contributions, perhaps involving abnormalities in dopamine receptor genes (Lobo et al., 2010).

Pathological gambling may develop in part because gambling follows a variable ratio reinforcement schedule when rewards occur, on average, every "X" number of times. This pattern of reinforcement produces behaviors that are highly resistant to extinction. Slot machines, in particular, produce payoffs on this type of schedule, maintaining high rates of responding by gamblers. Classical conditioning is also involved in maintaining this behavior, because gamblers learn to associate certain cues to gambling including their internal states or moods and external stimuli such as advertisements for gambling.

Cognitive factors also play an important role in pathological gambling. People with this disorder seem to engage in a phenomenon known as "discounting of probabilistic rewards," in which they discount or devalue rewards they could obtain in the future compared to rewards they could obtain right away (Petry, 2011). They also engage in other cognitive distortions many of which involve poor judgment of the probabilities that their gambling will lead to successful outcomes, as shown in Table 14.1.

The biopsychosocial perspective seems particularly relevant for understanding pathological gambling. According to the **pathways model,** the genetic vulnerability interacts with the poor coping and problem-solving skills of the pathological gambler to make the individual particularly susceptible to early gambling experiences, such as having early gambling luck ("the big win"). These, combined with sociocultural factors can propel the individual into more serious symptoms. The pathways model predicts that there are three main paths leading to three subtypes of pathological gamblers. The behaviorally conditioned subtype had few symptoms prior to developing the disorder but through frequent exposure to gambling, develops positive associations, distorted cognitions, and poor decision making about gambling. The emotionally vulnerable pathological gambler had pre-existing depression, anxiety, and perhaps a history of trauma; gambling helps this individual feel better. The third type of pathological gambler has pre-existing impulsivity, attentional difficulties, and antisocial characteristics. For this individual, the risk of gambling provides thrills and excitement (Hodgins & Peden, 2008).

pathways model
Approach to pathological gambling, which predicts that there are three main paths leading to three subtypes.

TABLE 14.1 Common Cognitive Distortions in People with Pathological Gambling

Type of Heuristic	Cognitive Distortions Derived from Heuristics	Example
Representativeness	Gambler's Fallacy	When events generated by a random process have deviated from the population average in a short run, such as a roulette ball falling on red four times in a row, individuals may erroneously believe that the opposite deviation (e.g., ball falls on black) becomes more likely.
	Overconfidence	Individuals express a degree of confidence in their knowledge or ability that is not warranted by objective reality.
	Trends in number picking	Lottery players commonly try to apply long-run random patterns to short strings in their picks such as avoiding duplicate numbers and adjacent digits in number strings.
Availability	Illusory correlations	Individuals believe that events that they expect to be correlated, due to previous experience or perceptions, have been correlated in previous experience even when they have not been, such as wearing a "lucky hat" that they wore when they won previously.
	Availability of others' wins	When individuals see and hear other gamblers winning, they start to believe that winning is a regular occurrence, which reinforces their belief that they will win if they continue to play.
	Inherent memory bias	Individuals are biased to recollect wins with greater ease than losses. They then reframe their memories regarding gambling experiences in a way that focuses on positive experiences (wins) and disregards negative experiences (losses). This causes them to rationalize their decision to continue gambling.
Additional cognitive distortions	Illusion of control	Individuals have a higher expectancy for success than objective probability would warrant.
	Switching and double switching	Individuals recognize errors and process gambling-related situations in a rational way when they are not actively participating, but abandon rational thought when they personally take part in gambling.

SOURCE: Fortune & Goodie, 2011

Researchers are beginning to investigate the possibility of treating pathological gambling with medications that target particular neurotransmitters. One set of medications are the opioid-acting medications to reduce the urge to drink in people with alcohol dependence, such as naltrexone and its long-acting form, nalmefene (Grant, Odlaug, Potenza, Hollander, & Kim, 2010). Another medication that shows promise is memantine, used as a treatment for Alzheimer's disease. People with pathological gambling showed improved cognitive control presumably due to the medication's effect on glutamate receptors (Grant, Chamberlain, et al., 2010).

Based on the pathways model, even if a medication is found that can reduce pathological gambling, individuals with this disorder would nevertheless require psychosocial interventions. Although many gamblers turn to help from Gamblers Anonymous, there are few studies of its efficacy. The most thoroughly studied intervention is cognitive-behavioral therapy. A typical cognitive-behavioral treatment would involve these steps. First, the clinician teaches clients to understand the triggers for their gambling by having them describe their pattern of gambling behaviors. For example, common triggers include unstructured or free time, negative emotional states, reminders such as watching sports or advertisements, and having some available money. The clinician would also ascertain the times when clients do not gamble. Clinicians use this information to help their clients analyze the times they gamble and the times they do not. Following this

MINI CASE

Pyromania

Floyd, a 32-year-old man, developed an intense fascination with fires and firefighting equipment as a child. By the time he reached adolescence, he had begun to set abandoned buildings on fire, because he found the experience to be exhilarating and sexually exciting. After graduating from high school, he applied to be a firefighter for the city, but he was denied a position because his psychological profile showed that he had difficulty controlling destructive impulses. He moved to a small town, where he knew he could join the volunteer fire brigade without any questions. However, since such a small town had few fires, Floyd began to deliberately set fires himself. At first, no one noticed anything unusual about the increase in the number of fires that had occurred since Floyd joined the department. After watching Floyd's reaction to the fires, though, the fire chief began to suspect that it was Floyd who was setting the fires.

assessment, clinicians continue in subsequent sessions to work on helping their clients increase pleasant activities, think of ways to handle cravings or urges, become more assertive, and correct their irrational cognitions. At the end of treatment, clinicians would help prepare their clients for setbacks using relapse-prevention methods (Morasco, Ledgerwood, Weinstock, & Petry, 2009).

Pyromania

People with **pyromania** deliberately set fires, feel tension and arousal before they commit the act, are fascinated with and curious about fire and its situational contexts, derive pleasure, gratification, or relief when setting or witnessing fires or while participating in their aftermath. To be diagnosed with pyromania, the individual must not set fires for monetary reasons or have other medical or psychiatric conditions. Arson is deliberate firesetting for an improper purpose (e.g., monetary gain), and an arsonist does not experience the relief shown by people with pyromania. Among hospitalized psychiatric patients, 3.4 percent had current symptoms and 5.9 percent had lifetime symptoms consistent with a diagnosis of pyromania (Grant, Levine, Kim, & Potenza, 2005). The majority of people with pyromania are male. Pyromania appears to be rare, however, even among arsonists. Among a sample of 90 repeated offenders, Finnish researchers found that only 3 met the *DSM-IV-TR* criteria for pyromania (Lindberg, Holi, Tani, & Virkkunen, 2005).

Pyromania appears to be a chronic condition if the individual does not receive treatment. Some individuals with pyromania, however, may switch to another addictive or impulsive behavior such as kleptomania or pathological gambling. An intensive study of 21 participants with a lifetime history of pyromania described the most likely triggers for their behavior as stress, boredom, feelings of inadequacy, and interpersonal conflict (Grant & Kim, 2007).

As is true for the other impulse control disorders, pyromania may reflect abnormalities in dopamine functioning in areas of the brain involving behavioral addictions. Treatment for pyromania that follows the cognitive-behavioral model seems to show the most promise, however. The techniques used in cognitive-behavioral therapy for pyromania include imaginal exposure and response prevention, cognitive restructuring of responding to urges, and relaxation training (Grant, 2006).

pyromania
An impulse-control disorder involving the persistent and compelling urge to start fires.

Trichotillomania (Hair-pulling)

A diagnosis of **trichotillomania** is given to individuals who pull out their hair in response to an increasing sense of tension or urge. After they pull their hair, they feel relief, pleasure, or gratification. People with trichotillomania are upset by their uncontrollable behavior and may find that their social, occupational, or other areas of functioning are

trichotillomania
An impulse-control disorder involving the compulsive, persistent urge to pull out one's own hair.

Individuals with pyromania are often fixated with every aspect of fire setting including lighting a match.

This man, like many who suffer from trichotillomania, has marked hair loss as a result of frequent and uncontrollable urges to pull his hair out.

impaired because of this disorder. They feel unable to stop this behavior, even when the pulling results in bald patches and lost eyebrows, eyelashes, armpit hair, and pubic hair. As individuals get older, they increase the number of bodily sites from which they pull hair (Flessner, Woods, Franklin, Keuthen, & Piacentini, 2009).

People with this disorder experience significant impairment in areas of life ranging from sexual intimacy to social activities, medical examinations, and haircuts. They may also develop a range of physical symptoms including the development of hairballs (trichobezoars), which settle in their gastrointestinal tract, causing abdominal pain, nausea and vomiting, weakness, and weight loss. They can also develop skin infections, scalp pain or bleeding, and carpal tunnel syndrome. Psychologically, they may suffer low self-esteem, shame and embarrassment, depressed mood, irritability, and argumentativeness. Their impairments appear early in life and continue through to middle and late adulthood (Duke, Keeley, Geffken, & Storch, 2010).

MINI CASE

Trichotillomania

For most of her childhood and adolescence, 15-year-old Janet lived a fairly isolated existence, with no close friends. Although Janet never discussed her unhappiness with anyone, she often felt very depressed and hopeless. As a young child, Janet lay in bed on many nights, secretly tugging at her hair. Over time, this behavior increased to the point at which she plucked the hair, strand by strand, from her scalp. Typically, she pulled out a hair, examined it, bit it, and either threw it away or swallowed it. Because her hair was thick and curly, her hair loss was not initially evident, and Janet kept it carefully combed to conceal the bald spots. One of her teachers noticed that Janet was pulling her hair in class, and, in looking more closely, she saw the bald patches on Janet's head. She referred Janet to the school psychologist, who called Janet's mother and recommended professional help.

Diagnosable trichotillomania is relatively rare, with an estimated current prevalence rate of 0.6 percent of the community population. However, trichotillomania may be underreported because people with this disorder are secretive about what they are doing and tend to engage in hair-pulling only when alone (Duke, Bodzin, Tavares, Geffken, & Storch, 2009).

In *DSM-IV-TR*, trichotillomania is included in the category of impulse-control disorders, but in *DSM-5*, it will move to the category that includes obsessive-compulsive and related disorders. In addition, the name will change to hair-pulling, which the *DSM-5* authors concur will be a better description of the disorder than calling it a "mania," which they regard as inappropriate for this disorder.

There may be two types of hair-pulling. In the "focused" type, which may account for one-quarter of cases, the individual is aware of having the urge to pull, and may develop compulsive behaviors or rituals to avoid doing so. In "automatic" hair-pulling, the individual is involved in another task or is absorbed in thought while engaging in the behavior. Individuals who fall into the automatic category of hair-pulling experience pronounced stress and anxiety. For people in the focused type, depression and disability are also likely to occur along with stress and anxiety (Duke et al., 2010).

Heritability seems to play an important role in trichotillomania, with an estimated 80 percent heritability (Novak, Keuthen, Stewart, & Pauls, 2009). Abnormalities in a gene on chromosome 1 known as SLTRK1 may play a role in the disorder; this gene is also linked to Tourette's syndrome (Abelson et al., 2005). Researchers have also identified abnormalities in SAPAP3, a gene related to glutamate which, in turn, is involved in obsessive-compulsive disorder (Zuchner et al., 2009). The neurotransmitters serotonin, dopamine, and glutamate are, in turn, thought to play a role in the development of trichotillomania (Duke, et al., 2009). Brain imaging studies of individuals with trichotillomania suggest that they may also have abnormalities in neural pathways in the brain involved in generating and suppressing motor habits; these pathways also seem to be involved in regulating affect (Chamberlain et al., 2010).

Corresponding to these abnormalities in neurotransmitter and brain functioning, the regulation model of trichotillomania suggests that individuals with this disorder seek an optimal state of emotional arousal providing them with greater stimulation when they are understimulated, and calming them when they are overstimulated. At the same time, hair-pulling may bring them from a negative to a positive affective state. Using the Trichotillomania Symptoms Questionnaire (Table 14.2), researchers conducting an online survey found that individuals who engaged in hair-pulling experienced more difficulty controlling their emotions than those who did not. There were subgroups within those who engaged in hair-pulling. These subgroups varied in whether they were more likely to experience boredom vs. anxiety or tension and in the overall intensity of emotions they felt that seemed to drive them toward hair-pulling. The researchers suggested that these subgroups on the questionnaire seemed to correspond to the automatic vs. focused subtypes of the disorder (Shusterman, Feld, Baer, & Keuthen, 2009).

TABLE 14.2 Trichotillomania Symptoms Questionnaire

1. Do you currently pull your hair out?
2. At any point in your life, including now, have you had periods of uncontrollable hair-pulling?
3. Do you (or did you in the past) experience urges to pull your hair out?
4. Do you (or did you in the past) try to resist pulling your hair out?
5. Do you (or did you in the past) feel relief when pulling your hair out?
6. Do you (or did you in the past) wish that the urge to pull your hair out would go away?
7. Have you been diagnosed with trichotillomania by a professional?
8. Do you, or did you in the past, feel shame, secrecy, or distress about your hair-pulling?

SOURCE: Shusterman et al., 2009

Various pharmacological treatments for trichotillomania include antidepressants, atypical antipsychotics, lithium, and naltrexone. Of these, naltrexone seems to have shown the most promising results. However, the results of controlled studies are not compelling and do not seem to justify the use of medications when weighed against the side effects that can include obesity, diabetes, neurotoxicity, delirium, encephalopathy, tremors, and hyperthyroidism, among others (Duke et al., 2010).

The behavioral treatment of habit reversal training (HRT) is regarded as the most effective approach to treating trichotillomania. Not only does this method prevent the side effects of medication, but it is more successful in reducing the symptoms of hair-pulling (Duke et al., 2010). However, for treatment-resistant individuals, a combination of medication and HRT may be required (Franklin, Zagrabbe, & Benavides, 2011).

In HRT, the individual learns a new response to compete with the habit of hair-pulling, such as fist-clenching. The key feature is that the new response is incompatible with the undesirable habit. When it was first developed several decades ago, HRT was given for only one session. Since that time, clinicians have extended the length of treatment and added several cognitive components, including self-monitoring and cognitive restructuring. For example, clients may learn to challenge their cognitive distortions such as their perfectionistic beliefs. Combining Acceptance and Commitment Therapy (ACT) with HRT is also shown to produce relief from hair-pulling symptoms. Cognitive-behavioral therapy can help in treating children and adolescents with trichotillomania, with very little alteration from the basic protocol used for adults. In one study, 77 percent of those who received treatment remained symptom-free after 6 months (Tolin, Franklin, Diefenbach, Anderson, & Meunier, 2007).

Intermittent Explosive Disorder

intermittent explosive disorder
An impulse-control disorder involving an inability to hold back urges to express strong angry feelings and associated violent behaviors.

The primary features of **intermittent explosive disorder** are aggressive outbursts in which individuals become assaultive or destructive in ways that are out of proportion to any stress or provocation. Their actions can cause serious physical harm to themselves, other people, and property. Like other impulse-control disorders, people with this disorder may feel a sense of arousal or tension just before having an outburst. Although they feel justified for their anger during the outburst, afterwards they feel genuinely upset, regretful, bewildered, or embarrassed by their loss of control.

An estimated 4 to 7 percent of people in the U.S. population have intermittent explosive disorder; of these, 70 percent have at least three outbursts per year with an average of 27 on a yearly basis (Kessler et al., 2006). People with this disorder are more vulnerable to a number of threats to their physical health, including coronary heart disease, hypertension, stroke, diabetes, arthritis, back/neck pain, ulcer, headaches, and other chronic pain (McCloskey, Kleabir, Berman, Chen, & Coccaro, 2010). People with this disorder often have co-occurring bipolar disorder, personality disorder such as antisocial or borderline, substance use disorder (particularly alcohol), and cognitive disorders.

Intermittent explosive disorder appears to have a strong familial component not accounted for by any comorbid conditions associated with the disorder (Coccaro, 2010).

MINI CASE

Intermittent Explosive Disorder

Ed, a 28-year-old high-school teacher, has unprovoked, violent outbursts of aggressive and assaultive behavior. During these episodes, Ed throws whatever objects he can get his hands on and yells profanities. He soon calms down, though, and feels intense regret for whatever damage he has caused, explaining that he didn't know what came over him. In the most recent episode, he threw a coffeepot at another teacher in the faculty lounge, inflicting serious injury. After the ambulance took the injured man to the hospital, Ed's supervisor called the police.

Intermittent explosive disorder involves sudden and usually unprovoked outbursts of anger that are overly aggressive in the context of the situation. Individuals with this disorder often feel they have little control over their behaviors during an outburst, and as a result may suffer from intense feelings of guilt and remorse once their anger has subsided.

Researchers believe that the disorder may result from abnormalities in the serotonin system causing a loss of the ability to inhibit movement (Coccaro, Lee, & Kavoussi, 2010). Other studies show altered EEG patterns that predispose individuals to these explosive outbursts (Bars, Heyrend, Simpson, & Munger, 2001).

Faulty cognitions further contribute to the individual's development of intermittent explosive disorder. People with this disorder have a set of negative beliefs that other people wish to harm them, beliefs that they may have acquired through harsh punishments they received as children from their parents or caregivers. They feel that, therefore, their violence is justified. In addition, they may have learned through modeling that aggression is the way to cope with conflict or frustration. Adding to these psychological processes is the sanctioning of violence associated with the masculine gender role, a view that would explain in part the greater prevalence of this disorder in men.

Given the possible role of serotonergic abnormalities in this disorder, researchers have investigated the utility of SSRIs in treatment. Though effective in reducing aggressive behaviors, however, SSRIs only result in full or partial remission in less than 50 percent of cases (Coccaro, Lee, & Kavoussi, 2009). Mood stabilizers used in the treatment of bipolar disorder (lithium, oxcarbazepine, carbamazepine) also have some effects in reducing aggressive behavior but there are few well-controlled studies (Jones et al., 2011).

Cognitive behavioral therapy can also be beneficial for individuals with this disorder. In one approach, a variant of anger management therapy uses relaxation training, cognitive restructuring, hierarchical imaginal exposure, and relapse prevention for a 12-week period in individual or group modalities. A controlled investigation of this model of therapy showed improvements in levels of anger, aggression, and depression that persisted for at least 3 months following treatment (McCloskey, Noblett, Deffenbacher, Gollan, & Coccaro, 2008).

14.2 Eating Disorders and Impulse-Control Disorders: The Biopsychosocial Perspective

The impulses that underlie the destructive or detrimental behaviors of people with eating and impulse control disorders seem to be ones that reflect an interaction of genetic, neurophysiological, cognitive, and social factors. Past psychological approaches to these disorders needed to provide reasonable doubt regarding the prosecution's argument that the defendant was sane. The Reform Act meant that the defense must now prove that the defendant fit the legal definition of insanity, which is a more difficult argument to make.

Individual states vary in the nature of the insanity defense that they use in criminal proceedings. Some states have moved toward separating the question of guilt from that of mental disorder by allowing the plea of "guilty, but mentally ill." The court does not exonerate defendants who use this plea from the crime, but gives them special consideration in sentencing.

Partly because of the storm of criticism following the Hinckley case, however, the court took a very different route in 1992. This time, the case involved a 31-year-old man, Jeffrey Dahmer, who confessed to murdering and dismembering 17 boys and young men and explained that he was driven to kill out of a compulsion to have sex with dead bodies. The trial took place in Milwaukee for the 15 murders that Dahmer claimed to have committed in Wisconsin. Dahmer's defense attorney argued that Dahmer's crimes could only have been committed by someone who fit the legal definition of insane. The jury rejected his guilty but mentally ill plea as they believed him to be responsible for his crimes and able to appreciate the wrongfulness of his conduct. He was sentenced to consecutive life terms for the murder of each of his victims. In 1994, Dahmer was killed at the age of 34 by another inmate.

Other highly publicized cases since Dahmer's have brought out other subtleties in the insanity defense as we currently construe it. In California, the Menendez brothers admitted to the premeditated murder of their parents in response, they claimed, to years of sexual and emotional abuse. The brothers, 23 and 26 at the time of the crime, admitted to the killings, but claimed they had acted in self-defense. Their defense attorneys presented the argument of "imperfect self-defense," asserting that they acted out of the mistaken belief that their parents were about to kill them, a belief that stemmed from a lifelong history of physical, emotional, and sexual abuse. The defense claimed that, on the night of the killings one of the brothers, in an altered mental state, retrieved his shotgun, loaded it, and burst in on his parents. The prosecution, which proved its case, claimed that the brothers instead were motivated by the $14 million they stood to inherit after the death of their parents.

The irresistible impulse defense came to light in the highly publicized case of Lorena Bobbitt, a Virginia woman who claimed to be temporarily insane as the result of years of physical and psychological abuse by her husband, leading her to cut off his penis. She

Lyle and Erik Menendez continue to serve life sentences in prison for murdering their parents in 1989.

claimed that at that point she was overcome with what she called "pictures," or mental images, of his abusive actions toward her. The jury concluded that she was temporarily insane and acquitted her of all charges of malicious and unlawful wounding. As mandated by Virginia law, the judge in the case committed Lorena Bobbitt to a state psychiatric hospital to determine whether or not she posed a danger to herself or others. After the 45-day period, she was released.

Yet another variant of the insanity defense occurred in the case of Andrea Yates who, in June 2001, drowned her five children in the bathtub of her Texas home. Yates had a history of profound postpartum depression following the births of her fourth and fifth children. Although her case seemed to merit the insanity plea, the court convicted her of capital murder in March 2002. In 2006, an appeals court overturned the verdict on the basis of the fact that one of the trial expert witnesses had presented false testimony relevant to her mental state at the time of the killings. In July 2006, the court moved her from a high-security mental health facility to a low-security state mental hospital.

The trials of Lee Boyd Malvo and John Allen Muhammed presented the case of two individuals who had committed homicides in which one individual but not the other committing the same crimes qualified for the insanity defense. The pair was arrested in October 2002 after committing sniper attacks in which they murdered 10 people in the Washington, D.C., area. The prosecution asserted that Muhammed, a man in his 40s, had undertaken the shooting spree and ordered 17-year-old Malvo to help him. Malvo's defense attorneys pleaded the insanity defense on the grounds that he was indoctrinated and therefore had a form of mental illness. Because he was a teenager under the power of a much older man, he did not know right from wrong. However, the jury rejected this version of the insanity defense.

The opposite situation occurred in the case of Theodore Kaczynski, known as the "Unabomber." Over an 18-year period, Kaczynski mounted a campaign from his cabin in Montana against the "industrial-technological system." He admitted that he killed three people and had maimed many others by sending package bombs to government addresses. From his history and extensive clinical evaluation, there was compelling evidence that he had schizophrenia, paranoid type. However, he refused to use the insanity defense as he did not consider himself to have a psychological disorder.

When Lee Boyd Malvo was 17, he and John Allen Muhammed shot and killed 10 people at random in the Washington, D.C., area in what were known as the "Beltway sniper attacks." Malvo's insanity plea was rejected by a jury and he was sentenced to six consecutive life sentences in prison.

Competency to Stand Trial

competency to stand trial
A prediction by a mental health expert of the defendant's cognitive and emotional stability during the period of the trial.

The determination of **competency to stand trial** pertains to the question of whether a defendant is aware of and able to participate in criminal proceedings against him or her. This determination is based on the principle that people should be able to participate in their own defense. To make this determination, a forensic expert evaluates the defendant's cognitive capacity, emotional stamina, and ongoing symptoms. In some cases, the court may demand postponing the trial until the defendant's symptoms subside, if necessary, by mandating that the individual receive medication. Although structured instruments are available for the purpose of making these determinations, the majority of forensic experts rely on their clinical judgment (Bartol & Bartol, 2012).

Understanding the Purpose of Punishment

Separate from the issue of competency to stand trial is the question of whether a mentally ill person who is convicted of a capital offense is able to understand the nature and purpose of a death sentence. The case of Scott Louis Panetti, which the U.S. Supreme Court heard in 2007, highlights some of the complexities of this question.

In 1992, Panetti killed his in-laws while holding hostage his estranged wife and their 3-year-old daughter. Even though Panetti had a lengthy history of mental illness and psychiatric hospitalizations, the Texas court sentenced him to death. In 2003, Panetti petitioned the Texas state appeals court to determine his competency for execution. Panetti asserted his belief that satanic forces had sought his execution to prevent him from preaching the Gospel. His defense lawyers claimed that since Panetti could not understand why the jury sentenced him to death, the death penalty would constitute cruel and unusual punishment and therefore violate the Eighth Amendment of the Constitution. The Texas Department of Criminal Justice objected to this argument, contending that capital punishment in such cases should not rest on whether or not a convict has rational understanding of the reasons for execution, but rather on the convict's moral culpability at the time he or she committed the crime.

In 2007, the U.S. Supreme Court blocked Panetti's execution and returned the case to the U.S. District Court in Austin, Texas. The Court based this decision in part on arguments that the American Psychological Association, the American Psychiatric Association, and the National Alliance on Mental Illness put forward. These organizations jointly submitted a brief stating that individuals with psychotic conditions, such as Panetti, may experience delusions and a disrupted understanding of reality. Also, these individuals may be unable to connect events or understand cause and effect, namely, the connection between the murder and the punishment.

For almost two decades the case of Scott Louis Panetti has been the focus of legal debate and controversy. Panetti's death sentence in Texas was overturned by the U.S. Supreme Court on the premise that Panetti lacked understanding of why he was being put to death.

Concluding Perspectives on Forensic Issues

As you can see from our discussion of forensic issues, there is an entire body of knowledge forming on the border between psychology and the law. Mental health professionals are playing an increasingly important role in the legal system and, at the same time, are finding that they must familiarize themselves with an array of forensic issues. Clearly, the areas of intersection between psychology and the law will continue to grow as society looks for interventions that are humane, ethical, and effective.

Mark was hospitalized for 5 days. While on the unit, health care professionals thoroughly assessed Mark, focusing on his suicidality and depressive symptoms. He attended group therapy and worked with a psychiatrist to change his medication regimen. Once he had stabilized and was no longer suicidal, he was released from the hospital. His parents picked him up and he decided to stay with them for the rest of the semester and to return to school for the following year.

Prior to his hospitalization, Mark's parents were not aware that their son was experiencing psychological difficulties. Much to Mark's surprise, they stated that they understood his need to stay home to recuperate. Since his parents lived several hours away from where he attended school, Mark and his therapist decided to have weekly telephone sessions in order to continue their work together. Their work focused on the relationship between Mark and his parents, and Mark used his time at home to learn to discuss how he felt that the pressure they had placed on him had been a source of much stress.

Dr. Tobin's reflections: Clinicians are sometimes faced with the difficult decision of hospitalizing their therapy clients. Mark's clinician performed the appropriate steps to determine his level of safety. He was in great need of hospitalization as he appeared to be an immediate threat to his life, thus the clinician was ethically bound to break confidentiality and commit Mark to the hospital.

Luckily, Mark and his clinician had a strong enough alliance that Mark felt he should come in for "one last session" rather than ending his life. This may have been a "cry for help," because Mark knew that the clinician would be able to help him.

Mark's first depressive episode was severe, lasting around 8 months. Usually, the more severe the initial episode, the more persistent and severe subsequent episodes will become. Considering that the current work with his clinician is the first time that Mark has received psychological treatment, a part of the treatment will be to help Mark gain a sense of insight into his psychological struggles. For instance, in the future, should Mark begin to notice the same pattern of symptoms that led to his current depressive episode, he may then recognize that his symptoms may turn more severe if he does not bring them to the attention of his therapist or psychiatrist.

Finally, conducting psychotherapy over the phone, or "teletherapy," is becoming increasingly a more common way of performing therapy and is covered by APA's Ethics Code. If both parties agree that it will be the best way to maintain the therapeutic alliance over a certain period of time, as in Mark's case, it may be a suitable alternative to stopping therapy altogether. Since Mark did plan on returning to school and continuing to work with his therapist, it appears that teletherapy was an appropriate way to continue with their work to that point and avoid a rupture in his progress.

SUMMARY

- Clinicians have various roles and responsibilities. We expect them to have the intellectual competence to assess, conceptualize, and treat clients whom they accept into treatment, in addition to having the emotional capability of managing the clinical issues that emerge. When beginning work with clients, they should obtain the client's informed consent to ensure that the client understands the goals of treatment, the therapy process, the client's rights, the therapist's responsibilities, the treatment risks, the techniques that the clinician will use, financial issues, and the limits of confidentiality.

- Confidentiality is the principle that the therapist must safeguard disclosures in therapy as private. With only a few exceptions, the content of therapy is privileged communication; that is, the clinician may not disclose any information about the client in a court without the client's expressed permission. Exceptions to confidentiality include instances involving mandated reporting and duty to warn. Mental

health professionals are mandated by law to report information involving the abuse or neglect of children or other people who are unable to protect themselves. The duty to warn involves the clinician's responsibility to take action to inform a possible victim of a client's intention to do harm to that person.

- In their relationships with clients, we expect clinicians to adhere to the highest standards of ethical and professional conduct. They are to avoid inappropriate relationships, such as sexual intimacy with clients, and must maintain neutrality and distance in their dealings with clients. In overseeing the business aspects of psychotherapy practice, mental health professionals face various challenges, particularly when operating within managed health care delivery systems. Sometimes clinicians must serve in roles that present unique ethical challenges (e.g., expert witness, child custody evaluations, and evaluations of people with dementia).

- Clinicians are sometimes involved in the process of commitment, an emergency procedure for the involuntary hospitalization of a person who, if not hospitalized, is likely to create harm for self or others as a result of mental illness. Hospitalized clients have the right to treatment—the right to a humane environment with appropriate amenities, in addition to liberty and safety. Clients also have the right to refuse unwanted treatment, unless a court deems that the client is at risk of harming self or others without needed intervention. Clients also have the right for placement in the least restrictive alternative to treatment in an institution.

- The major forensic issues that pertain to the field of mental health involve the insanity defense and the competency to stand trial. The insanity defense is the argument that the lawyer acting on behalf of the client presents, which states that, because of the existence of a mental disorder, the law should not hold the client legally responsible for criminal actions. Various controversies have emerged during the past two decades regarding the insanity defense, as courts have struggled with issues of assessing a defendant's responsibility in well-publicized cases involving violent assault and murder. The determination of competency to stand trial pertains to the question of whether a defendant is aware of and able to participate in criminal proceedings against him or her.

KEY TERMS

A

acceptance and commitment therapy (ACT): A form of cognitive therapy that helps clients accept the full range of their subjective experiences, such as distressing thoughts and feelings, as they commit themselves to tasks aimed at achieving behavior change that will lead to an improved quality of life. 90

active phase: A period in the course of schizophrenia in which psychotic symptoms are present. 199

acute stress disorder: An anxiety disorder that develops after a traumatic event, with symptoms such as depersonalization, numbing, dissociative amnesia, intense anxiety, hypervigilance, and impairment of everyday functioning. People with this disorder may reexperience the event and desperately avoid reminders of the trauma. These symptoms arise within the month following the trauma and last from 2 days to 4 weeks. 115

adaptive testing: Testing in which the client's responses to earlier questions determine the subsequent questions presented to them. 65

agnosia: The inability to recognize familiar objects or experiences, despite the ability to perceive their basic elements. 304

agoraphobia: Intense anxiety about being trapped or stranded in a situation without help if a panic attack occurs. 103

akinesia: A motor disturbance in which a person's muscles become rigid and movement is difficult to initiate. 309

alcohol myopia theory: Proposes that as individuals consume greater amounts of alcohol, they are more likely to make risky choices because the immediate temptation of the moment overcomes the long-term consequences of the behavior. 331

allele: One of two different variations of a gene. 72

Alzheimer's disease: A form of dementia characterized by progressive and gradual cognitive deficits due to severe cerebral atrophy. 304

American Law Institute's (ALI) guidelines: Guidelines proposing that people are not responsible for criminal behavior if their mental disorder prevents them from appreciating the wrongfulness of their behavior. 393

amnestic disorders: Cognitive disorders involving the inability to recall previously learned information or to register new memories. 302

amphetamine: A stimulant that affects both the central nervous and the autonomic nervous systems. 335

amyloid plaques: A characteristic of Alzheimer's disease in which clusters of dead or dying neurons become mixed together with fragments of protein molecules. 313

analog observations: Assessments that take place in a setting or context such as a clinician's office or a laboratory specifically designed for observing the target behavior. 61

anorexia nervosa: An eating disorder characterized by an inability to maintain normal weight, an intense fear of gaining weight, and distorted body perception. 355

anterograde amnesia: Amnesia involving the inability to remember new information. 328

antisocial personality disorder: A personality disorder characterized by a lack of regard for society's moral or legal standards. 231

anxiety: A future-oriented and global response, involving both cognitive and emotional components, in which an individual is inordinately apprehensive, tense, and uneasy about the prospect of something terrible happening. 102

anxiety disorders: Disorders characterized by intense, irrational, and incapacitating apprehension. 102

anxiety sensitivity theory: The belief that panic disorder is caused in part by the tendency to interpret cognitive and somatic manifestations of stress and anxiety in a catastrophic manner. 104

anxiolytic: An anti-anxiety medication. 344

aphasia: A loss of the ability to use language. 304

apraxia: A loss of the ability to carry out coordinated bodily movements that the individual could previously perform without difficulty. 304

asociality: Lack of interest in social relationships. 201

Asperger's disorder: A pervasive developmental disorder in which a child maintains adequate cognitive and language development but becomes severely impaired in social interaction. Children with this disorder also develop restricted, repetitive, and stereotyped patterns of behavior, interests, and activities. 267

Assertive Community Treatment (ACT): Where a team of professionals from psychiatry, psychology, nursing, and social work reach out to clients in their homes and workplaces. 220

attachment style: The way a person relates to a caregiver figure. 85

attention-deficit/hyperactivity disorder (ADHD): A behavior disorder involving problems with inattentiveness, hyperactivity, and impulsivity. 270

autism spectrum disorder: A term currently used by many researchers and clinicians proposed in the *DSM-5* to replace the diagnosis of autistic disorder. 262

autistic disorder: A pervasive developmental disorder involving massive impairment in an individual's ability to communicate and relate emotionally to others. 262

automatic thoughts: Ideas so deeply entrenched that the individual is not even aware that they lead to feelings of unhappiness and discouragement. 90

avoidant personality disorder: A personality disorder whose most prominent feature is that the individual desires, but is fearful of, any involvement with other people and is terrified at the prospect of being publicly embarrassed. 238

avolition: A lack of initiative, either not wanting to take any action or lacking the energy and will to take action. 201

axis: A class of information in *DSM-IV* regarding an aspect of the individual's functioning. 28

B

behavioral activation: Behavioral therapy for depression in which the clinician helps the client identify activities associated with positive mood. 188

behavioral assessment: A form of measurement based on objective recording of the individual's behavior. 60

behavioral interviewing: Assessment process in which clinicians ask questions about the target behavior's frequency, antecedents, and consequences. 61

behavioral medicine: An interdisciplinary approach to medical conditions affected by psychological factors that is rooted in learning theory. 136

behavioral perspective: A theoretical perspective in which it is assumed that abnormality is caused by faulty learning experiences. 86

behavioral self-report: A method of behavioral assessment in which the individual provides information about the frequency of particular behaviors. 61

binge eating: The ingestion of large amounts of food during a short period of time, even after reaching a point of feeling full, and a lack of control over what or how much is eaten. 356

biological perspective: A theoretical perspective in which it is assumed that disturbances in emotions, behavior, and cognitive processes are caused by abnormalities in the functioning of the body. 72

biological sex: The sex determined by a person's chromosomes. 168

biopsychosocial: A model in which the interaction of biological, psychological, and sociocultural factors is seen as influencing the development of the individual. 8

bipolar disorder: A mood disorder involving manic episodes—intense and very disruptive experiences of heightened mood, possibly alternating with major depressive episodes. 179

body dysmorphic disorder: A somatoform disorder in which individuals are preoccupied with the idea that a part of their body is ugly or defective. 126

borderline personality disorder (BPD): A personality disorder characterized by a pervasive pattern of poor impulse control and instability in mood, interpersonal relationships, and self-image. 240

bradykinesia: A motor disturbance involving a general slowing of motor activity. 309

brief psychotic disorder: A disorder characterized by the sudden onset of psychotic symptoms that are limited to a period of less than a month. 207

bulimia nervosa: An eating disorder involving alternation between the extremes of eating large amounts of food in a short time, and then compensating for the added calories either by vomiting or other extreme actions to avoid gaining weight. 356

buprenorphine: A medication used in the treatment of heroin addiction. 348

C

caffeine: A stimulant found in coffee, tea, chocolate, energy drinks, diet pills, and headache remedies. 345

case formulation: A clinician's analysis of the factors that might have influenced the client's current psychological status. 35

case study: An intensive study of a single person described in detail. 20

catatonia: Extreme motor disturbances in a psychotic disorder not attributable to physiological causes. 201

childhood disintegrative disorder: A pervasive developmental disorder in which the child develops normally for the first 2 years and then starts to lose language, social,

and motor skills, as well as other adaptive functions, including bowel and bladder control. 267

classical conditioning: The learning of a connection between an originally neutral stimulus and a naturally evoking stimulus that produces an automatic reflexive reaction. 86

client: A person seeking psychological treatment. 26

client-centered: An approach based on the belief held by Rogers that people are innately good and that the potential for self-improvement lies within the individual. 92

clinical interview: a series of questions that clinicians administer in face-to-face interaction with the client. 49

clinical psychologist: A mental health professional with training in the behavioral sciences who provides direct service to clients. 27

clinician: The person providing treatment. 27

cocaine: A highly addictive central nervous system stimulant that an individual snorts, injects, or smokes. 336

cognitive behavioral therapy (CBT): Treatment method in which clinicians focus on changing both maladaptive thoughts and maladaptive behaviors. 90

cognitive perspective: A theoretical perspective in which it is assumed that abnormality is caused by maladaptive thought processes that result in dysfunctional behavior. 89

cognitive restructuring: One of the fundamental techniques of cognitive-behavioral therapy in which clients learn to reframe negative ideas into more positive ones. 90

commitment: An emergency procedure for involuntary psychiatric hospitalization. 388

communication disorders: Conditions involving impaired expression or understanding of language. 281

community mental health center (CMHC): Outpatient clinic that provides psychological services on a sliding fee scale to serve individuals who live within a certain geographic area. 39

comorbid: The situation that occurs when multiple diagnostic conditions occur simultaneously within the same individual. 34

competency to stand trial: A prediction by a mental health expert of the defendant's cognitive and emotional stability during the period of the trial. 396

compulsion: A repetitive and seemingly purposeful behavior performed in response to uncontrollable urges or according to a ritualistic or stereotyped set of rules. 112

computed axial tomography (CAT or CT scan): A series of X-rays taken from various angles around the body that are integrated by a computer to produce a composite picture. 67

concordance rate: Agreement ratios between people diagnosed as having a particular disorder and their relatives. 20

conditioned fear reactions: Acquired associations between an internal or external cue and feelings of intense anxiety. 104

conduct disorder: A development-related disorder that involves repeated violations of the rights of others and society's norms and laws; the childhood precursor of antisocial personality disorder in adulthood. 279

contingency management: A form of behavioral therapy that involves the principle of rewarding a client for desired behaviors and not providing rewards for undesired behaviors. 89

conversion disorder: A somatoform disorder involving the translation of unacceptable drives or troubling conflicts into physical symptoms. 123

coping: The process through which people reduce stress. 131

counterconditioning: The process of replacing an undesired response to a stimulus with an acceptable response. 88

Creutzfeldt-Jakob disease: A neurological disease transmitted from animals to humans that leads to dementia and death resulting from abnormal protein accumulations in the brain. 309

cultural formulation: Includes the clinician's assessment of the client's degree of identification with the culture of origin, the culture's beliefs about psychological disorders, the ways in which the culture interprets particular events, and the cultural supports available to the client. 35

culture-bound syndromes: Recurrent patterns of abnormal behavior or experience that are limited to specific societies or cultural areas. 31

cyclothymic disorder: A mood disorder with symptoms that are more chronic and less severe than those of bipolar disorder. 183

D

day treatment program: A structured program in a community treatment facility that provides activities similar to those provided in a psychiatric hospital. 39

deep brain stimulation (DBS): A somatic treatment in which a neurosurgeon implants a microelectrode that delivers a constant low electrical stimulation to a small region of the brain, powered by an implanted battery. 79

defense mechanisms: Tactics that keep unacceptable thoughts, instincts, and feelings out of conscious awareness and thus protect the ego against anxiety. 82

delirium: A temporary state in which individuals experience a clouding of consciousness in which they are unaware of what is happening around them and are unable to focus or pay attention. 299

delusion: Deeply entrenched false belief not consistent with the client's intelligence or cultural background. 200

dementia: A form of cognitive impairment involving generalized progressive deficits in a person's memory and learning of new information, ability to communicate, judgment, and motor coordination. 303

dependent personality disorder: A personality disorder whose main characteristic is that the individual is extremely passive and tends to cling to other people, to the point of being unable to make any decisions or to take independent action. 248

dependent variable: The variable whose value is the outcome of the experimenter's manipulation of the independent variable. 14

depersonalization disorder: A dissociative disorder in which the individual experiences recurrent and persistent episodes of depersonalization. 142

depressant: A psychoactive substance that causes the depression of central nervous system activity. 327

derealization: Condition in which people feel as though they are living in a dream and that their surroundings are not real. 142

developmental coordination disorder: A condition characterized by marked impairment in the development of motor coordination. 282

deviation intelligence (IQ): An index of intelligence derived from comparing the individual's score on an intelligence test with the mean score for that individual's reference group. 53

Diagnostic and Statistical Manual of Mental Disorders (DSM): A book published by the American Psychiatric Association that contains standard terms and definitions of psychological disorders. 28

Dialectical behavior therapy (DBT): Treatment approach for people with borderline personality disorder that integrates supportive and cognitive-behavioral treatments to reduce the frequency of self-destructive acts and to improve the client's ability to handle disturbing emotions, such as anger and dependency. 242

diathesis-stress model: The proposal that people are born with a predisposition (or "diathesis") that places them at risk for developing a psychological disorder if exposed to certain extremely stressful life experiences. 75

differential diagnosis: The process of systematically ruling out alternative diagnoses. 34

diffusion tensor imaging (DTI): A method to investigate abnormalities in the white matter of the brain. 213

disorder of written expression: A learning disorder in which the individual's writing is characterized by poor spelling, grammatical or punctuation errors, and disorganization of paragraphs. 281

dissociative amnesia: An inability to remember important personal details and experiences; is usually associated with traumatic or very stressful events. 141

dissociative fugue: A dissociative disorder in which a person, confused about personal identity, suddenly and unexpectedly travels to another place and is unable to recall past history or identity. 142

dissociative identity disorder: A dissociative disorder, formerly called multiple personality disorder, in which an individual develops more than one self or personality. 139

disulfiram: Known popularly as Antabuse, a medication used in the treatment of alcoholism that inhibits aldehyde dehydrogenase (ALDH) and causes severe physical reactions when combined with alcohol. 330

DNA methylation: The process that can turn off a gene as a chemical group, methyl, attaches itself to the gene. 75

double-blind: An experimental procedure in which neither the person giving the treatment nor the person receiving the treatment knows whether the participant is in the experimental or control group. 15

Down syndrome: A form of mental retardation caused by abnormal chromosomal formation during conception. 257

dual-process theory: A theory regarding alcohol use proposing there are automatic processes that generate an impulse to drink alcohol and controlled, effortful processing that regulates these automatic impulses. 330

Durham Rule: An expansion of the insanity defense based on determining that the individual was not criminally responsible if the unlawful act was due to the presence of a psychological disorder. 391

duty to warn (or otherwise protect): The clinician's responsibility to notify a potential victim of a client's harmful intent toward that individual. 385

dysfunctional attitudes: Personal rules or values people hold that interfere with adequate adjustment. 90

dyspareunia: A sexual dysfunction affecting both males and females that involves recurrent or persistent genital pain before, during, or after sexual intercourse. 164

dysphoria: The emotion of sadness. 178

dysthymic disorder: A mood disorder involving chronic depression of less intensity than major depressive disorders. 178

E

eating disorders: Diagnosis for people who experience extreme disturbances in their everyday diet along with possible distress or concern about their body weight. 354

ecstasy (MDMA): A hallucinogenic drug made from a synthetic substance chemically similar to methamphetamine and mescaline. 341

ego: In psychoanalytic theory, the structure of personality that gives the individual the mental powers of judgment, memory, perception, and decision making, enabling the individual to adapt to the realities of the external world. 82

ego psychology: Theoretical perspective based on psychodynamic theory emphasizing the ego as the main force in personality. 84

electroconvulsive therapy (ECT): The application of electrical shock to the head for the purpose of inducing therapeutically beneficial seizures. 79

electroencephalogram (EEG): A measure of changes in the electrical activity of the brain. 65

emotional dysregulation: Lack of awareness, understanding, or acceptance of emotions; inability to control the intensity or duration of emotions; unwillingness to experience emotional distress as an aspect of pursuing goals; and inability to engage in goal-directed behaviors when experiencing distress. 242

emotion-focused coping: A type of coping in which a person does not change anything about the situation itself, but instead tries to improve feelings about the situation. 133

encopresis: An elimination disorder in which the child is incontinent of feces and has bowel movements either in clothes or in another inappropriate place. 290

endophenotypes: Biobehavioral abnormalities that are linked to genetic and neurobiological causes of mental illness. 74

enuresis: An elimination disorder in which the child is incontinent of urine and urinates

for childhood separation anxiety disorder: Informant, age, and sex differences. *Journal of Anxiety Disorders, 24*(8), 946–952.

Alpert, H. R., Connolly, G. N., & Biener, L. (2012). A prospective cohort study challenging the effectiveness of population-based medical intervention for smoking cessation. *Tobacco Control.*

Altarac, M., & Saroha, E. (2007). Lifetime prevalence of learning disability among US children. *Pediatrics, 119 Suppl 1*, S77–83.

Alzheimer, A. (1907/1987). About a peculiar disease of the cerebral cortex. *Alzheimer's Disease and Associated Disorders, 1*, 7–8.

Andreasen, N. C. (2010). The lifetime trajectory of schizophrenia and the concept of neurodevelopment. *Dialogues in Clinical Neuroscience, 12*, 409–415.

Anton, R. F., O'Malley, S. S., Ciraulo, D. A., Cisler, R. A., Couper, D., Donovan, D. M., . . . Zweben, A. (2006). Combined pharmacotherapies and behavioral interventions for alcohol dependence: the COMBINE study: A randomized controlled trial. *Journal of the American Medical Association, 295*(17), 2003–2017.

Archer, T. (2011). Physical exercise alleviates debilities of normal aging and Alzheimer's

Psychopathology and Behavioral Assessment, 33(2), 137–158.

Bars, D. R., Heyrend, F. L., Simpson, C. D., & Munger, J. C. (2001). Use of visual-evoked potential studies and EEG data to classify aggressive, explosive behavior of youths. *Psychiatric Services, 52*(1), 81–86.

Barsky, A. E., & Gould, J. W. (2002). *Clinicians in court: A guide to subpoenas, depositions, testifying, and everything else you need to know.* New York: Guilford Press.

Bartol, C. R., & Bartol, A. M. (2012). *Introduction to forensic psychology: Research and application.* Los Angeles, CA: Sage Publications.

Killam, C., Cautin, R. L., & Santucci, A. C. (2005). Assessing the enduring residual

Risperidone treatment for aggression-resistant symptoms of chronic military

68(11), 1016–1022.

T

tardive dyskinesia: Motor disorder that consists of involuntary movements of the mouth, arms, and trunk of the body. 215

target behavior: A behavior of interest or concern in an assessment. 60

tau: A protein that normally helps maintain the internal support structure of the axons. 313

theoretical perspective: An orientation pertaining to individuals choosing to undergo sex reassignment surgery. 169

transvestic disorder: Diagnosis applied to individuals who engage in transvestic behavior and have the symptoms of a paraphilic disorder. 155

transvestic fetishism: A paraphilia in which a man has an uncontrollable craving to dress in women's clothing in order to derive sexual gratification. 155

traumatic brain injury (TBI): Damage

symptoms, health status, family background, and life history. 49

uplifts: Events that boost your feelings of well-being. 133

V

vaginismus: A sexual dysfunction that involves recurrent or persistent involuntary spasms of the musculature of the outer part of the vagina. 164

validity: The extent to which a test ...

SUBJECT INDEX

Bold locators indicate definitions of terms.